THEODORE DREISER

𝔍𝔬𝔲𝔯𝔫𝔞𝔩𝔦𝔰𝔪

VOLUME ONE

Newspaper Writings, 1892–1895

THE UNIVERSITY OF PENNSYLVANIA DREISER EDITION

THOMAS P. RIGGIO
General Editor

JAMES L. W. WEST III
Textual Editor

THEODORE DREISER

Journalism

VOLUME ONE

NEWSPAPER WRITINGS, 1892–1895

EDITED BY

T. D. NOSTWICH

University of Pennsylvania Press · *Philadelphia*

upp

Copyright © 1988 by the University of Pennsylvania Press

Library of Congress Cataloging-in-Publication Data
Dreiser, Theodore, 1871–1945.
  Journalism / Theodore Dreiser : edited by T. D. Nostwich.
    p.   cm.—(The University of Pennsylvania Dreiser edition)
  Includes index.
  Contents: v. 1. Newspaper writings, 1892–1895.
  I. Nostwich, T. D., 1925– . II. Title. III. Title: Theodore
Dreiser, journalism. IV. Series: Dreiser, Theodore, 1871–1945.
University of Pennsylvania Dreiser edition.
PS3507.R55A16   1988
070'.92'4—dc19
[B]   87-38083
                                                           CIP

Printed in the United States of America
Designed by Adrianne Onderdonk Dudden

CONTENTS

"HEARD IN THE CORRIDORS"

THEATRICAL REVIEWS

St. Louis Republic

THIRD DISTRICT STORIES

𝕿𝖔𝖑𝖊𝖉𝖔 𝕭𝖑𝖆𝖉𝖊

𝕮𝖑𝖊𝖛𝖊𝖑𝖆𝖓𝖉 𝕷𝖊𝖆𝖉𝖊𝖗

𝕻𝖎𝖙𝖙𝖘𝖇𝖚𝖗𝖌 𝕯𝖎𝖘𝖕𝖆𝖙𝖈𝖍

ALLEGHENY STORIES

𝕹𝖊𝖜 𝖄𝖔𝖗𝖐 𝖂𝖔𝖗𝖑𝖉

ILLUSTRATIONS

PREFACE

Theodore Dreiser's literary apprenticeship began in the gritty world of big-city journalism, which in the 1890s attracted a fraternity of talented writers like Stephen Crane, Abraham Cahan, Upton Sinclair, and Jack London. In June 1892, Dreiser wrote his first news story for the *Chicago Globe*. Though he received a pittance for his labors, the twenty-year-old newsman fancied himself on the way to literary fame and fortune. Three years later, a disillusioned Dreiser abruptly quit the field by walking out of Joseph Pulitzer's New York *World*, where as a space-rate reporter he was being paid, like a garment worker in the city's sweatshops, by the inch.

Between Chicago and New York, Dreiser did some promising work on newspapers in St. Louis, Toledo, Cleveland, and Pittsburgh. He never realized the dream of having his own byline, a column the public would read because his name appeared above it. Yet he was talented enough to get good assignments—drama critic, special-feature writer, investigative reporter—on the *St. Louis Globe-Democrat*, the *St. Louis Republic*, and the *Pittsburg Dispatch*. At times, he was encouraged to depart from fact and invent material, as when he wrote the "Heard in the Corridors" column for the *Globe-Democrat*, which consisted of stories told by travelers in the corridors of St. Louis's major hotels. In these slight sketches Dreiser created what amounts to his first body of fiction. All together, the subjects he covered in these years supplied him with raw material for later novels and stories, as well as for a large book about his newspaper days.

Four years after leaving the *World*, Dreiser began writing his historic first novel, *Sister Carrie*. When he later came to tell the story of that book, he dramatized it as coming to him swiftly and somewhat involuntarily, even mystically, as a name on a yellow sheet of paper. The impression he cultivated thereafter was that he had written nothing before *Sister Carrie* that had any bearing on the novel—an idea that has been challenged only in recent years. The publication of this first volume of Dreiser's early journalism puts into clearer focus the long foreground that resulted in such an extraordinary start as a novelist. T. D. Nostwich's meticulous, pioneering research has uncovered a great body of Dreiser's newspaper work. Of the 106 articles in this edition, 59 have not been identified previously, and only 4 have been reprinted elsewhere. The presentation of the early journalism expands the Dreiser canon with writing that the author never intended as a serious demonstration of his talent. Nevertheless, these articles and stories tell us a great deal about the young Dreiser and are valuable as a new source for critical and biographical inquiry.

Dreiser could turn out run-of-the-mill copy as well as anyone, but a surprising amount of this work contains, at least in embryo, the themes, subjects, and style found in his later fiction. In the less routine items, familiar Dreiserian turns of phrase and even whole passages survived the copy editor's pencil. Such articles demonstrate how early Dreiser's literary sensibility and ideas were fixed. This record of daily journalism also allows us to construct a rough log of his whereabouts in years for which we have little hard evidence. Since his specialty was the interview, there are numerous occasions when Dreiser himself appears in the role of anonymous reporter, asking questions and responding to a great range of issues—and so inadvertently providing a glimpse of himself as a young reporter.

This volume continues the Pennsylvania Dreiser Edition's tradition of publishing authoritative texts of writings that either survive only in manuscript or are inaccessible to the specialist and general reader alike. Nostwich transcribed the texts from original newspaper files and, when these were not available, from microfilmed reproductions. He devised the editorial principles, wrote the historical and textual essays, supplied the notes, and compiled the apparatus and index. The general editor, the textual editor James L. W. West III, and associate editor Arthur D. Casciato proofread the text and verified the contents at each stage of preparation.

Richard De Gennaro, before leaving the University of Pennsylvania as director of libraries to become director of the New York Public Library, established the Dreiser Edition on a formal basis and provided steady support and encouragement. Neda M. Westlake labored as the first general editor of the Dreiser Edition at a time when to do so required a large act of faith. Without their efforts, this project would have remained a scholarly daydream.

THOMAS P. RIGGIO
General Editor,
The University of Pennsylvania Dreiser Edition
July 1987

ACKNOWLEDGMENTS

I thank the University of Pennsylvania for permission to quote from manuscript materials in its possession and Harold J. Dies of the Dreiser Trust for permission to quote from *Dawn, A Hoosier Holiday,* and *Newspaper Days.*

I am deeply in debt to my good friend Neda M. Westlake, former Curator of the Charles Patterson Van Pelt Library Rare Book Collection, not only for making the vast University of Pennsylvania Dreiser Collection readily accessible to me but for her careful comments on my historical and textual essays and for her kind assistance, advice, and encouragement over several years.

Of the many reference works used to prepare this edition certainly the most important was *Theodore Dreiser: A Primary and Secondary Bibliography,* compiled by Donald Pizer, Richard W. Dowell, and Frederic E. Rusch. Particularly useful was its identification of many newspaper stories.

The Center for Research Libraries in Chicago loaned me microfilms of the *St. Louis Globe-Democrat,* the *St. Louis Republic,* and the *Pittsburg Dispatch,* which greatly expedited the preparation of this edition.

Joy Gleason and her staff at the Newspaper and General Periodical Center of the Chicago Public Library expended much time and effort in tracing volumes of the *Chicago Globe.*

I am thankful as well to three other institutions that made available to me microfilms of newspapers: the Library of Congress for the *St. Louis Globe-Democrat,* the University of Minnesota for the New York *World,* and the Ohio Historical Society for the *Toledo Blade* and the *Cleveland Leader.*

Many staff members of the Iowa State University Library took a kind interest in the progress of this work and assisted me in innumerable ways. I particularly remember the good help of Elaine Campbell, Donald Pady, and Susan Rafter.

Special thanks are due also to Robert H. Elias for invaluable aid in confirming Dreiser's authorship of certain articles; to Cathy Reilly, Librarian of the St. Louis Municipal Police Department, for supplying vital information about that department in the 1890s; to Melba Browning of the Microfilm Division of the St. Louis Public Library for locating several elusive newspaper articles; to Blair F. Bigelow for permitting me to transcribe his photocopy of Dreiser's first newspaper story.

Four other people generously took time to answer questions: Bill Feustel of the *St. Louis Globe-Democrat;* Karl E. Gwiasda of the Iowa State University Department of English; John Molyneaux of the Rockford, Illinois, Public Library; Wesley I. Shank of the Iowa State University Department of Architecture.

Thomas P. Riggio and James L. W. West III have my admiration and gratitude for their skilled transformation of my massive and unwieldy manuscript into a publishable form.

Lee Ann Draud, of the University of Pennsylvania Press, has exercised her considerable editorial skills in making the book finally fit for exposure to the public.

Preparation of this edition from the initial stages was facilitated by assistance in the form of released time and grants-in-aid from the Iowa State University College of Sciences and Humanities, the Graduate College, and the Research Foundation.

The Department of English at Iowa State University was especially considerate in providing me with research assignments, research assistants, and funds for reproduction of printed and manuscript materials.

I am profoundly grateful for the early encouragement of two good friends and colleagues, Richard Herrnstadt and Keith Huntress. The first-named gentleman I thank especially for his thoughtful criticism of my historical and textual commentaries.

My labors were lightened by the following people who turned the arduousness of proofreading into something like a pleasure: Jane Nolan, Ann, Elisabeth, and Sarah Nostwich, Janet Searls, and Sunanda Vittal.

Assuredly I could not have completed this book without the practical assistance and the unflagging, tender sympathy of my wife, Ann. To her, as well as to my sister, Mildred; my daughters, Elisabeth and Sarah; Elisabeth's husband, Chris; my sons, Mark, Paul, and Michael; and Michael's wife, Sara, I dedicate that portion of this edition that is my own.

T. D. N.

THEODORE DREISER

Journalism

VOLUME ONE

Newspaper Writings, 1892–1895

Chicago Globe

1 - CLEVELAND AND GRAY
THE TICKET.

Cleveland and Gray will be the ticket. This was decided upon last night at a meeting of the leaders of the party held at the Richelieu hotel in the apartments of ex-Secretary Whitney.

This momentous result was achieved almost solely by the efforts of Mr. Whitney, who has been moving heaven and earth to destroy the last vestige of opposition to Mr. Cleveland.

It is a concession to the Tammany men, who dictated the nomination of ex-Gov. Gray for second place. Gray was Hill's choice for the tail end of the ticket should the latter have been nominated, but as the Tammany men learned that this was impossible, they took what they could get—the second place.

At 8:30 o'clock p.m., the president-makers began to quietly drop in and were quietly shown up to the apartments of Mr. Whitney, where stood his private secretary, who ushered them to the apartment where the meeting was to be held.

At 9:30 all were present and the doors were barred.

After deliberating for an hour and a half, it was found that Mr. Cleveland's strength in the convention would be enough
[Two lines illegible.]
selection by the national committee for temporary chairman was acquiesced in, and Mr. Wilson, of West Virginia, was decided upon for permanent chairman of the convention.

Gov. Abbett, of New Jersey, will place Mr. Cleveland in nomination, and will be followed by Senator Voorhees, of Indiana, who will second his nomination. After considerable deliberation the Indiana delegation swung into line and the thirty delegates from that state will be solid for Cleveland. Sixteen of Ohio's delegates will cast their votes for Mr. Cleveland and one vote from South Carolina is also counted for Cleveland.

The Indiana delegation, in return for their solid vote for Cleveland, will receive the western end of the ticket, and ex-Gov. Isaac P. Gray of that state will be nominated for vice president.

The party leaders decided to lay aside the favorite sons and recognize the importance of New York and Indiana in the November contest where the popularity of the opposing sons will be tested.

The platforms presented by a majority of the various state delegations are in the hands of Mr. Whitney, but action has been deferred and will be left to the national committee for final composition.

Ex-Secretary Whitney was seen shortly after the caucus and said: "We have 601 voters without the New York delegation and Mr. Cleveland will be nominated on the first ballot. Ohio gives us sixteen votes and South Carolina one. The Indiana delegation is desirous of Gray for the vice presidency and he will be the nominee. I wish you would say that the statement to the effect that Mr. Gorman had written me a letter declining to allow his name to come before the convention is unfounded. In justice to Mr. Gorman I wish to deny this, as it is absolutely untrue. I can not say as to whether the Hill delegation will join us or not. We do not need them."

An air of entire satisfaction was plainly visible upon the faces of the attending democrats of the secret session and all confessed themselves as satisfied with the result, considering it as final.

[21 June 1892, p. 1.]

2 - CHEYENNE, HAUNT OF MISERY AND CRIME.

The belated pedestrian who goes into the district bounded by State, Van Buren, Sixteenth streets and the river literally steps into the bedrooms of scores of sleepers, who on hot nights stretch their weary limbs on the hard pavements. Others recline against posts and barrels or slumber with bodies well nigh nude protruding from windows that open into hot, stifling rooms.

The streets are walked the night long by sick men with haggard countenances; by drunkards and footpads and other characters lost to all semblance of manhood.

The houses are low, mean and poor structures sunken below the street level. It is a territory wherein is crowded a great portion of the vice and crime of the city.

Heat is always the factor that brings forward in disgusting and sickening prominence the awful condition of these beings. No one can realize from a distance the condition which prevails in the locality. The eye must behold it, the ear must listen to the wailing before the heart can comprehend.

Chicago is a city of heterogenous population. It is a city of sections and of nationalities, each bearing distinctly special features. The masses are home-loving people, who are honest and industrious. The rapid growth and commercial prosperity have brought together the various nationality types of the world, and its streets resound with a babel of tongues endeavoring to speak intelligently the English of Uncle Sam.

The more ignorant of the foreign classes huddle together in districts and live there much as their means allow. It is a spectacle to behold these people in their own quarters—poor, ignorant and depraved—eking out a seemingly purposeless existence.

In that section of the city known as Cheyenne, bounded on the north by Van Buren street and on the east by State street, extending thence south and west to the river, dwells a curious conglomeration of foreign residents. The small frame buildings, low and weather-stained, hold thousands of beings.

The streets are always alive with people, not the hurrying, self-absorbed population of the other portions of the city, but rather with the idlers of life; with those who labor for existence merely. They line the streets seated on barrels and boxes or stroll up and down with a vague unrest in their eyes. Italians and Arabians mingle together and eye one another with the mistrustful glance of suspicious ignorance.

Their small apartments where they live—a dozen in a single room—are too small to remain in, and the first breath of heat drives them, as water drives rats, from their dens.

They parade the sidewalks in faded, shapeless garments and find enjoyment in brawls and the more fiery brands of whisky.

From here go forth the Greek and Italian banana peddlers and organ grinders. They wander the city over in search of charity, gather pennies from the hands of innocence and bring them here to pay for their beer—for their food they gather along the way.

Throughout the day the women linger about awaiting the return of their husbands at nightfall. When darkness comes the merriment begins and the police are given sufficient occupation to keep them from dozing. The patrol is in good demand and is probably the most respectable and respected vehicle which enters the locality. When the heat is oppressive the residents lie awake on the sidewalks, in the door-ways and on the roofs until far into the night.

Drowsiness overcomes the oppressive sense of heat. They fall asleep. No grass or trees vary the everlasting monotony of musty, aged and stained buildings.

When it rains they pack themselves like sardines in the ill-smelling apartments up rickety old stairways, and opening out on dark, dusty halls. From surrounding basements issue the sickening heat of laundries, or equally as bad, the fumes of whisky and the odors from the underground restaurant. The alleys reek with decaying garbage and human filth, the vile odors carrying disease and death to those already weakened and enervated by such environment. No really healthy face greets the eye. No ray of intelligence beams from the faces of the wandering, jaded inhabitants. They are all alike and attract no attention but for the haggard looks, the ragged garments and the filth of person.

Filth is the common condition and it can readily be seen why, for within the entire district it is safe to say that there are not 200 bath tubs.

Children go about with wan, peevish faces—faces plaintive from early suffering and neglect.

Entering the district at midnight and wandering along the broken wooden pavements, ill-lighted by lamps and avoided by the police, the nerves tremble at the threatening appearance of the whole neighborhood. From out of windows where glow spluttering lamps the faint cries of infants are heard. Women lie with their heads on their arms and almost nude, panting for a cooling breath as a relief from the stifling air. On the sidewalks men lay face upward with arms outspread muttering and going over some quarrel of daylight hours.

In a yard facing on Sherman street lay a family of Italians sleeping on the bare ground.

Here was a mother and a half naked child pushed arm's length from her; a father and son lay huddled a short distance away. As the midnight wanderer paused and viewed the scene the child rolled about feverishly and uttered a whimpering cry of pain.

Men with besotted brains came reeling along the walks cursing and mumbling at some hated foe; and others with shuffling footsteps shambled along in the shadows seemingly afraid of even the dim light of the locality.

Although the district is patrolled by an officer for every block, a circuit of one block was made three times without discovering that dignitary.

In a three-story brick south of Polk street on Pacific avenue live fifty families of Greeks, one room being allotted to each family. The structure has only a few windows and the atmosphere is naturally stifling. The doors opening into the hall each contained a half smothered sleeper whose head and arms were stretched out into the hall with famished eagerness. It reminded the spectator of a row of bodies on the slab at the morgue.

One little Italian staggered homeward along the almost deserted streets. Into the alley between Clark and Dearborn streets he turned and guided himself along to a rickety old two-story frame that filled the back half of a lot, occupied in front by a two-story brick containing a saloon and flat. Here laying on a wooden walk and on the rat eaten floors were women and men in all kinds of positions.

Some were asleep and others tumbled about in fitful wakefulness. How, in case of a storm, the number so lying about could find space to sleep in the house remains a mystery. Cattle could not be crowded into a meaner pen. These same people line the streets during daylight with supplicating, out-stretched hands. Often the men are in the hands of a contractor, who lets them for hire for a stated sum to corporations. He draws the money and pays to these ignorant and pitiful tools a sum barely sufficient to keep body and soul together. That a city in twenty years has drawn together such a mass of vice, misery and crime, is a fact worth pondering upon. They are here to stay and to be assimilated eventually as Americans.

Those people, far from their native country, their friends and relatives, jumbled into a polyglot mass, live, grow and die in squalor. Apparently they never rise above a purely animal conception of life.

Over them all the night wind softly breathes and the stars look down in their serene purity. On they sleep with white faces upturned from the pavement.

And so the midnight finds them.

What can be done for them? How can they be uplifted? They nestle in the very arms of free education and are not aroused.

Let the wise of the world ponder. Let human pity extend a helping hand.

[24 July 1892, p. 3.]

3 - FATE OF THE UNKNOWN.

What becomes of the unknown dead? Comparatively few of Chicago's citizens know, yet the answer to this question is simple—they are buried.

A visit to the county morgue proves interesting to anyone. Many go, longing yet fearing to see beneath the glass the face of one, in life, near and dear, longing, for often the knowledge that death has solved the mystery of a disappearance takes away a suspicion of shame that may have surrounded the fate of the missing, fearing, because no matter how one may sin, love remains in spite of shame.

The only other people who visit this place where death's victims are in state, except for those whose business forces them there, are those who go from morbid curiosity. To these an accident or a murder is a boon, but the morgue is the only place that can give them thorough enjoyment. They gaze with eager interest on the dead and on the relatives and friends of the forms which lie with closed eyes and rigid limbs on the slabs.

Of all the bodies brought to the morgue, two-thirds are identified. These, after the formality of an inquest, are removed by relatives or friends and, presumably, given a funeral and Christian burial.

The one-third, however, are entered on the records as unknown. The inquest is held, a verdict, "an unknown man, found drowned in Lake Michigan," is the result, the verdicts varying only in place and cause of death in the several cases. Occasionally, but seldom, the unidentified body is that of a woman. In all instances the course of procedure is the same and it is as follows:

The body is taken to the morgue and is thoroughly examined. A minute description is taken of it and of the clothing and of everything which may have been found on or near the deceased. The place where the body was found, by whom and at what time, color, age as near as may be judged, the height, weight, build and every detail of face, form, apparel and circumstance is noted.

Then the body is placed on a truck or slab under one of the glass cases. Here it becomes a veritable "stiff" for the temperature is kept at about 30 degrees—2 degrees below freezing point. Here the body remains for an uncertain time. Perhaps it is recognized and identified. If not, it is kept for a month or more. At any rate it is kept until all probability of its identification has passed.

Then the doctors take a hand and in that hand is a knife. Limbs are separated from the body and tissues from the bones. Arteries, veins, muscles and tendons are laid bare and science progresses and scientists receive valuable information—perhaps.

And then? And then the end, so far as mortals know—the grave. A cheap coffin, six feet of earth, a headstone bearing a number only and the potter's field has gained an addition.

The morgue-keeper was asked for some stories of unidentified bodies. He replied:

"An unknown has no story."

[11 September 1892, p. 3.]

4 - SWINDLERS.

There is now in operation at No. 144 Madison street a fake watch auction which is conducted right under the nose, so to speak, of the Young Men's Christian association. All kinds of jewelry and watches are being auctioned off at prices that are fabulously ridiculous. An auctioneer is all day receiving the bids of the cappers and pluggers for the firm, and occasionally a jay or interested citizen who would like to buy good jewelry cheap offers a bid. Prices are set and bids made in rapid order and once in a while a capper will buy a watch just to give the game a semblance of honesty. After paying for it he will take a turn around the block and drop in again when his identity has likely been forgotten by the crowd of suckers that is inticed into the place.

That the auction is crooked and an open swindle would seem to be self-evident to almost anyone and yet there are those who will bite at almost anything. For the benefit of these the snares that are set for them should be pointed out.

The auction goes on from early morning until midnight, or just as long as a stranger will venture into the room. The skinners offer a fifteen jeweled, gold-filled Dueber case, Hammond movement watch for $10. If this handsome offer fails to draw the money, a charm is thrown in, and the whole auctioned off to the first stranger who ventures to bid.

The moment a stranger bids, no matter what his offer may be, they close with him. None of the cappers bid higher and he is forced to stand by his bargain.

The auctioneer asserted that the case alone could be taken back to the manufacturers, the Dueber company, and $18 would be paid for it. Yet the whole will be sold for $10 straight.

"Come on now, who's the next?"

Occasionally a stranger buys, and then there is great glee in the camp. To say that the bargain is a genuine one would be madness, and yet they work a rather festive game on the purchaser. They go so far as to show him a good watch, and which in all probability would cost from $50 to $70.

If the watch suits him and he agrees to buy, they make sure to change it and palm off a brass-cased affair worth in all probability from $3 to $4.

The Young Men's Christian association looks down on this with none too amiable eye. The crooked game is not in its building, or the association would close it in a hurry. They are bemoaning, as it is, their inability to stop the auction. The game is plain to anyone. Officers pass the door and fly cops drop in once in a while, but the game goes merrily on.

The Gaelic association can not play football. The Marlowe opera-house can not open on Sundays, and Garfield Park is warred against most persistently, but such open faced swindles as these are permitted and glossed over by the mayor and the most righteous chief of police.

Chief McClaughry is in the hands of the clock and watch thieves and they triumph in their power. Steve Douglas is their attorney, and he has told the "majah" that he will make him the next mayor.

While in truth Douglas has no influence in the counsels of his party, being considered a fat nonentity, yet he has "conned" McClaughry into believing otherwise, and the chief has sold his soul for the evanescent mayoralty bubble.

Douglas sits upon the chief's body like some stuffed and bloated vampire, fattening on McClaughry's carcass while the latter actually believes he is being "doctored," and in truth he is, but not in the way he thinks. When Douglas gets through with him he will find that he has been staking his hopes upon a pillar of adipose which will utterly collapse in the hour of need.

[6 October 1892, p. 1.]

5 - FAKES.

The fake auctioneers lately closed by the police will receive their licenses again and will conduct their illegal business at the old stand. Mayor Washburne has decided that the places can not be kept shut, illegal as their business may be.

On the evidence presented to the police department in reference to the mock auction jewelry and cigar places the department closed up one, the most conspicuous, at No. 144 Madison street. After this good start a lull came and it looks as though the police have been overpowered by their own success. Nothing further has been done and the only evidence of their whilom incidental triumph is about to be removed. Ever since George P. Thayer's auction permit has been revoked he has haunted the city hall and has patiently waited at the door of Inspector Ross. Three days of such persistent "hanging on" has brought him numerous interviews with Ross, McClaughry and Mayor Washburne, and the result has been very favorable to his cause. The mayor after counseling with the city law department finds that nothing can be done except to return to the auctioneer his license.

For $300, the license fee charged, cheap goods of all kinds may be auctioned off in anywhere from one to forty places providing permits, that the city grants gratis under the original license, be taken out for each separate place. By this simple arrangement the entire fake business now in the city may be operated by one party or by the co-operation of a few in order to save money. By this simple plan also the thirty dives now running are controlled by two or three professional dealers.

Mayor Washburne, Chief McClaughry and Inspector Ross have a systematized explanation to offer, and they recite it in clockwork style. Mayor Washburne said:

"The city law department has looked up the law governing the appeal of this man's lawyer, and find that there is nothing to be done other than to issue a license. The man is willing to pay $300 and conduct his place respectably."

"Does not his record debar him from obtaining a license?"

"I am advised not by the department."

Major McClaughry's explanation was simply ditto and Inspector Ross' was a second edition called down through the speaking tube. Inspector Ross added to the above explanation a satirical comment upon the decision.

"I realize that these people are sharps and that their shops are nuisances. We can and will close them up as fast as we can secure evidence against them. We have three men detailed to watch them but they have yet to report any 'queer work' at any of these places. We can not take the word of outsiders in this matter. We must have evidence in the way of bad jewelry and defrauded strangers, or the word of our detailed officer, otherwise we are powerless."

"If citizens see the crookedness of the places and ask you to investigate, why can not your officers see it?"

"I can't imagine."

"Then if your men can not see the evil, why is not the ordinary citizen's evidence taken?"

"Well, never mind, we will look into these places and see how they are operating. Send us any evidence you happen to gather, please."

The numbers of nine shops now operating in the downtown portion were left and the promise gained that they would all be closely investigated.

The goods in the auction shop at No. 238 South Clark street are a fine line of shams. The place is operated by a Mr. Zuckermann, who also operates the cigar auction at No. 169 Madison street. Mr. Zuckermann keeps four cappers or "shillabers," as they are called.

"A queer line of watches that fellow keeps," said an ex-shillaber of the place. "He keeps watches and all kinds of jewelry, glass diamonds, guns, cutlery and musical instruments. The watches are brass and the case names on them are forged. So are the numbers and names of the movements. Zuckermann sells false Dueber and Boss cases, and almost every movement you can think of. They are all shams and brass.

"One watch is called the 'Success.' It is the worst fake of the lot; solid brass and one that they 'palm off' most frequently.

"His musical instruments are cheap imitations. Violins cost $5 and they are sold for from $30 to $50. He sells a 'Parker' gun. That name is also forged. It is not a Parker gun and he buys it for less than $10, and auctions it off for $40. That is the way they all do business. The whole list of saleable articles could be gone over and the same things proved against them as against the watches. They are all shams."

Another told how the "shillabers" are drilled. It is a second repetition of "Fagin," in "Oliver Twist."

"They are drilled to follow the auctioneer's every move and look," said this party. Names and words are taught them, and whenever an auctioneer gives vent to one of these they are to act on it at once. Now, for instance, the auctioneer says "Hutze" during his conversation. That means bid me 50 cents higher on this article. The shillaber immediately bids fifty. The word "Rot" interpreted means bid me $1 higher. The phrase "Buy it, buy it," is a signal for the "Shillabers" to stop bidding, as the stranger becomes somewhat weary. When the auctioneer draws his hand down the lappel of his coat he means "scatter," as an officer is usually present. These few safeguards are known only to the trusted "shillabers."

The terms and phrases used by the "shillabers" are characteristic of the business. "Running" a customer means getting him so excited that he does not realize "where he is at." "Packing" signifies scaring or shaming him into purchasing, and so it goes through a long list of professional terms of more or less service to the "shillabers."

According to these wanderers no device is too low or petty, no argument too mean to use and no price too exorbitant to ask. To those vampires every stranger and innocent is lawful prey, whom they swindle without compunction. When called before Inspector Ross they are allowed to offer their victim his money back. Even allowed to argue with him from the standpoint that he is a poor man, that if he sues and closes them up that they will not pay him at all, and that it would be best to receive back his money and drop prosecution. This is why the police can not close them up.

A pure and verdant rustic, a stranger, who, with bulging carpet bag, faded umbrella, and wind tossed whiskers, enters their precincts to their unadulterated joy. To such as these they propose to sell their snap jewelry regardless. Such a one, a reporter for the *Daily Globe*, yesterday walked into No. 238 South Clark street.

The *Daily Globe*, for such emergencies, keeps a reporter with triumphant terra cotta hued World's Fair whiskers.

His entrance was the signal for a grand rush on the part of the shillabers, who surrounded him while the auctioneer quickly drew forth a "success" watch and began to expatiate upon its manifold charms. The intended victim's looks being so perfectly innocent their arguments were full of joyous superfluities totally foreign to the demands of the occasion.

"Here, my friend," began the auctioneer, "here is a fourteen-karat, gold plated, fifteen jeweled watch, with an Elgin movement and a Dueber case. You can take it anywhere and get $40 for it in a minute. Why, my friend, one lid alone is worth more than we ask.

"I'm bid $7, I'm bid $7, 'hutze,' I'm bid $7.50, I'm bid $7.50."

"My friend," said the auctioneer leaning over the counter in a confidential manner, "you will be getting a great bargain if you buy this for $8. My friend, I'm getting old and gray headed. I wouldn't deceive you for the world. Take this watch now; give me $8 for it and you will never regret it."

This touching appeal failed to "fetch" as was intended. A smaller watch was drawn forth and the auctioneer held it temptingly aloft.

"Here's a watch," began the shark, "pawned to us by a lady from Colorado. It's a fine watch that you can present to your mother or sister." This last was said with grinning significance. "It's a genuine double duplex movement, the case is genuine vermicelli, warranted for twenty years. Here's an $8 chain that we will throw in and you can take the whole lot for $8.50."

The offer was too much. It was cloying to the "bargain" desire in the rustic's breast. It was richly sickening and it defeated its own purpose. The reporter hastily withdrew while the "shillabers" talked of north winds and corn silks as exemplified in the retreating jay.

[16 October 1892, p. 1.]

6 - ARRESTED.

Joseph Zuckerman, the proprietor of the auction shop at No. 228 South Clark street, was arrested yesterday afternoon charged with violating section 1437 of the city ordinances.

The warrant was sworn out by Louis Zitenfield, a former employe and "capper" for Zuckerman. Zitenfield appeared before Justice Glennon at 3:30 o'clock p.m. in company with another "shillaber" of the same auction shop. The warrant was shortly placed in the hands of Detective Walker, of the Central detail, who proceeded to the auction shop in company with a *Daily Globe* reporter.

When Detective Walker entered the shop, only two auctioneers and three cappers were present. Mr. Zuckerman was out.

The detective had not waited two or three minutes when Zuckerman came hurrying in. Mr. Zuckerman was met by the detective, who said:

"Is your name Zuckerman?"

"It is," was the reply.

"Then I have a warrant for your arrest."

"Can you wait a few minutes for me?" said the prisoner.

"No; my orders are to bring you at once to the Central station; you can come, of course," said the detective, persuasively.

"Oh, yes, of course I'll come," replied Zuckerman, with a grimace, and with that he handed over his umbrella to the cashier, while Detective Walker locked his arm in his and marched him off north on Clark street.

A few dry commonplaces were indulged in between the detective and Mr. Zuckerman on the way to the station, but they failed to arouse any enthusiasm on the part of the fake auctioneer.

"Kind o' sloppy," said Mr. Walker.

"Yaas," was the only reply.

"It's nice weather, though."

"Yaas."

Then Mr. Zuckerman took occasion to ask:

"Might I stop and see a friend?"

"Oh, no; better come on down. He will do that for you."

"But," suggested the prisoner, "you have not read the warrant to me."

"Oh, well, it's enough when I say I have it. I will read it to you in the station. Won't that do?"

"Ye-as," dryly remarked Mr. Zuckerman, and with that the conversation ended.

Once in the city hall the prisoner was ushered into the presence of Inspector Ross.

"Well," said the inspector, coldly, "what will you have?"

"This is the man you sent me out for," broke in Officer Walker.

"Oh, yes, well take him to the desk sergeant."

Mr. Zuckerman was taken to the desk sergeant, where the warrant was read to him and his name booked on the charge preferred. His name being booked Mr. Walker said:

"I'll have to search you now."

"I haven't anything dangerous on me," protested the prisoner.

Detective Walker's answer was not in words. He deliberately passed his fingers into the prisoner's vest pocket and drew forth the contents. During this trying ordeal, so unpleasant to Mr. Zuckerman, the prisoner nervously edged about and explained to everyone who approached that he was there simply because a discharged employe had seen fit to revenge himself in such a cruel manner.

His story was many times interrupted and he frequently began anew, because many of the gentlemen whom he started to address had no interest in his case and were rude enough to tell him so. Mr. Zuckerman's possessions were not many, though fairly valuable.

Detective Walker took out and examined three lead pencils, some tooth picks and small cards, two of Mr. Zuckerman's stock watches, a copy of the *Daily Globe* and two purses filled with money. As to the two watches, the prisoner explained that he had taken them to a jeweler, not being a jeweler himself, to have them repaired, and that he was just bringing them back to his jewelry shop. Mr. Zuckerman was then requested to make himself comfortable until the Harrison street station patrol could be called, that he might ride to that point.

"Can I send for some of my friends," requested Mr. Zuckerman. "I have some friends and I can get bail."

"Oh, you will be given a good chance," said the desk sergeant, reassuringly, "but not here."

A few minutes later the patrol drove up and Mr. Zuckerman was transferred to the Harrison street station, where he was locked up and his friends notified.

Mr. Zuckerman was still waiting for his friends last evening.

The trial is set for 9:30 o'clock this morning, when Mr. Obermeyer, counsel for the city law department, will prosecute the case for the city. Mr. Zuckerman has for his attorney Mr. B. Schaffner. The prosecution will be based upon the last half of section 1437, which reads as follows:

> Any auctioneer or person being present where any watch, plate or jewelry is offered for sale, who shall knowingly, with intent to induce any person or persons to purchase the same or any part thereof, make any false representation or statement as to the ownership of, or character or quality of the article so offered for sale, or the owner or pretended owner of such article or articles, shall on conviction thereof, be subject to a fine of $50, and if such false representation is made by such auctioneer, or by any person with such auctioneer's knowledge and consent, the license of such auctioneer shall be forfeited.

The two "shillabers," who were formerly in Mr. Zuckerman's employ are prepared to swear that they misrepresented the jewelry sold by Mr. Zuckerman, to strangers and with his full knowledge and consent.

"There is no question," said Mr. Obermeyer of the city law department, "that the evidence of these two 'cappers' is sufficient to convict this auctioneer. He can be fined $50 and costs and on the strength of that I can recommend that the mayor revoke his license. The work that the *Daily Globe* is doing is a righteous one. You can depend upon me to give you all the assistance within my power."

The warrant, in the first place, was taken by the two "shillabers" in company with a reporter to the office of Chief McClaughry. Word was sent in that these warrants had been finally procured in spite of the police department and now would the major be kind enough to serve the warrants; also that information was in the hands of the *Daily Globe* which was sufficient to convict the proprietors of other auction shops now in operation. The major had no time. He couldn't possibly listen. The many strangers coming to Chicago must be protected and in promoting that very desirable end the mock auctions would not be considered. The police department in general was rather "chilly" toward the innovation of actually swearing out a warrant for the benefit of the public, but they could not refuse to act. The work had been done for them.

[19 October 1892, p. 1.]

7 - THE RETURN OF GENIUS.

There was born, once upon a time, a great Genius. His younger years were spent in poverty and sorrow. Yet his brain teemed with noble thoughts and grand purposes. One day, his heart filled with sorrow and despair, he wandered about viewing all that was rich and gorgeous, and the iron bitterness of fate entered his soul. He groaned aloud in the depth of his misery.

"Oh, that I was famous. Oh, that fame was mine, and riches, and pleasure. Even the world I would forsake if my name could be assured to posterity."

Musing thus he hurried to the woods and fields and by the side of a silver brook threw himself down and anguish filled his soul.

Then there came to him, above his outcry against fate, a gentle voice, sweet with sympathy, saying: "Thou, poor fool. Hast thou not genius? Is not the world before thee? See, it lies here! Rise! go forth! hew for thyself a path! make for thyself a name!"

He raised up his woebegone face and seeing no one cried,

"Who speaks?"

"The God of Genius," answered the voice. "Go and strive and I will assist thee."

The genius only buried his face again and sighed, "Would that I had never been born."

Then came the voice again, saying: "What wilt thou?"

"I would that my name may live through all time," answered the genius.

"On one condition shalt thou have glory and an undying fame."

"All conditions will I obey if only my name is hereafter assured."

"I will give thee fame even now, and riches, and ease, and an undying name, only thou shalt not hear nor see thy own glory."

Then Genius arose and was comforted.

"Go, then," said the voice, "and gather from the fields a handful of poppies. Breathe the perfume from these thrice and thy wish will straitway come to pass."

With great joy the Genius went his way gathering here and there from fragrant nooks a handful of poppies, and when these had been gathered he returned to the brook, threw himself by its side and breathed the perfume thrice. Then there came to him a glorious fancy and he was transported to a mansion of silver. In it were ornaments of gold and precious stones, and luxurious furnishings, such as mind could hardly conceive.

All around sounded the voices of birds and the murmur of silver brooks and the air was burdened with the delightful odors of strange and beautiful flowers.

"Oh!" cried Genius, "now am I happy and my fame will be perpetual."

Slaves dressed in gorgeous attire anticipated his every wish and daily brought him tidings of the world without, written on sheets of pure gold. Sweet voices nightly sang his praises from without, saying: "Thy name is forever famous."

Time rolled on and curious longings entered his heart. They were at first as whisperings of some evil counselor, and for a time he spurned them from him. They would come to him, however, and again was Genius unhappy.

"Oh," he thought, "that I might see the world again. What is greatness and glory but to enjoy. That I might see the world bow and smile, that I might feel its glances of admiration and hear its words of praise. Even can I forget riches and ease for that. Had I but that added to my happiness my cup would then be full to overflowing."

Scarcely had the thought come to him than he heard the voice saying: "I have given thee gold and silver and luxurious ease. See! You have delights granted to no other. Thy name is also forever assured. Wilt thou hear voices of praise? Then, insomuch is thy name forgotten. Wilt thou have the admiration of humanity? Then in that degree will thy name be forgotten. Wilt thou mingle with the world and have it bow to thee? Then dies thy name with thee."

The Genius thought long and deeply and was not comforted. No more was there delight in his gorgeous surroundings. No longer murmured the brooks to him in whispering melody. Everything seemed to have lost its harmony. Time brought only a longing to be great among men.

"I will go," he cried. "I will mingle with men and be of them. They are nearer to me than silver and jewels; nearer to me than words of praise and gorgeous luxury. Fling wide the doors! I am through with this life. I will again seek mankind," and he hurried from the palace.

On the last step stood a fair maiden bearing a lute and holding in her hand a bunch of poppies. "Breathe of these thrice or thy world will be ever lost," she said and the Genius, stooping, inhaled their fragrance.

Then was the brook again as before. Then again he realized his life and its terrors, and looking upward cried, "Oh, that my dream was still," but a voice whispered: "Go! Make for thyself a palace. From it thou canst never leave. In thine own hand is the power—the strength. Achieve thine own glory. It is for thee and thee alone to do this. In effort, will thy genius be sharpened. Aid from the gods would but destroy thee."

And the genius listened to these golden words and returned to men.

Carl Dreiser.
[23 October 1892, p. 4.]

St. Louis Globe-Democrat

A work of such magnitude as the present construction of the great St. Louis Union Depot bears features of interest that call for consideration from all the city's inhabitants and the population of the great State of Missouri. Common knowledge it is that the great railroads terminating in this city have banded together for mutual profit and the glory of the City of St. Louis to build, not the second largest and finest depot in the United States and the world, but actually the first. Common knowledge goes farther and covers the fact that the great enterprise is located on Market street, facing north, and extends from Eighteenth street to Twentieth, a beautiful stretch of two blocks, or 600 feet. Many have watched the progress of the work and visited frequently the now famous section devoted to this colossal passenger station. Many thousands of the readers of the *Globe-Democrat*, however, have not viewed the structure in progress, nor indeed have a tangible idea of the magnitude of the undertaking. For this reason pains have been taken to gather correctly a mass of technical facts and to present them lucidly in order.

The constant growth of St. Louis has attracted through a score of years a number of great trunk lines which find in this city a convenient and profitable point for termination. As a terminal point for great trunk lines St. Louis is unsurpassed, lying, as it does, in the central portion of the Union and of the Mississippi Valley, and really standing as an open gateway to the great West, Southwest and Northwest. Since the days of the early Astors and other great fur companies St. Louis has held the position of a terminal point; a place where, after a long journey from the East, travelers might stay to recuperate and gather their supplies for enterprises that lay farther to the south and west. All stories of Western life and adventure usually include an opening chapter sentence which reads: "We reached St. Louis on the ———, and stopped for," etc. The "Capt. Bonneville," of Irving, did; Mark Twain relates it of his expedition to the Rockies, and other writers of minor fame have added their mite to the evidence. Dickens, too, paused and wondered in the Mound City.

Gradually great trunk lines have centered here until now there are twenty-one railroads having entrance, six of which have St. Louis for their eastern or western terminal point. These are the Big 4, the Louisville and Nashville, Missouri Pacific, Ohio and Mississippi, St. Louis, Iron Moun-

"The Grand Waiting Room" (*St. Louis Globe-Democrat*, 11 December 1892, p. 28).

THE GRAND WAITING ROOM.

"The New Union Depot" (*St. Louis Globe-Democrat*, 11 December 1892, p. 28).

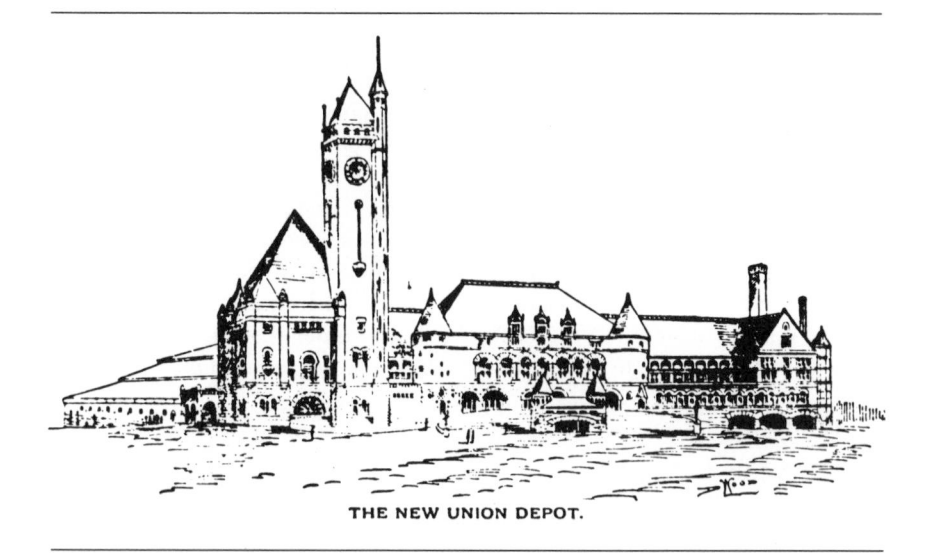

THE NEW UNION DEPOT.

tain and Southern, and the Wabash Railroads. St. Louis is fortunate above many cities in having her railroads bunched together and entering the city through one great artery. This obviates, in a great measure, the many grade crossing accidents or murders, as the metropolitan vernacular terms them, and makes possible a great union depot, where, as in the present instance, interests and personalities do not blind the business foresight of the great railroad magnates involved. The great trunk lines, in conjunction with the Merchants' Terminal Railroad Association, and the various other roads having entrance here have long worked in harmony and mutually profited by it. But the traffic has outgrown the accommodations. The Union Depot that long served the needs of St. Louis as a sixth and seventh rate city now falls far short of her needs, her dignity and her pride as a metropolitan center. The demand for better accommodations became frequent and resulted in the structure now in process of erection. The present scheme is the outgrowth of long consideration of the special needs of this city, coupled with a knowledge of its certain future greatness and prosperity.

Hubert P. Taussig, Chief Engineer of the Merchants' Terminal Railroad Association, representing the combined interests of the various roads jointly enjoying the depot privileges, first called for plans and specifications for a great Union Depot in 1890. This call met with at least a dozen responses from architects and engineers. These, at a somewhat later date, Mr. Taussig presented to the Board of Directors, composed of representative members of the various railroad corporations concerned, and awaited their choice. After some deliberation the entire set of plans was rejected, and for a time the matter was apparently dropped. The Executive Board, however, was merely looking about for competent architects and civil engineers, on whom to rest the great charge of building the depot. These were eventually found in the persons of Theodore C. Link, of Link & Cameron, who designed the plan for the depot proper, and George H. Pegram, Consulting Engineer of the Missouri Pacific Railroad, who designed the train shed, the largest in the world. Another important feature which required the genius of a third, was that of the track system, for the best convenience of all the roads. This task was really one of the most difficult and was admirably designed by Hubert P. Taussig. These men worked separately for awhile, each mapping out splendid plans and mentally figuring a passenger station to fit them. When Mr. Pegram, the designer and contractor, was informed of the name of the architect, Mr. Link, he went at once to consult with him. After speaking of the great enterprise awhile, Mr. Pegram took occasion to remark:

"I don't see how I am to build a train shed less than 200 feet high, according to the width called for."

"Great heavens, man," cried Link, "my depot tower is only 222 feet high."

The prospect of such miserable proportion eventually induced Contractor Pegram to calculate on nothing higher than 100 feet, which was accordingly carried out.

It is proper here to introduce the main feature of the entire depot question, namely, that of how the suitable site was procured. Long before any plans had been arranged for a depot, as regards design or architectural beauty, the question of a suitable, convenient site had been weighing on the minds of the interested Directors of the various corporations. No site could be more convenient for all parties concerned than the one chosen, and yet the residents and owners of land in that quarter seemingly least suspected that designs were had upon the ground. Indeed, whole areas within a radius of two miles of the old depot were alternately selected and rejected by hordes of speculators with selfish intentions. Land on the opposite side of Market street is exceedingly valuable just now, a half dozen transactions in the neighborhood of $600 a foot having taken place since last summer. The railroads, through their agents, managed, however, to secure the ground at a very reasonable figure, the entire cost being in round numbers about $1,000,000.

Through the section now occupied by the depot, train shed and "throat" of tracks, four streets should pass east and west. These are Eugenia street, Clark avenue, Spruce and Poplar streets. These four do not include the bounding streets north and south, which are Market and Randolph streets. Nineteenth street, if continued through the section north and south, would divide the property into equal parts. Thus the section actually includes twelve blocks of property and also the additional space where the streets should be dedicated by the city to depot purposes. This section of land contained a frontage of about 3600 feet.

If it had been known that the Terminal Railway Association intended to build a depot there the property would have been bought up and held for a good round figure. Nothing less than $800 per front foot would have been asked, and in the end $800 would undoubtedly have been paid for it. At that rate the cost of the land would have been $2,880,000. As it actually was, the Terminal Association secured the land for $1,000,000, or about one-third as much.

Early in the spring of 1890 the Terminal Association, through its agents, began the purchase of realty in that vicinity. The company discreetly refused to allow any of its former agents to secure options or purchase ground for it. The Directors feared that the matter might get wind and be blown about among the property-owners, forever barring the hope of a reasonable purchasing price. Through a dozen small real estate dealers the corporation first operated, and later, when sufficient land had been purchased to give the enterprise a firm standing, condemnation suits were begun. The balance of the frontage was secured at a more reasonable figure. A few, however, profited by the great enterprise. Several property-owners surmised the scheme, and demanded not only a high figure for the property desired by the company, but made haste to purchase land in the immediate vicinity, especially that fronting south on Market street. Various individuals in inner depot circles profited by their foreknowledge substantially. The property adjoining and facing the depot is now largely in the possession of speculators and dealers. It will no doubt change hands several times before the builder and user secures it.

The great task was then in the hands of three masters of special lines, Messrs. Link, Pegram and Taussig. They modified their various calculations into an harmonious whole, and, the land question being disposed of, work was eventually begun. This auspicious and very desirable event occurred in April, 1892. After months of planning, consulting and rearranging the great project was at last started and the old buildings on the proposed site were wrecked. This, however, was the work of months, and blasting-powder was not infrequently used. When completed the depot will stand as a monument of the enterprise and constructive genius of St. Louisans, for all of the men engaged in mapping out the great work are residents here. The effect on the vicinity of the location is yet hardly to be foreshadowed. It is safe to say that the depot will drive from the locality all residents and change it to a truly business portion.

The first great division of the work is the depot proper. This division is in the hands of Theodore Link, who designed the entire building, and called for bids according to his specifications. The materials used for the walls and exterior decorations are Bedford limestone and enameled and red pressed brick. The structure is a rather free treatment of the Romanesque school. The exterior presents to view a front of solid Bedford stone, beautifully chiseled and decorated with turrets and towers of varying dimensions. Two sides only are of Bedford stone. They are the Market and Eighteenth street prospects. The Twentieth street side is of red brick, but it can not be seen by the ordinary pedestrian, being partly hidden from view by the train shed extension that runs along the Twentieth street side.

A casual observer would say that the building was composed of three separate architectural groups, harmoniously blended into a charming whole. From the east and west, parallel with Market street, terraced approaches lead to the main entrance, a fine, broad flight of steps and landings that lend vigor and variety to the front aspect. The central building, or one-third, is strongly contrasted with the east and west one-thirds, being of more even, square proportion, with a high, slanting roof that stands prominently out and above the roofs of the east and west wings. This central portion is given entirely to the two waiting rooms, the general and grand. The two upper stories of the east and west wings are devoted to office rooms. In order to give the central portion prominence these two upper stories on either side are set back from the main front line of the structure a distance of some 20 feet. The eastern end or one-third has for its distinguishing feature a tall square tower modeled somewhat after the style of the Italian Campanile. It is topped by a conical roof that protects an arched and pillared balcony, which can be reached by a spiral iron staircase. This tower stands 222 feet high on a base 30 feet square. It will be ornamented with high narrow windows and four great clock dials, facing the four points of the horizon. These dials will be illuminated at night by electrical arc lamps from within. This portion will be four stories in height, or one more story than the general height, which is three.

The Eighteenth street side will contain an entrance-way and staircase, 50 feet wide, leading down to the Eighteenth street promenade that extends along the east side of the train shed for its entire length. The west one-third is of three-story uniform order and serves a second purpose of the great station. This purpose gives a distinguishing feature to this end in the shape of three great archways at the extreme west portion, through which the various vehicles will pass to the baggage room and the main promenade. There is an entrance for carriages only under the great terrace or porte-cochere leading up to the main entrance. Carriages can drive from Market street through a kind of half-moon driveway, to the central entrance, which is a doorway that opens out upon the midway landing of the grand staircase. This staircase leads from the general waiting to the grand waiting room.

Thus, one can either walk up the outer flight of steps into the grand waiting room, or can drive in a carriage to the central entrance-way and ascend a half of the grand flight into the same room. From the carriage-way arches at the west end to the sidewalks on the east end is a gradual rise of 15 feet. The basement of the depot is on a level with the tracks under the train shed. The first floor is just a little above the Market street level. The rise of 15 feet hides a portion of the first story at the east end, but the effect is not deteriorating to any perceptible degree. The rear or south wall of the depot joins the extension of the great train shed. This wall will rest on a base of Bedford stone 3 feet in height. From that a wall of enameled brick 9 feet in height will spring, and above that again buff-colored bricks will be used. The windows of the entire structure are set deep into the thick walls, and give to the whole an appearance of massive solidity. The slay line of the roof is neatly and frequently broken by the varying size of the three portions, which, with the roof turrets, dormer windows and pinnacles, give a splendid finish to the entire structure.

Passengers entering the depot from the train will pass first into the general waiting room on the ground floor. This room, according to plans, will contain a floor area of 10,000 square feet, inlaid with mosaic. The walls will be of cream enameled brick to the ceiling, 18 feet above the floor. The ceiling will be painted and highly decorated. To the right and left of the south entrance the east and west walls will contain the ticket windows, eighteen in number, evenly divided. The east wall is to have nine railroad ticket offices; the west, nine sleeping-berth offices. This side will also contain a sub-station of the general Post Office for the sale of stamps and money orders. In the center of the room will be the bureau of information, a circular glass screen, where information on various railroad topics will be stored and dispensed.

Facing the south entrance will be the grand staircase, which leads to the grand waiting room above. On the first landing the entrance for carriage passengers will be situated. This inlet is on a level with Market street and under the terraced approach which leads to the main entrance above. This staircase will be of solid brass, with ornaments of bronze, and 20 feet wide. The middle landing and turn will contain 1200 square feet of floor space, and besides the staircase, two elevators will connect the general with the grand waiting room. From the west side the general waiting room connects with the lunch rooms, barber shop and bath rooms, and these rooms will be finished in Italian marble. From the last a corridor leads to the immigrants' waiting room, which will be a well-appointed, plain finished apartment, with walls of enameled brick and oak trimmings. The remainder of the ground floor will be taken up with rooms of sale, a public telephone room and the great carriage concourse at the west end.

The grand waiting room on the first floor above will be the feature of this great work. This room will contain a floor area of 12,000 square feet. The height from the marble mosaic floor to the rib-arched ceiling will be 60 feet. The dimensions will be 60 by 120 feet. The walls, exclusive of the many niches and balconies, will be of Scaglione marble, giving the room a cream-yellow tone. This great area will be uninterrupted by pillars or fountains of any kind. The other decorations will be of gilt. The arched ribs of the ceiling will be studded with many incandescent lamps, some 3000 in number.

The center of the north wall of this room will contain a great product of the skill of the workers in glass, a window 20 feet square. This window will be of colored glass and contain some allegorical allusion to the progressive arts. The figure glass of this window alone will cost nearly $3000. About the east, north and west sides a receding balcony will look down upon the splendid scene. Three great chandeliers, composed of several hundred incandescent lamps, will be suspended from the center of the arched ceiling. From the east the smoking and waiting room for gentlemen can be reached. On the west the ladies' parlor adjoins. This room will differ from the general decorations in that it will be finished in oak and leather. From the west end also of the grand waiting room a corridor leads to the grand dining hall. An attempt will be made to decorate this room in very delicate shades. Polished oak, gold and mirrors, with a dado of real African marble 5 feet high about the base of the walls, will complete the scheme. The service of this hall has not yet been decided upon, but no doubt will be in keeping with the splendor of the decorations. The remaining two stories of the station will be divided into offices, 100 in number. The fourth story of the eastern one-third will be occupied by the telegraph service of the various roads. Pneumatic tubes will run from this room to the office of the train dispatcher, who will be guided by the telegraph instructions.

An estimate of the magnitude of the task can be gained from the following facts: Four million bricks will be used, 20,000 square feet of marble, 1200 tons of iron and 2,350,000 little blocks of mosaic will be laid in the floors. The cost of the plain glass used will be nearly $15,000.

Work on the building is well under way. The foundations for the west half are already in. Two of the three stone carriage-way arches are completed. The third is only half constructed. Running east from this the walls lessen in completeness, until at the farther end men are still digging for the foundation. Immense derricks are upon the ground and great blocks of stone and granite are swung lightly into place. The construction of the building is in charge of J. Willard Adams, of this city. Mr. Adams stated to a *Globe-Democrat* reporter that after the foundations were in a large force of bricklayers, carpenters and stone-cutters would be put to work, and that in a few weeks the building would take definite form. At present there are less than 100 workmen on this branch of the work.

The second division of the great work is the train shed. The credit for this really wonderful dome belongs to Mr. Pegram, who takes it with a modest unassuming that is in little proportion to the magnitude and accompanying honor of the work. Mr. Pegram drew the plans, and on December 4, 1891, called for bids for the various conditions according to his specifications. The train shed is really more striking than the depot itself, being the largest constructed steel and iron shed in the world, and really a triumph of engineering skill. Working under forced conditions as to length and width, while at the same time limited as to height, Mr. Pegram brought about a harmonious entity that to many seemed impossible and even foolish to attempt. It stands 601 feet in width, 700 feet in length, and yet is only 100 feet high, which would be the same as a shed 100 feet in width and length and only 16.6 feet high. To make a train shed of the latter dimensions look imposing is beyond human skill; yet under similar conditions and proportions that are in the exact ratio of 16.6 to 100 feet, Mr. Pegram has succeeded in constructing a magnificent train shed that is truly imposing, while at the same time fulfilling all the requirements of a great metropolitan depot. At first various materials were proposed. It had not been decided for instance, until the work was well under way, whether the glass of the skylights should be set in wood or copper, or whether all steel should be the constructive metal or iron. The uncertainty of the relative strength of each material made the task all the more difficult. These obstacles have indeed not yet been entirely overcome, as to what metal or glass or kind of wood will be used in the different instances. However, the work proceeds apace and the questions will be decided when the call for material comes.

The original specifications for the train shed, which have been since largely carried out, are as follows: The roof of the train shed forms an arch of 600 feet radius, 700 feet long, 30 feet high on the sides and a height of 100 feet from the base to the center span of the arch. Support is given the roof by forty-four outer columns, forty-four intermediate and twenty-four middle columns, increasing in height proportionately with the upward slant of the roof. These columns are spaced 60 feet apart lengthwise of the shed (or receding from the depot to the yards), and forming five spans in the width (parallel to the depot), three spans of 145 feet and two of 92 feet, making a total width of 604 feet. On these columns rest the eighty-four trusses and twenty-seven rafters that support the roof. A truss is a frame that supports weight between pillars or columns. A good illustration of a truss is the side of an iron bridge. The top cords of the trusses form the beautiful arch of the roof. The bottom cords of the trusses are formed of I-bars and they hang in chains over the columns, so furnishing the support. A central skylight, 25 feet high and 40 feet wide, rests on the roof and extends for the entire length, or 700 feet. From this as a backbone lateral skylights, 30 feet wide and 10 feet high, run down the roof on either side at regular intervals of 30 feet. To the regular train shed an extension will be added that will cover a space of 42,000 square feet, between the depot proper and the train gates. This space is 70 feet wide and extends from Eighteenth to Twentieth street. The entire central skylight and half the width of the extension or auxiliary shed, some 21,000 square feet, will be covered with white ribbed glass, set in copper. The sides of the cross or lateral skylights will be covered with sheets of white ribbed glass, 8 feet in length, set in steel bars. Slots will be put in every section of the lateral and central lights, at short intervals, for ventilation.

The trusses, or simply the iron work at both ends, will be covered with corrugated iron, merely for looks, below which a curtain of glass, set in steel, 40 feet in depth and 500 feet in width, will be hung. The effect of this curtain on the appearance of the shed proper will be properly conceived when the illustrations are glanced at. In constructing the shed the best materials are being used. No wood is used except for sheathing. This sheathing is of tongued and grooved heart yellow pine, and is covered with tin on the outside. The inside will be polished and varnished. In due time the iron work will be properly painted and decorated. The great expanse of roof will appear from the ground as though it were oil-finished. Incandescent and arc lights will be supplied from a power house on the ground. Hardwood platforms, 12 feet in the clear, will be laid between the thirty-two tracks running parallel into the depot, and will be guarded from intrusion by a fence and gates of iron of handsome design. The effect of all these accouterments, the lights, many trains, wonderful distance of the roofs, etc., will be a fitting preparation for the appreciative senses before entrance is made into the grand depot. A few figures as to the weight, number and cost of the various materials, such as glass, iron, wood, etc., will not be out of place here.

The estimates call for 6,000,000 pounds of steel, 1,000,000 square feet of hardwood, 120,000 square feet of glass, or about three acres. There will be 52,250 square feet of cast, galvanized and corrugated iron; 475,000 square feet of varnished roof in view, and the cost of the superstructure or train shed itself, exclusive of the track system and depot proper, will be $600,000. Along the Eighteenth street side a 50-foot platform will be constructed for the use of promenaders exclusively. Beginning with the train gates, or 70 feet from the rear depot wall, on the Twentieth street side, a baggage room will extend 300 feet southward. This will be the most complete quick-service room in the country, and every facility will be had for speedy and safe transfers of chattels. Sale stands and counters of all kinds, as well as branch offices and service cards, will be confined within the limits of the extension or auxiliary sheds, along the line of the train gates and fence. Under this shed no engines will stand puffing vile smoke. Trains will be backed and left in the inclosure until within a few minutes of starting time, when the locomotive will back in and connect.

The third division of the Terminal Association Columbian enterprise, the planning of the tracks, was placed in the hands of Engineer Taussig. His plan for the great station is certainly unique. The system as arranged will have thirty tracks, varying in length from 400 to 1200 feet. This entire number will converge into a bottle-shaped junction or throat at the south end of the four main tracks. These main tracks branch off to the east and west into a system of two main parallel tracks. The whole forms a figure resembling a wine glass or bottle, as will be seen in the accompanying illustration. Trains coming from the east must seemingly pass by the south end of the train shed on the outer track, running north and south. When the shed has been passed the engine will be reversed and the train backed in over the curved Y on to its respective track. This leaves the train ready to start again without switching the cars about in the yards. The trains coming from the west will run east past the train shed, and so back in, in a similar manner. Trains from and for the west will occupy the west half of the train shed; trains from the east the eastern half. The division is as follows:

West half—Wabash, St. Louis, Keokuk and Missouri, St. Louis, Kansas City and Colorado, St. Louis, Iron Mountain and Southern and St. Louis and San Francisco roads. These all come in from the west, passing under the Twenty-first street bridge.

East half—Wabash, Chicago and Alton, Burlington, Cairo Short Line, Big Four, Illinois Central, Louisville, Evansville and St. Louis, Louisville and Nashville and the Ohio and Mississippi Railroads.

The roads will be connected with the new station from the mouth of the Eads tunnel, that runs under the city from the big bridge to the present Union Depot, by four main tracks. Two of these tracks will be used for passenger trains exclusively; the other two for freight. Under the train shed the tracks will be arranged in groups of two, spaced 22½ feet apart. This intervening space will be used as a platform. It is the intention to inclose the entire station so that access to trains can be had only through the train gates next adjoining the depot. This will prevent accidents and confusion, and will also assist in espionage when it is needed. Exit can be made either through the depot proper, or by way of Eighteenth and Twentieth streets. After submitting many plans, covering every possible location between the present site and the old depot, and not excluding Washington square, where the new City Hall stands, the plans for the present location were submitted and accepted. The switches will all be controlled by the interlocking system. From one point near the station all the switches and connections will be controlled. It will be impossible for the man in the switch tower to give the right of way to more than one train at a time. This system prevents all possibility of collision, for in throwing one switch by the lever all other switches are locked and danger signals thrown into place as a warning. The starting time of all trains will be signaled by lights and signs, so that the watch of the engineer will be useless as a criterion to start by. The length of the tracks under the sheds, if stretched in a line, would be about ten miles. The cost of the entire system will be nearly $200,000. The tracks will be of steel and rock-set.

The following data in regard to the large train sheds of the world is furnished:

St. Pancras, England, is 248 feet wide.

Grand Central Depot, New York, 200 feet wide.

New Pennsylvania Railroad station at Jersey City, 256 feet wide by 658 feet long, covering twelve tracks.

New Philadelphia and Reading Railroad station at Philadelphia, 260 feet wide by 800 feet long, covering fourteen tracks.

Proposed new Pennsylvania Railroad station at Philadelphia, 306 feet wide by 647 feet long, covering sixteen tracks.

Union Passenger Station at Frankfort, Germany, 552 feet wide by 600 feet long, covering eighteen tracks.

New St. Louis Union Depot, 601 feet wide by 700 feet long, covering thirty-two tracks.

[11 December 1892, p. 28.]

9 - MR. WATTERSON ON POLITICS.

Henry Watterson, the far-famed Kentucky editor and orator, is comfortably ensconced at the Southern, and will remain until Saturday morning. His mission in St. Louis is to deliver his popular lecture on "Money and Morals," which he does this evening. Mr. Watterson is accompanied on his tour by his wife and private secretary. To obtain an expression from the great editor on political topics of present interest a *Globe-Democrat* reporter visited Mr. Watterson and presented a few questions for discussion.

"I have not any special knowledge, I believe, on the points you speak of. It is hardly worth while talking on political topics. Still, if you will report my language verbatim and not make alterations, I will consent to an interview."

Upon being assured that his words should not be misinterpreted, Mr. Watterson sought out a secluded corner and remarked: "Well, now, what is it that you wish my opinion on?"

The sentiment was expressed that probably Mr. Cleveland had other reasons for opposing Mr. Murphy than those recently published in New York and telegraphed to the *Globe-Democrat*. It will be remembered that Mr. Cleveland in the published interview said that he opposed Mr. Murphy in the senatorial contest believing that Mr. Murphy was not a sufficiently broad and experienced man to represent the great State of New York in the United States Senate. Mr. Cleveland expressed the opinion also that there were other men more able than Mr. Murphy, and also that Mr. Cockran would suit him fairly well.

"Why does Mr. Cleveland oppose Mr. Murphy in the senatorial race in New York?" was asked, "and why should Mr. Cleveland advocate the candidacy of Bourke Cockran, when in the Convention hall last June Mr. Cockran so bitterly opposed the naming of Mr. Cleveland as the party leader?"

"Well," said Mr. Watterson, "Mr. Cleveland has stated himself why he opposed Mr. Murphy. I know of no other reason. These facts, however, remain, that Mr. Murphy was Chairman of the New York delegation in the National Convention that indorsed Mr. Hill, and Chairman also of the New York State Central Committee. In New York men are rated according to their actual power; not according to any literary or oratorical abilities they may possess. I don't know that Mr. Cleveland has expressed any preference for Mr. Cockran. If he has, it is because Mr. Cockran represents the qualities which Mr. Cleveland declares are conspicuously absent in Mr. Murphy. But I imagine the reason why Mr. Cockran is being urged by the opposition to Mr. Murphy is rather a flank movement against Mr. Murphy than a genuine preference for Mr. Cockran. If Mr. Cockran had been the original choice of Tammany it is likely that those who are now singing his praises so loudly would be assailing him precisely as they are now assailing Mr. Murphy, although they would not have the claim of inexperience and unsuitability which they are urging against Mr. Murphy to urge against Mr. Cockran. I think it unfortunate that Mr. Cleveland feels it a necessity to take any part whatever in the election of a Senator from the State of New York. At the same time it seems hard that he should not have some representative from his own State in the Senate of the United States on whom he can rely for hearty sympathy and support."

"It is said, Mr. Watterson, that Col. Dan Lamont will get a Cabinet position, probably that of Postmaster General. Have you any opinion on that subject?"

"I know absolutely nothing of Mr. Cleveland's intention," continued Mr. Watterson, "respecting his Cabinet. But I have had an impression that Col. Lamont will be a member of his political family."

"You probably think that Mr. Whitney will secure the leading position in the list of Cabinet offices?"

"I think Mr. Whitney ought to and will be able to command any place within the President's gift. My understanding is, however, that Mr. Whitney's great and varied money interests will not allow his taking office."

Asked as to whether Isaac Gray, of Indiana, deserved well at the hands of the President-elect and whether he will get an office from Mr. Cleveland, Mr. Watterson stated that that was something he did not know anything about. Of Gov. Francis and the prospects of a political plum falling over the river into Missouri, Mr. Watterson expressed himself as equally ignorant.

"I have the highest regard for Gov. Francis," said the great editor, "but knowing nothing about the matter I don't care to discuss it."

As to Mr. Carlisle, the probability of his becoming a member of the Cabinet and his attitude on the silver question, Mr. Watterson seemed more willing to talk. In answer to the question, "Will Mr. Carlisle be a member of the new Cabinet?" Mr. Watterson replied:

"Mr. Carlisle has undoubtedly been offered the secretaryship of the Treasury, and he is being urged to accept it, not only by Mr. Cleveland, but by an overwhelming majority of Democrats all over the country. He expresses the logic of the situation in many ways, and is a conceded master of the economic and fiscal questions which will press upon the new administration. He has thus far hesitated to accept the proffered honor because he is well satisfied where he is, and being a poor man, dependent upon his salary as a Senator and his law practice, which would be cut off if he accepted the Treasury, he does not feel himself able, from a money standpoint, to make the sacrifice. But I believe the end of it will be that his objections will be overruled and that he will be the next Secretary of the Treasury."

"Do you think Mr. Carlisle will retreat from his present attitude toward the silver issue?" was asked.

"It is a mistake that Mr. Carlisle has ever been an extremist on the silver question. In the sense that Mr. Stewart and Mr. Jones, of Nevada, and Mr. Teller and Mr. Wolcott, of Colorado, are free silver men, Mr. Carlisle is not a free silver man; that is to say, he does not belong to that category of financiers. He is simply a bi-metallist who believes in gold and silver and paper convertible into coin on demand as the money of the land; but he realizes that the whole silver question is in an experimental and transition state, and his intellectual and political character is a guarantee that he would engage in no financial adventures. It is Mr. Carlisle's conservatism, not less than his abilities and experience, which commend him to the new President as well as to the business interests of the country as a safe head of the Treasury Department at this time."

"If Mr. Whitney refuses the Secretaryship of State, who do you think Mr. Cleveland will finally select?"

"From actual knowledge, or even from direct intimation, I have not the remotest idea. I see the names of three gentlemen mentioned by the newspapers. They are Senator George Gray of Delaware, ex-Senator Eustis of Louisiana, and ex-Minister to England Phelps. There are some very positive objections to this latter gentleman, whose abilities and accomplishments are admitted, but who is a man of limited American sympathies, cordially disliked by a large section of our foreign born citizens, himself a citizen of the little Republican rotten borough of Vermont, and certain if he is made Secretary of State to bring no strength but some actual weakness to the Administration. Moreover, if Mr. Collins, of Massachusetts, is to be a member of the Cabinet, and it is said he will be, the naming of Mr. Phelps for Secretary of State would be out of question. Nevertheless Mr. Cleveland is a man of his own head in these matters and is not likely to let a stumbling block like that trouble him. Mr. Gray, of Delaware, is a strong man, and his appointment would make a place in the Senate for Mr. Bayard, whose return to public life seems to be desired by the President-elect. Ex-Senator James B. Eustis, of Louisiana, was at one time arrayed as one of Mr. Cleveland's severest critics, but he is in many ways better qualified for this important post than any other Democrat within Mr. Cleveland's reach. Mr. Eustis is a man of great legal learning, of powerful intellectual calibre, of large experience in foreign languages and affairs, having a commanding address and an ample fortune. He would make not only a great Secretary of State but a great political adviser."

"What are the Democrats going to do about the tariff?" was asked.

"The Democratic party is charged with the business of conducting the country from the high scale of protective duties to a low scale of revenue duties, to which the party is irrevocably committed. Twice by overwhelming majorities the people have commanded this change—in 1890 and 1892. During the campaigns preceding those general elections the issue was squarely made by the Democrats and met by the Republicans, with the result of an increasing vote in favor of the free traders and against the protectionists. The platform on which Mr. Cleveland was elected is unequivocal. My understanding is that Mr. Cleveland is not behind the terms of that platform in his convictions and purposes. And I confidently look, therefore, within the next four years, to see the McKinley system supplanted by a free-trade system, reached by methods so conservative and rational as to compass the revolution without any serious disturbance of the manufacturing interests of the country."

"Would you restore the sugar tax?"

"Why, certainly. Under the specious pretense of furnishing the people a free breakfast table the Republicans put tea and coffee on the free list, when Brazil immediately put an export duty on coffee, which failed to cheapen coffee in the degree expected, whilst leaving sugar upon the dutiable list. Two years ago the McKinley bill put raw sugar on the free list, leaving a duty on refined sugars for the benefit of the Sugar Trust and giving a bounty of $10,000,000 to the domestic producers of raw sugar, thus cutting down the revenues by about $50,000,000 and increasing the taxes of the people by the sum of $10,000,000 of bounty, making a difference in all of about $50,000,000 to the Treasury, and therefore against the taxpayers. Meanwhile every other article on the breakfast table—knives and forks, plates and saucers, grandmother's big cup and baby's napkin ring—are taxed to the moon, and this they call a free breakfast table. The first thing we do will be to smash the sugar bounty and restore sugar to the revenue yielding schedules. In that way we shall get about $50,000,000 of the $250,000,000 we must get through the custom houses. Tell my old friend, the editor of the *Globe-Democrat*, to put that in his pipe and smoke it good."

"What about whisky and tobacco?"

"The two ought to yield an average of $125,000,000 annually of internal revenue, just as they stand, without any change or increase, leaving the additional $25,000,000 that may be needed to support the Government and pay the pensioners, or any additional sums that may hereafter be needed to be got out of the well-regulated income tax."

"In case Mr. Carlisle takes the Secretaryship of the Treasury would you be likely to succeed him as Senator?"

"Nothing could induce me to take public office of any sort. I settled that matter definitely ten years ago, when I might have gone to the Senate without opposition. I know of nothing more distasteful than the servitude and insecurity of official life in the United States, nor any occupation which pays so scantily upon the investment required of those who enter it. If Mr. Carlisle takes the Treasury the scramble for his place will be free for all and anybody's race; but nobody is thinking of me in that connection, for everybody in Kentucky knows that if I should be elected I would not go to Washington to take the oath of office."

[6 January 1893, p. 4.]

10 - THEOSOPHY AND SPIRITUALISM.

Mrs. Annie Besant, the famous theosophist of London, was visited yesterday afternoon at the Southern Hotel by a *Globe-Democrat* reporter in quest of theosophical knowledge. Responding to an invitation to come in the reporter found Mrs. Besant engaged in trimming a basket of pink roses and placing them in a jar of water. It was suggested that in view of the fact that so few Americans understand the meaning and the scope of theosophy it might be best to take verbatim an explanation of the new belief and publish it. Mrs. Besant stated that her present work in America is simply to spread theosophical knowledge, and that for this reason her lecture here and elsewhere would be largely devoted to its underlying principles.

"What is theosophy?" was asked.

"The word of course means the wisdom of God and the principle of it; the marked belief of it is the reincarnation of souls. We believe that theosophy contains the solution of this world's ills; its science applies to the solution of the labor problem and the rehabilitation of society in general. Theosophy teaches that brotherhood is the natural and necessary normal condition of the world. The world to-day has a wrong standard. Whatever religions may teach the highway along which civilization is at present advancing is self interest and not the interest of all. People believe that personal success is and should be the aim of every one; that without this aim the world, or rather civilization, would not advance."

"Do you believe then that the race can advance when this self interest has been removed or transferred to interest in the welfare of others?"

"Certainly. No doubt you imagine that success is yours because you placed before yourself a certain aim, a personal aim to be sure. You believed that because you followed this and left others to take care of themselves you have achieved your aim and stand superior to your brothers. Nevertheless you are unhappy. Men set up before themselves a false God; they follow a misleading standard. Though they achieve every honor that this world can bestow and everlasting fame they are still unhappy. Men attain their objects and their self ends, simply because the rest of their brothers have equally personal objects and selfish aims. Where an entire community stands with brotherhood as the underlying principle, personality and selfish aims can not be accomplished. So, then, we believe that this selfish standard should be changed to one of brotherhood."

"What can you do with poverty?"

"Poverty is a disease from which both the poor and the rich suffer. There is in this life an element of ether in which and through which this disease thrives and spreads. It is not alone the poor that suffer. All nature is outraged, sinned against by poverty inasmuch as poverty is a crime against nature. The rich being a part of this great nature can not escape the results of the sin. In poverty is bred disease, which enters into the domain of the rich, causing suffering and death. They can not escape it, and it were best to open their eyes and remove the disease than to endeavor to flee from it."

"You do not recognize, then, a controlling principle—a God?"

"No, we do not. If there is a God, the order of this life is then manifestly unjust. Some beings are born with ability and strength, some with dulled senses, with weaknesses and with deformities. If you say that a just being has sent a weakling into the world to battle on equal terms with strength and ability, then you simply admit that the controlling influence is unjust. Instead of accusing a divine being with being partial, we turn to the individual himself and find a solution of the apparent discrepancy in reincarnation."

"You mean, then, that souls are born over and over?"

"Yes, that is it. Instead of saying no thanks to myself for my ability to write, to sing, no thanks to myself for my strong physique, we believe that all thanks are due to yourself and no one else. In your former state, in that life that you can not remember now, you took care of yourself. You cultivated those accomplishments which the world terms genius. You say you do not remember that past. Certainly not. You do not remember your early childhood, nor one-hundredth part of all the small, even interesting happenings that go to make up your life; and yet those events influence your existence and the temporary impressions they created go to make up your present capacity. I believe that some time in the progress of every man's life, or future life, he will remember all his former state and be able to see by what a marvelous process he has progressed through the different stages. Every human being can thank himself for his condition, for in those former conditions he cultivated those parts that are admired in his present existence. If he was weak then and disregarded the laws of that condition he is weak now, and vice versa."

"Are there souls in a lower and a future state at present, and can we communicate with them?"

"The souls in the lower state are the races of men now on earth. There are many persons below us in mental capacity; the souls in a higher state are about us, and in that period between the death of the body and the assuming of the next. You know that we can communicate with those about us, and I believe that we can communicate with those who have left the body. All souls are progressing, that is the 'ego' in man is progressing. The Indian that dies now will undoubtedly return in a higher state, assuming the body of a Caucasian. After death the soul is a perfect intelligence, remembers the past and concentrates the energy and strength of all its progress here on earth preparatory to a re-entrance into the world. With these we communicate. This world is guided by countless intelligences, each one entering into the affairs of individuals, may be into the affairs of a race or a nation. Any number of persons about us are guided by the counsels of their friends, are domineered by the interests of others. These also are influenced by the spirit world. Every person ought to be strong enough to control their own existence, but many are not. These souls may be dragged back from their period of rest (that is between the death of the body and the reincarnation) by stronger minds here on earth."

"Do you remember anything of your former existence here on earth?" was asked.

"Oh, yes, I remember a great many things relative to my former existence. I don't care to go into details as to time and place, however, as that is a private affair and very liable to be misunderstood by the public. I expect to return again after my death. In that period of rest I expect to have full consciousness and to exercise an influence here on earth until such time as I shall have returned in another form."

[20 January 1893, p. 12.]

11 - BURNED TO DEATH.

One of the most appalling and disastrous wrecks that has occurred in years followed the negligence of a switchman on the Big Four road at Wann, Ill., yesterday morning. Passenger engine 109, drawing the Southwestern limited express of four coaches, headed east for New York, crashed into an open switch a half mile north of Wann, a joint station of the Chicago and Alton and the Big Four roads, where seven oil tanks stood in line on the side track. The result was a fire, and later an explosion in which life and property were destroyed. The dead number six and the wounded twenty-two. The following is a list of

THE DEAD.
[List of names omitted.]
FATALLY WOUNDED.
[List of names omitted.]

The crashing of the engine into the side-tracked oil tanks was not disastrous in itself. The consequent explosion and fire that occurred two hours later caused the terrible havoc, but not among the passengers. It was the sightseers from Alton, Ill., who suffered the loss of life and limb. The Southwestern limited train that leaves St. Louis in the morning for New York and arrives at Wann at 8:48 a.m., was thirteen minutes late. At

"General View of the Wreck" (*St. Louis Globe-Democrat*, 22 January 1893, p. 1).

Wann, which is a flag station, there is no side-track, but a half mile farther on, opposite the little cluster of houses known as Alton Junction, several tracks are laid side by side with the main line to permit switching and the taking on of cattle from a stock yard which is there. On one of these tracks seven oil tanks filled with refined lubricating oil and consigned to the Waters-Pierce Oil Company, of this city, were left standing by the switch engine of the Vandalia Line, which brought them there from Beardstown, Ill. The switchman who has charge of this section is R. Gratten, who, it is said, is both a switchman and a barber, managing to eke out a precarious existence by combining the salaries of the two. To this gentleman's door is laid the entire blame by more than one employe of the Big Four. Last evening, it is said, he left Alton Junction, his home, for parts unknown.

When the limited arrived the switch was still open. Rushing along at a speed of fully forty miles an hour the limited rushed into the switch and on, fairly over the tanks, splitting two of them in twain and throwing the rest crushed right and left. The engineer, Webb Ross, and the fireman, Dick White, both saw the danger. White swung himself from the side of the flying train and ran out across the fields. Webb Ross stood manfully to his post, reversed the lever and threw on the air brakes, but to no avail. The velocity overpowered all opposition. Ross stood the shock and still found time to leap from the cab. Almost instantly, however, the burning oil had spread about the engine and the ground was a seething sea of flames. Into this he plunged—a break for life. The flames burned away his garments and scorched his body into a blackened mass. He emerged from the flames only to fall dead at the top of the bank that led from the track. Next to the engine was the baggage car and cafe car, the occupants of which were badly shaken up and thrown to the floor. The same condition affected the passengers of the three remaining palace cars, but further than that no one of the thirty passengers was injured. They rushed to the doors on realizing the catastrophe and made good their escape. The flames soon spread from the tank to the cars, and for several hours they burned fiercely in the morning breeze. In the baggage end of the first car were the mails, eleven pieces of baggage, and a corpse, which was being forwarded from the Southwest to Boston. The body was that of Mrs. Morrison.

The passengers gathered about the blazing wreck and began looking for any one who might need assistance. The villagers from the little town of Alton Junction rushed to the scene; word was telegraphed to St. Louis, Alton and neighboring points, and the company ordered a wrecking train with a score of physicians to the scene. The news of the burning wreck brought hundreds of sightseers from Alton, which is only three miles north of the wreck. They gathered about viewing the flames and chatting idly. At 11 o'clock the horrible addition to the already shocking story was made. Two of the remaining tanks, apparently not yet affected, reached the climax of self-containing heat. An explosion followed that shook the ground for miles about. Seething, blazing oil was showered upon the onlookers, thrown high in the air and over on to the comfortable cottages of villagers who lived by the roadside. The scene that followed beggars description. Many forms were instantly transformed to blazing, screaming, running, rolling bodies, crying loudly for mercy and aid. These tortured souls threw themselves to the ground and rolled about on the earth. They threw their burning hands to tortured, flame-lit faces, from which all semblance to humanity had already departed. They clawed and bit the earth, and then, with an agonizing gasp, sunk, faint and dying, into a deathly stillness. The horrible holocaust had been accomplished. Five souls had been burned into eternity and twenty-two had been maimed, blinded, burned into an unsightly condition, that made every face blanch and every heart shudder. In all this awful holocaust distraction and frantic fear held sway.

People perfectly safe and unharmed stood wringing their hands, crying out in useless fear or rushing madly to and fro in almost an agony of despair. The explosion gathered together all those who had previously left the wreck, or had as yet not heard of it. They gathered in throngs, but their presence was ineffective and entirely useless. Water would not quench the hissing, flaming oil, and more than that, water was not to be had. The little village of Alton Junction has no water supply except a few wells. The explosion drove the shattered mass of iron with fearful velocity far across the fields. Some of it fell close at hand, however, and pinioned the bystanders beneath its weight of molten heat. The wires overhead leading to St. Louis were melted, fell to the earth, severing all direct connection with the city. The only alternative was to bring aid from Alton, Ill., three miles away. At 11:30 a.m. the train arrived bearing the medical staff of St. Joseph's Hospital, with the exception of Drs. W. R. Haskell and T. P. P. Yerkes, who had left in the early morning in response to the first call for aid. The second call brought Drs. W. H. Haliburton, E. Guelick, Figenbaum, Scheussler and Fisher, of Alton; also Drs. Gross and Thomas, of Gillespie. They hurried from the wrecking train to the scene and superintended the removal of the bodies. Shutters and cots were brought from various little homes and the moaning victims were wrapped in blankets and cloths and carried to the Big Four station at Alton Junction. The scene at the little frame depot was exciting. A great crowd stood about and blocked the entrance way to the various rooms. One by one the litters came, borne by strong, willing citizens, who drove back the morbidly curious and filed into the little depot waiting room.

Here the couches were arranged side by side, and over each one a physician bowed for a few minutes to see just how serious the wounds were. Nothing could be done, for no lint or ointment could be applied that would ease the blackened flesh and bones of the half charred frames. Every now and then the cover was slightly raised to see if life still remained. The gents' waiting room would only hold five bodies, and when that number had been laid side by side the north room was cleared of benches and the coming litters arranged in this also. There were still others, and out on the platform they were tenderly cared for by the self-appointed nurses. The others were carried across the fields to the little cottages, where the families ministered all that could possibly ease their suffering. By 12 o'clock the Mattoon accommodation train was ready to depart for Alton. In the four coaches and baggage car the dead and the dying were deposited. The work of loading the dead and dying was another appalling spectacle. Out from the waiting room were borne the litters and gently lifted into the cars. From out the little cottages the wounded were again borne, followed by all the villagers, talking and gesticulating, but in a mournful, subdued manner. When the train had been filled the signal was given and the hospital train was off. Notice was telegraphed to the Alton Police and Fire Departments, who prepared to assist in removing the bodies from the train to St. Joseph's Hospital, which stands on a hill overlooking the city. The accommodation stopped some seven blocks south of the regular station to permit of a short cut to the hospital. At this point were gathered a score of wagons, prepared to do duty as ambulances. Here, too, had gathered hundreds of the local residents who had heard of the awful wreck. It was with difficulty that the crowd was forced back from the cars and the bodies lowered. Then started the succession of wagon journeys to and from the hospital that in no time lined the way with thousands of people gaping and talking in an anxious, nervous manner. From every window and doorway, in back and front yards, on the stoops and hanging on the fences that lined the way the people looked out and down upon the procession.

From the railroad track to the hospital gate is three straight blocks, ascending very rapidly to the crest of the hill, where St. Joseph's stands. The ascent was necessarily slow and gave ample time for the crowd to satisfy its curiosity. Before the hospital door another immense throng was gathered, anxious and almost determined to view the unrecognizable faces that passed on litters through the entrance-way. Inside all was confusion and hurry. Dr. Haskell, the physician in charge, returned with the train and hurried to and fro, gathering about him his staff and urging his assistants to great speed. The sick of the hospital are attended by the Sisters of Charity, and they busied themselves in taking the suffering to the respective rooms. In a little while three rooms on the main floor were filled with the wounded. The sick that had occupied them were borne out into the hall or carried into other rooms less crowded. The work was lovingly, anxiously done. Each sigh and groan of pain found an echoing response in the heart of the self-sacrificing attendants. One room was cleared for surgical purposes, but was not used until all of the first train had been cared for. The scenes in the rooms where the wounded were removed from the rough temporary litters into the snowy couches were heart-rending. The removal was necessary, however, and much as the victims shrieked and groaned, the work went on. Lying on the couches, the dirty, oil-soaked rags were cut away from the bodies and laid bare the horrible work of the burning oil. The hands and faces of all were scorched, torn and bleeding. The lips and noses were swollen and distorted, and the eyes were either burned out or were flame-eaten and encrusted with blood and dust. The hands of many were burned to a crust, fingers were missing and arms broken. Several of the victims when uncovered were found to be without cuticle, the flames having cooked and burned it until it either clung to the clothing in removal, or fell away of its own accord.

When all arrangements had been made the public were admitted. An eager throng of mothers, fathers, wives and daughters hurried along the aisle and into the chambers of suffering. Here they viewed each face, but in many cases without avail, for the forms and faces were unrecognizable. By dint of questioning many of the sufferers were induced to reveal their names. These were taken down by the Mother Superior, Mary Joseph, who preserved the list to guide the inquirers. Soon by each bed, with anxious, tear-stained faces and disheveled appearance, stood the relatives and friends whispering words of comfort into the dying ears, sobbing words of cheer that were half-choked in the utterance. Many of the patients recognized the voices of friends and relatives and moaned appeals for aid, for to be spoken to, cheered, lifted up and the like. In the main hall stood a throng of anxious parents whose boys had gone down to the wreck in the early morning and had not yet returned. They appealed to the physicians, the Little Sisters and the attendants generally for information concerning their missing children. A *Globe-Democrat* reporter entered the chamber of suffering and went from couch to couch inquiring from the distorted occupant his name, age and address. After a long period of waiting and gentle questioning the list was completed and he returned to the hall. To those inquiring the list was read, and as the last name was spoken and "that's all" ejaculated a score of sighs were heard, for many an anxious heart knew that the loved one was not in the list.

At 3:30 p.m. the second hospital train that had been sent to Wann by the railroad company returned to Alton. At Wann the same scenes were reenacted, and at Alton the same crowd lined the way to watch the progress of the painfully thrilling work. This train brought four bodies from the scene of the disaster. They were those who had since been prepared for the journey, having missed the first train. The progress up the hill was none the less interesting. The throng at the gate, though having watched without food or drink during the long hours of the morning, were none the less eager in their looks nor none the less backward in pressing forward to look at the bodies. More order prevailed inside the hospital with the coming of these bodies. The work of the noon hour had nerved the attendants and practiced their ability in taking care of the unfortunates. So they were received and placed with rapidity and ease. In the temporary department of surgery the unfortunates were borne one by one. In this three surgeons stood ready with knives, cotton and lint bandages and plenty of ointment. The victims were stretched out, their clothes cut away, and their wounds dressed and bandaged. Most of them were horribly burned all over, instead of in splotches, and every breath of air seemed to give them the most intense pain. The majority were fully conscious of their awful condition and asked to be handled carefully. Some were stronger than others and wanted to move about.

Several begged to be killed, that they might be free from their pain. "Oh, I'm blind," moaned one; "I feel that my eyes are gone. Oh, I could stand all, everything, I could be burned with satisfaction, I could be crippled or deformed forever, but to be without eyes, to have the light shut out forever, that is too much. I want to die! I want to die!" and then a loving mother bowed low over the moaning form and buried her tear-stained face and misery-convulsed form in the clothing that shielded her son. Several little boys were among the victims, and their moanings were the source of much distress to all the others. Still others were only slightly injured, and deeply congratulated themselves upon their luck in escaping at all. One of these, Charles Hammond, a track-walker for the Big Four, had escaped with the loss of his hair, several severe scalp wounds and a burned hand. He sat in the corridor of the hospital solemnly viewing the proceedings. In reply to questions from a *Globe-Democrat* reporter Mr. Hammond said: "I am a track-walker for the Big Four, traveling between Venice and Alton at night time, and my home is at Alton Junction. My work was all done, of course, and I was sleeping soundly when my wife woke me up to tell me of the horrible wreck. I jumped up and ran over to the place. There was nothing that I could do. Water would do no good, and so I stood looking on. I had started to stroll away when the explosion occurred. I intended going north to the Junction Station, but I had not got 70 feet away before I was knocked to my knees by the crash of the tank. I felt the hot oil light on my head and hands and felt the fearful burning sensation. To relieve myself I buried my head in the earth and threw dirt over my hands. Then I ran away. I don't know how fast. Here at the junction I met a physician who bandaged my head and hand. Then they put me on the wrecking train and I came here. The sound wasn't so loud as it was stunning. I didn't look back much. All I wanted was to get away. The man that had charge of the switch at that place was a fellow by the name of R. Gratten. He kept a barber shop and attended the switch at the same time. The company hired him simply because he was cheap. I know that he has gone out of the country already, and they won't find him soon. It's a shame that a railroad company should be allowed to hire men to do work in that manner, risking the lives of passengers, simply because it is cheap."

The scene at the wreck late in the afternoon was one of vast destruction. The burning oil had been thrown for a distance of 800 feet and more, and had set fire to two little cottages that stood facing the track. The little dwellings belong one to a man by the name of Jones, and the other to Car Inspector Emery, of the Big Four. They could not be found, however, as they had gone to Alton with the hospital trains. On the track where the seven oil tanks had stood a line of melted, rusted car trucks and piles of ashes lay. Lying in a molten heap among them were the gnarled remnants of engine 109, and back of it the ashes of the four coaches with bars of twisted protruding iron completed the side-track picture. To the east a wrecking train brought from East St. Louis lay, and to this the gang of wreckers carried whatever they saw fit to remove. The work of clearing the debris from the main track was soon accomplished, and trains plied to and fro at will. A small crowd of sightseers was gathered about the place, but always at a discreet distance from an oil tank that had not yet exploded, and which was credited with being perfectly empty. They plodded to and fro, each one bent upon gathering some little stick or piece of iron as a souvenir or memento of the great disaster. A little north at the station the bodies of the six dead lay in order awaiting the coming of the Coroner. One of these was identified by a watch upon his person which bore his name—Edward Miller. A singular feature of his death was that his watch stopped at 11:10, supposedly the time of the great explosion which buried him beneath a mass of heated iron. The telegraph operators and station employes generally were very cautious about their remarks. They professed ignorance of the number and names of the dead, and the extent of the damage. Their orders, they said, was to keep still, and that if they talked they were liable to lose their positions. The porter of the Wagner sleeping car that was attached to the train was found sitting morosely alone on a box near the station at Alton Junction. He refused to give his name, but the badge on his coat read "Wagner 474." He said that the first knowledge he received of the calamity was when he was tossed over the back of a reclining chair and lay flat on the floor. He said the jolt was fearful and every body in the car was more or less tossed about. When the occupants recovered their feet and wits they hurried to the door. The oil from the tanks was already flowing towards the cars, a regular wave of flame, which gave little time for any one to leave in. Many of the passengers hurried away towards the station, fearing further trouble. "I did not stay long," said the gentleman. "I knew there was goin' to be more trouble, an' so I just pulled off. I came down here, and I didn't go back nuther, nor I ain't agoin'. I've been in wrecks before, an' I know enough now to git out an' away jist as far as the Lord 'ull let me," and with that the porter lapsed into silence and refused to be disturbed by further questions. The station agent at Wann said that he thought the company had lost something like $200,000 by the fire. "The company won't pay anything to all these sight-seers who gathered about here to view the ruins. They have no business here, and, of course, if they come to grief it is no fault of the company's."

In the City of Alton the news of the wreck was the topic of the hour. The streets there had the appearance of a county seat upon the arrival of some big circus. Everybody was out of doors. The streets were promenaded by the inhabitants; the store fronts were occupied by crowds of gossiping residents who collected together for the sole purpose of recounting the enormity of it and of recalling the great wrecks of the past. The depot station was the resort of another class who vaguely imagined that each incoming train would bear peculiar intelligence relative to the matter that might not be had elsewhere in the city. The offices of the local newspapers were scenes of vast activity, and the floors of the same were strewn with paper on which was scribbled more than a dozen introductions to the wreck. Sister Mary Joseph, the Mother Superior of St. Joseph's Hospital, was one of the calm central figures around which a dozen excited assistants revolved with more or less rapidity, according to her directions. The sight of the mutilated forms, while it stirred her heart into expressions of sincerest pity, failed to upset the goodly common sense and directing ability that characterized her every word. To a *Globe-Democrat* reporter Mother Mary said: "We have dealt with the victims of wrecks before. They come to us very frequently, and we try to do all that human charity can do. This is not the first time that I have watched the incoming of wounded souls by scores. Two years ago there was a wreck, eight miles north of here, in which three were killed and some fifteen of the wounded were brought here. No, I have had experience and I give it with all my heart to the suffering souls about me. I only trust that their pain may be less now than before."

Among those who were witnesses to the explosion were J. H. Maupin and Robert Curdy, real estate men of Alton. Mr. Maupin, in company of J. H. McPike, was advancing toward the scene of the wreck and was about 200 feet distant when the explosion occurred. The force of the shock for an instant turned them back and separated them. Mr. Maupin in relating his experience says:

"For a short while I made Nancy Hanks time in the opposite direction. But quick as I was, the flames overtook me and burned these holes you see in the back of my coat. As soon as the heat subsided sufficiently to admit it, I hurried to the scene and did all in my power to alleviate the sufferings of the victims. I saw a man running toward me in a sheet of flame. Just as he got to me he fell. Pulling out my knife I cut, as best I could, the blazing garments from off his body. When I had succeeded in extinguishing the flames, I stopped only long enough to ascertain that his name was Richardson, and then hurried on to assist the other unfortunates." In the meantime Robert Curdy and others were engaged at different points in their heroic efforts.

Mr. Curdy said: "I think the force of the explosion must have spent itself in my direction. Although I was 600 feet distant when it occurred, the flames swept by me and passed in a sheet over my horse and rig, which were standing near. I can hardly describe the noise. It was not like a cannon, nor like thunder, but more as the rushing of a mighty force of air. Looking around me I saw boys and men running in all directions through the fields.

"One man headed toward me. I did not recognize him, but I called to him to stop, which he did. I had my knife in hand, and as he halted, I rushed up to him and cut and slashed away through the sheet of flame until there remained not a vestige of his original habiliments. I tried with my voice to console him in his awful plight as with my hands I did what I could to alleviate his pain. He recognized my voice, and, with his burned and sightless eyes turned toward me, he managed to inform me that he was my old friend, James Murray. In pulling off the sleeve of his coat, the skin of his hand stuck to it and came off like a glove, the nails with it. I threw dust over him, and rolled him in the dirt. When I had extinguished the flames, little was there in that charred but breathing mass having any resemblance to James Murray. Others hurrying up took him in charge and, bundling him into a wagon, bore him to his home in Alton, where, I hear, he still lives."

"Over near the house, on the embankment and to the west of the scene of the horror," continued Mr. Curdy, "lay the smouldering remains of a boy of 14 or 15 years of age. It is supposed his name was Hagerman. I shouted to the fleeing ones to walk, not run, as running but fanned the flames. Hurrying on I overtook Willie McCarthy, a lad of 13. After I had done all I could for him, and with scarcely a bit of clothing left on him, he lay down and in his agony rolled over and over on the snow and ice. By this time the crowd of helpers had swelled considerably, and finding Mr. Maupin we jumped in the rig and whipped up toward Alton to secure increased medical attendance. To every one we met we hastily communicated the sad intelligence of the second disaster and the dreadful plight of the victims. Houses were stripped of bed clothes, pillows and the like, and a multitude of tender and sympathetic care-takers was soon in attendance. On the road we met several doctors urging their steeds to the limit of endurance. In a short time after our arrival at Alton every available physician was speeding on his errand of mercy."

[22 January 1893, pp. 1–2.]

12 - SIXTEEN DEAD.

The hope that the wounds of the injured of Saturday's great wreck and oil explosion at Wann, near Alton, Ill., would not prove fatal, is fast fading. When the morning light of the Sabbath yesterday dawned upon St. Joseph's Hospital at Alton, where nearly all the victims are now lying, four more had passed away. At 9 o'clock another gave up the struggle. A 5:15 p.m. another died, making six for the first twenty-four hours in the hospital. Three bodies, namely—W. H. Miller, Daniel Harris and W. H. Mantz—were found about the wreck under peculiar circumstances, that would indicate that there are more yet unrecovered. One suffering soul, John Burke, who can not possibly live, was found near the wreck and brought to the hospital to die.

A revised list at dark shows sixteen dead and fourteen more who can not possibly recover.

[List of names omitted.]

The above list includes only those who are known. Rumor has it that the number exceeds the printed list. Many were severely injured, but having friends and relatives in the adjoining stations to the wreck, made their way to their homes and have since given no account of themselves. The number of those who were scorched by the rushing heat has not been estimated, but it is safe to say that every one present was more or less injured. Many who found that their clothing was on fire, tossed away their clothes and fled as best they might.

The deaths for the day make a fearful story. John Lock lived until 3 o'clock Sunday morning, when death relieved him from the torments his injuries had thrown him into. Lock was a glassblower, and came to Alton a few years ago from Pittsburg. He has a wife and child to mourn his sudden demise.

Edward Maupin, the young man from St. Charles, Mo., also died during the night. He, too, was burned from head to foot, and at the time of the explosion his clothes were torn from his body.

Henry Penning, an old man, who resided at Alton Junction, was another to die during the night. Like the others, he was burned fearfully, and it was but a question of time in his case.

Daniel Harris, another one of the victims, died on the Sabbath at his home, near Alton Junction.

Wm. Miller, father of Edward Miller, also died yesterday. This family is the most terribly afflicted of any whose friends or relatives were in the explosion. The son, Edward, was killed outright, the father died yesterday, and three other sons, Frank, Julius and Henry, are badly injured, and Frank may die.

William Edwards, of Alton Junction, died yesterday morning at his mother's house, on the outskirts of the little village.

William Shattuck, of Upper Alton, also died late Saturday night at the hospital. Yesterday he was carried to his home for burial.

Charles Wilkinson, the little Alton boy, died at 5 o'clock Sunday afternoon.

To realize the scope of the sad disaster one must pay a visit to St. Joseph's Hospital. By the bedside of the wounded through all the long hours of Saturday night and Sunday the friends and relatives kept anxious vigil. No service was left undone, no sigh passed unheeded. A majority of the patients are past medical assistance. All that can be done for them has been done, and now they are left to the strength of their own constitutions. If they have been blessed with superior physical strength the chance of living is, of course, better, but nothing short of superhuman strength can save their nervous system from complete exhaustion. Those who yesterday begged for release from pain were ministered to during the long hours of the night by the Angel of Death, and relief came with a convulsive, yet restful, sigh that freed the spirit from the tortured frame. It would have been almost impossible, had it not been deemed unnecessary, to compel the relatives to leave the hospital. The nuns, worn by constant watching, were glad to accept the assistance of any one, and especially the assistance of those to whom the lives of the injured were dearest. One room contained seven of the most seriously wounded. Over each cot was pinned a little slip of paper, on which was written the name and the address of the occupant.

As Dr. Yerkes slowly moved from one to the other his only comment, delivered in a solemn whisper, was "dying." "No, they can't live," said he. "It is useless to hope in such cases as these. Most all of them have great burns, where the nerves are laid bare. Their eyes are burned out. Their ears are great, swollen sores, or mere crusts. They have breathed in the flames and the fumes of the burning oil, and, as a consequence, their mouths and throats are raw and bleeding. It isn't a question of remedy or nursing. It is simply a question of physical strength and time, and no body, no nervous system, however strong, can stand for any length of time the ceaseless irritation and stinging pain that accompanies their every move. This has been a peculiar and awful accident. I never passed through anything like it, and I never want to again. Such aggravated cases of physical agony I have never witnessed before and I never want to again."

Everything possible is being done under the supervision of Mary Josephine, the sister in charge of the hospital. It was found impossible to secure enough linen bandages, and a request was read in every church at the morning services calling on all to contribute what soft linen they had to spare.

One by one the victims are giving up the struggle. At 9, at 10 and at 12 o'clock respectively Saturday night a soul was released. At 4 in the morning another died and at 9 another. Then a break came in the line of departing spirits. The remaining eleven who will die possessed a little more of physical strength than their brothers, and they linger on a little longer. The work of the attendants was one of pitying love, and as each of the weakened mortals gasped his last the covers were lifted away and the cots noiselessly borne out from the room into the dressing room, where the bandages were readjusted, the sad, pain-marked faces straightened and the lips pressed together. Then they were wrapped in winding sheets and borne down stairs and out into the Morgue, where they were laid side by side to await the coming of their struggling comrades above, who moaned and sighed a longing for but a minute of rest or for eternal peace.

With the rising of the sun the number of visitors increased, and these took, in part, the places of the worn watchers of the night, who sought some obscure couch where they might lie down and rest. As the morning waned the crowd increased. Dr. Haskell returned after but a few hours of rest, and resumed charge of the good work. He hurried from chamber to chamber, inquiring after his charges and expressing the hope that a few at least might recover.

Perhaps the most pitiful scene of all was that enacted at the side of the cot of little Willie McCarty, the 13-year-old lad who received so many fearful wounds in the awful explosion. The boy was literally covered with sores, his eyes were completely ruined and his body scarred and burned beyond recognition. On Saturday when he was borne into the room his boyish vitality would not permit of rest nor quiet. Then he cried loudly for aid, begged that he might be lifted up and moved about, for he felt an inward unconquerable resistance against the awful thought of lying still and of dying. Despite the appeals of his mother and the almost stern yet necessary warning of the attending physicians he stretched out his scorched and bleeding arms that he might cling to his mother's neck. At that time he kept up a constant struggle, rolling and tumbling to and fro. Yesterday his vitality showed signs of exhaustion. He no longer moved about, nor did he talk continuously. The change was not for the better. The wounds were if anything more irritating, but the strength was less. It was the apathy of death that had set in. By the cot, with eyes swollen and reddened from weeping, sat Mrs. McCarty, bending over at every fresh sigh of pain to murmur words of love and cheer into the dying ear. The only response was a feeble, pitiful wail, "I want to die, I want to die."

By 6 o'clock p.m. no further deaths had been reported at the Hospital, but the patients were gradually sinking and only a few hours of life was thought to be theirs.

A second scene of bitter, sorrowful reality was that witnessed by many, namely, the interior of the little brick Morgue back of the hospital. Within its chilly walls by 10 o'clock in the morning, the bodies of five of the victims who had died during the night, were ranged side by side on litters, their faces hidden by the white winding sheets that were placed over them. One by one the visitors came and lifted from the faces the bandages, searching as they were for their friends. The sight was as painfully sickening as it was sad. The work of the boiling oil and flames could now be distinctly seen. It was awful to look upon. The arms, shoulders, necks and faces of the dead were literally eaten into in a hundred places. These little spots, no larger than a penny, were thick and deep, and the ravages of the most virulent form of small pox could not have left scars such as these poor souls would have been compelled to have borne had they been able to stand the pain and recover. The inflammation fled from these wounds with the heat of the body and left the flesh tightly drawn and stiff. This only distorted more their awful condition and vivified the terrible range of their sufferings.

At 10:45 a.m. Coroner Thomas Kinder, of Madison County, arrived with a jury at St. Joseph's Hospital and immediately began taking testimony in the various cases. A separate verdict was returned in each case, but the testimony was taken in bulk. The separate verdicts were returned on the general testimony. The jurors were E. F. Banage, B. Fahrig, L. Fahrig,

Wm. Platt, F. Volbracht and Wm. L. Fairman. A table was arranged at the north end of the hospital hall, with writing materials and chairs, and about this the jury gathered.

The first witness called was Frank Brannage, a teamster of Alton. He said that upon hearing of the wreck on Saturday morning he, in company with a friend named John Maul, secured a buggy and drove to Alton Junction. They fastened the buggy to a neighboring tree and approached the wreck. He noticed that the five oil tanks were surrounded by fire and that various portions of the flat cars were ablaze. He said he staid within 30 feet of the tanks and general wreck for fully fifty minutes. All this time he noticed that the rivets of the oil tanks were giving away, and that from the tank cap a flame was burning, which was gradually increasing in size and height. Then he went north to the little station at Alton Junction to look at the body of Webb Ross, the engineer. From here, with his companion, he returned to the buggy and drove off to a neighboring bar-room some 150 feet distant from the oil tanks. In the doorway of this building he stopped to view the increasing flame. He said that at this time the flame was fully 50 feet high and shone bright over the tree tops. A dull, hissing roar accompanied the blazing. "I told the fellows who were with me that I thought we had better go away for the tanks were going to explode. A great crowd had gathered by this time. When I started away there were fully fifty others who went along. We all went west and north from the tanks. Before we had gone 100 feet, however, the tank exploded with a stunning puff. Every one in the crowd cried out and all broke into a run. We heard cries of pain, but did not stay to look about, being too fearful of getting hurt. Before the explosion I saw several people digging about the place where Engineer Webb Ross fell. I don't know what for. I did not hear any railroad employes tell any one that they should go away or that the tanks were liable to explode. There were quite a number of railroad employes on the ground, however, engaged in removing the original wreckage."

The next witness sworn was Louis Deneau, a glass-blower, who works in Alton. Deneau said that he lately came from Montreal, Canada, and had but recently obtained employment. Upon hearing of the wreck he, with a companion, went to Alton Junction to look at it. He walked about the wrecked engine and tanks and viewed the body of the dead engineer. At that time the tanks were surrounded by fire and a flame was blazing upward from the cap of the tank fully 50 feet high. He became scared and started to go away. When he had gone a distance of 1500 feet the tank exploded. Without turning to look back he struck into a run away to the north. While he was running he felt some of the burning oil light on the back of his neck. He threw his hand up, and in doing so severely burned it. Then he smelled the burning of cloth and saw that his overcoat was on fire. He threw off the garment and hat and put dirt on the back of his neck. Then he went to the depot, where his wounds were dressed. He had not heard any railroad employe, nor in fact any one, urge the people to leave on account of the danger.

James Maupin, Jr., upon being sworn, testified as follows: "Two gentlemen, McCurdy, Pike and myself, left Alton upon hearing of the wreck at Wann and got there at 11 a.m. We mingled with the crowd about the wreck, near the oil tanks and the crushed engine. At that time the flames from the oil of the other wrecked tanks were about the four remaining tanks, two of which exploded later on. The cars on which the oil tanks stood were burning fiercely, and I thought the tanks must soon topple down. A great crowd was there; I should say 300 people. I noticed that the rivets in the tanks were loosening and giving way, and that a flame which was burning from the top of the tank cap was gradually increasing in size. The sound of the burning oil was like that of a lighted gas well. I made the remark that I didn't know that oil in tanks would burn that way and make so much noise. I said that I thought the tanks were dangerous and that they would explode. I looked at my watch and found that it was just 11:40 a.m. We had hitched the horse and buggy in which we came about 1500 feet away, off near the Edwardsville road. After strolling up to the Alton Junction station, where the body of Webb Ross had been, we turned by to go to our rig. To reach our rig we had to pass the tanks again, which we did about 200 feet west of them. Just as we got directly opposite the tanks exploded. The report was not loud, but it was dull and deafening—more of a shock. A wall of fire sprang up over the tree tops, I should say fully 200 feet high. The great crowd that was gathered about broke and ran. It seemed as though flying balls of fire pursued the crowd. The oil fell in flaming drops just like a rain of fire. Any number of people passed me running, and it seemed as though everybody's clothes were on fire. I helped three different persons. One of them was a stranger to me, but I understand that he spells his name just like mine. Most of the people were throwing off their clothes as they ran. Lots of them had stripped off even their shirts to the wrist and were trying to unbutton the wrist buttons. Quite a number got their hands fearfully burned because they could not loosen the buttons. I helped three of four who were covered with flames. I threw dirt on them, cut away their boots and clothing and smothered part of the flames with my overcoat. I should say that I saw more than forty persons running away with their clothing and persons on fire. I saw the wrecking train on the ground and quite a number of railroaders working there, but I did not hear any one advise the crowd of the danger nor order them to keep away from the tanks."

The next witness, Physician-in-chief Haskell, testified to the death of five persons in the hospital.

After hearing others who testified in a similar manner the jury returned verdicts in the cases of Wm. Shattuck, Henry Penning, Willie McCarty, John Lock and Edward Maupin. The verdict ascribed the death to the burns received, caused by the explosion of the oil tanks at Wann on the Big Four road. The verdict did not hold the Big Four road responsible. This verdict was reached at 8:30 p.m. yesterday.

Wm. T. Fairman, the foreman of the hospital jury, was interviewed by a *Globe-Democrat* reporter immediately after the verdict. Mr. Fairman said: "There was a sentiment, rather strong at first, among the jurymen against the railroad company. It seemed as though the company should have been held responsible for the trouble. I thought myself that such a verdict would be returned, but after we listened to the evidence it was deemed advisable not to cast any reflections. These injured people were all there out of curiosity, and although the evidence did not show that the men were warned away by the railroad employes, yet it was brought out that everybody apparently knew of the danger and expected an explosion. In that case, of course, we could not hold the railroad responsible. While I realize the magnitude of the catastrophe, I do not see where the company is to blame, speaking strictly of the five cases in which we returned verdicts."

A second jury, in charge of Coroner Kinder in person, sat over the bodies of Edward Miller and Charles Harris at Alton Junction. The evidence introduced was the same. The jury returned separate verdicts of accidental death, but did not censure any one.

Coroner Campbell, of East St. Louis, held an inquest yesterday on the body of Timothy Houlihan, who was injured in the wreck at Wann on Saturday and died early yesterday morning. The jury heard the evidence of several witnesses and finally decided that Houlihan's death was the result of an accident caused by the negligence of the managers of C., C., C. & St. L. Railway employing an incompetent man to attend the switches. Houlihan was born and reared in East St. Louis and has a large circle of friends.

The scene of the wreck is still a source of much interest, for it is firmly believed by many that all the dead have not yet been recovered. Yesterday morning the bodies of W. H. Miller and Daniel Harris, the aged father of Charles Harris who was burned to death by the explosion, were found in the immediate vicinity of Alton Junction. A little later in the day William Mantz was found half a mile from the scene of the wreck dead from a multitude of burns and scars. The presumption is that he tried to wander to his home, which was in that direction; that his strength had failed him and burning with the agony of a hundred wounds he had sunk down by the wayside and expired. His wife, who saw him depart in the morning for the scene of the wreck, worried greatly over his failure to return, and went later to Alton to discover if possible whether he, too, was numbered among the dead. Her anxiety was destined to be transformed into an agony of sorrow.

John Wilkinson, the student of Wyman Institute, who died at 5:15 p.m. in the hospital, was found bleeding and groaning on Sunday afternoon near the water tank at Alton Junction.

A rumor that could not be verified was current late last night that ten other students of Wyman Institute were missing. It is more than probable that the lapse of a few hours will develop some startling features to the already awful list of casualties.

O. L. Gratton, the missing switchman, turned up at the depot yesterday morning safe and sound. He disclaims all intention of running away, and denies that he was the cause of the wreck.

The Big Four road, according to the local railway officials, has lost between $100,000 and $125,000 by the wreck. Altogether twenty cars were burned, and to this must be added the cost of the seven tanks and the oil they contained.

The little village of Alton Junction presented a desolate, mournful appearance yesterday. The remains of the wreck had not yet been cleared away, although a wrecking train was there and a gang of men were at work. About the ruin a number of straggling sightseers were gathered. They moved about picking up bits of iron and wood, minutely examining the condition of the remaining oil tanks and shattered mass of iron that remained of the others. To the west of the tracks were the ruins of the two little homes that but lately graced the now desolate section. About the village stores knots of men were gathered, discussing the now rather worn topic of the explosion. In front of the village church another class of good citizens stopped and chatted over the horror before they entered to pray and again after the service before they wended their separate ways. In many of the little homes, in fact, in a majority of them, there was cause for worry enough. Nearly one out of each family received some slight face or scalp wound, and these had to be carefully nursed for fear of their growing worse. One could see, by strolling through the forsaken lanes, many a face peering out through the front window across the field, but invariably decorated with a bandage of linen or a patch of porous plaster. Whatever the pain in these instances might be, the victims found consolation in the fact that they were not among the dead or the dying, nor yet were they seriously disfigured, as many of those who will recover will be. Most of them were inclined to heave a sigh of relief as they speculated upon the scene of Saturday morning and listened to a recital of the woes of the others.

An idea of the force with which the oil tanks exploded may be gained from the fact that a fragment of iron weighing fully 125 pounds were hurled to the east of the spot for a distance of 2000 feet, landing out in the center of a neighboring corn field. The blazing oil was tossed for a distance of 1600 feet in every direction. Thanks to long standing conditions the village of Alton Junction stands considerably farther west, and so the little cluster of homes were beyond the reach of the flames. Being without water or fire protection of any kind the little place would have been at the mercy of the flames and a scene of desolation would have followed in the train of the already too disastrous events of that morning.

[23 January 1893, p. 10.]

13 - GUIDED BY SPIRITS.

Prof. J. G. Leonard, the famous clairvoyant, arrived at the Southern yesterday morning from the West. Prof. Leonard dabbles in the mystic sensations of the spirit, the something beyond that is ever a source of wonder to mankind. He combines the powers of the mind-reader with that of the mystic, and foretells with ease the future and many things that one would deem the most secret thoughts of his own nature. A *Globe-Democrat* reporter visited Prof. Leonard yesterday afternoon to ascertain, if possible, the extent of his powers.

"You believe, of course, in spirits, do you not?" was the opening suggestion.

"Yes, I believe in spirits; the souls of men from all times are about us. They have been growing in intelligence of human affairs just as human beings acquire education by observing men and things about. The great minds of the world are here; they no doubt influence our lives, suggest the great thoughts that come to us and prompt us to do those successful deeds that make us famous and great. These spirits are the men who have been upright and progressive in the past. They choose the person whom they intend to guide in his infancy, and all through his life his powers are guided by their counsels. All spirits do not possess the same ability. Some of them can read the future better than others. Their mental ability gauges their powers in that mystic realm, just as it, with the assistance of other spirits, gauged their measure of success here on earth."

"Are all the spirits good and able to assist human beings?"

"Not all of them. There are those whose evil tendencies here on earth limited their success and injured the lives of others. Their spirit after death often seeks, in fact, is ever seeking, to influence the lives of others, not to do evil, but to retrieve through the good of others their own evil actions of the past. Their efforts in this line are forever futile. They tell you to do so and so. It will help you. You feel the invisible instruction, you do as this prompting bids you, and you fail most ignobly. That is partly your fault, partly that of the spirit. You should have had better intelligence. So should the spirit. Your loss grieves you, but it grieves that evil spirit that sought your own good more. That is the future punishment—the desire to do good for others and forever being compelled to see that desire leading human beings into trouble."

"Do you believe in a God—a controlling influence that is back of all this force?"

"Yes, I believe in a controlling spirit. In how much this spirit influences the actions of men I cannot tell; I should say very little. The pervading spirit is his. I believe that we have desires leading us to fulfill the divine purpose. The departed souls have desires also that lead them to endeavor to fulfill the divine purpose. That pervading spirit which you and I know to be separate from our mental judgment is the power that guides the universe. So it is that the souls of the dead endeavor to guide us, but some of them wofully fail. A man is less his own master than he himself is willing to admit in his inmost conscience."

"Do these spirits have companionships?"

"Yes, indeed. They have full consciousness of the existence of each other and often work in harmony. I have to influence and guide me three separate bands of spirits of which I am fully conscious. I know them by name, and know when I ask for information from whom it comes. They invariably answer my appeal. I do not care to give all their names. Some I will give though. Did you ever hear of John Foster, the famous medium from New York State? Well, he is a member of a band of spirits who during their lives dabbled in the black art, as it is called. He, with others, desires and does perpetuate his powers here on earth with me. I have still stranger influences over me, however, namely, a band of Indians—an Indian chief by the name Mighty Water, and a second called Black Eye here on earth, and a third, a squaw known as Red Hand. They assist me continually; I can almost hear their voices. I do not believe in all that many Spiritualists claim, but I do believe that spirits can be called back into visibility, providing, of course, the powers of the medium are equal to the demand. However, I have never tried that myself, and I do not think that I shall."

"What becomes of the soul of a man who commits suicide?" was asked.

"That soul is no more. A soul that endeavors to force itself into the spirit realm is contradicting the natural law of the universe. The result is eternal death."

"What of the spirit of an idiot, or has it one?"

"I believe that an idiot has a spirit, but not as an idiot after death. Whatever evil influence it was that caused the child to be born without sense is relaxed and removed by sickness and death. How many insane people do you think recover consciousness at death? Have you seen them dying? Did you notice that their eyes brightened, and a look of intelligence shone there? Did it not seem as though they wanted to say something—to tell you of another world? That is the reawakening that is completed when the spirit bounds free from the body."

Prof. Leonard has ability to prove his assertions. With apparent ease he repeated the history of the visitor, read his aspirations and predicted the result of them. While the Professor was without the room a name and a question were written on separate slips of paper, neatly folded and placed in the pocket of the reporter. When Mr. Leonard returned he was requested to state what was written on the separate pieces. He requested that he might have the privilege of passing the folded slips across his forehead. After doing this he repeated the name and the question. He also answered the question, which was relative to a future occurrence. A deck of cards lay on the table. As the visitor arose he lifted one and looked at it. Laying it back, he questioned: "What card did I see?" "The eight of hearts," was the reply, although Mr. Leonard had been busily engaged in a far corner of the room and could not possibly have observed the action. Mr. Leonard has a somewhat remarkable history, which includes innumerable successes and the acquiring of a fortune of $100,000. He leaves here for the South to-day.

[24 January 1893, p. 12.]

14 - AN IRON FIRM GOES UNDER.

The MacMurray-Judge Architectural Iron Company, with office and works at the southeast corner of Twenty-first and Papin streets, filed papers of assignment in the Circuit Court yesterday. The company is financially embarrassed at present. Through its attorney, Leverett Bell, the company assigned in favor of its creditors. The Mississippi Valley Trust Company was made the assignee and took charge at once. The liabilities are estimated at $69,000, and assets at $150,000. The officers of the company are Arthur J. Judge, President; Arthur J. Judge, Jr., Secretary and Treasurer; and Directors, Sylvester C. Judge, John C. Lullman, J. W. MacMurray and R. E. MacMurray. The assets include the real estate, machinery, buildings and stock on hand. The outstanding accounts are with numerous small creditors, the largest account being estimated at no more than $4000. The company is one of long standing. A few weeks ago a number of wage suits were filed in Justice J. Spaulding's court.

Arthur C. Judge was seen by a *Globe-Democrat* reporter last evening at the works. "We are only temporarily embarrassed," said Mr. Judge. "A great deal of our money is tied up in contracts which we can possibly alter. In this condition we have been affected by other failures, the principal one being that of the Wiener building, in Kansas City, which was started and never completed. Then, too, trade has not been the best, although it has been fairly good, and competition has been close. We have a large number of unfinished contracts on hand, which, when completed, will help us a great deal. I estimate that we have $50,000 worth of contracts on hand at present. To-morrow we will shut down, but on Wednesday the doors will open again, and we will continue business as before. There need be no fear as to all contracts not being paid. One hundred and twenty-five men were constantly employed."

[7 March 1893, p. 11.]

15 - AN HYPNOTIC SEANCE.

That mystic influence which the modern public, along with the masters of it, are pleased to term hypnotism or mesmerism, was forcibly illustrated last evening by Prof. LaRoge, of this city, who resides at No. 807 North Fifteenth street. Prof. LaRoge calls himself a professor of mesmerism and hypnotism. By these powers he endeavors to develop latent psychical powers, and stands high in the estimation of all those who have had occasion to witness his performances in this line. Last evening a select gathering of friends and invited skeptics assembled at Hazenstab's Art Gallery, near the corner of Sixth and Olive, on Sixth street. The gallery in question is up one flight of stairs, and is a very large, spacious room, almost square, with little, low windows looking down on Sixth street, and a ceiling that is none too high. The visitors began dropping in about 7:45 p.m., and by 8:30 a fairly large audience of quizzical inquirers sat chatting in parallel lines along the east and west sides of the room.

Prof. Laroge is a small man of perhaps 28 years of age, with fair hair and small, deep-set eyes that in the glamor of a few incandescent lamps looked as though they might be steel blue. In a nervous manner he strolled to and fro, awaiting the arrival of the guests, and during that while he discoursed upon his powers to a *Globe-Democrat* reporter.

"I am going to give a few tests this evening," he said, "in the line of hypnotism and perhaps clairvoyancy that will interest you. A great many are skeptical as to the truth of this influence of one mind over another, but I propose to show that one mind does dominate another in a manner most marvelous to relate. The subjects I have with me are men whom I have picked up here and there, and they are completely dominated by my power."

The "limited number" having gathered by this time, the Professor broke off his discourse and strolling to the center of the room requested the attention of the guests.

"Now," said the Professor, "is there any one here who is desirous of testing this hypnotic power in their own persons? If there is I do not want you to be afraid to say so. I promise you that while you are in this condition I shall not make you do anything that you would not wish to do before your friends."

There was no response to this query, and finding no one who was willing to become a subject, the Professor called two of his own subjects and seated them at the extreme south end of the hall on two plain wooden chairs. The subjects were James Reynolds and Joseph Emerson, two very humble and plain-looking men, evidently possessed of little will power of their own.

When they were both seated the Professor approached Reynolds and requested him to assume an upright position, putting his arms to his side and drawing his feet close together. He began by waving his right hand before the subject's face, then gradually approaching and moving both hands over the subject's head. The longer he smoothed the subject's forehead and hair the lower drooped the eyelids. The head began to nod as of one going to sleep; the muscles relaxed, the eyelids finally closed, and the head suddenly fell forward on the breast. Laroge then removed his hands, and, snapping his fingers close to the subject's ear, cried, "Wake up! wake up!" and the subject showed signs of reviving consciousness. When he eventually did open his eyes in response to repeated finger calls it was only to stare at the thumb and forefinger of the mystic hand that were close to his eyes. Then the thumb and forefinger moved away and the patient arose from his chair and humbly followed. When he reached the center of the room the professor said:

"See all the people about you; look at them; they are making faces at you."

This statement seemed reality to the patient. It grieved him also. He bent forward, first bowing to some indefinite object and protruding his tongue; then to another and another, while the mystic smilingly observed him, and called for a broom. Some one brought a broom.

"See here," said Laroge, putting the broom in his hand, "here is a banjo, a nice instrument; you can play the banjo, can't you?"

"Yes," said the subject.

"Well, take it now. Sit right down here and play for us."

The subject took the chair indicated.

"Now play," continued the mystic, "and sing, too, some old familiar piece that you know."

For awhile Reynolds only thrummed the straw with his fingers and moved his left hand along the frets, stopping every now and again to put some ill-sounding string into harmony. It finally thrummed to his satisfaction, and he broke out in a weak, piping, plaintive voice to sing the "Man in the Moon" and sang it, too, but it was rather sad singing to hear. While he was playing Laroge put his hand to one end of the broom handle and held it firmly. All at once the subject dropped it as though it were red hot, sprang to his feet, closely inspected his hands for traces no doubt of blisters and scorched skin. In a dazed way he picked up the broom again and examined it. Then he returned to his chair, seated himself and began to mournfully thrum the straw, keeping time with his head and his foot in a most harmonious manner.

Prof. Laroge then took up a position behind his chair and placed his left foot on one of the lower rounds of it. With his left hand he grasped the back, and simply waited for an effect. Reynolds did not move.

"Your chair is growing hot," said the mystic, "awful hot. It will burn you. Don't you feel it?"

Then the effect came. The patient leaped from the chair with every expression and movement of pain. He examined his hands, his coat-tails and his trousers, and then approached the chair again. Before this he paused and stretched out his hands as one might over a kitchen stove of a cold morning. He bowed low over it and seemed to feel its heat and finding it growing too hot, moved away from it. The professor endeavored to assure him that such was not the case, that the chair was perfectly cool, and all that, but with no effect.

"It is cool," said Laroge. "The chair is not hot. See, I will sit on it myself," and, suiting the action to the word, he sat down.

"Now, you sit down," continued Laroge. "Come sit down," and the subject did so, but sprang away again, exclaiming, "It's too hot! It's awful hot!"

"Oh, no, it isn't," said Laroge; "but never mind," and waving his hand before the subject's eyes, he handed him a silk handkerchief and said:

"Here is a baby. Do you see it? Can't you hear it cry? Rock the poor baby to sleep." Reynolds took the handkerchief to his arms, and, sitting down, began to rock to and fro, crooning the while some old lullaby that is now almost forgotten. While doing this Laroge snapped his fingers and told him to "wake up," which he did, looking perfectly calm and sensible.

La Roge then approached the second subject, Joe Emerson, and performed the same tactics with him as with Reynolds until he had him standing in the center of the room. Then he closed the subject's eyes and passed his hands up and down the body from head to foot. As this stroking progressed the body of Emerson stiffened and seemed ready to fall. It was caught, however, and lowered to the floor much as one would lower an upright log. The mystic then called for assistance, and placing two stout wooden chairs back to back, but some 5 feet apart, he, with the assistance of several others, lifted the stiffened body to the top. The neck rested upon one round of the chair's back while the heels rested upon the other. All hands were removed, and the body lay in that condition without a tremor. Several of the guests were then invited to mount the body, and rest upon it but all declined. "Well, help me up, then," said Laroge, and with the assistance of several he was lifted up, and stood upon the stomach of the subject, even jumping in his endeavor to make it fall, but with no effect. Next he stood beside it, and reaching out his hand, held it over the body, which insensibly moved toward it. He then placed his hand beneath the back and below, and moved it down toward the floor when the body immediately bent in that direction. Other guests becoming emboldened by this time, when requested by Laroge, sat upon the body just to prove that it could not be bent. When all were convinced a few snaps of the finger brought the subject to himself, and he sat smiling as cool and undisturbed as though nothing had happened.

The third test was that of clairvoyancy, and for this purpose Reynolds was again called into use. La Roge again put Reynolds under the hypnotic influence, and passed him into the hands of a guest, a well-known skeptic, for his own use. The visitor took the subject's hands and commanded him to visit Bloomington, Ill.

"Are you there?" said the speaker. "Yes," said the patient. "Well, now, go to ——— ——— street and tell me what you see." The subject, after a few moments of silence, responded and said:

"I see a two-story frame house, with a small lawn and a brick walk in front."

"Are there any trees?" was asked.

"Yes," came the answer.

"What kind?"

"Palm."

"Go into the house, and as you go count the steps."

"I will," said the subject, and then began to count, "one, two, three, four—"

"No; that is wrong," said the director; "count again."

"One, two," said the subject.

"Yes; now go in. Go in to the parlor to your right."

"You need not tell me," said the subject; "I know where to go; I can see it."

"Well, what do you see?"

Then began a long description of articles in the room. Pictures were described by the subject, the carpets' color told, the furniture and its arrangement described. Wardrobes and drawers were opened, papers and books handled. The kitchen was entered and described, and the contents of a cupboard related. Certain kinds of pie were observed, and the subject refused to come away until he had eaten a piece.

Then he was told to return to St. Louis, which he did by the aid of imaginary wings. Once in St. Louis, he was directed to a certain room, which he entered, lighted the gas and described its contents. He saw familiar objects, and told how they looked and what they were. This description went on until all queries were exhausted and he was given into other hands. A watch was placed at the back of his head, and he was told to look at it and tell the time. After a few moments of study he was able to say, "Twenty-five minutes of 10," which was the exact time registered by the watch.

While guests were questioning him, needles were passed through the skin, and from the wounds no blood issued.

The subjects, when spoken to by a *Globe-Democrat* reporter, expressed utter ignorance of all that had taken place, felt no pain and no inconvenience of any kind. Said Reynolds:

"I met Prof. Laroge a year ago. I like him very much. I often go with him to such places, and he does what he likes with me."

"Could you refuse the Professor anything?" was asked.

"I don't know," said Reynolds. "I don't think I could. He never asks much of me; but he could make me come. I can't stay away even if I wanted to."

[17 March 1893, p. 4.]

16 - MAJ. BANNERMAN EXPLAINS HIS DEFEAT— COL. BUTLER RETIRES FROM POLITICS.

Maj. James Bannerman and Col. Ed. Butler, the ex-candidate and the ex-boss of the Democratic funeral train, presented widely different aspects yesterday afternoon and opinions that were equally well diverged. Maj. Bannerman had returned to the saddlery business about 9 a.m., but people generally—to say nothing of mournful Democrats in particular—were not inclined to give Maj. Bannerman a rest. That individual sat in his front office, surrounded by friends, when a *Globe-Democrat* reporter called to inquire how it all happened. Somebody must have said, "I told you so," for Maj. Bannerman was a little flushed and his words just a little warm.

"The *Globe-Democrat* wants to know how it happened," was the opening statement.

"I don't know," replied Maj. Bannerman. "Not enough Democratic votes in St. Louis to elect me, I suppose. I'm still a Democrat, however, and just as ready to go down in my pocket for $500 to contribute to a Democratic campaign fund to-day as I was yesterday. I'll remain in that condition for some time to come, I think."

"You have no hard feelings then especially?"

"None in the world. I have no use for a Republican, and I never will have. I will always put up money to knock out one of them if I live a thousand years."

"What in your estimation was the one particular cause of your defeat?"

"The *Globe-Democrat*. It came into line for the Republican party for the first time in years as regards municipal elections, and it elected the ticket. I know of no other influence."

"Don't you think your interview with an afternoon newspaper reporter hurt you somewhat?"

"Not a bit. I stated then my exact opinion, which I hold to now; and I rather think it helped me than hurt me. I polled the full Democrat vote, I think."

"How about the labor vote, Judge Krum's letter and the Council ticket? Were not they a detrimental influence?"

"The labor vote did not hurt me at all. I know that I had my full share of that. As for Judge Krum, I don't think he or his letter had any influence. Judge Krum is a well-known local lawyer, with changeable opinions; in fact, a hale fellow well met, but that is all. I know Judge Krum, and I think I have gauged him. As to the Council ticket, that ticket was all right. I know the members of it personally, and I know them to be good fellows as well as honest. They were poor—of course, they were—but that doesn't say that they were going to the Council to be boodlers just because the Council only pays $25 a month to each member. I know lots of rich fellows who are Councilmen, or who have been, and they are the d——dest lot of crooks. There are more rich Councilmen that are crooked than there are poor ones.

"It comes down to the fact that St. Louis is a Republican city, and it is hurting her reputation. If it isn't, then what has become of our Northern Missouri trade? Chicago is getting it. Chicago is a Democratic city and a white city. It went Democratic much to its own credit this time. Do you think for an instant that Democratic merchants in Missouri or in the Southwest are coming to a black-hearted Republican city like St. Louis to buy when they can go to the Democratic merchants of Chicago instead? Not a bit of it. St. Louis is losing her trade and she will lose more of it. Look at Philadelphia. See how it dwindled and died out after the war. The merchants there lost almost every dollar they had because they were a lot of black-hearted Republicans. New York—a Democratic city—got all the trade, and Philadelphia has never recovered and never will until it becomes a Democratic city."

"What do you think of Maj. Bernheimer?"

"Oh, he's a man of narrow ideas and acts out of his character. No, I didn't get the votes, that's all. In the wards I expected to poll most—like De Menil's, Bernheimer's and Noonan's—I got least, and, along with the mugwumps and the *Globe-Democrat*, I didn't win."

Maj. Bannerman emphasized his remarks ever and anon by a few irreligious exclamations, which showed that he was ill at ease.

Col. Ed. Butler was out and around with a broad smile and a satisfied look. The defeat of his party did not interfere with his horse-shoeing business, and one of the employes at the shop, at Tenth and Walnut streets, stated that "the Boss" had "been down," but had gone home to dinner. When called up by telephone Mr. Butler stated that he would wait the coming of the *Globe-Democrat* man at his house, No. 2304 Pine street. Mrs. Butler answered the door bell at that number, and called to her husband that some one had called to find out whether he was still alive.

"I'm still living," said Col. Butler strolling in, "and I feel as good as I did yesterday, if not better. I suppose you want to know how it all happened. Well, you know as much as I did. We didn't get enough votes."

Here Col. Butler sat down and began a dissertation on local politics generally, in which every point of the situation was covered.

"I attribute Bannerman's defeat to three things. First, the labor vote was against him—without reason, of course; but it was against him, and a very powerful factor it was. The next was Maj. Bannerman's interview. That was very bad, and it was used against him with serious effect. He should not have talked that way. The third reason was the Council ticket. Bannerman could not carry that Council ticket. There were other influences at work. Judge Krum's letter was one of them, and the late beginning the Democrats made with their campaign was another. The Democrats were too sure this time. They had been successful last fall in the country and the State, and they rested easy on their oars until it was too late. They began campaigning when there was hardly time left.

"The Republicans were aroused to the situation. They were alert, better organized, and had more money than the Democrats. They spent more money by a good bit than the Democrats did. Then the *Globe-Democrat* was in line for them, and they could not have wanted more. They had a good strong ticket and they won. Bannerman had the odds against him, and he had the Council ticket to carry. Now, I have nothing in particular to say against that Council ticket. I will say it was not a suitable one.

"As for Mayor Walbridge, I count him an excellent man, and he will make a strong, decent Mayor. He never was any one's tool, regardless of what the Democratic newspapers say, and he never will be. He is a man with broad views, and St. Louis can well be proud of him.

"As for myself I am out of politics entirely. I have a good business, and I do not need to tamper with parties. I am getting too old, and I want to rest. There are plenty of younger leaders running about, and they are getting too swift for me; I can not keep up with them. By the time the next Mayoral campaign rolls around I will be 59 years old. You may feel sure I won't want to enter into the rush then. No, I'm really done with it all, and I'm proud of my record. There is not a man to-day who can say that I ever made a dollar out of politics, or ever wanted to. I never held an office, I never asked for one, and I never would have accepted one as a gift, for there is no money in it. I have been in politics for amusement and for the good I could do other people."

[6 April 1893, p. 5.]

17 - A GIRL FRIGHTFULLY OUTRAGED.

Sergt. Matt Cummins received information yesterday morning in a meager way that Ida America, a 9-year-old girl, had been outraged about three weeks ago in a stable on the south side of Wash street, between Seventh and Eighth. The Sergeant hunted up the girl and found that she lived with her grandmother in the rear of 914 North Eighth street. The grandmother when seen stated that about a week ago Ida had complained to her of soreness, and suspecting nothing extraordinary paid no attention to the little girl's talk. Yesterday morning, however, she cried with pain and she was taken to the City Dispensary. Dr. Jordan upon examination found that not only had the girl been outraged, but she was also suffering from a disease. The child was treated by the Doctor, and on being returned to her home her grandmother did not care to inform the police. However, Sergt. Cummins heard of the case and at once set out to investigate. He found that Ida had been enticed into the stable by a Russian Jew named Solomon Schwartzman, 17 years old, and the little girl says he is the brute. The police have been instructed to arrest Schwartzman wherever he may be found.

[11 November 1892, p. 9.]

18 - HIS NECK IN A NOOSE.

"Hang the scoundrel! Pull him up! Let's finish him now; we've got the chance." These and a score or more of angry expressions, similar in language and accent, emanated from a furious mob of indignant citizens congregated in the alley, just south of Cass avenue, near Thirteenth street, yesterday afternoon. The mob filled the alley, spreading out half way across Thirteenth street, and extending half a block west. It struggled and surged toward and retreated from a shouting, struggling object almost in the center of the angry throng. Round the neck of this object could be plainly discerned a noose fixed at the end of a long clothes line. The other end of the rope was in the hands of determined men, and frantic efforts were made to throw it over the projecting arm of a pole supporting an alley electric light.

The struggling object did all in its power to prevent this. Both hands were clinched about the noose. Teeth and feet were freely used in a desperate endeavor to repel the would-be lynchers. Minutes that seemed hours passed. Windows in surrounding residences were opened and heads of women and children appeared therein. All breathlessly watched the battle for life of the one against the multitude. Those in the windows knew not what occasioned this uproar, and probably prayers emanated from more than one pair of lips for the safety of the object.

The object was Wm. Crawford, over whose head now hangs a ten years' sentence for murder. He lives with his mother, a midwife, at No. 1423 North Thirteenth street. Crawford is a small man, but a giant in strength. Madly he plunged, dragging his assailants hither and thither. The strain was intense. Suddenly he slipped the noose over his head, and, with a rush, battled his way through the mob and made for his mother's house, where he took refuge. The neighbors say the house was surrounded until the arrival of Sergt. John O'Sullivan and Officer McSheehy, ten minutes later.

The cause of the mob's fury was an alleged attempt of Crawford to criminally assault Annie Cox, 10 years old, who lives with her parents at No. 1308 Cass avenue. It was immediately behind this number where the mob gathered. Annie is simple-minded. She was sent by her mother to bring up some kindling wood from the coal-shed located in the rear of the house. She had been gone only a few minutes when the mother heard her screaming for help. William C. Cox, the girl's father, is just convalescing from a severe spell of sickness. He was sitting in his front parlor when his wife rushed in and told him that Annie was calling for aid. Cox ran down the back steps leading into the yard. As he reached the bottom step Annie emerged from the shed. Her dress was torn and her hair disheveled. She rushed to her father and informed him that Crawford had tried to assault her.

In the meantime a number of young men had hurried to the scene. Their numbers were augmented each second. Crawford was standing near the shed from which the little girl had run. They caught and held him while others went to learn what occasioned the cries. When the girl's story was heard, the scene before described took place. The mob was in earnest, and only Crawford's strength saved him.

The facts as given were obtained partly from neighbors and partly from the child's father. Cox lives in a neatly-furnished suite of rooms on the second story of the number given above. A *Globe-Democrat* reporter visited him last night, but the father was averse to talking.

Annie was lying on a bed. She was unable to sleep, owing to the shock to her nervous system. The father partially narrated the child's story of the assault, which is incorporated with the foregoing. He said that he would apply for a warrant to-day.

The police, after investigation, concluded that there was very little basis to the charge of attempted outrage, and would not arrest Crawford. They report that Annie made a similar charge against another man some eight months ago. This charge, the police claim, proved to be without foundation, and they think likewise in the present instance.

Crawford bears a bad reputation. About four years ago he murdered Herman Holthouse in a saloon brawl, near Tenth and Mullanphy streets. He was tried for the crime in the Criminal Court last March, was convicted of murder in the second degree and sentenced to ten years in the Penitentiary. The verdict was appealed to the Supreme Court, where it is still pending. Crawford is out on $10,000 bonds. The police say that he is constantly in trouble.

[5 December 1892, p. 7.]

19 - ISAAC DUTCHER'S DAUGHTER.

Miss Eugenia Dutcher, a highly respected and accomplished lady, was arrested last evening by Detectives Crowley and Gaffney on a charge of shoplifting and locked up at the Third District Station, where she is now confined. As to what prompted Miss Dutcher in taking the articles she is charged with stealing is a mystery both to the police and her aged father, who called to see her at a late hour last night. She is charged with abstracting small articles from the following places, all of which were found on her when arrested: D. Crawford & Co., Sonnenfeld's, Barr's Grand Leader and Famous. The articles taken by Miss Dutcher were tooth-picks and toys of every description for children.

Miss Dutcher kept house for her aged father, Isaac V. W. Dutcher, who resides at No. 4243 Finney avenue. Mr. Dutcher was one of St. Louis' fruit commission merchants and an honorable and highly respected citizen. He retired from business a few years ago, and has since been living at the above number. When he called at the station last night to see his daughter the poor old gentleman wept like a child at the cell door behind which his daughter was confined. He would have fainted had not Turnkey Hennessy held him up on his feet. He said he could not understand why his daughter took the articles from the store, as they were for children, and he had none; furthermore he always gave her any amount of money she needed to purchase presents with. The daughter cried and moaned bitterly, saying that she did not know what made her do it. She did not need any of the property, but some influence seemed to urge her to steal.

Last night Mr. Sonnenfeld called at the station and stated that he would not prosecute the woman. Miss Dutcher is being held until the other named firms are heard from.

[23 December 1892, p. 9.]

20 - A PENSIONER'S ADVENTURE IN ESSEX ALLEY.

Last night James Briscoe, colored, and a G. A. R. man, living at 807 North Tenth street, appeared at the Third District Station and wanted Sadie Trueheart, colored, arrested. Briscoe, it appears, draws a pension, having received a leg wound during the late war. Yesterday he received his $80 for the quarter. He left part of this money at his home, and then went out to enjoy himself. He went to a saloon and grocery at Tenth and Carr streets, where he met the Trueheart woman. She invited him to her home, situate in Essex alley, between Seventh, Eighth, Wash and Carr streets. Before her departure she took $5 from his pocket, he says, and also induced him to go for a can of oysters, some crackers and celery. He returned to the house with the eatables, and when he reached the door found everything dark. He knocked at the door, and as he did so a shower of bricks came through the window on him. A brick grazed his head, and up flew the crackers and celery. When he reached the center of the yard he was surprised to see a negro's head peeping out of the window from Sadie's apartments warning Briscoe to keep away from his woman. Briscoe, with the bucket of oysters in his hand, rushed into the Third District Station and related his experience to Sergt. King. He wanted both the woman and her man arrested. Officers Fanning and Kavanaugh were detailed, but when they reached the house found that both had fled. Later, however, Sadie was locked up on a charge of robbery. As Briscoe says he will prosecute her, a warrant will be applied for this morning.

[20 January 1893, p. 9.]

21 - SUFFERINGS OF A DESERTED FAMILY.

Mary Stifel, with two small children, aged 11 and 6 years, in a half-clad night almost frozen from the cold and sleet. The mother and the two children were crying from cold and hunger. She told Sergt. King that they had been living in one room at 1409 North Ninth street, her husband having deserted her some time ago. She was obliged to work to support herself and children, but as she was sick and her feet began swelling she had to give it up. Yesterday her rent was due and her landlord ejected her and her household effects. They found shelter in a coal shed in the rear, but feared being frozen to death if they remained there last night. They had already spent a day there without a bite to eat. Good-natured Sergt. King at once gave her an empty cell near the stove, while Turnkey Hennessy hustled about the station and secured all the old clothes he could, and made a bed for the trio. A *Globe-Democrat* reporter, in the meantime, purchased sardines, lobsters, cheese, sausage, bread, cakes and rolls, upon which the family feasted.

[27 January 1893, p. 9.]

22 - IRREGULARLY ISSUED.

There's an ugly mystery surrounding the death of a baby at No. 1415 North Sixteenth street. It died nearly a week ago, but as yet it lies unburied in an old chip basket that serves as a bier for its remains. Maggie Daly, wife of Dan Daly, the pugilist, who died sixteen months ago at St. Vincent's Asylum, is the infant's mother. The father of the little one is said to be in Chicago. According to the statements of Mrs. Daly he acquired this relationship only after drugging her. Dr. Thomas F. Dunnigan, of 1625 North Sixteenth street, made out the burial certificate. The certificate he wrote was made out yesterday as "the infant of Mrs. John Crowley;" the date of death as given by the physician is "February 5" and the cause as "inanition." As a matter of fact the child died early on the morning of February 2.

Last Friday Mrs. Hannah Lane, residing at 1882 O'Fallon street, notified Mortuary Clerk Jacks at the Health Department that there was a dead baby at 1415 North Sixteenth. Jacks told Mrs. Lane to notify the Coroner, which was done. Yesterday afternoon Mrs. Lane heard that the infant was still unburied and again informed the Coroner. This time the matter was turned over to the police, who at once began to hunt up the facts. As a result of the investigation Coroner Frank will probably see fit to hold an inquest over the dead child to-day or to-morrow.

Mrs. Hannah Lane was visited at her home, 1832 O'Fallon street, last night by a *Globe-Democrat* reporter. "I was called out of bed to attend Mrs. Daly," said she, "last Tuesday night. I was feeling quite sick, and did not want to go. As the women who came were quite certain that the case was a very urgent one, I got up and went down to No. 1415 North Sixteenth street, where Mrs. Daly was. The child that was born was a splendid, big, healthy boy. I left both doing very well, and called again next day. This time, however, I did not get to see Mrs. Daly for her mother, Mrs. Ford, refused me admittance. I understand that she was terribly angry with her daughter over her indiscretion. I also understand that on the day before Mrs. Daly was delivered her mother drove her out of the house. She came back, though, before the child was born. After calling at the place and being denied admittance to the mother, I considered my duty done. The next day, Thursday, I learned that the child was dead. Being down at the City Hall, I told the Health Department clerk of the child's death, as no certificate had been issued. To-day I was greatly surprised to learn that the baby was not buried. I thought of course that it had been disposed of days ago. Of course I don't know how the baby died. All I do know is that when I last saw it on Tuesday night it was as jolly and healthy a child of its age as I ever saw."

Mrs. Ford, mother of Mrs. Daly, appeared at the door when the reporter called at her house. At the first mention of the word "baby," the old lady begged the visitor to talk in whispers, and began to cry. "Oh, it's a horrible thing," she sobbed, "but the baby just died, that's all. There's nothing to be asking questions about. Dr. Dunnigan gave Maggie a burial certificate this morning. Maggie has gone up to the undertaker's now. It'll be buried to-morrow. Please keep still and don't let the people know."

A call fifteen minutes later at the same place was answered by Mrs. Daly herself, who stepped out on the little porch with a shawl around her shoulders. She began to sob before saying a word. "What'll the people say? What'll the Dalys say?" she wept. "Oh, I wouldn't have had this happen for a million dollars! There's two poor little children, Dave's children, that'll get all the disgrace! What'll I do, what'll I do. I wish I was dead."

"Have you been to the undertaker's?"

"Sist!" exclaimed Mrs. Daly, putting her finger to her mouth. "Sist! No, I haven't been there. I told my mother that I had. Oh, I don't know what to do. I am afraid to do anything and afraid to keep still. Here's the certificate the doctor made out. Do you think it's all right? I don't even know when the baby died. Wednesday night I was so sleepy, having had no rest for two days. I nursed it at midnight and then again at 2 in the morning. When I woke up at 5 it was dead, with its little face down on the mattress."

"Why did you have it made out in a bogus name?"

"Because I didn't want the Dalys to know about it. They don't know anything about it yet. There is my brother in the house, too. He didn't know anything about it. I'm going to take the baby up to Cullinane's undertaking place at Jefferson avenue and Dayton street."

Mrs. Daly drew her shawl up over her head with a shivering sob. Then, as if taking a sudden resolve, she stepped into the house and emerged in a moment with a basket. "I'll take it right up there now," she exclaimed; "I guess they'll take it."

"I don't see how it all happened," she continued, slipping and tripping with uncertain steps over the ice-covered walk. "I don't know how it happened."

When poor Mrs. Daly got to Sixteenth and Carr streets she said she'd get a friend to go to Cullinane's with her. "I've got a lady friend living at 1610," she remarked. "I guess I'll go in there."

She went through the gateway and up to the door of the house with her sorrowful burden. When she reached the door she rang the bell and was admitted. She did not come out again.

Dr. Dunnigan was in a very perturbed state of mind last night. A couple of visits from the police and the newspaper men led him to believe that he had "put his foot in it" very emphatically.

"I've known that girl for years, and took her word. She came to me and told her trouble and asked me to shield her as much as possible. I didn't even see the baby. Well, she said its father was named Crowley; so, to get her out of a bad scrape, I just wrote down what you saw. I've even forgotten myself what I wrote. She told me the child was weak, so I put the cause of death as inanition. Goodness gracious, I wish I hadn't signed that paper."

At midnight the Cullinane people answered by telephone that no one with a baby in a chip basket had called.

[7 February 1893, p. 4.]

23 - KIDNAPED FROM ST. ANN'S.

It is rarely that a case of kidnaping is reported from St. Ann's Asylum, as those who are compelled to place their infants in that institution are usually too glad to have them remain there. The police of the Third District, however, are working on a kidnaping case that was reported to them a few days ago by the Sisters. A Mrs. Lambkin, who resides at 2635 Sullivan avenue, is charged with having done the deed, she being assisted by her husband and her mother. The child is 17 months old, and has golden hair and large blue eyes. It is said to be one of the handsomest that the asylum had.

From what information could be obtained last night it appears that Mrs. Lambkin is not the mother, but had merely raised it. She was so much attached to it, though, that she and her husband loved it as their own. The babe, when but a few months old, was given to Mrs. Lambkin to raise by the Sisters of St. Ann's. They would not reveal its real mother's name. A few weeks ago the Sisters went to the residence of Mrs. Lambkin and took the child back to the institution. Mrs. Lambkin grieved very much over the loss and wept bitterly. Nothing more was thought of the incident by the nuns, as they were impressed with the idea that the matter was ended. Such, however, proved not to be the case.

On Monday, shortly before noon, Mrs. Lambkin, in company with her mother, paid the asylum, situated at the corner of Tenth and O'Fallon streets, a visit. As they neared the door leading into the building they were joined by the husband of the woman, who is a teamster, and who halted his team of horses and wagon in front of the entrance. He remained on the rig while his wife and mother-in-law entered. Mrs. Lambkin asked to see the child which she had so tenderly nursed. The Sister in charge granted the request and got the baby. When the child was brought in to the sitting room, where the two ladies were waiting, Mrs. Lambkin asked that she be allowed to take the little one in her arms. She fondled the child and had hardly pressed the little one to her bosom before she made a dart for the front door, followed by her mother and the Sister. When the front door was reached, the Sister, who appeared to be quite a sprinter, caught up with the two. She made an attempt to seize Mrs. Lambkin and the child, but was prevented from doing so by the mother. The daughter had safely reached the outside when the alarm was raised in the asylum.

More than twenty-five Sisters from all parts of the building rushed to the struggling member. It seems that when Mrs. Lambkin reached the pavement she made an attempt to get on the waiting wagon. Two nuns, however, rushed upon her and began pulling her back. Mr. Lambkin, seeing that his wife was held a prisoner and that she could not defend herself, as the child was in her arms, came to her rescue. He freed her from the women, and his wife and the babe disappeared. A score of habited religieuses reached the pavement and they soon took after Mrs. Lambkin and the baby. Meanwhile the woman's husband and her mother made their escape in an opposite direction in the wagon. The Sisters chased the fugitive up streets, through alleys and into hallways. They were joined by Officer Maher and a number of other policemen, but none were able to overhaul the fleeing woman and her burden. When within seeing distance Mrs. Lambkin boarded an elec-

tric car of the Mound City line at the corner of Ninth street and Cass avenue
and went north.

[8 February 1893, p. 4.]

24 - BREAD WAR IN LITTLE RUSSIA.

The Russian Jews, who are so thickly settled in the Third Police District,
are rapidly falling in the ways of Americans. Carondelet has just recovered
from a bread war, and now one that will probably end in trouble is on between Franklin and Cass avenues, west of Broadway. For a long time a few
bakeries have controlled the cake and bread trade in Little Russia, and
they allowed no one to enter in the field. They manufactured and sold
mostly what is known as kosher bread, which is white twists and black or
rye bread, prepared in conformity with the religious requirements. These
loaves were sold at 5¢ each, or three for 10¢. Those who had a monopoly of
the bread trade among these Russians were M. Goldberg, on North Eighth,
L. Schneider, on Biddle, and M. Kaiseer, on North Seventh street. A few
days ago, so it appears, Jacob Kohn, a baker, opened a shop at 622 Carr
street, in opposition to what Kohn called a trust. He was assisted by his
beautiful wife, and they soon made friends and began getting the trade.
Then the other bakers began cutting prices, selling two loaves for 5¢ to
drive Kohn out of the business. Kohn yesterday displayed a painted muslin
sign with the picture of a loaf of bread and Jewish lettering to the effect that
he also would sell two loaves for 5¢. This sign he tacked over the door, and
his rivals at once had similar ones made and placed over their doors. Thus
the war went on. Late yesterday afternoon one Abraham Graber, who, it
seems, is one of Kohn's rivals, rented the store adjoining Kohn's place, and
soon had the place stocked up with bread. He had a sign printed in the
Jewish language, which was fastened over the door, announcing that he
sold three loaves of bread for 5¢, and that he had come to stay. Kohn would
not come down in his price last night, but it is expected that he will be
compelled to do so to-day.

The police of the Third District are watching the bread war very closely,
as they fear trouble before it is ended.

[10 February 1893, p. 9.]

25 - SHOT BY A MAD HUSBAND.

A faithless wife and an indiscreet lover caused a tragedy yesterday that will find its expiation in the death of the wife and the probable future death of the lover. Eugene Borrman entered his home at No. 2016 Carr street yesterday afternoon at 3:10 p.m. He was prepared for vengeance, for he opened fire with a five-shooter Smith & Wesson revolver on Tim Reagan, the paramour of his wife, who was in the room with him. Some of the neighbors must have informed Borrman of Reagan's presence, for his opening exclamation was: "You ——— ———, I have been looking for you, and now I've got you." Then he fired. The first shot was aimed well and to kill, for it struck just above the nose, glancing from left to right and grazing the bone of the forehead. The work seemed effective, for Reagan uttered an exclamation of pain and fell to the floor. A second shot, fired to supplement the work, missed its aim entirely. At the firing of the second shot Mrs. Borrman ran toward her husband to stay the fearful work. The third shot aimed at her struck her right arm above the elbow, breaking it. Seeing that her husband's rage was boundless, she turned to run past him. While running he turned after her and fired a fourth shot, which entered her left side above the hip and came out through the groin, passing entirely through her. She then staggered to the porch and fell. Borrman again turned his attention to Reagan, who had recovered consciousness and was preparing to leap out of the south kitchen window. As Reagan jumped Borrman fired a fifth shot, without effect, however. Then he left the house and strolled toward the E. C. Simmons Hardware Company, for which firm he occasionally did teaming. Reagan, with the blood streaming from the skin penetration, limped away toward Twenty-first and Biddle. At that point he came in contact with Officer Barney Reagen, of the Third District, to whom he appealed for aid. Officer Reagen called the patrol and he was taken to the City Dispensary.

The sound of the shots on the second floor of No. 2016 aroused the entire neighborhood, and the sidewalk and yard were soon filled with people. Officers from the neighboring beats arrived and took charge of the premises. A patrol was called and Mrs. Borrman was taken to the City Dispensary. When Borrman reached Ninth and St. Charles streets he lingered about the delivery portion of E. C. Simmons. Officer McDonnell, of the Third District, followed him from the scene of the shooting and accosted him. Borrman gave himself up without any trouble, and was locked up at the Third District. The officers at the scene of the shooting opened a temporary office in a neighboring Chinese laundry, much to the disgust of that worthy, where they made out the official report.

At the Dispensary Mrs. Borrman and Tim Reagan were examined by Dr. David Nichols, who dressed their wounds and sent them to the City Hospital. To Dr. Nichols Reagan told his story. He said that he was visiting Mrs. Borrman at the time of the shooting, and that Borrman suddenly opened the door. He carried a revolver in his hand and aimed at Reagan. After the first shot Reagan said that he became senseless and did not see what was going on until the fourth shot was fired. Then he jumped out of the window. Mrs. Borrman refused to say anything, being in a kind of stupor. At the City Hospital the twain were received by Dr. Heine Marks, who examined their wounds. When seen by a *Globe-Democrat* reporter Mrs. Borrman was stretched on a litter in the women's ward, much in the same condition as that in which she arrived. When taken from the house she was almost denuded, as was Reagan. Mrs. Borrman was in a kind of stupor, and talked incoherently. This condition was not the effect of her wounds, but rather from drink. The woman had been drinking all the morning. When questioned she answered with difficulty, and cried continuously.

"Were you in company with this man Reagan when you were shot?" was asked.

"I don't know," she answered. "I don't know who I was with. As sure as I am lying here almost dead, I don't know anything about it."

"Did you know that Reagan was shot, also?"

"Was anybody shot? Who was it? I don't know of anything, honestly, I don't."

Here Mrs. Borrman began to cry again, and further questioning proved futile.

In the lecture room of the Dispensary Reagan was stretched out on a litter. The blood from his forehead trickled down over his face and had clotted in his eyebrows and mustache. His appearance portended more serious effect than was really present. Reagan had been drinking also, but was sober enough to understand his situation. To a *Globe-Democrat* reporter he said: "I was in the house at the time of the shooting. Borrman fired two shots at me when he came in and two more at his wife. When he fired at me I felt as though some one had struck me and I saw stars. Then I fell to the floor. I woke up in a minute and crawled to the window and opened it. Borrman was in the other room, and as I jumped he fired again. I struck the brick walk below and hurt my feet, then I limped out the back way and over to Twenty-first and Biddle, where the officer arrested me. I have known Mrs. Borrman for three years now. I have been to the house before, but Borrman never knew it. I went there yesterday because I had been drinking all the night before. She had been drinking, too. When Borrman came in we were both sitting on the lounge. I don't know Borrman, only by sight. He has seen me before, and I heard that he had been looking for me. He threatened to kill me once before, I heard. Mrs. Borrman has been married thirteen years that

I know of, and she has three children. The little girl was at school when I came, but the two little boys were down in the yard. Is she badly hurt?" inquired Reagan of Dr. Marks.

"Yes," said the Doctor; "she is seriously injured, and may die."

"Humph!" ejaculated Reagan, "she got it a good deal worse than I did, then, for I ain't hurt. My eyes are all right, it's just a skin wound."

Reagan is a heavy built, stolid looking Irishman, with a full shock of sandy-colored hair and mustache. He weighs 170 pounds, is 30 years old, and employed as a day laborer in Kenkinnely's quarry on Florissant avenue. Mrs. Borrman looks as though she might be of Irish extraction. She is 28 years old, of full, plump figure, with a blonde complexion and reddish-brown hair. In the Third District Station Eugene Borrman, the husband, is locked up. He was rather taciturn when visited last night, and refused to talk.

"Will you give the correct spelling for your name?" was asked.

"No, I won't," came the answer.

"What is your age?"

"Forty-three," said Mr. Borrman, who then turned away. He turned around, however, and came back to the bars, saying: "I haven't anything to say; you can write up what you please; I done my part and I'm going to quit. If anything's against me it'll come out at the trial, so it don't make any difference."

Borrman is a small wiry-looking person, with dark sharp eyes and clearly outlined features. He is employed by Morris & Glorris, teamsters, who have their barns at Twentieth and Carr streets. The firm lets wagons to wholesale merchants and employs men to drive them. Reagan stated that some one must have carried information of his presence in the house to Borrman, because of the latter's coming home during his working hours. Reagan's wound is so slight that in several weeks it will be healed. Of Mrs. Borrman's wounds Dr. Marks said that he did not think she could possibly live. It was stated by residents in the neighborhood of 2016 Carr that Borrman had shot his wife once before for a similar offense. The children of Borrman have been taken in charge by neighbors, who will care for them until Borrman is set free. No. 2016 Carr is a plain two-story brick dwelling, the second floor of which is reached only by a back stairs. The landing of this stairs forms the porch where Mrs. Borrman ran to and fell. The house was locked up, and over the entrance an empty bird cage hung, almost symbolical of the deserted home.

[22 February 1893, p. 12.]

26 ~ A FAST YOUNG RUSSIAN-AMERICAN.

Charles Siegel, 14 years old, was arrested last night by Officer Callahan, of the Third District. The arrest was made upon complaint of the boy's father, Meyer Siegel, a Russian, who lives at 816 Biddle street. The father says that the boy has been in this country but a few years and has already fallen into the ways of the fast American youngster. He doesn't want to work and prefers to "shoot craps" all day. Last night he came to his home and demanded some money from his father. That was refused him, whereupon he wanted to beat his parent. He will be sent to the House of Refuge to-day.

[10 April 1893, p. 3.]

27 - [HARRY HALL]

"The finest bits of scenery that I have ever witnessed occur right about the town of Bloomington, Ind., which lies about due east of St. Louis," said Harry Hall, of Mount Clemens, Mich. "The country about there was the earliest settled portion of Indiana, and it now contains the least portion of that State's population. The land is very hilly and full of gravel and rocks. It is, in a great measure, useless for cultivation. The farmers have learned this, and they have left it severely alone, many portions of it having never been plowed at all. This land contains many high hills and rocky ravines that wind about among the hills and lose their waters in underground passageways, only to reappear again at some point further on, and tumble along over rocks and falls in a most picturesque manner. But one feature that was always interesting to me was the many little graveyards that dot the country. Seemingly every old farm house had a graveyard of its own, and now, the original owners and users being all dead, these little plats of ground are walled in and left to molder and decay. No one thinks of using the rocky land, and so these little spots are perfectly safe from destruction. In some of them a dozen members of the family are buried, the last probably having been laid to rest away back in 1845. Since then many summers of weeds and wild roses have flourished, and little pine trees, that were originally planted for decoration, have grown into tall trees, that forever keep the graves beneath their shadow. While at college there, I have often with a companion entered these sacred precincts, trampled down the weeds and righted the little tombstones, yellow with age, that had long since fallen to earth and buried even the inscribed virtues of the departed deep in the earth. In the winter time, when other trees are leafless, great flocks of crows resort to these pine clumps and create a most noisy rendezvous. I have watched them on cold winter days cawing and screeching in the pine branches, and with every gust of wind flying out and circling about as if unable to hold their position against the wind. So it goes. The hardy pioneers of Indiana's fame are tucked away in little forgotten patches left to the care of the wind and the rain, and furnishing a winter shelter for carrion crows against the cold north winds of January."

[14 December 1892, p. 7.]

28 - [ALBERT JONES]

"**I** once stopped in a haunted house," said Albert Jones, while sipping
lemonade in the Lindell annex. "That was in the beginning of my theatrical
career, some four years ago. I was a rather ambitious young roustabout. I
wanted to go on the stage, but somehow my talents were not appreciated by
the profession. Then I proposed starting a minstrel troupe of my own, and I
did so. With a local companion named Neff, I began making arrangements
and soon had a crowd of local talent gathered about me who were ready
to accompany me on a tour, and receive their salary in proportion to the
net proceeds of our engagements. I ordered lithographs and billed several
neighboring towns. Then we started. The Jones and Neff combination, after
a successful run of four nights in four different villages, struck Huntington,
Ind. We were not rich enough yet to put up at a hotel, but we did the next
best thing, we secured a vacant house and slept in that. Every man had his
blanket. Oh, we were ambitious; there is no question about that. This house
adjoined the Huntington Medical School, and the upper floor was once used
for a dissecting room. That's why the house stood vacant. On moving out the
students forgot to remove a plain square pine box that lay in one corner,
and which contained a well-strung and articulated skeleton. When we discovered the remains we took counsel with one another and discussed the
advisability of sleeping elsewhere; but finally we concluded to throw the
skeleton out and sleep all together in one room downstairs. There were
eight of us, and, after piling the respected departed out into the wood shed,
we wrapped our mantles about us, as Bryant says, and lay down to pleasant
dreams. My dreams were weird. Finally I awoke and imagined that I heard
footsteps up-stairs in the ghost's chamber. Neff lay near me and I shook
him. He listened and said that he heard them. Then we awakened the whole
company and bade them listen. They did so. We all heard the tramp, tramp,
tramp of the ghost above. I rolled up my blanket and prepared to immigrate.
So did the company. At last Neff said he heard the stair door open that led
down into our room. We immediately adjourned to the yard and surveyed
the second floor in the moonlight. We couldn't hear anything nor see anything. We were in a quandary as to what to do. The town watch came by
and, attracted by the confabulation in the front yard, came in and joined.
We told him the circumstances. One member offered him a 'nip of the serpent.' Then he said he would go up and see. We went along. There was
nothing up there. We decided to try and sleep once more. With the exception of a few strange noises, that might have occurred elsewhere in the
neighborhood, we heard nothing. Next day we secured new quarters and
immigrated, but we couldn't explain the footsteps. I do believe it was that

skeleton." "What became of the company?" asked a bystander. "It busted at Lafayette, Ind., and I went to Chicago and I've been successful ever since."

[21 December 1892, p. 7.]

29 - [PAUL DRESSER]

"**N**o, thanks," said Paul Dresser to a coterie of genials in the parlor of the St. James. "I never smoke, although I like tobacco very well. Why don't I? Well, I'll tell you," continued Mr. Dresser, with a promising smile of a good story. "I once caused the death of a friend of mine by smoking, and since then I have kept a solemn vow never to smoke again. Years ago I was foreman in a powder mill down in Connecticut, about twelve miles from Hartford. I had a good friend who worked under me, a steady, promising young man, and I took considerable interest in him. It was our custom to spend the noon hour together before the mill door eating and chatting. The work in the mill filled the clothes with the powder constituents in great quantities, and in a little while our apparel was highly inflammable. Regardless of this, we were wont to smoke, although we used lid-covered pipes. One day while smoking before the door I opened my pipe to force down the tobacco, seeing that it didn't draw well. My finger knocked some sparks and ashes on my friend's coat, and in a moment his body was enveloped in flames. He jumped and started to run down to the little stream that ran in front of the mill. The wind only fanned the flames more, and by the time he reached the stream he was burned beyond cure. We took him to Hartford, where his wounds were dressed, and where he received the best care, but he only lingered a few days. This fact worked upon me and I have always thought myself guilty of crime in that respect. The young man was so bright and promising that it seemed all the worse to have him die in that manner. I quit smoking then, and I have never touched tobacco since. When a man is young he does not take into account the serious risks that he runs to satisfy a mere moment of desire."

[24 December 1892, p. 5.]

30 - [JOHN M. MAXWELL]

"Talk about fame and honor and all that," began John M. Maxwell to a *Globe-Democrat* reporter, "I have almost got over all that. A man that gets above starvation nowadays is doing excellently well, but the man that lays up $20,000 is really successful, although I didn't think so a few years ago. In those days I was given to writing poems about the fading shadow, beautiful snow, etc. I had three or four plays, some thirty poems, the half of a comic opera, two philosophical essays, the first three chapters of a long novel all written and a salary of $12 a week. I was given to reading "Thanatopsis" and Carlyle's "Hero Worship," and the more I read the more inflamed I became at my poor position in life. Eventually I decided to cap the climax and write an epic poem and then starve to death. The world would then find out what a master mind had lived unappreciated. Well, sir, that epic was the making of me. I let it occupy all my spare moments and shirked my work to go off in a corner and write a few lines about the great trombones smashing the heavenly spheres together. The result was that I got fired from my position as collector for an easy-payment firm and went forth to seek a job. Then I eased up on literary work. I didn't have half the ambition to starve to death and let the world discover my masterpieces when I should lie a stiff and soulless corpse, not half. All I wanted was due assurance that I was going to eat regular. Well, my quest didn't pan out well, and I began to worry most fearfully. To close it all the house where I roomed caught fire and all my brainy efforts evaporated in smoke. That completed my reformation. When I secured work in a wholesale dry goods house I earned my salary and studied to learn the business. I have had better luck since then and now I'm a commercial tourist. I don't want to discourage any literary genius, but, by the way, I don't think a real literary genius could be discouraged or turned aside at all."

[29 December 1892, p. 7.]

31 - [CHARLES BRANDON]

"I was once lost in a cave," said Charles Brandon, dropping his pen in the writing-room of the Lindell and turning smilingly towards a *Globe-Democrat* reporter. "My experience is laid in Kentucky, where I visited some friends a year ago. I was always anxious to explore a cave, and when I heard of the near proximity of one I proposed to visit it. One morning I asked Harris, my friend, to lead the way, and he did. We bought several hundred yards of sheep twine, trimmed up a couple of torches and wended our way to the cave. The entrance was a rocky aperture in the side of a beautiful wooded hill, and we slipped down to the first landing in a trice. Some little distance in we fastened the twine and then moved on. The twine gave out just where our progress led us to a large arched aisle like that of a church. We did not turn back, however. Here we set up a tall white stalagmite that had fallen to earth, and tied to it the end of our twine. About a hundred feet farther on the aisle ended and a ragged, perpendicular wall arose. We climbed this, hand over hand. At the top was an opening that looked through into a great chamber and down into the smooth surface of an underground stream. We crawled through and I sat down near the entrance. Harris climbed down to the stream. I wanted to keep near to the entrance so as not to lose track of it. After watching Harris moving about in the distance for a few minutes I glanced about to take a reassuring glance at the aperture. I could not see it. I made a move toward the place, but the entrance was not there. I looked about, and further on I saw several, but I knew that I had not moved away 10 feet. My nerve departed. In an instant I felt clammy and cold. Then I cried out to Harris. The hollow sound of my voice astounded me. Harris came hurrying up the rocky ledge and stood beside me. 'What's the matter?' he said. 'I can't find the entrance that we came through,' I exclaimed. We both looked, but in vain. It was gone. We looked at one another with blanched faces. I murmured something about 'awful,' and Harris simply weakened and sat down. I had visions of death, of chattering ghosts in that miserable vale, of starving to death and of wandering about in that rocky blackness, a mumbling, chattering maniac. The more I thought the weaker I became. The blood rushed to my head. I lost my balance and sunk down. When my head struck the rock I was wide awake. My torch was sputtering on the ground. I looked about. Right before me I saw the entrance way. I might have rolled through it. Then I jumped up and it was gone again. But I knew the trick. It was hidden by an overhanging ledge and that was why I could not see it. We crawled through and hurried along the aisle. We untied the twine and followed it a great deal faster than we had entered. Regardless of bumps and bruises we hurried on and reached the entrance. Then we climbed out. I rejoice in the memory of that experience. Yet I don't care to repeat it. The memory is plenty for me."

[30 December 1892, p. 7.]

32 - [OLNEY WADE]

"Speaking of people who are the victims of passion or of a habit," said Olney Wade, of Elizabeth, N.J., who is at the Lindell, "the most remarkable case I know of was that of a young Dane by the name of Christian Aaberg, who came to America in 1883. This young fellow, not over 26, was the son of a Danish nobleman, a member of the Danish Parliament and a man of high intellectual accomplishments, coupled with suave refinement. The characteristics of the father were those of the son, with the exception of the son's passionate nature, which led him to many excesses, of which the most prominent was that of drink. His father tired of his wild escapades at home, and bestowing an annuity on the young man forced him to leave the country. He came to New York, where I met him. His career was a remarkable one. He plunged into everything sensuous and debilitating. His annuity he sold for temporary pleasure, and at last found himself compelled to look for work or starve. He secured a position running the elevator for the firm I now represent. This Dane could talk on the most inspiring themes. His knowledge was seemingly limitless, and his discourses on the purpose of life, the affinity of character and like subjects were marked by sincere thought and appreciation. Through the Danish Consul at Washington he communicated with his father, and after many promises secured $70,000. With this he bought a small but really beautiful farm in Pennsylvania and went to live on it. The closing chapter of the story was that he was found in his room some few months after in a drunken stupor. The table was set with the finest of wines and liquors, and mingled with them were books by the master minds of the world. He had drunk himself literally to death, for he never awoke from that condition."

[27 January 1893, p. 7.]

33 - THE THEATERS.

[Excerpts]

HAVLIN'S.

Miss Rosabel Morrison, the handsome and talented young daughter of Lewis Morrison, and the original *Marguerite* of her father's production of Faust, will appear at Havlin's Theater this afternoon in the late Henry De Mille's great railroad play, The Danger Signal. The play is a good one, and considerably above the average "locomotive drama." Among the sensational effects introduced is a monster iron locomotive propelled by steam, a snow plow, a freight train and a cannon ball express. Paul Dreiser, the famous song-writer, will greet his many friends who know him through his melodies. Next Sunday afternoon, Jas. H. Wallick's Bandit King.

SIVALL'S WONDERLAND.

If the good citizens of St. Louis don't enjoy themselves at Wonderland this week it will only be because they don't attend. By far the best bill of the season has been provided in both curio halls and theaters. Peter Sampson, the Russian strong man, who literally broke his way out of a Siberia prison, will show how he did it. Maletta and Madeline, the Zulus, will exhibit their savage arts. George Lippert, the three-legged man, will astonish many, and the stake and four soldering irons used to burn the negro Henry Smith at Paris, Tex., will excite horror in the beholders. George Derious' funny comedy Jocko will be produced on the stage.

[12 February 1893, p. 30.]

34 - THE THEATERS.

[Excerpts]

GRAND OPERA HOUSE.

The Crust of Society is the latest play to reach us from Paris via the translator's pen and the stage carpenter's craft. It tells in polished language of the excess of immorality in the world, and especially in women. It tells how the social outcast must create and live in a world of her own after she falls. It tells how the man in the case is still smiled on by society, despite his known crimes. But it tells not how this state of things may be remedied. The hero of the story, instead of reaching out his arm to help the fallen, does all in his power to keep her from reforming by putting every obstacle in the way of her match with the man she loves and who loves her. The Crust of Society is adapted from the younger Dumas' novel, "The Demimonde." Of the twelve characters in the play ten are either ostracised by society or ought to be. Notwithstanding the unhealthiness of the drama's tone it is a splendid effort from an artistic standpoint. The members of Mr. John Stetson's company are all excellent players, and seem to have been selected especially for the requirements of the characters they take.

Elita Proctor Otis plays *Ernestine Echo*, Carrie Turner, *Mrs. Eastlake Chapel*, and Jane Stuart, *Violet Esmond*. Messrs. Joseph E. Whiting, Harry St. Maur, David Elmer and Joseph Foster and Miss Helen Kinnaird, Miss Jane Lovejoy and Miss Hennings make up the company. Next week the Grand will have Modjeska.

HAVLIN'S.

Dramatic art of the present day is measured by the amount of excitement the playwright can work in in three or four acts. His heroes and heroines must get right out and prove themselves heroes and heroines. Half hour love scenes don't go any more, for in that time goodness knows how many real interesting wrecks might occur. The Danger Signal, in which Miss Rosabel Morrison appears to advantage at Havlin's, is certainly a play of the present. Climax follows thrill and thrill climax from the first to the last scene. A "cannon-ball" express crosses the stage at the rate of fifty miles an hour, a snow plow plows, a freight train "freights," and other equally exciting incidents keep coming until the story is done. Miss Morrison has few equals in her line of work. Paul Dresser, one of America's foremost song writers and an actor of ability, plays *Corporal Yost* in the Danger Signal. Next week Havlin's has James H. Wallick's Bandit King.

[13 February 1893, p. 9.]

35 - MISS FAY'S SEANCE.

The exhibition of "spiritual manifestations" given by Miss Annie Eva Fay at the Grand Opera House Sunday night has created considerable comment among certain circles. In the ranks of the Spiritualists the exhibition has had the effect of confirming already long-established beliefs. Among the skeptical, however, the feeling of unbelief has been only strengthened, and a new impulse toward "finding out" the causes of the phenomena has been given. One of the most pronounced of the latter class is Dr. J. K. Bauduy, who attended the "seance." Dr. Bauduy was one of the committeemen appointed by the audience to remain upon the stage while the performance was going on, and, if possible, detect and expose any attempt at trickery.

"Miss Fay gave a very clever exhibition of sleight of hand," the physician said when questioned, "and I was greatly pleased at her expertness. She is certainly an adept in her art—or her confederate is. I must say that she conducted her exhibition in a very fair manner, indeed, for every opportunity was given us for investigation, and, during the whole performance, the lights were burning brightly. In this regard she beats any of the other alleged mediums I have seen, who always turned down the lights before performing their tricks. But that is as far as I can praise. That she was aided by spirits or other influences from any but our own physical world, I do not believe and do not admit. One thing that struck me as being very patent was the fact that all her tricks are old. She does almost the same, if not the identical list of tricks and illusions, that the Davenport Brothers did years ago. They were afterwards exposed, if I remember rightly, but where or by whom I forget. She does nothing new. Another thing, that she must even admit herself, is the fact that her exploits or manifestations or tricks are by far poorer than those performed by the East Indian jugglers and by other magicians. Yet they are free to say that their deeds are all done by physical means. If she were aided by the spirits does it not seem probable that she would do things out of the range of human performance?

"Of course I can not say how Miss Fay tricked us or how she did not. I am morally certain, though, that she had a confederate very well concealed somewhere about that cabinet who threw out the musical instruments and made all the racket as soon as the curtains were drawn. Miss Fay was tightly bound, I'll swear to that, when she was inside the room. Just the instant the curtain was drawn the 'manifestations' would begin, which proves beyond doubt that she had some one helping her. She never stirred at all, for her assistant did the work. But how he did it I cannot guess. When we were in the 'circle' I held her hands tightly in mine and know that she did not release them, though the 'manifestations' went on just the same.

"It is said that Miss Fay can give the same sort of an exhibition in any private drawing room without preparation. Now, I'll bet you she can't come here in my office and do it. If she will do it I'll begin to believe in Miss Annie Eva Fay as a spirit medium."

[21 February 1893, p. 4.]

36 - MODJESKA AT THE GRAND.

The initial performance of King Henry VIII. by Mme. Modjeska and her company was given at the Grand last night under very favorable auspices. The throng attending was large, fashionable and not over critical, and the players excellent from the tragedienne down to the meanest in the cast. Few if any of Shakespeare's plays have ever been produced with such a wealth of scenery and such truthfulness of costuming and detail. *Katherine of Aragon*, the spurned wife of *Henry*, is the main female character in the drama and the one taken by Modjeska. *Katherine* is undoubtedly one of Shakespeare's grandest daughters, and despite the fact that she is so seldom seen, deserves for her womanly traits to rank with *Portia, Rosalind* and *Ophelia*. Mme. Modjeska's conception of the part is nearly faultless. Her interpretation of the unfortunate Queen's grief at being cast aside, her efforts to win back her faithless husband's love, her meekness up to the point where meekness becomes weakness, and then when that point is overstepped, her magnificent denunciation of *Cardinal Wolsey*, all prove her claim to genius. Mr. Beaumont Smith, a St. Louis actor, is cast as *Buckingham*, and last night fairly surprised his friends by his splendid work. Otis Skinner, one of the best leading men in the country, makes a robust but not overartistic *Henry*, and Guy Lindsay, another St. Louis boy, an excellent *Surrey*. John Lane's consummate acting in the part of *Wolsey* can scarcely be too highly praised. Mrs. Beaumont Smith speaks a sweetly natural *Anne Boleyn*. Taken as a whole Modjeska's Henry VIII. commands admiration. It scarcely possesses all the necessary qualities of interest, however, to make it a popular piece in repertoire nowadays. Next week Fanny Davenport will appear at the Grand in Sardou's Cleopatra.

[21 February 1893, p. 5.]

37 - THE THEATERS.

GRAND OPERA HOUSE.

The almost cloying gorgeousness of Sardou's Cleopatra, which opened at the Grand last night, and in which Fanny Davenport moves with becoming grace, will delight many who have need of such gorgeousness to enjoy a play. Miss Davenport has her admirers in great number, and these are easily thrown into ecstacy by the sensuous movement that pervades the piece. The old theme never tires when interpreted fittingly with the shade of character that is lent to every move and look and sound, all of which makes up the glamor of it all. Perhaps it is to sit and envy *Marc Antony* his tragic fate that draws many to the piece. Certainly Melbourne McDowell makes a shapely and striking *Antony*, with a goodly share of ability thrown in. Fanny Davenport as *Cleopatra* interprets what one might deem the most truthful character of the Egyptian Queen. Still there are shadows of weakness over it all.

OLYMPIC.

E. S. Willard last night opened to a large audience at the Olympic in the role of *Cyrus Blenkarn* in the Middleman. Probably all who saw him knew the theme and the story beforehand. It is of the soulful inventor who saw glory in the invention and not in the fruit of it; endeavored for years with nerve-destroying persistency to accomplish his aim; met misfortune and reverse; met the shame of his much-loved daughter and finally triumphed in invention, and gloried in it also, if only for the revenge it would bring to a broken spirit. It isn't *Cyrus Blenkarn* after all: it's E. S. Willard. With the shadow of a mystic about him he has been able to express himself aloud before the world, and the world has bowed low. The Middleman is strong; it is human. Willard affects the human role. In the present age of earthly struggle humanity wants more of the human, and Willard can give it. On Wednesday evening he will appear in Judah.

[28 February 1893, p. 9.]

38 - JOHN L. OUT FOR A LARK.

Since ex-Champion John L. Sullivan arrived in St. Louis early Sunday morning he has experienced one continual round of excitement. He has dallied with the "black bottle" as only John L. can dally with it, and, although sober enough on Sunday to speak his lines in The Man from Boston without betraying to the audience his exhilarated frame of mind, he was not so successful at the performance last evening. It was with considerable difficulty that Sullivan was assisted into his stage costume for the first act when carried into his dressing room after arriving at the theater in a carriage from a merry time had with convivial society throughout the afternoon. As he reeled on to the stage the large audience immediately took in the situation and a great titter was heard all over the house. One man of gigantic proportions who was seated in the parquet and could not contain his merriment "ha-ha'd" right out. Sullivan scowled savagely at the man and moved up toward the footlights and addressed the audience as follows before entering upon his lines:

"Ladies and gentlemen: Did you ever see a mug? Well, there's one. (Pointing to the man who had given vent to his merriment.) He don't know a good thing when he sees it. He thinks I'm drunk. But I'm not. I go on like this just to give the newspapers a chance. That mug is ignorant. I know a little something. I went to school with my father and mother. I learned to spell and read and know things. If that mug comes up here on the stage I'll show him he isn't in it with me."

Here the big fellow stopped, amid great applause, and attempted to go on with his lines.

The thrilling drama soon became a ludicrous farce-comedy as John L. substituted here and eliminated there. In the course of the evening he handled his leading lady so carelessly that the paint on her left cheek was rubbed off, giving the woman much pain and embarrassment. He delivered several impromptu speeches before the close of the show, saying on one occasion: "You people would like to see me stripped, wouldn't you? Well, I'll fool you. I won't strip to-night."

Mr. Sullivan at last accounts was still enjoying himself early this morning.

[28 February 1893, p. 9.]

39 - THE BLACK DIVA'S CONCERT.

Mme. Sissieretta Jones, the new singer whom a delighted public is pleased to term the Black Patti, appeared last evening at Exposition Entertainment Hall, it can not be said in a delightful programme, but a delightful programme was not necessary. What songs and instrumental solos were introduced were undoubtedly interpolated to give Mme. Jones a rest. To say that her singing is grand sounds tame. It is all and more than one could wish. It swayed the large audience at will, and the applause that followed the different numbers and encore selections was wild and long. Her singing reminds one of the beauty of nature and brings back visions of the still, glassy water and soft swaying branches of some drowsy nook in summer time. She trills the chromatic scale to perfection, and varies it in a manner too rich to describe. Her last notes sometimes die away in a long sweet strain. "Comin' Thro' the Rye," "Suwanee River," and other popular encores when rendered by her seemed to express the composers' ideas to perfection. The other artists were Miss Benchley, Miss Mittie Smith, James H. Harris, J. Arthur Freeman and James W. Grant. Another concert will be given to-night.

[1 April 1893, p. 8.]

40 - THE THEATERS.

[Excerpt]

GRAND OPERA HOUSE.

Minnie Seligman (Cutting) opened last night to a full house at the Grand in Archibald Clavering Gunter's dramatization of the popular novel, "My Official Wife." Mr. Gunter's facile pen has handled the situations of the novel in a strong manner. What is more, he has added considerably to its merit. The plot is born of a phase of Russian law relating to marriage. *Col. Lenox*, an ex-American army officer, takes across the Russian border a woman whom he claims as his wife. The Russian law declares her such, holding him answerable to all the duties and responsibilities of a husband. The theme is of course of a Frenchy turn, but the American public seems determined to have more of the same constantly. From the status of present public opinion the play is strong and well acted. It seems to be the prevailing opinion that the power of good acting is to suggest and excite the sensual nature. Tried by any other standard a host of the present celebrities would fall flat and into obscurity. However, William F. Owens as *Col. Lenox* is quite natural, and Miss Seligman as *Helene Marie*, the fair nihilist, is quite dramatic. The remaining members of the cast are meritorious. Next week Miss Marie Tempest in The Fencing Master.

[10 April 1893, p. 10.]

41 - THE THEATERS.

[Excerpt]

GRAND OPERA HOUSE.

For a second time this season the Crust of Society opened to a large audience at the Grand Opera House last night. Probably the theme may not be dramatic nor heroic. There is nothing heroic in the character of a fallen woman who endeavors to pose as pure and good in the eyes of even one, to that one's detriment. Possibly it is not even dramatic in the modern sense, but it is interesting, moving and valuable in a mood. The story of the Crust of Society is that of a fallen woman who desires to reform, to push herself up into respected society, from which her birth, her disreputable father and her own actions have barred her. To do this she secures the affection of a young army officer, and endeavors by his money, social station and good name to place herself in a high social station. A diplomatic, though rather blase, former lover endeavors to save the young officer from a union with the adventuress, of whom he knows only too much. The warning comes too late; is ineffective. Such a theme is not pure nor elevating; it is awfully real and disgustingly terrible. The moral law that despises deception and fraud in all creation despises it most of all in a woman. The play furnishes cause for reflection, and leaves one to change a sudden curtain-fall decision with the maturer reflection of years and experience. Next week, Ali Baba.

[25 April 1893, p. 4.]

42 - THE THEATERS.

GRAND OPERA HOUSE.

Ali Baba opened to a crowded house at the Grand last night, beginning its third successful engagement in this city this season. The manifold beauties of this spectacular production are well-known to theater-goers here, and pleasant memories are retained of enjoyable evenings spent in witnessing the bewildering beauties of the jeweled cavern, the atrocious movements of the two score Bagdad robbers, the sparkling realism of the mountain water-fall tumbling down from high, craggy cliffs, and scattering its moon-lit spray as a back ground to the shining armor and accouterments of the band of forty thieves. Few can forget the palm-environed terrace outside of Ali Baba's palace, with its prismatic fountain playing in the moonlight. The quaint old oriental mill, the heights of Bagdad and the culminating tableau, the birth of the butterfly, are all impressively beautiful and not easily forgotten. Eddy Foy, as usual, added his grotesque humor to the novelty of the situations, and as usual it was very taking. The chorus of the extravaganza is wonderfully costumed and drilled, and comes very near being all that one might desire a chorus to be in such an extravagant dream of the beauties of the Orient.

HAGAN'S OPERA HOUSE.

Miss Jeffreys Lewis appeared last evening at the Hagan Opera House in La Belle Russe, David Belasco's grand romantic drama. The play, like others by the same noted author, is beautifully consistent and closely adheres to the idea of one central figure around which all the scenes and events are logically laid. It deals with a Russian heroine, *Geraldine*, and in this character, which Miss Lewis created, she has achieved an enviable fame. When she last produced that drama in this city the St. Louis Lodge of Elks, No. 9, made her an honorary member of their order, presenting her with a beautiful diamond badge and many floral tributes. Her work is unquestionably artistic and brilliant. The audience in attendance last evening seemed to appreciate her efforts thoroughly. La Belle Russe will be continued to-night, Tuesday and Wednesday matinee. Wednesday and Thursday evenings Sardou's Clothilde will be given. Friday and Saturday evenings and Saturday matinee will be given to Forget-me-not, in which Miss Lewis appears as the beautiful *Stephanie de Mohrivart*. Saturday evening's performance concludes the regular dramatic season of the Hagan, and the house will be closed for the summer.

POPE'S.

Peter Jackson's pugilistic ability is certainly remarkable and very entertaining to observe. As a pugilist in Uncle Tom's Cabin, although the plot does not call for any such character, he is quite pugilistic and natural. When the curtain went up on that time-worn, barn-storming production last evening at Pope's, it went up on a full house. Perhaps the balcony and gallery made the audience a little top heavy, yet nevertheless it was a full house. Many are undoubtedly inquisitive concerning Jackson's acting in the character of *Uncle Tom*. All excitement in this direction may as well subside, for Jackson doesn't act. He can not be tried by any standard known to the play-going public. Tried by that other standard lately developed by such worthies as John L., Corbett and their confreres of Thespopugilistic fame, he does quite well. In fact he is even better than the standard, and manages to lay aside that very suggestive, not to say sluggestive, air of trouble-picking which accompanies constantly his guild brothers. The four-round set-to between him and young Choynski is worth seeing. The company is fair and the scenery is excellent. Next week Dr. Carver in the Scout.

HAVLIN'S.

Havlin's Theater was crowded yesterday afternoon to the doors when Ada Gray opened in East Lynne. As there were no other afternoon entertainments in the city, Providence having interfered, the crowd might have been attributed to that, but it is polite to suppose that it was all due to East Lynne's attractive powers. The role that Ada Gray sustains in East Lynne is a very difficult one. There is constant need of strong emotional work after the opening half of the first act, which need increases as the play proceeds, until in the last act a most trying climax is called for. Ada Gray ably sustains the character of the unfaithful and deeply repentant wife throughout, and does very effective work in the several climaxes. She long since established a reputation for herself in this one play, and her acting has become so familiar to the public that comment is quite unnecessary. The support given her is not above the ordinary and might be improved. The week's business will evidently be large. Saturday evening closes the Havlin season.

STANDARD.

A week of copyrighted specialties was inaugurated last night at the Standard, where the Marie Sanger Burlesque Company opened with its aggregation of bright specialty stars. The performance began with A Heavenly Time, given by the company to the audience, and it seems to be named well enough. For a "gorgeous galaxy of goddesses" and a "gingery aggregation of gods" it did very well indeed. As a last half of the burletta an olio of specialties were introduced, opening with Fox and Ward in clever songs, dances and jokes; Annie Whitney, a vocalist of merit, sang "After the Ball," and Frank Latona followed in a comical representation of a musical tramp with his eccentric mule "Ginnie." Brown and Harrison, Gallagher and Griffin and Nettie Von Bieg all added their mite of merriment to the bill. The performance concluded with a short operatic satire, A Neapolitan Maiden. Next week, Weber and Fields, with their own company.

[1 May 1893, p. 10.]

St. Louis Republic

43 - THE BOY'S BODY FOUND.

The fire of Sunday night that destroyed one life and about 150 horses of the C. M. Crum Livery and Boarding Stables at Channing avenue and Locust street destroyed also the books of that firm with the records of the boarders and the value of their property.

The principal incident of the morning's work at the scene of the ruins was the recovery of the body of Edward Queenan, the 7-year-old son of James Queenan, the barn foreman. At an early hour the grief-stricken father made his way to the ruin and awaited the cooling off of the charred and steaming debris, when the search for his child might begin. Hook and Ladder Company No. 5 was on duty in charge of Assistant Chief Hester. The members of the company began their operations at the southeast corner, just below where the Queenan family had lived.

The charred rafters and mass of bricks were removed, and there, beneath the mattress and springs of a bed, the body of the child was found, charred and flame-eaten until only the trunk was left, and that an almost unrecognizable mass. What remained was removed to the Greerson Livery Company's barn, corner Thirty-third and Locust streets, where it was prepared for burial. The burial occurs to-day at 2 o'clock from the livery company's office. The body will be buried in Calvary Cemetery. The lad was 6 years and 10 months old and had but lately started to school.

The father, James Queenan, has taken up his abode temporarily at No. 307 North Channing avenue, over a tailor shop, where several rooms were fitted up for him by kindly neighbors. The shock of the calamity appears to have dazed him and he seems uncertain about the necessity of anything in particular.

When the child's body had been recovered the attention of the workmen was directed to the dangerous condition of the toppling walls, still standing. The effect of the water and flame upon the mortar had been to soften and crumble it. Ropes and ladders were brought and shortly after great masses of brick and mortar came tumbling down with a cloud of dust and a crash that was deafening.

Then the attention of the City Sanitary Department was called to the number of decaying horses in the ruins and to the fact also that the stench was becoming unbearable. The department sent several great vans to the ruins and while one gang of men was at work removing the brick another was engaged in dragging out the charred bodies and packing them into the wagons, after which they were hauled away.

Chief Lindsay of the Fire Department was present throughout the morning and afternoon, supervising the work, and a squad of policemen in charge of a Sergeant kept back the crowd of idlers and sight-seers who gathered about for want of anything better to do.

According to C. M. Crum, the president of the company, the loss of the books will entail considerable trouble and worry before anything like a complete and satisfactory account can be given. With the assistance of Mr. Crum and Barn Foreman James Queenan, whose child was burned, a partial list of the horses, saved and perished, was made out from memory, and is herewith presented.

[List of names omitted.]

Mr. Crum says there must have been 125 horses cremated, which leaves 44 unaccounted for.

Almost all the persons who had lost horses or had found them dropped around to look at the ruins. The burned building presented a disgusting sight with its endless shade of red, ill relieved by the black, charred wood and the bloody, half-covered carcasses of the animals. Here and there a phaeton wheel or hub lay submerged, and a few posts still stood erect in the center of the wreck.

Mr. Crum discussed the fire in a rather melancholy mood. "I can't imagine how it started at so late an hour. I haven't the slightest idea. I was not feeling well last night, but when I heard of the fire I got up and came here. Mr. Queenan's loss was the worst of all. I am sorry for my many customers—the men who had fine horses and rigs in my stable. Some of them have lost a great deal. Besides the 125 horses in the stable we had 150 rigs of all descriptions, the average price of which can be safely placed at $300. Some of those who boarded two horses at the barn kept three and four rigs with fine trappings that represented a large price. I lost several good horses myself. I did not own the building and do not know Mrs. Powell, the lady from whom we leased it. I suppose, however, that it is fully insured. We had a large stock of feed on hand on the different floors and a considerable number of buggies. I carried $17,000 insurance, which will partially cover my losses."

"Will you rebuild and enter the business again?"

"I think so. I can't just tell. It will take some time before all matters are straightened out and then I will consider rebuilding."

The two-story brick building just west of the livery barn, which was formerly occupied by the Graves Carriage Company and which is owned by Sheehan Bros., was damaged fully $3,000. The three-story stone-front house at No. 3410 Washington avenue, owned by Mrs. O'Marks, caught fire at 12:30 a.m. and was damaged $200. At 2:40 a.m. fire broke out again in the same house and did $1,000 additional damage. The property was fully insured. A family living opposite the barn on Channing avenue anticipated the heat of the summer sun and decorated the front windows with bright colored awnings. The intense heat of the fire, however, anticipated the summer sun and withered the awnings until they floated upward in smoke form.

Bookkeeper B. Alexander spent the entire morning driving around looking up the boarders of the firm and ascertaining their losses. All of those who kept horses in the barn owned at least one, and several owned three and four fancy driving outfits. The loss, as estimated correctly by *The Republic* yesterday morning, will reach a little over $100,000. The building, which is owned by the Crittenden estate, was insured for $18,000.

The building at 517, 519 and 521 North Channing avenue, owned by P. Schmitt, was badly damaged in the rear; insurance, $3,100.

The two-story brick dwellings at 3402, 3404 and 3406 Washington avenue, owned by P. Schmitt, were badly damaged in the rear; insurance $1,500. Furniture of tenants damaged $500; insurance, $700.

Nos. 500 to 512 Channing avenue, owned by Bart Brennan, slightly damaged walls; insurance, $12,000.

No. 3408 Washington avenue, owned by Mr. Gerherty and occupied by C. A. Overfield, damaged contents $200; no insurance.

Frank C. Case was insured $600 on horse and vehicle; B. W. Clark, $500 on horse and wagon; J. R. Lewen, $250 on horse and buggy; James Hopkins, on horses and vehicles, $1,500, and William D. Hemenway, $150 on horse and buggy.

———

Residents in the vicinity of the Crum Livery Stable fire are much exercised over the outlook of having the carcasses of the 130 or more horses sacrificed in Sunday night's holocaust left festering in the ruins for several days to come. It is the duty of Colonel Ed. Butler to see that the remains are removed, but with the force employed yesterday but little progress was made in the work. Not more than 20 carcasses were carted away. The residents in that vicinity were informed by a Police Sergeant that it would probably take four or five days to complete the work of removal. The odor from the ruins is already offensive and in three or four days it would become simply unbearable. Such a nuisance at this season would become a grave menace to the public health. The neighboring residents resolved to see that something is promptly done. A committee, consisting of Messrs. Marcus Bernheimer, M. E. Paddock, J. J. Fisher and Dr. Comstock, called upon Mayor Walbridge yesterday to lay the case before hm. He had gone to Collinsville and will not return until to-day. The committee then called upon Chief Harrigan of the police force. He was not in, but later informed the committee by telephone that the matter would be attended to to-day. Not yet satisfied, the committee declared their intention of seeing the Mayor as soon as he returns.

In the meantime the Board of Health had acted in the matter. A resolution was passed at yesterday's meeting requesting the Mayor to place 60 workmen this morning at the task of removing the dead animals. It will be an interesting question whether Colonel Butler and the Merz Company will receive the benefit of the labor of these men, or whether the wages of this emergency force will be charged to the contractors, whose special business it is to see that such nuisances are abated. It is understood that the carcasses of these animals will be very valuable to the Mertz Company. Will the company receive them gratis after the city has paid doubly for delivering them to the Mertz concern?

[23 May 1893, p. 7.]

44 - "I'M LUCKIN' FER MER WIFE."

Sam Jackson, an old negro with long, white hair, called at the Four Courts yesterday and told Assistant Prosecuting Attorney Estep a long tale of woe. On entering the door he bowed very low, saying:

"Is dis de boss Atturney's offis?"

The Attorney nodded, and Sam proceeded: "I'se luckin' fur mer wife Sousanna. We lives down to Greenville, Miss., an' she jes' pick up an' leab me two weeks ago wid a yaller nigger. I seed dem goin' an' I runned 'cross de kentry jes' in time to see dem gittin' on a boat. De boat lef' befo' I cud caitch it an' I cut 'cross de kentry to de nex' lan'in' befo' de boat got dere an' waited. But de boat went on by, an' I seed dem on de daick laffin' at me, I did. Dat made me as mad as a yaller jackit, an' I took de nex' boat an' wurked mer way up here. Dase right here in town, an' I wants a warrant fur der 'res'. Kin I git it?" The wife hunter paused, and Mr. Estep told him to make an effort to get her. He went away and in a short time returned and asked the attorney to give him a note to the "yaller nigger," ordering him to deliver the wife. The attorney told him he could not do such a thing, and Jackson replied that the "yaller nigger" said he would not turn her over unless he brought a note. Jackson left when the attorney told him to try again to get his wife back and if he failed to come back this morning and get a warrant.

[26 May 1893, p. 12.]

45 - HIS OWN STORY.

Sam A. Wilson, the picturesque train robber, arrived over the Missouri Pacific Railroad last night from Lebanon, Mo. The prisoner was in charge of Detective Pat Lally of the Missouri Pacific Railroad and Sheriff F. Y. Jones of Laclede County. The party brought along the $500 in silver that Wilson gave up, and also the satchel that he left lying at the roadside near the scene of the robbery. They left the train at Tower Grove Station and took the street car into the city. At the Four Courts an immense crowd assembled to get a glimpse of the robber, but missed him. The people gathered on the Twelfth street side and the police brought Wilson in through the Clark avenue entrance.

Wilson was taken direct to Chief Harrigan, who talked with him about the robbery. The bandit again explained how he accomplished his work. He was given supper, after which he was placed in the holdover, where he remains until a warrant can be issued. The officers hold $1,075 of the captured money as evidence. Wilson only used $49 of the sum stolen.

Wilson is tall, slim, awkward and in appearance the last person in the world who would perform such a daring deed. He explains that the reason he had no accomplices was because of a failure to get his "pals" to stick on a former occasion. His father notified the Sheriff of Laclede County, and expects to get a part of the reward offered for the capture of the bandit.

LEFT: "Sam A. Wilson" (*St. Louis Republic*, 4 June 1893, p. 1); CENTER: "Sheriff Jones" (*St. Louis Republic*, 4 June 1893, p. 1); RIGHT: "Detective Lally" (*St. Louis Republic*, 4 June 1893, p. 1).

Wilson is 26 years old and has a wife and three children. He is a telegrapher, and has had several years' experience in railroad offices. Lack of work and need of money is the reason given for the robbery.

The pistols used to intimidate the train men were cheap affairs, not much better than toys. The two cost less than $3.

The lean, lone Missouri Pacific train robber, the-entire-seven-in-one Sam A. Wilson, arrived in St. Louis at 6:20 o'clock last night over the Missouri Pacific from Lebanon. The order of his coming was reversed by the officers who had him in charge. They were Detective Lally of this city and Sheriff F. Y. Jones of Laclede County, Missouri, of which the county seat is Lebanon. Wilson was scheduled to arrive over the St. Louis and San Francisco road at 6:30, and such information was given out by the police. The order was changed to give the movements of the party as little notoriety as possible. When the San Francisco train arrived at Pacific Wilson was transferred to the Missouri Pacific fast mail, due there a little later, and it was on the run from Valley Park to St. Louis that a *Republic* reporter came up with him and made his acquaintance.

"My name is Sam A. Wilson," said the slim highwayman, "and I live with my wife and three children in my father's house on a farm near Lebanon, Mo. My children are a boy and two girls aged respectively 7, 5 and 3 years. My father is 56 years old and my mother 48. My own age is 28 and I am the oldest of two boys.

"When I robbed the train at Pacific it was after long deliberation—some four or five months, I think. My object, of course, was to obtain money, and I tell you I needed it. I needed money very bad, because I had been out of work a long time with no prospect of getting any. I hung around Lebanon for awhile in a kind of aimless way. My father is poor, owning only a small farm. I own nothing. Not only that, but I owe money for almost everything that my family and myself have had in months. For groceries, clothes, liquor and everything else. I believe that the total amount of debts must be near $900. People were pressing me for money and I really didn't know what to do. I have worked around railroads nearly all my life as an operator, train dispatcher, agent, etc. When I was 17 years old I got tired of farming. The life was too dreary for me and I persuaded my father to send me to school at Stockton, Mo., where I studied telegraphy for several months, and then went to work as an operator. I've worked at Richland and Arthur, this State, at Austin, Tex., at Wichita, Kas., and other places.

"I learned a good bit about railroading and railroad men. I came very near knowing something about them nearly a year ago. I needed money when I was working at Richland, and I thought then I would rob a train. I worked around and took four or five fellows about town in with me. They were mere hangers on who had nothing to do and wanted money. Every one of them blowed about what they would do and how they would stick by me, but before the time came they backed out. Someone gave the scheme away and I dropped the matter entirely. I said then that the next time I wanted to hold up a train I would go it alone.

"Well, three or four months ago I began to try and think of some way to get out of my debts and trouble. I thought of robbing a train, but I hadn't decided upon any plan until a few weeks ago. At first I intended to cross the river and hold up one of the Mobile and Ohio express cars. Then I began to think the river might worry me and I almost decided not. Just about that time someone else held up a train at Cairo, and I thought that the road people might be well prepared for anyone else who would attempt to hold up another. That and the river made me change my mind and decide to stay on this side.

"About three days before I held up the train at Pacific (Sunday, May 21), I decided to hold up the Missouri Pacific. My choice of Pacific came about from a combination of three or four things. I came to St. Louis about two weeks before that and went to work in Lemp's brewery. I worked there 11 days. On the Saturday night before the robbery I bought a stick of dynamite and went out to Kirkwood, where I stayed over Sunday. While I was there I went out into the woods and set off one of the sticks just to see how it would work."

"Did it work?" asked someone.

"You bet," said Wilson. "It blew a good deep hole in the ground and tore up things generally. Monday I came back to St. Louis, secured a suit of clothes and bought these revolvers."

Here Sheriff Jones exhibited two bright new revolvers of 38 caliber, American make, from which all the bullets had been carefully extracted.

"I got them of the Meacham Arms Company and the McLean Hardware Company. One cost me $1.50 and the other $1.35. I had a valise with me, the one that was found, and I packed my things in that and went out to Kirkwood the same day—Monday. I intended to send that valise home with all my spare clothes in it. I intended to express it from Kirkwood. I forgot it, however, and that night I started to walk for Pacific, having fixed upon that as the nearest point. I walked in a roundabout way to Washington on the other side of Pacific, so as not to excite suspicion. I came through Washington the next day (Tuesday) and went on to Pacific. I looked at the road until I knew it fairly well. There were three or four people around the depot at Pacific, but they never noticed me. I learned the time that the train arrived and then went back about a mile and placed my satchel as a mark at which place the train was to stop. When the train pulled in that night, I got on the blind baggage, just back of the engine, as the train pulled out.

"The engineer saw me but he didn't say anything. He probably took me for some poor fellow who was just trying to steal a ride. When we got to traveling real fast, I climbed up on the tender and sized up the two fellows. The fireman said: 'What do you want?'

"'I want you,' I said.

"Then he kinder laughed, said he guessed I wanted the engineer. I pulled out my two revolvers and leveled them. He opened the door and started to shovel in some coal, but I told him I guessed he didn't need to, and ordered him to quit. He only threw on one shovelful and then stopped. The engineer came in from the outside, where he had been riding, and took his place. The fireman just stood and looked at me as though he was making a study of my face so he could tell me the next time he saw me. We were coming near, I thought, about that time to where I left the satchel, and I ordered the engineer to stop her. He did, and then I told them to climb down and come back to the express car with me. They both came and walked ahead of me. I ordered the express messenger to open the door, but he wouldn't, and so I blew it open. I took out three sticks, just as the fireman said, and put two back in my pocket. I saw several people sticking their heads out of the train, and I fired four shots just to frighten them. I mistook the express messenger's assistant for the messenger himself, and so I made the messenger climb out. When I saw my mistake I made him get back in and open the safes for me. Then I climbed in myself."

"Were you not afraid that one of those three outside would grab you, when you climbed in? They certainly knew by that time that you were alone."

"Well, you see, I jumped in very quick and I kept my revolvers in hand. Sometimes I had a revolver in each hand and sometimes I had the two in one. That's the way I threw out the packages of silver. Then I got out and made the fireman give me a lift. No one offered to move, and I started to walk north towards the hill. When they couldn't see me any more I pulled the old handkerchief off my face and turned my hat back. I had my hat turned inside out and pulled down over my ears, and I tore it getting through a barbed wire fence—see," and Wilson took off his hat and pointed out the torn lining.

"It was awful hard walking through the fields with that heavy load. I could hardly get along. Finally the sack broke and a bundle of silver fell out, but I didn't have time to stop and fasten it together again. I let it lie and made my way to a thick bushy patch about a half mile north, where I let down.

"I stayed in that brush all that night and all the next day until evening, when I struck out and went back to find my valise. I knew if the people got hold of that they would get me. I stopped the train at the wrong place—past where I put down the satchel, and when I looked for it that night it was gone. I went back and got my money and started to find a haystack, where I could sleep. I did find one some distance south of where I held up the train, and I slept in that haystack for two or three nights. I forget which now. Then I started for Lebanon. I determined to go home because I was under bond to appear in court there to answer a charge of assault. My father went on my bond for $1,000, and I knew that if I did not return they would take all he had. I couldn't do that. He has done too much for me, and I decided to go home. I walked every step of the way carrying that package of money. I passed through Moselle, Stanton, Rolla and Dixon, but no one ever said anything to me or seemed to notice me. I walked over four days before I came to Lebanon. When I got there I took a roundabout way and came up to the back entrance of my father's house. My children were out in the yard and I told them to run in and tell mother and my wife to come out. They all came out. Mother was very pale and my wife was crying. They wanted to know what I had done and I told them to keep quiet, that I hadn't done anything. I went to the barn then and stayed there until the Sheriff came for me."

"Why did you carry all that silver from Pacific to Lebanon?" was asked. "Why didn't you hide it and go back after it another time?".

"Well the family needed money and I thought it would be best to bring it along."

"What made you keep those two revolvers on your person?"

"I started to go home, and I determined to get there. I carried those revolvers just to make sure that no one stopped me. No one could have stopped me, either. I hung about the house for a day or so and left it with my father to decide what I should do. I could have escaped, but that mortgage was still hanging over me and I could not. I did not get as much money as I expected to, and after this bond had been paid there would have been nothing left. My father went and consulted a lawyer, who advised him to have me give myself up.

"Father notified Sheriff Jones and Friday he came out to the farm to get me. I didn't offer any resistance. I had given my revolvers to the family to keep in the house. I did not want to offer any resistance and I didn't."

"What made you give up the $500 in silver?"

"Oh I thought that the Judge would be a little lighter on me if I did that."

"Weren't you just a little afraid to tackle a whole train alone?"

"No; I was just as cool as I am now. I guess the fireman can tell you that."

"Did you know that the Governor was on board?"

"I didn't know anything about the train or the people on it until I came home last Wednesday. I saw a *Republic* then and read all about it. Do you think they will be hard on me?" asked Wilson.

"They ought not," was the answer. "Any man who has nerve enough to hold up a train alone ought to be set free and receive a gold medal."

"If they could see," continued Wilson, figuring out in his mind the whole jury system at once, "my three little children they wouldn't be very hard on me, I think. I hope I'll get a light sentence. I'm sorry now that I did it. I wouldn't do it again. Just the same if I had sent that satchel home as I intended from Kirkwood they never would have got me in the world. A man could do most anything he pleased and get ahead of these people around here."

"What made you buy blank cartridges?"

"I bought those blank cartridges just to fool with. I only wanted them to fire off around the house. When I held up the train I had real lead, 38 caliber, and I meant business."

The revolvers in question were a goodly pair of glistening Americans, 38 caliber, and were carried for exhibition purposes by Sheriff Jones of Laclede County. The $500 in silver returned by Wilson was neatly arranged in a small yellow valise that ably belied its looks as to weight. This valuable little package was carefully used by Sheriff Jones as a foot rest during the journey. The party made probably as interesting looking a group as one would be liable to run across in many a day's journey.

Wilson is all that has been said of him—a long, lean, lank, sickly-looking, ague-shaken farmer, nearly 6 feet tall. His eyes are not over large, of a strong gray color and shaded by eyebrows of a sandy hue and not very heavy. He wears a small mustache of a faded sandy color, while his face is covered with a stubby growth of sandy hair of several weeks' standing. His arms are long, and he moves them in a languid way, as though they lacked muscle. Wilson was dressed in a suit of mixed cotton and wool, of a color that was almost anything from a black to a brown. It was ill-fitting and gaunt-looking, as most clothing purchased in country stores is. Wilson's hat is small, steel blue felt of the prevailing style. It long since lost its shape, having been crumpled and crushed into a mere zone of cloth. On the occasion of the robbery Wilson turned it inside out and pulled it down very close to his ears. His whole figure looked worn and slipshod, and he walked with bent head and a kind of sinking at the knees as though his legs were tired. His manner was entirely open and goodnatured. He seemed to have no fear or worry of any kind, and no desire to keep anything back. At times he smiled as though he enjoyed the glory of it all, and at other times seemed to feel just the least weary of it.

Pat Lally, the Missouri Pacific's detective chief, sat opposite the robber, and beside him sat F. Y. Jones, Laclede County's Sheriff. He is a typical Missourian of the plain, rough order, dressed in ill-fitting clothes, and wearing a black beard. His eyebrows are quite heavy, and he crowned his shaggy head with a large, broad-brimmed black hat. The trio took matters pleasantly and discussed the situation in the most nonchalant manner.

The chase for an interview with the train-robber was an affair that was as interesting as any other part of the proceedings. It was given out by the authorities that Wilson was coming to St. Louis over the St. Louis and San Francisco road. In their eager desire to throw as much darkness and secrecy over Wilson's arrival as possible, Detective Lally and Sheriff Jones transferred the prisoner to the Missouri Pacific fast mail at Pacific. *The Republic's* representative left St. Louis at 4 p.m. on the Valley Park accommodation, which reaches Valley Park at 5 o'clock. There a wait was made until the train bearing Wilson passed at 5:30. When the train arrived at 5:33 p.m. it was found that Wilson was not aboard, but had been transferred to the fast mail. Only 10 minutes remained until the Missouri Pacific train would pass through Valley Park, some three blocks north of the St. Louis and San Francisco depot. A quick run was made across the open prairie, and at the Missouri Pacific station it was learned that the train bearing Wilson did not stop and would not stop. The gentleman who vouchsafed this pleasing information was busily engaged hanging aloft on a hook the Valley Park mail sack. There was little or no time to parley, as the train could be heard in the far distance faintly rumbling forward. Every possible plea was urged, and finally a last one caused the agent to swing down the red lantern board out towards the track which caused the engineer of the rapidly moving train to slow up. The cars dashed past the depot fully 200 yards before the train was brought to a standstill. After a good hard run the representative of *The Republic* clambered on and entered the smoking car, much to the surprise of the little party who had it all to themselves. Upon arriving in St. Louis the party left the train at Tower Grove Station and took the Chouteau avenue line downtown, thus avoiding the crowd at the depot. For the entire length of his journey Wilson was the center soul of a crowd of gaping sight-seers, who were content if they could stand within 10 feet of him and watch his every move.

Detective Pat Lally, chief of the Missouri Pacific's force, who has gained considerable notoriety for what he didn't do in the case, desired to offer an explanation of the matter.

"On the night of the robbery," said Mr. Lally, "I was on the train in the car that was between the smoker and the sleeper, about the fifth car from the engine. I was talking with Burns, the brakeman, and the conductor most of the way. At Pacific I got off and chased several tramps off of the platform who were preparing to steal a ride. When I returned into the train there was no one about that I could see. When the train slowed up one and a half miles out of Pacific I was sitting with the conductor, who was counting his checks and tickets. He got up and asked me to hold his checks for him, as he wanted to go outside and see what the trouble was. I did so, and in a few minutes he came back and told me that the express car was being robbed. I looked out the window, but just then the dynamite went off and I concluded that the fellows were experts. Then four shots were fired and I naturally supposed there were a number of men in the job. I did not think it policy to go out against such a layout as that and so I just kept quiet. I don't think that I ought to be blamed so much in this matter, as the supposition was quite natural and everybody in the car seemed to look at the matter in the same light."

Immediately after the robbery, on the night that it occurred, Detective Lally went to work on the case. As soon as it became light enough to see he repaired to the scene, where he was joined by Detectives Viehle and Allender. While scouring the woods some of the money dropped by the lone robber was found. It was the first clew as to the direction that the man had taken. Further on a lot of papers, checks and similar articles belonging to the express company and the Missouri Pacific Railway were found in a lot of weeds, where Wilson had thrown them. Then came the finding of the valise with the papers, letters, etc., bearing his name.

Positive that Wilson was the man, the work of running him down commenced. Detective Lally proceeded to Lebanon and, falling in with Station Agent Edward Sheehan of the Frisco Railroad joined forces with him. For days they skirmished around Lebanon, the home of Wilson, and other places he was in the habit of frequenting, coming in contact several times with Detective Furlong's men, who were also on the same errand. Finally, when Wilson returned home, Sheriff Jones of Laclede County stole a march on the two and bagged the man with the assistance of Wilson's father.

When Agent Edward Sheehan, who came in with Wilson last night, was seen, he said that when he heard of the train robbery and the daring manner of the highwayman he at once came to the conclusion that Wilson was the man. He had known Wilson for at least 15 years, and knew he was bold enough to attempt anything single-handed. The following Saturday Agent Sheehan met Wilson's father in Lebanon and asked him where his son was. He was informed that Sam was in St. Louis. Still positive that Wilson was the man wanted he called at the home of the father the following day to obtain more information about Sam, only to learn that he was still absent and had not been heard of lately. The following day Wilson left his home and went to Lebanon, where he called on Agent Sheehan and asked what he wanted with Sam. He was told about the train robbery and the suspicion that he was the man wanted. He agreed to surrender his son when he put in an appearance at the farm. From day to day the old man called on Agent Sheehan and consultation followed. Thursday morning at his visit the senior Wilson said that he had learned that his son would be home before long, and the father agreed to take Agent Sheehan to his house and the two would bring the boy to Lebanon, providing the old man could have the $300 reward. The father left Agent Sheehan after agreeing to return.

Instead of returning the father called on Judge Wallace, and through his advice secured the assistance of Sheriff Jones. The two proceeded to the Wilson farm, and when the boy showed up he was taken into custody.

When Wilson boarded the train at Pacific, shortly before the robbery, he fell in with a tramp who was riding in the blind baggage. Sizing up the man he came to the conclusion that he was just the man he wanted in stopping the train.

"Say, cully, will yer help in holding up this train? There is a lot of boodle in the express and we kin whack up, see?" said Wilson, at the same time handing the man one of the two revolvers he had.

"Nixy," replied the tramp. "I'se bad enough stealing a ride from the company, but yer kin betcher life I will not steal their coin."

After the refusal Wilson paid no more attention to the tramp.

Wilson was not brought to the Four Courts until about 8 o'clock, after he had been in the city an hour and a half. He was taken before Chief Harrigan and made a full confession. He took his capture good naturedly, and said he was ready to stand the consequences.

"Why did you not call on Governor Stone when you held up the train?"

"If I had known he was aboard I would have paid my respects to him."

"Would you hold up another train?"

"If I had to I would."

"Were you not afraid you would get killed?"

"Well, if anyone had resisted I would have disappeared as quickly as I could."

After the interview Wilson was given his supper and then locked up in the "holdover" to await the issuance of a warrant against him by the authorities of Laclede County.

A large crowd awaited the arrival of the train bearing the noted lone robber with a hope of getting a glimpse at him. When the Frisco train, on which he was supposed to be, pulled in it was quickly learned that Wilson had been transferred to a Missouri Pacific train at Pacific, Mo., and had been taken off at Vandventer avenue. The crowd made a rush for the Four Courts, and after waiting an hour and a half, saw him being brought up Clark avenue and taken in the main entrance. A grand rush was made in that direction, and the crowd followed the train robber and his escorts into the office of Chief Harrigan. It took the united effort of Sergeants O'Malley and Allen and several detectives and policemen to eject those that were not wanted.

The money sack, the revolver and the stolen money amounting to $1,075, including what was found in the wheat field by the detectives and what was found on Wilson, are in possession of Chief Desmond and will be used as evidence against the man. A search is still being made for $140, which was lost by the robber in his flight after the robbery. Wilson only succeeded in spending $49 before he was captured.

Detective Viehle, who was out searching for Wilson, is still out of the city, but will return to-day. He may be able to make more revelations.

All was excitement yesterday at the Four Courts over the capture of

S. A. Wilson, the Missouri Pacific train robber. Chief Harrigan received two letters from Detective Lally in the morning mail, which were written the day before, showing how the chase was going on, which eventually ended in the capture of the daring robber.

The first one was as follows:

Crocker, Mo., June 2, 1893. — Major L. Harrigan, Chief of Police: *Dear Sir*—Myself, Viehle and Sheriff Imboden got here this morning. Three of Furlong's men came up as far as Dixon with us. There they got off and got horses. Wilson was in Hancock yesterday morning and bought a suit of clothes, hat and shoes, for which he paid 16 silver dollars. Nobody in Hancock had nerve enough to arrest him. There were two other men with him, but the people did not get to recognize them, as they kept quite a distance from Wilson. It is thought that one of those men was Hyatt, and that him and his partner stopped over one night with Hyatt's father, who lives one and one-half miles from Hancock. Wilson stayed all night with the agent at Hancock, W. H. Wilson, who is a cousin. We learned here this morning that a hack passed through here this morning at 4 o'clock with four or five men in it, and we naturally supposed they were Furlong's men going to Selkirk. This is where all of Wilson's relatives live. Viehle and Imboden are after them on horseback. I am going to Lebanon and get Dick Goodall and come the other way and meet them. I think that within a very few hours Wilson will be in jail in St. Louis and if possible we want to be on the winning side and bring him in ourselves. Furlong is making a great fight to get him, but I think that we will win. Wilson said in Hancock that if he was arrested they would have to go East for him. His sister-in-law lives here. Everyone seems to be under the impression that he will try to get to see her. We have her watched closely. I think that Wilson is making for home, and as I said before I will get to Lebanon and get Dick Goodall and try and head him off. Viehle and Imboden will catch up with Furlong's gang easy enough, and I believe pass them easy enough. Imboden is a hustler, and he knows this country better than anybody. I will write or wire any new developments. Truly yours,   *P. M. Lally.*

The letter from Lebanon was as follows:

Lebanon, Mo., June 2, 1893. — L. Harrigan, Esq., Chief of Police: *Dear Sir*—Sam Wilson's father has been in town all morning. He places all confidence in the world in the Frisco agent here, Ed Sheehan. He told Ed that he wants his son to give himself up. Old man Wilson wants to get the reward. He went home about noon. He is coming and Sheehan will get a livery here and go with the old man down to Atoka P.O. This is Wilson's old home. It is 18 or 20 miles from here, and the old man will see if he can't see his son and have him go into St. Louis with him and give himself up. He does not know where he is, but thinks he is down there. Viehle and Imboden and I think some of Furlong's men are down there now. It may be they will get him before the old man gets there. I am satisfied that Wilson is down there, but thought it was best for me to stay here and watch old man Wilson and the young Wilson's wife. Sheehan will try to let me know where to go to meet them on the train. If he does I will possibly ride into St. Louis with them. This is the programme at present. I wrote you this morning from Crocker. I will write you or wire you again if anything turns up to-day. Very respectfully,   *P. M. Lally.*

Chief Desmond brought forth the valise found near the scene of the robbery yesterday and allowed its contents to be examined by the reporters. It was through letters found in this grip that the detectives succeeded in capturing Wilson. The valise is an ordinary one, of medium size, containing wearing apparel, papers, letters and two or three books, among which is a dictionary and a pocket encyclopedia. The letters are mostly from a lady of Hancock, and from their tone it is surmised that she is much the worse for having met and loved Wilson. Among the papers are several life insurance policies in favor of his wife, Mrs. Laura Wilson. One of the policies was issued by the Life Insurance Association of the Order of Railway Telegraphers for $2,000, another for $3,000 in the International Association of Ticket Agents and one by the Travelers' Insurance Company of Hartford for $2,000. There were about a dozen letters of recommendation from the San Francisco Railway officials given Wilson at various times when he severed his connection at one place and removed to another.

Among other things in the grip is a lot of green goods circulars, and a small ladle which is looked upon with a great deal of suspicion by the detectives. This is a little iron affair, and is just such an instrument as would be necessary to a full fledged counterfeiter. The ladle has an opening at the top and a little hole in the bottom through which the melted solution runs into the molds. It is barely possible that Wilson has been engaged in a large and lucrative business of counterfeiting. In addition to the ladle, however, is a small pamphlet of printed instructions regarding the use of certain plating materials referred to. This is the most probable theory as to the use of the ladle.

The most important things the grip contained were four percussion caps and several feet of fuse.

It was Wilson's carelessness in leaving these things in the grip that led to his capture. The day after the robbery Detective Allender learned at the Meacham Arms Company that a man had bought three sticks of dynamite and 50 feet of fuse the day before the robbery. Wilson was the purchaser and he said that he wanted it to kill fish by exploding the dynamite under water. Wilson first asked for 15 feet of fuse, but he was told that the company would not sell less than 50 feet. While at the store Wilson acted very suspicious, requesting that dynamite of full 70 per cent strength be given him.

Wilson's description was furnished by Manager J.R. McBeth to Detective Allender. This is not the first case he has been connected with. Six months ago he was arrested with five others for conspiracy to rob a train at Hancock, and he is now out on bond for that offense. Wilson is known here by W. C. Hammond, superintendent of telegraph of the Missouri Pacific, he having appointed him to a position at Piedmont, Mo., several years ago.

[4 June 1893, pp. 1–2.]

46 - WHO GETS THE REWARD?

The enthusiastic party of detectives who brought Sam A. Wilson to this city on Saturday night had even so early as Sunday noon partly dispersed and returned to their homes. The first of the party to leave was R. P. Goodall and Agent E. J. Sheehan of Lebanon, who came to St. Louis to collect from the Police Department the amount due them for their work in hunting down Wilson. Whatever the amount was that the department owed them or whether the Chief recognized their claim or not is not known. It was learned from Sheriff Jones, however, that the twain left well satisfied.

When the party arrived in this city Sheriff F. Y. Jones, E. J. Sheehan and R. P. Goodall took rooms at the Heefner House, opposite the Four Courts, so that they might be near should any midnight marauders attempt to carry off the Police Department. It was here that Sheriff Jones was yesterday afternoon enjoying the shade and the fresh air from the pinnacle of a wooden chair tipped back against the side of the building. In a short conversation Mr. Jones was brought to express himself quite freely upon the subject of Wilson's deserts, and also as to whom the reward of $300 belongs.

"Who do you think ought to get this $300 reward?" was asked.

"Why, myself, of course. I arrested him."

"You will take the money back with you, then?"

"Yes."

"There seems to be an impression that Wilson's father ought to have the money, since he persuaded his son to give himself up."

"Yes, he informed me, but according to the provisions made by the express company the money belongs to me. I may give a portion of it to Wilson's father, or to Wilson's wife. I believe I will give it to her, as she is very poor, and now she hasn't anyone to help her and the children. I feel sorry for her, anyhow. She's a good woman."

"How does Wilson's family stand in the estimation of the people at Lebanon?"

"He comes from a good, honest family. They are all poor, but Wilson's father is as honest and square as any man you ever saw and his mother is a mighty good woman. I've known them for years."

"Do you think Wilson deserves to be dealt lightly with?"

"Well, I'm inclined to be lenient with him. You know a man can't help but admire nerve, and his act certainly does break the record. He's not a bad sort of a fellow at all, but he's got a record that is just a bit shaky."

"He owns up to having meditated train robbery once before, but that's about all, isn't it?"

"Well, not exactly. He was concerned, with several others, in an assault case. Three or four of them tried to hold up a man for his money, but I reckon Wilson was led into it as much as anything. He has wonderful nerve, and that is always creditable to a man. He might do better if he were let go. I believe that if I were a Judge I would give him a light sentence."

Mr. Jones also stated that Wilson's brother and cousins were noted for their bravery, and he believed that they possessed a larger amount of that personal quality than most of the inhabitants out his way. Sheriff Jones leaves to-day for Lebanon, having ended his work in the case by surrendering Wilson and reaping the reward.

Sam A. Wilson was visited in the holdover at the Four Courts yesterday afternoon, where he is sojourning for the present. When the reporter called he was endeavoring to sleep, lying upon the hard wood bunk in his cell in the far east end of that dingy apartment. He responded to the friendly greeting with great alacrity and expressed himself to the turnkey who opened his cell door and allowed him to pass out into the little stone court as being glad to get out of that cold cell.

"I didn't sleep very well," said Wilson, in answer to an inquiry after his welfare. "This place is such a miserable hole that I can't sleep. I wish I was out again and free."

"Who, in your estimation, ought to get the $300 reward offered for your capture?"

"My father, of course."

"It is said that Sheriff Jones will get it."

"Well, I don't think it belongs to him. My father persuaded me to give myself up and carried the information of my whereabouts to him. Still Jones told me that he intended to give the money to my father."

"Do you think he will do so?"

"Certainly I do. Jones is a man of his word. He's one of the whitest men I have ever known and he's not mean-hearted. He treated me nice. He allowed me to ride without irons and gave me some time to visit my wife and children before I left Lebanon. I'm certain that if Jones hadn't been along the other fellows would have had me weighted down with irons. I know Jones will do as he says."

Wilson seemed slightly more cognizant of his predicament than heretofore. It is plainly apparent that he is inclined to be open-hearted and frank. A man of not over vast experience nor worldly wisdom, he possesses nerve and coolness. The talk as to his being insane has begun to reach his ears, and he apparently appreciates the ludicrousness of the theory. Heretofore he has been free in the discussion of his deed, because everyone seemed to marvel at it, but now he is beginning to understand that his soundness of mind is being questioned and he seems anxious to allay any such suspicions. He constantly asseverates his knowledge of the folly of his deed and wishes that he might be free. He never fails to question anyone as to the number of years they think he will get, and to ask their judgment as to whether a light term would not be justifiable.

Yesterday morning Detective Viehle and Sheriff Imboden of Pulaski County arrived. Imboden comes to straighten out the matter of his expense and emolument for his services in connection with the case. They leave to-day. Just how long Wilson will be held in the holdover is not known. He will probably be tried in either Franklin or this county, although the laws of Missouri provide that anyone connected with a crime against a State corporation having branches throughout the State or traversing it, as a railroad, may be tried in any county within the State that the corporation may elect.

Governor Stone was speaking to a friend last evening about the circumstances which prevailed at the time the robbery was committed. "I should like to see the conduct," said he, "of the men who have commented upon the action of the man or men at the time the engineer, fireman and express messenger were holding up their hands and only one man on the train with arms. A burglar is a bad customer to attempt to handle if he should force an entrance into your bedchamber, and under the same circumstances would you expect men to leave the car without a weapon and attempt to disarm a man who had everything and everybody covered with his guns?

"Of course, had the exact situation been known the result might have been different, but as it is no one was hurt and the robber has been caught. This was my first experience in being held up by a train robber, and I will say that none of the passengers, so far as I know, were frightened. On the contrary, we rather looked upon it as a joke."

"Are you going to call on Mr. Wilson?"

"No," said the Governor, reflectively, "I shall not have time."

A warrant charging highway robbery will be applied for to-day against Wilson at Pacific, Mo. He will be taken to that place by Detective Viehle, so Chief Desmond says, and may be given a preliminary hearing. If he is arraigned it would not be much of a surprise if he pleaded guilty.

[5 June 1893, p. 3.]

47 - THE TROUBLE STILL ON.

"**N**o, sir; no siree!" emphatically announced Congressman Charles F. Joy, as he kicked over his legal waste basket in an attempt to "get comfortable," and then deliberately curled his patrician lip as he looked upon a sketch of Colonel Gus V. R. Mechin which a *Republic* reporter had idly, but injudiciously dashed off in his presence.

"Gus. V. R. Mechin can't bluff me, even if one or two misguided cranks do call him Colonel."

The exciting remark just quoted took place on the seventh floor of the Bank of Commerce Building in the office of that muscular athlete and all-around Congressman, Charles F. Joy. The cause of his excited exclamation was the statement made by Mr. Mechin that the Owls could wipe the Elks off the face of the earth with one hand in a game of baseball.

"Mechin can talk all he wants to. He can stand out on the corner and sway about with a baseball bat and illustrate how he is going to do us up, but I say he ain't, nor his whole nine ain't; and what I say means business."

At this juncture Mr. Joy slackened up a moment, which gave *The Republic* representative time to secure a fan. The visit to Mr. Joy's office was made for the purpose of announcing that Sportsman's Park could be secured for Monday, July 17, or some date quite near that, on which day the two clubs may meet and lay the much mooted question as to "which can lick" forever to rest.

The Republic reasoned that if nine strong men, having eaten nine large dinners, and really feeling like nine heavy weight Samsons, felt called upon to go out on the seventeenth day of July and muss, swipe, swab, mop (or any other kind of) up the earth with nine other large and enthusiastic St. Louisans who should come out for the same purpose, why it ought to take advantage of the cyclonic soiree. It felt that it ought to do this, even though there might be "blood and hair and the ground tore up," because of the hundreds and thousands of innocent babies whose lives are endangered by the intense heat of the long summertime and who are pining and dying away for want of fresh air. It feels certain that there are 10,000 people in St. Louis who will go out to Sportsman's Park on July 17 and enjoy the fray and the rolling together of the 18 muscular gentlemen just to aid the babies. So *The Republic* hurried forward and secured the park for the occasion named. Then Mr. Joy and Mr. Mechin were visited with the intelligence. The information was of all things most soothing to their ferocious desire "for gitten at one another."

Mr. Joy said that he had not kicked in anybody's rib for some time and Mr. Mechin said that the taste of the last ear he chewed off had completely

LEFT: "Eager for the Fray" (*St. Louis Republic*, 20 June 1893, p. 4); RIGHT: "In Fighting Trim" (*St. Louis Republic*, 20 June 1893, p. 4).

faded away, so that both are pining for the enemy and the enemy is equally pining for them. The contest is to be for nine innings only and no gouging. Any kind of bat from a rail to a board fence is permissible, and no one will be permitted to hit the ball twice at the same time. These particulars are the only ones agreed on.

"Mr. Mechin says that you can't play ball," was suggested to Mr. Joy.

"I can't, eh!" answered the Congressman. "Didn't I play right field last year? Didn't I catch the ball in three innings and wasn't I dressed up in a brown and white ball suit. Mechin can talk, but we'll get out and color the mud with his nine. They can't play. A mere lot of scrubs, all of 'em. Wait 'till you see me," and Mr. Joy leaned back with a vision of himself in a brown and white suit nimbly moving around on the turf and catching the sphere with one hand.

While he was engaged with this ethereal vision the reporter sneaked out and visited Mr. Mechin at his office on Chestnut street.

"Mr. Joy called you and your nine a lot of scrubs," was the opening remark.

"He did, did he?" said Mr. Mechin. "Did Joy call me a scrub? When did he say I was a scrub?"

"He didn't say you were a scrub; he said that you are one."

"I are one," meditated Mr. Mechin.

"That's what he said."

"Well he ought to know. He can't pitch, catch or hit the ball. We'll just wallop him all around and won't half try. Didn't I knock the ball over the fence last year. Didn't I run clean around to third base without stopping. I don't care if they did get me out at first, I ran to third and not one of 'em dared to stay me," and here Mr. Mechin indignantly wiped his perspiring forehead.

"Who will you have in your nine?" was asked.

"Let me see. I've got a list here." A piece of paper was produced and from a scrawled list of characters Mr. Mechin began to read as follows:

"Gus W. Neimann, he's with August Gehner & Co.; Fred Smith, the real estate man; Joe Duffy, in the same business; Otto Stifel, the brewer; Walter Ashton, the engineer; Ed Ambler, the oil dealer; Geo. Mathews, the oil dealer; A. A. Aal of the Parisian Cloak Company and me. I'm with August Gehner."

"Who have the Elks got?"

"Now you're coming to the scrubs," said Mr. Mechin. "He ought to call me a scrub. They've got France Chandler of the Wabash Railroad, Allen McDowell, their grand lecturer, Stanislaus Kehrmann, the florist; John M. Chesbrough, the assistant general passenger agent of the Vandalia; Chalmer D. Colman, George Durant, the telephone man; Al Vallet of the Council and Jimmy Kern, the liquor dealer. Anybody can tell by reading those two lists, who is going to get the worst of it. I tell you right here that we're going to play ball and win, and that we are going to have the honor of netting the Fresh Air Fund a big sum." Mr. Mechin also said that the members of his nine intend to wear each a different costume which shall be representative of the great geniuses of the world. They propose to emulate the various sages in the matter of dress for at least one afternoon. Mr. Mechin poetically remarked, "We're no common baseball skates. We're intellectual St. Louisans and we propose to make a cultured showdown and don't you forget it."

The following telegram was received by Mr. Joy last evening from Chalmer D. Colman, who is at present in Detroit attending the meeting of the Supreme Council of Elks:

> *Mr. Charles F. Joy,* St. Louis, Mo.: The Supreme Council has just decided that if we Elks don't beat the Owls and win the gate receipts the St. Louis Council will be fired out of the order. I protested, but they would do it.
> *Colman.*

Mr. Joy said that the Supreme Council need not be afraid; that if the local council didn't "wade in and kick up the mud" they ought to be fired out. Mr. Joy afterwards explained that "kicking up mud" was the elite Congressional term for winning out, which he had picked up in Washington. As *The Republic* reporter was returning from the office of Mr. Joy he came across Mr. Mechin, armed with a ferocious look and a baseball bat. His progress north on Broadway indicated that he was on his way to Joy's office for the purpose of creating trouble. By rare and most unheard-of strategy Mr. Mechin was inveigled into enjoying a glass of beer. This gave ample opportunity for preserving Mr. Joy, who was notified. The latter gentleman immediately borrowed a silk hat and left for Washington, to stay a week. While this internecine feud is much to be regretted, and while both Mr. Joy and Mr. Mechin are prone to allow their wrath to obtain the "best holt" on them whenever their baseball talents are called into question, yet the object to be attained by having the feud come to a climax and the several gentlemen to bruise one another being so worthy, *The Republic* is pleased to assuage and condone their conduct as much as possible. Mr. Mechin is now preparing the score cards and training his cohorts for the fray, while Mr. Joy is busily engaged scheming and mapping out various strategic moves whereby he proposes to dump the Owls so prodigiously far and hard that they will not return for a year. Meanwhile the thousands of little infants who are to be taken out into the country by the money so obtained, whose cheeks are to blush redder and whose eyes are to sparkle brighter because of the boon so obtained, are toddling forward to the joyous days "After the Ball" game and stand ever as an indulgence and forgiveness for any and all blood that may be spilled upon the occasion rapidly approaching. The game will be undoubtedly the most entertaining event of the summer, and it is equally without doubt that the affair will be a society event.

[20 June 1893, p. 4.]

48 - TEACHERS AT THE FAIR.

Special to The Republic.

Chicago, Ill., July 17. — Providence seems to be right with *The Republic* and its World Fair guests at present. The evening sleeper, full of teachers who left St. Louis Sunday night to visit the great World's Fair at the expense of *The Republic*, were greeted by such a day as caused many residents to comment upon its superiority over those preceding. A tour of Jackson Park that lasted from 11 o'clock a.m. until 6 p.m. was made, and, while it wearied the pretty school marms, it satisfied their curiosity for the time being. Providence, Phil Dean and *The Republic's* especial emissary were right with them to the close of the day.

When the Chicago and Alton night train with the beautiful special sleeper Benares attached pulled out of the Union Depot in St. Louis for the World's Fair, the sleeper was filled with the 24 school teachers, a few of their relatives and as many friends. Never was there a jollier or more light-hearted assemblage than that which caused "Benares" to resound with merry voices and laughter. All the young school teachers had trooped down to the car with oh, so many bundles, because, forsooth, somebody had said that it was foolish to take a trunk. They climbed into the sleeper to look at it and then climbed out again to bid their friends good-by and then back into the sleeper again, where they remained until Monday morning.

Of course they all placed their bundles and satchels in the wrong place and equally of course they were informed of the fact by the most genial of all conductors, who just more than "laid himself out" to be accommodating, after which there was more of joyous laughing and teheeing until the train gave a sharp start. The start was productive of 24 little screams from the 24 little school marms, who immediately stated that the train must be going, after which explanation of the situation all fell again to enjoying the pleasure of the previous subject under discussion. Prof. Soldan, the genial principal of the High School, was on board and, realizing that all the young ladies had at one time or other, been pupils of his, he took it upon himself to guide them in a fatherly way, which made everything even more merry than before. Then came the long night ride, and what a pleasant ride it was, to be sure. Like all thoughtful little school marms *The Republic's* especial 24 had brought along the daintiest little lunches and boxes of candy and flowers. By the time the train had reached Alton a "dove" party had been formed in the drawing-room at one end of the car; everybody was invited, and, what was better, everybody came. Even the most genial of all conductors and the mighty porter deigned to stick in their heads just to see how things "were coming." Such high carnival as was held then and there can hardly be fitly described. It grew more merry with each succeeding moment and by 11 o'clock all were singing the latest and most pleasant of popular airs.

The good and serene Prof. Soldan set the example, of course, by retiring to his berth, and then, one by one, all the rest disappeared behind the shadowy curtains for the night. By 7 o'clock Monday morning all the guests were astir. The berths were put up, and after the morning ablutions a light repast of coffee and rolls was indulged in by almost all. From Joliet to Chicago is but a little way, but the ride became interesting, especially the last few miles, where the Alton winds among long lines of warehouses and tall buildings into the Union Depot. There the party were met by Phil Dean, who had the great Columbia tally-ho present, horns, bugle and all. The party mounted, stacked on their bundles, and with a crack of the whip, a loud bugle call and a murmur of excitement the tally-ho moved away from the gaze of an admiring throng which had gathered. Its route lay along Adams street to Michigan avenue, into which it turned off for the Varsity. The coach was the one feature of the thronged thoroughfares, and from Adams Street Bridge to the Varsity entrance it was the object of unnumbered admiring glances. Once at the Varsity Hotel, a pleasant five-story brick structure with comfortable hallways and large rooms, the teachers dismounted and with but little delay were assigned to their rooms. It was 8 o'clock when the train pulled into Chicago, 9:15 when the tally-ho reached the Varsity, and 9:45 when the entire party sat down to breakfast.

After breakfast tickets to the Fair were provided for all the guests, with which, headed by *The Republic*'s representatives, the party adjourned to the World's Fair entrance, only five blocks from the hotel. At the gate the rounds of that wonderland began, and rounds without end it was, to be sure. The party walked but a short distance along the Midway Plaisance until the great Ferris wheel was reached, towering as it does 250 feet above the ground. Into this the entire cortege was escorted, and by no less a personage than Mr. L. V. Rice, the superintendent of the wheel, who was pleased to accompany the party and explain to the ladies, as guests of *The Republic*, the points of interest about the great revolving baskets or chambers. Coming out of this the party was conducted by devious paths thronged with sight-seeing humanity and edged by endless lines of gay bazars, where the nations of the earth exhibit their choicest products, on to the great Turkish bazaar, where the Musselmans hold forth in great numbers. The exquisite productions of the Orient were decidedly alluring to the young teachers, whose propensity to go shopping is well known. There was then such a running hither and thither from one stand unto another as was sufficient to baffle all attempt at unity in the party and cause no end of calling and

counter-calling until all were again under the wing, so to speak, of the so-
licitous envoys of *The Republic.*

Then followed a visit to the dancing Coryphies of the Ottoman Empire, a
pilgrimage to and through the German Village, with its excellently arranged
cottages and lawns, a visit to Libby Glass Manufacturing Exhibit, with a
learned elucidation of the same by Mr. Dean, and a tour of the Woman's
Building. From here the journey lay to the Missouri Building, where the
party rested itself and registered itself to its undoubted heart's content.

By the careful foresight of *The Republic* representatives lunches had
been brought along. These then were carried to the shores of the restless
murmuring Michigan, where, in sight of the rolling waters and fanned by a
pleasant lake breeze, the guests seated themselves in a group upon the
grass and dined. Being so refreshed and recuperated, all felt able to exam-
ine the contents of the German Government Building, the Ceylon exhibit,
the Canadian and the English buildings in turn. It was in coming out of that
latter building that the Viking ship was spied, quietly rocking on the lake
waves on the shore. This was duly inspected, as well as the neighboring
man-of-war Illinois, which was at anchor close to the great lake pier. Then
came a walk through the Liberal Arts Building, as well as the Mechanics'
and the electrical exhibit. It was journeying from booth to booth and from
aisle to aisle within the walls of these great temples that the company
whiled away the remaining hours of the afternoon and returned late in the
evening weary and hungry, but enthusiastic, to the Varsity and its excellent
dining service.

The evening was given over to the inspection of Buffalo Bill's great Wild
West circus, tickets for which had been kindly provided by the management of the same. The beauty and value of this nightly performance shall be
given further description, but not at present.

The whole day was spent really in satisfying that untold desire, which
exists in the mind of every visitor to the Fair, to see everything at once and
mighty quickly at that. To-day will see a different kind of "touring for inspection." More time will be given to individual exhibits, now that *The Republic*'s merry guests are impressed with the immensity of it all. Some of the
buildings passed through yesterday will be revisited and others, not yet
thought of, taken in. One thing is certain, the Irish village and Castle
Blarney will not escape the attention of the party to-day. The blarney stone
must be kissed if it takes the last effort of every "schoolmarm's life."

[18 July 1893, p. 7.]

49 - THE REPUBLIC TEACHERS.

Special to The Republic.

Woodlawn Park, Ill., July 18. — "*T*he Republic's school teachers!" This exclamation is put here to show that certain glorious things are being done which plain flow of language can not come near describing. This is the end of the second day of their visit to the Fair Grounds and it has been spent most enjoyably. There are just three facts that have developed themselves most prominently so far. They are, first, that the sun does not set as it does in St. Louis, the east being in the wrong place; secondly, the whole show is just too sweet for anything, "cute" and "funny" being barred; thirdly, it is just bewildering. These three facts have been carefully compiled by *The Republic's* representative, who called upon every member of the great World's Fair party for an expression of opinion. Nothing is going on at the World's Fair that the party isn't going to witness before it completes its tour, but the right now of it is the best part of the whole show. *The Republic's* representative seriously considered the necessity of writing a poetical harangue upon the subject of the tour last evening, but the task was too much—not for lack of words, but rather because of the immensity of the grand task.

To-day the sun shone out gloriously. The cool breeze from off Michigan's restless bosom was enthusing. The Fair Grounds were sprinkled and crowded with people, but the best of it all was that *The Republic's* party got off from the Varsity Hotel early and stayed at the grounds until late in the evening. It is not hard to tell of the number of buildings visited, but it is to tell of all that was seen. In the first place only the Horticultural, the Fisheries and the Liberal Arts buildings were visited, with the exception of a few shows on the Midway Plaisance, which were entered just to wind up the day pleasantly.

A man could get into the Liberal Arts Building and trail around from place to place for a year and not get tired. He would simply start out walking, looking in this case and that shelf, peering down into this depth and up to that height, climbing these stairs up and those down, until he would grow weary and go home. Next day he would start in again and after a long while he would come back to the place that he started from and begin to look at the selfsame things that he saw when he first started out, but that wouldn't make any difference; really he wouldn't know the difference. That's what people are coming to up here. *The Republic's* correspondent saw several of its own select party looking at the same things three or four times over. Several times he ventured to tell them the difference, but it was always in vain. They would deny having been there before.

The Fisheries Building was also visited after the party came out of the Horticultural Building. After viewing the mountains of plants and the forests of flowers in the first-named building, the 40 odd members of "*The Republic's* push," for such is the name they are becoming to be known by, contented themselves with crowding their noses up against the glass water-filled cases in the Fisheries Building, and came near scaring the life out of the poor fishes. There was one fish in the building that created a good laugh all around. It was the "Common skate," according to the large gilt letters above. It was the ugliest humpbacked creature that ever cut salt water. It came forward and put one eye up to the glass in the most familiar manner. Then Miss Muenchen remarked:

"Now, just look at that fish; how fresh it is."

"Don't you believe it," said Prof. Soldan; "that fish is a salt water fish. I know him from away back."

"You wouldn't know him from a sway-back, would you?" smiled Miss Boyle, which caused several smaller fish to faint, and made a distant clock which was about to strike 12 stop short and strike only 8.

From the Fisheries Building the Liberal Arts Building was entered. Its wiley depths were sauntered through for over an hour, by which time all were hungry, and adjourned accordingly to the lake shore, where the boxes were opened and food devoured. There a cocoa pavilion was entered. These little places have been built by the manufacturers of cocoa and chocolate. The one entered by the teachers was fitted out in old Holland style. The ser ⁄ing maids wore jolly little Dutch caps and served the beverage in little China cups that were decidedly pretty.

After this slight dissipation a return was made to the Liberal Arts Building. For several hours the St. Louis school exhibit was dived into. Every marm must needs find what her own little pupils had sent, and in the excitement of tearing themselves away several lost their umbrellas. Their sorrow was, however, soon drowned in the joy of the free gifts which many exhibitors give away. Books, periodicals, pictures, souvenirs of all kinds and descriptions were heaped upon the teachers just as soon as the clerks in charge learned that *The Republic* had charge of them. It did look for a while as though many of them would have more than they could carry.

A visit was made to a vaudeville theater in the Midway Plaisance. James J. Corbett was boxing there and after his bag-punching exhibition and his three-round contest *The Republic* reporter secured him and brought him out to shake hands with all the girls. It was delightful. The fair girls gathered about him and wanted to tell him how much they thought of him. Miss Sullivan was the only one in the crowd who hung back a moment. She said he had disgraced the family name. From here the forty odd went into Cairo street to see the sights. The day's tramp concluded with a late inspection of the grand night illuminations, after which the party returned to the hotel.

[19 July 1893, p. 6.]

50 - THIRD DAY AT THE FAIR.

Special to The Republic.

Chicago, Ill., July 19. — Wednesday the third day of the visit of the school teachers from St. Louis to Chicago under the patronage of *The Republic* passed away pleasantly enough. Now it is nighttime and sitting on the balcony that ornaments the second floor of the Varsity Hotel, the "forty odd" had much of interest and pleasure to reflect over. The evenings are too cool here, so that sitting on the balcony is not exactly comfortable without wraps. Maybe there is a slight dampness in the air that causes the strings of the banjo, that one of the group is playing, to sound just a bit off on the high frets, but that does not stop the young ladies from dancing, which they have been doing ever since their evening meal. This day has not been warm. None of the days here seem to be, for although the sun's rays beat down with terrific force, the breeze from off the lake blows them away. They fall only with somewhat of a soothing warmth. After tramping all day long from "post to pillar," as it were, and back again, to sit on a balcony and enjoy the cool of nighttime is very enchanting.

From one you may look west and see the heavens one vast blaze of lurid fire, the reflection of the spectacular representation in pyrotechnics of the siege of Sebastopol. To the north, only two blocks away, stands the great Ferris wheel, lighted brightly by many electric lamps, and whenever the wind blows good and strong the noise of the grinding cog wheels that revolve it about can be distinctly heard. Directly east tower the main buildings of the Fair within full view. Their many domes and spires are lighted up by thousands upon thousands of electric lamps, until the whole appears as some enormous piece of silk lace and drapery, spun of flaming silver and molten gold. From the topmost pinnacle of the Administration Building gleam out with all the power of a gorgeous eye the streaming rays of the electric searchlights. Someone stands aloft, away up there, and by some process sways them to and fro, as though in search of some far distant object, and, as their rays gleam out a white and widening hue across the sky, the whole distant prospect is lighted up and distant many blocks one may see people walking, distinguish the finer outlines on buildings and see small objects. Every now and again the path of the light leads across the hotel front, and it is as if there were a prolonged flash of lightning. It is thus environed that the "forty odd" pass the evening after the day.

This morning the members of the party lingered just a little longer in their couches, probably because of extra fatigue the day before. It was fully 10 o'clock before all had sauntered down to breakfast and secured their luncheons preparatory to starting. At that hour all were gathered together and escorted to the Woman's Building. A cursory visit had been paid to this building on Monday, but to-day a protracted stay was made. The never-ending row of show-cases was glanced through; delightful paintings, manuscripts and relics were examined and the confused variety of materials gathered were studied for fully three hours. It was in this building that Prof. Soldan and party were lost. To-day, however, the crowd managed to hang together and so came out intact.

The "forty odd" are much given to discussing matters and at any moment the leader is liable to pull up, gather about him the remaining members and consult about some point of interest. It matters little where they stand. They are just as liable to stop and pack some doorway as to gather on the broad highways that lead among the buildings outside. The guards don't understand how it can happen that so many people gather so suddenly in one place. To-day Phil Dean drew up and inquired: "Say?" In a moment the entire company was close about him. He only desired to know the pleasure of the party as regarded the next building to be visited—whether it should be so and so or something else. While this was going on a guard hurried up and edged himself by sheer force into the heart of the crowd.

"Anything the matter here?" he inquired of the astonished young ladies.

"No, sir," was the reply.

"No one sick, I trust?"

"Not at all," was the rejoinder.

"Merely deciding where to go, that's all."

"Beg your pardon," said the guard, "it looked as though someone was hurt," and with that he bowed himself out.

A similar "confab" in front of the entrance to the Cairo street caused an official investigation, which, however, did not prove fatal.

The decision of the party after leaving the Woman's Building was to visit the California Building. This structure is by far the finest of all the State structures and contains an exhibit worth looking at. Talk about your fruits! This is where the young ladies got a chance to look at some of the real kind. The many artistically designed booths which are mostly built up of bottled and transparent jarred fruits were each visited in turn. The "house of beans" was looked upon with interest, as well as the sphere of oranges and the pyramid of grapes. After indulging somewhat in orange cider the party moved off to the Missouri Building. Quite a number of patriotic St. Louisans were on hand as usual looking for someone from "down home," and they were not disappointed. It was on the topmost floor of this building that the party opened their lunch boxes and sat down to enjoy dinner.

Some little time was spent in playing and dancing about the reception rooms on the second floor, and then all were taken through the Florida Building, which is just next door. Here some beautiful modeling in butter was examined as well as other exhibits. The Idaho and Montana buildings came next in order for their due share of attention, between which and the Missouri Building, which stands near at hand, the remaining hours of the afternoon were divided. To-night the term of several of the guests who won only three days' tours expires, and they will leave for home accordingly. The expression of satisfaction gathered from them indicates decidedly the pleasure and complete success of the tour.

The Republic's party is of interest in itself. In the first place, it is evidently the largest party at the Fair. Everywhere it has been remarked, and hundreds of people have stopped and turned to gaze upon the jubilant procession. All the members are on the best of terms, and merriment is at no time lacking. The party has a leader who knows the grounds, has written most of the interesting features and has mapped out each day's work with something like mathematical precision.

Some amusing comments on the party are heard. In the Turkish Bazaar in the Midway Plaisance a Turkish Jew stood with his hand to his chin watching the approaching crowd, just outside his stand.

"Zee, zee," he remarked to a neighboring salesman, "at muzzy be a churge party. Hi! Hi! not? Some religious," and then he did his very utmost to attract the attention of the members and have them "come buy."

The second comment overheard was by two gay and sapient looking ramblers.

"Bob!" called the first to the second. "Look! See 'em! Sunday school party er I'll eat my hat."

"That's what," said Bob. "They hang together all right," with which Bob and the other moved away.

It was in the Horticultural Building on the second day that two very sedate ladies with green goggles and extra large chatelaine bags encountered the solid "Forty Odd." They also stopped.

"Just look," said one.

"Yes," sententiously remarked the other; "school teachers."

"Do you think?"

"Do I think? I know. I've not been a school teacher 20 years for nothing."

Probably as interesting divertisement as may be found anywhere inside the World's Fair city is the famous show of Buffalo Bill—Colonel Cody's Wild West. This genial gentleman of much record, kindly extended tickets to the "Forty Odd" for Monday night and had them all visit his splendid exhibition. He did more. He waited at the entrance for them and as they entered he pressed forward to shake hands with each one and to bid them hearty welcome. They were then treated to a delightful programme. Colonel Cody has a great show, and it was thoroughly enjoyed.

[20 July 1893, p. 4.]

51 - WILL SEE EVERYTHING.

Special to The Republic.

Chicago, Ill., July 20. — Nobody will be able to tell the school teachers anything about the World's Fair when they get back to St. Louis. There is no question about this. If there is any stray knowledge stored away in some dim forsaken corner that has not been brought out yet, it's going to come out, that's all. The day was just as delicious as usual. Just as cool, as bright and as enthusing as any of the preceding three, which goes to prove what a warm friend Providence is to the teachers and *The Republic*, whose especial care they are in. Besides doing the Fair, or "faring well," as the term goes now, the party is making sundry excursions into the regions about the grounds, such as the hotel district south, Washington Park west, and even on the lake east. This morning they went through the usual morning proceedings which invariably wind up at the Sixty-first street entrance to the Fair. The gate-keeper at Sixty-first street is getting quite familiar with the party. "Aha," he invariably remarks, "Back again? well I'll be blessed, but these teachers are having a good time."

Frank Rigler, the chief clerk of the Bureau of Press Admissions, has also become deeply interested in the Fair-going young teachers. This was at first considered as something barely possible, and not probable; but the young ladies have, as usual, won, and now the genial Frank never fails to ask all about them every time he gets within hailing distance. If there is one man connected with the Fair whose duties are of a difficult as well as a delicate nature it is those of Mr. Frank Rigler. There is scarcely a publication in the country that has not applied for admission passes, whether they have given any space to the Fair or not. All day long Mr. Rigler has to contend with a waiting line of editors and reporters who work on the Podunk *Wrestler*, the Marysville *Bam Fizz*, the Orientsburglet *Resounder* and other great journals. But while all of them don't get passes, they all go away feeling that at any rate Mr. Rigler is a gentleman.

To-day's work was of considerable interest because it took in the Agriculture Building where Brother Zachariah, just in, of course, was present in great numbers just to see what his fellow farmers are accomplishing in other parts of the world.

It's sickles to mowing machines that Bro. Zachariah or Zebulon has broad rolling acres of land with waving fields of grain, a great old farmhouse and barn. Bro. Zachariah, if he's a bit thrifty, does not come up among "these bum-busted sharks and gol-dinked man-eaters" unless he is well-heeled and knows that everything is going "jist as slick to hum."

So to-day the teachers saw the farmers, and they were pleased. That building contains an immense amount of agricultural products that one would never hear of anywhere except within the spacious walls of its beautiful rooms. Here, as elsewhere, one may walk around and around and all at once find one's self looking at the same object as in the beginning.

Machinery Hall was visited among the first places, that great exhibit of mechanical science, which is one continual roar from sunrise to nightfall. Then came a second visit to the Horticultural Building, the California Building and again the Missouri Building, where, as on the previous day, dinner was eaten.

The New York Central and Hudson River Railroad exhibit was also visited. Nothing could be prettier than the train of Wagner vestibule cars Columbus, Pinzo, San Salvador, Ferdinand and Isabella—the trappings of which are gorgeous.

Mr. Soldan, the genial sponsor of the young ladies, has positively degenerated into the "wit" of the "Forty-Odd." He has given himself over to much drawing of comparisons and much composition of comical tales, wherewith to regale the crowd. Only to-day he propounded the query why the "Forty-Odd" were like the American flags. Upon all deserting the contest he gave out as the explanation that the members of the party were all stars and Mr. Dean was the stripe. He also had the members of the party endeavoring to give facts about fish which would augur their possession of intellect; finally, he explained by saying that they were noted for moving in schools.

The letter-writing mania has come upon the young ladies, one and all. Throughout the grounds in the different buildings there stand little "nickel-in-the-slot" boxes which contain Columbian Exposition postal cards. These are beautiful samples of the colored engraving art and they come out two for a nickel. The young ladies are wasting their substance most recklessly in buying the cards. Then they go off to some noted point and sit down to write. If all of their acquaintances don't receive postal cards from a score of places within the Fair it will be simply because their financial resources become strained. The Fair officials certainly knew something of human nature, and especially female human nature, when they put those slot boxes in the grounds.

When the Missouri Building was forsaken at 1:30 p.m. the party made a swift detour of the Art Palace, which is right across the way south from the Missouri Building, and then visited the Manufactures Building for the third time; however, the entire afternoon was spent within the limits of the Columbian exhibit. The great sculptors and painters of Italy have splendid exhibits and one might spend days within the darkened limits of that little extreme southwest corner which is filled with the most delicately carved, painted and sculptured articles, of which there are hundreds and thousands. A few of the party, under the guidance of Phil Dean, left however, for the Convent of "La Rabida," where they spent something like an hour and then returned to the Varsity. To-night over half of the teachers returned to the grounds to witness the magnificent illuminations. A gondola party was also formed and a glide taken about the lagoons.

A second party preferred to visit South Park, two blocks distant from the hotel and row upon the lake there. The moonlight has been so inviting, the air so cool and the shadows cast so soft that none could resist them. It is now that the thought of returning is becoming a kind of sorrowful reflection.

[21 July 1893, p. 2.]

52 - FIFTH DAY AT THE FAIR.

Special to The Republic.

Chicago, Ill., July 21. — The teachers spent this their fifth day entirely in the Art Palace, with the exception of about one hour and a half spent in the Missouri Building at lunch time. The day was announced by the leader of the party, Mr. Phil Dean, as "Free-for-all day." That of course meant that Mr. Dean did not feel like working. Everybody was to pull out for himself and see what he chose, which, besides being a divertisement, would prepare the members of the party for the last great day, to-morrow, in the Midway Plaisance. It was suggested, however, that the Art Palace receive the consideration of all as being the most interesting collection within the grounds. That suggestion was followed unanimously.

To-night the party divided up into groups, one going to Lincoln Park, another to the Fair Grounds, and the third remained at the hotel forming a "piazza squabble," which is the latest for tete-a-tete on the balcony. The teachers are rejoicing at present over the good time they have had. It is only the shadow of returning home and leaving the Varsity and the White City that is troubling them. The shadow of the end is already streaming out towards them and soon it will be over them.

Six in all went "gondola chasing" last night. "Gondola chasing" is not gondola rowing. It means looking for a gondola. The fact is that everybody at the Fair has the idea that he must go gondola riding before he leaves. They all want to choose some romantic tour, when the moon is beaming down kind of silvery like and the stars cast a thousand diamond reflections in the rippling waters. Then they all wait until evening and go to get a gondola. That is, the first ones to the lagoon get a gondola and row about. Pretty soon all the gondolas are gone and you can't get one for love or money. Then a lot of other people who want to go gondola riding come up and ask whether they can get one, and if they can't, why can't they? They sit around and look out on the water and wish some of the people out rowing would get tired. Every time a gondola goes by there is a chorus of "There goes one," but it goes on just the same and doesn't stop. Then they all get up and walk on to the next renting booth and sit there and wait until it's too late and they have to go home because the lights are going to be put out.

Miss White was anxious to go, and so the party went out and walked around and around until very near 10 o'clock, but they did not go out on the water. Some one said they would, if the water was solid enough, but it was not and so the whole scheme fell through. A number of the girls have decided that they are not going to be satisfied with just one week, but are going to stay over several weeks more. More of them are coming back again in September to spend a few more weeks looking about. At the same time the party that will return to-night to St. Louis will be quite large.

The management of the Hotel Varsity deserves exceeding credit for the kindness with which they have attended to the wants of the party. The treatment could not have been better. The Varsity is an excellent hotel.

As a general thing the early hours of the night after a day at the Fair are very pleasantly spent. The "Forty odd" divide into smaller parties and are out for any kind of sport in which they can find amusement. Rowing seems for many to be a favorite manner of whiling away the hours. Washington Park affords that pleasure. It is located within two blocks of the hotel in which the school teachers are staying. The pond is a very large one, but not very deep, and so there is no danger of death from drowning. Once in a boat with the free air and the heaven above them, the young and pretty school teachers lose all their dignity. Their songs fill the air and their laughter echoes from shore to shore. Many of the 40 entered a rowboat for the first time in their lives in this city, but were much pleased with the satisfaction of being on the water under such conditions. Muscles are being hardened and appetites increased. Altogether when the "Forty Odd" return to St. Louis they will be a very healthy looking lot.

Rowing is not the only way of spending the evening when the teachers are weary of sight-seeing. They gather in crowds and indulge in story-telling, relating their experience as teachers. Amusing topics are always selected. Miss Julia Barclay holds the palm for the most laughable story yet related. Her story ran as follows:

"Several months ago my class took up the words 'divine' and 'defense.' I explained what the two meant and then asked my scholars to give me sentences containing one of them. One little boy who is particularly bright was the first to raise his hand. When I gave him permission to rise and speak he gave the sentence: 'The vine climbed over the fence.'"

"I had an experience equally as laughable," said Miss Julia Sullivan, when the laughter had subsided. "One day my class came across the word 'lightsome.' None of my scholars knew what it meant, and I tried to explain by saying that the room we were in was full of light and therefore it was lightsome. One of my boys, thinking he understood the meaning of the word, arose and gave me the sentence: 'I must go and light some matches.'"

The appetites of the teachers have not diminished during their stay here. Every morning every one, before leaving the hotel to spend the day at the Fair, is given a nicely put up package of lunch, consisting of good and substantial food, fruits, cakes and other eatables. At noon the "Forty-odd" gather in the Missouri Building and laugh, chatter and devour what they have been given. The crumbs left are hardly enough to provide a meal for one of the sparrows so common in St. Louis.

Prof. Soldan on all occasions is ready to make someone the victim of a joke. His latest is very good. Every teacher is provided with a meal ticket so that she can be identified in the dining-room. To-day Prof. Soldan, after dinner, approached Miss Higgins, who was standing talking to several other teachers, and remarked: "I see you cannot eat without a punch." She, thinking that he meant some kind of a drink, denied the charge, saying the only beverage she drank was coffee.

"You are mistaken," replied the Professor; "I saw the cashier punch your meal ticket."

On another occasion a teacher was examining a pretty landscape painting in the Art Gallery. She uttered: "Oh, how nice!"

"Why, of course," replied Prof. Soldan, who had read the card underneath the painting. "I see it comes from Nice, France."

[22 July 1893, p. 2.]

53 - LAST DAY AT THE FAIR.

Special to The Republic.

Chicago, Ill., July 22 — At this writing, the nineteenth hour of the sixth day, which is the last of the St. Louis teachers' stay at the World's Fair, at least as a party, it may be safely stated that there is really nothing they have not seen. Some of them are expressively singing, "We won't go home till morning," and so ends one of the largest and most interesting expeditions that ever entered the Fair gates. The World's Fair catalogue or official guide names all the buildings and tells what each contains. If the teachers have not examined each individual article closely it is only because time has been too precious. At one certain hour or another during this last week they have been near them one and all.

The mention of official catalogues cannot be passed over without relating a little incident that occurred outside the Administration Building the other day. A couple of young fellows, employes of a refreshment stand concessionaire, were crying out their wares: "Come on, now," said one. "Get your nice ice-cool official watermelons! The real administration watermelons! The only authorized edition of official World's Fair watermelons— 20 cents a slice!" The novelty of the manner in which the youth cried his wares collected a crowd and the crowd bought his official watermelons, so that after all there was method in his mad humor.

One of the ladies came over into the Missouri Building at 10 o'clock yesterday morning to deposit her lunch box with the post office clerk, who has charge of such things. Then she entered the Art Palace and two hours later returned to the Missouri Building. "Don't you know," she said, "I just walked into the Art Palace. I just had time to see a few of the lovely pictures, not more than 4, and don't you know when I looked at my watch it was noon—really 12 o'clock. Now you must believe it, won't you." The listener agreeing to believe it, he was left to ruminate upon the indefiniteness of time and the mutability of all things earthly.

The "Forty-odd" has become a poor name for *The Republic's* party now. The week has seen the departure of those who only came for three days. Tonight more are leaving and every now and again some one of them will be seen moving here and there with a bundle or satchel, which means a departure. Those that remain contemplate a boat ride on Lake Michigan some time Sunday. Some of these young ladies, who only won three-day trips to the World's Fair, are lingering over with the party, paying their own expenses. A number of these are going on the lake trip, if it turns out as planned on Friday night. Some of them are going to church, too, Sunday morning.

Among the experiences indulged in outside the Fair have been the beauties of Washington Park and a boat ride on its pretty lake; a ride on the elevated road; in the evening, a trip over some of the North Chicago lines and a tour through Lincoln Park. An evening spent near the Yerkes Fountain, with a stroll along the north-shore drive, and finally a very circumspect pilgrimage into the central portion of the city, where the great, tall buildings were inspected, completed this week. Not all, of course, did these things, but a good many of them did.

To-day was spent rather enjoyably at the World's Fair. It may seem somewhat trite to remark that the sun shown out clear and the cool breezes blew from the lake, but they did just the same and no mistake. This morning the party rode over to the Stony Island avenue gate and went directly to the Missouri Building, where the members stored their lunch boxes. Some six of them made off for the Art Palace, while the others went to the Government Building. The latter party between 10 o'clock and noon visited several other buildings, including the Illinois State Building and the Wisconsin exhibit. An hour for lunch at the Missouri Building brought all the members together again. From that time until 6 o'clock to-night they did not separate. A ride was taken about the grounds on the Intramural Railway, and after that they all went into the Midway Plaisance, the first time since Tuesday. The Turkish theater, Cairo street and Hagenbach menagerie were all taken in, in turn. Those who are not going home to-night have arranged no specific plans. They will probably spend the hours in strolling about or resting in the balcony.

There have been numerous incidents of interest which have occurred during the week which so far have not been related. The one that afforded the most momentary excitement, of course, was an alarm of fire, which was turned in supposedly from the Mining Building. It was at night, during the progress of some very interesting illuminations which were going forward. A great crowd had turned out, every building, grass plot, walk and bench was filled with humanity, strolling, standing, lying and in all kinds of conceivable postures. Suddenly, the great fire whistle on the Machinery Building wailed out its alarm. Another such a long, wild, unearthly sound could not be conceived of. The escaping steam rushes out in varying degrees of force, such as can only be illustrated by citing the example of a voice going through the "do-re-me" of the musical scale. No human voice, however powerful, or by what passion moved, could sigh, moan, wail, yell, screech as that fire whistle does, and then sink through the same varying sounds, down and back to the sigh again, where it ceases.

The entire party was standing near one of the entrances of the Manufactures Building, by which passed the broad roadway on through several spacious courts and right by the Mining Building. Scarcely had the whistle ceased than the clang of the gongs on the different fire conveyances were heard to be approaching in the distance. The broad roadways, walks and squares were massed with human beings. A roadway had to be made for the rushing horses and it seemed as though hundreds would be dashed over and killed by rushing horses. All at once they turned into the main stretch, passed the Manufactures Building, the gongs clanging most furiously. Hundreds of voices cried out the imminent danger to the others, and, as though from right beneath the maddened feet of the flying teams the crowd surged back upon itself—the pathway was made. Then they came, engine after engine, hose reels, and ladder trucks excellently guided, all over the lagoon bridge towards the Mining Building. A fire then augured the loss of thousands of lives, but as it happened it was nothing more than a momentary scare.

Another thing that happened illustrated quite forcibly how easy it would be to create alarm. There has been no railroad wreck within the World's Fair Grounds or outside of it this week. Yet one afternoon someone spread the statement one had occurred inside the grounds. How it started, or why, could not be learned, but it was started and that was sufficient. *The Republic* representative happened to be traveling about the grounds at that time at a fairly rapid rate and everywhere the rumor was flying. From expressions dropped here, it was plain that the rumor was creating excitement. The size of the wreck grew of course in the mouthing of it, and it was but a little time until several parties gave it out that only a few hundred people were killed and several thousand injured, this being actually correct and no mistake.

Another thing that has caused considerable comment among the young ladies has been the manner in which the inhabitants of the Orient and Eastern Europe travel about the streets of the city, stroll through its parks and enter its stores. These Turks, Arabs, Hindoos, Japs, Egyptians and others fix themselves up as fantastically as possible for no other reason than to attract attention. They all love to be admired and, as ugly as many of them are, they will smirk and grin upon observing the slightest glance cast in their direction. One meets them by day in the central portion of the city, standing hands on back, staring about in an easy interested way. They ride on the elevated road and cable lines, stroll in the parks, smile at you from benches, and, indeed, from almost anywhere else where one may go of an evening.

They all went to see the illuminations last night, and ah! indeed they were worth visiting. The White City is grand. It is beautiful by day, with the blue sky above, the changing colors of the waters of Michigan to the east of it and the glorious sunbeams flooding its arches and spires, its pillars and domes, as they stand so distinct and clear, out against the sky. There is not one who does not delight in the coolness of the air, the endless splash of the waters on the sands of the shore. None could fail to appreciate the beauty of the well-kept lawns, so richly green, that are curbed in by winding walks, so graceful in their contour and shaded by beautiful trees and shrubbery. Then it is that one is reminded of what the ancient Athenian capital must have been like. How its temples and public buildings, its statuary and its public ways must have adorned the ancient hills of Hellas. One can understand, looking at the group of buildings so gracefully sweeping away on every hand, why the Grecians were proud and how it came that men could meditate the sublime philosophies that characterized that mythic age.

But at night, when the sun has set, when the long shadows have all merged into one and the stars begin to gleam out over the lake and the domes of the palaces of the White City, then it is that the World's Fair is superb and then alone. Soon its spires are fringed with ropes of fiery gold. The many pinnacles are capped with flaming crescents and crowns of light until the walls are brighter illuminated than by day and the shadows of the trees melt into nothingness. How the statuary gleams, a silvery brightness in the glare of the lights that rest upon them! It is then that the Fair Grounds seem a garden of the gods.

It was to this garden that the party strolled last evening that they might see the illuminations. It did seem as though the beauty of the place could not be improved upon, but that was an error. The description lacked the story of a sky that shed stars of silver, purple, emerald and gold. The picture drawn told nothing of the magic fountains that far outvie in splendor the glory of the fountains of the East, whose flowing waters were only of yellow and gold.

Out on the open plaza, between the Mining and Machinery buildings stands numerous groups of statuary. They are only beautiful, however, because they deck the marble walls that confine the waters of the lagoon. On either side of this body of water stand the mounds of rocks which twice a week are turned into rushing fountains of waters besides whose glory, the misty mingling colors of the rainbow pale and fall short. Last night among all the glory of the nighttime festivities they burst forth towards the sky. The leaping waters seemed only to leap high in their glory that they might be kissed by the bending, descending showers of pyrotechnics, so gorgeous alone of themselves that the eye seems surfeited.

A crowd was gathered to see it, a massive crowd, a surging throng. The sight-seers came in droves—armies, thousands. They crowded the benches, walks, bridges, balconies and pavilions that stand about. They made one black and motionless mass. From such a groundwork of humanity up sprang the waters. High they leaped, rolled, rushed and then curved and gracefully descended to the surface below. In their very leaping they were transformed. First they were all a white, shadowy mist, then massy, cloudy foam, and then a million falling pearl drops. Now comes the pink of it—the red, the purple, green, orange, blue, silver and yellow.

While all watched in silent admiration, three Viking boats came drifting over the waters of the lagoon chained close together and moving by the pleasure of a dozen pairs of silent dipping oars. They were filled with singers, and as they neared the flaring waters their voices were uplifted in song—melody that was harmonious, inspiring, divine—much because of its strength and purity, more because of the Edenic charms that abounded about. It was only when the whistle wailed out its reminder of the lateness of the hour that the fountain ceased, the pyrotechnics were discontinued and the lights on the buildings began to die out. Then the great enthusiastic mass tramped its way out and rejoiced that it had been fortunate enough of all the world's children to have seen such a display.

[23 July 1893, p. 6.]

54 - FEVER'S FRENZY.

Fever dethroned the reason of John Finn, a *Republic* carrier living at 2828 Chouteau avenue, and caused him to almost murder his four children yesterday morning. As it is, horribly beaten, their faces covered with marks of violence, their skulls fractured and crushed, the four—Johnnie, Willie, Mamie and Annie, the eldest only 13 and the youngest 5—lie at the City Hospital, while the father, with his throat dangerously cut, and afflicted with typhoid fever, rolls restlessly on another cot, unconscious of his terrible deed and its possible consequences.

At the hospital the father and Willie, whose cases are most serious, were placed in one ward on the second floor. Johnnie, who will probably recover, is on the main floor, while Mamie and Annie, the two little girls, were placed in the female ward on the second floor.

The home of John Finn, *The Republic* carrier, is a plain, square, red brick building containing six rooms, three down and three up stairs, at 2828 Chouteau avenue. The home is of ancient style, with only windows in front. The doors and porches are all on the east side, facing the west wall of the store building next door. The Finns occupied the three lower rooms. The front room they used as a sitting-room and parlor, the middle as a sleeping-room, it containing three beds, and the back or rear room was the kitchen, opening from two doors into the yard. In the sleeping-room the crime was committed.

"The Home of John
Finn" (*St. Louis Re-
public*, 9 August 1893,
p. 1).

"Scene of the Crime"
(*St. Louis Republic*,
9 August 1893, p. 1).

John Finn has been sick for three weeks with a kind of bilious fever, which Dr. Heine Marks of the City Hospital now declares was the preliminary stage of typhoid fever. Dr. Jones of Ewing avenue and Manchester road was treating him. Finn had not been so sick that he was confined to his bed, but was wofully ill at ease. In fact, relatives of the family say that he has been ailing for over a year. About two weeks ago he hired someone else to deliver his papers and on last Friday took to his bed. Saturday he was about again but little better. Yesterday morning he awoke at an early hour troubled with a burning fever. He was uneasy and moved about the three rooms on the lower floor, sitting down now, and again walking to and fro for rest. His wife, Mary Finn, awakened also and heard him complaining of severe pains in the head and of his fever. About 8 o'clock she said that she would call Dr. Jones. While preparing to leave, Johnnie, the elder son, 13 years old, who had in the past helped his father to carry papers, complained of illness. His mother brought him a glass of milk and afterwards placed the glass on the mantel. Her husband laid down on one of three beds in the room next to the kitchen. On another lay Willie, 11 years old, and Johnnie, 13, with their elder sister, Mamie, 7 years old, stretched at their feet. Annie, the 5-year-old daughter, was in the cot.

Leaving them thus Mrs. Finn left the house and started for Ewing avenue and Manchester road in search of Dr. Jones. She visited the Doctor's house and returned on her way home. Coming back she met Officer Joe McKenna of the Fifth District going towards her house. A crowd of people had gathered about the dwelling, in the yard and in the house. Coming up she was informed that her husband had attempted to kill his four children. The shock almost prostrated Mrs. Finn with grief and fear. She ran through the crowd and through the open doorway into the sleeping-room, where lay the children bleeding and moaning. Her husband lay delirious upon the bed where she had left him. At the sight she fainted.

It seems, according to his fitful tale told to Dr. Marks and later to his wife at the City Hospital, that lying there upon the bed after his wife's departure his fevered imagination was greeted by a vision of something indefinitely grand, the eternal home of the faithful, the heaven of the world's children. There was that in it all which called him away from earth and his physical being, and he realized that his death hour had come. With the vision came the thought that going thus to a realm so pleasant it would be good to have his children with him—to take them away from a world of pain and have them as companions in the beyond. Death was nothing for such a goal. Murder meant nothing. It was only fatherly love to release them all into such happiness. It was a religious frenzy that prompted him to rise—a burning desire to make real the glory of his dream. He arose and rushed to the kitchen. Behind the stove hung three flatirons, black, plain and heavy. The first he seized and returning to the bedroom began the awful work.

There was method in his madness. It was for eternal bliss that he was striking the murderous blows. He would release their souls in order—first the eldest, last the youngest. Willie, the 11-year-old boy, was first. The father lifted the iron and pounded him fiercely over the head. The blows were probably five in number, for the boy's skull was crushed; three scalp wounds are marked and the eyes were bruised by one blow. The child was left in a senseless condition, in which he will linger no doubt until his death.

Johnnie was next. The insane frenzy of the vision had not moderated. He had gloriously released Willie and now Johnnie would be free. He must have struck the boy three times, for besides having his skull fractured the lad's right cheek bone is crushed and his lip cut. He only desisted, believing the boy dead. So the mad fury hurried him on. The handle of the flatiron broke completely off after one of his blows. Returning quickly to the kitchen he seized the other two and brought them to the task.

Mamie, the 7-year-old daughter, was beaten over the head until her skull was fractured and she lies as one dead. Annie, the youngest and brightest of them all, suffered a similar fate.

Now then was his work completed—all but himself. He could not die from blows delivered by the iron in his hand. A pair of scissors were near by, a pair of scissors and his razor. Tossing the flat iron under the bed he seized the shears and jabbed at his throat. The point entered somewhat over a half-inch. A second slash he made, but only to cut the skin and no more.

Here the delusion must have ended—the reality forced itself upon his returning senses. It may have been that the sight of the crime of his own hand caused him to faint away. At any rate the work was not completed.

When Mrs. Monahan, who lived above on the second floor, came down attracted by the noise, Finn was senseless upon the floor and about him lay the battered and blood-stained children—mere heaps of senseless flesh, upon the beds and the carpet. They must have offered resistance to his deadly assaults. His clothes were torn and his shirt hung bloody and in shreds from his back.

Mrs. Monahan, who had hurried down from above, no sooner saw the scene than she fled to the street and gave the alarm. Valentine Roth, a tailor, first put in an appearance. Then other neighbors came, and even strangers found an officer and brought him to the house. An ambulance was immediately sent for and came at 9:15 a.m. The two girls partially recovered consciousness during the time and were removed to Dr. Boogher's office at Chouteau and Ewing avenue, from whence they were conveyed to the hospital. Captain Keeble and Sergeant Patrick Gaffney took charge of the premises and ministered, with the assistance of the neighbors, to the mother, who swooned at the sight and to the children until the ambulance came. The rapid treatment which the latter received during the interval between the blows and the arrival at the hospital will probably result in the saving of the lives of three of them. Still the wounds about the head are of a questionable character, no certainty existing as to the result.

The wounded man when seen at the City Hospital lay on a cot fairly gasping for breath. When approached by the reporter he at first refused to say anything, but after questions were repeatedly put to him, by an effort Mr. Finn gathered up his faculties and gave rational answers between his moans of agony.

"Well, this morning," he said, "after my wife left, the beautiful sunshine—God's own sunshine—came into my head. It was a beautiful dream, and it filled my head and the whole room and I heard it say to me: 'If you'll kill your children and yourself you will all go straight to heaven and to God.' I jumped up from the bed and went into the dining-room and got the flatirons. I first struck Johnnie and then the others. In hitting Johnnie I woke up Mamie, who sat up in bed. I then struck her in the top of the head, breaking the iron handle. I ran into the kitchen and got the other two irons and tried to kill my other children. Oh, I don't know hardly what I did. I was burning up with the fever so. I am so sick. How are my children?" he asked eagerly.

"They are all right."

"Thank God for that. I would not harm a hair of their heads."

"How was it that you did not want to kill your wife, too?"

"I did not want to kill her. I wanted to go to heaven and take my children with me. If Mary wanted to go she could come all right."

The wounded man then fell back on his cot exhausted.

———

When *The Republic* reporter called at the plain, old-fashioned brick on Chouteau avenue yesterday afternoon the mother, a slim, dark-haired, dark-complexioned woman of some 48 years of age, sat in the kitchen back of the sleeping-room, where Finn for three long weeks had lain restless and in pain. The front sitting-room was filled with inquisitive and curious relatives and neighbors, who edged close up to one another and talked away in a doleful strain. Out in the kitchen sat Mrs. Finn, and near her two sisters, who could do nothing to assuage the dazing grief which was upon her. She crouched as though alone, staring vacantly at the wooden floor, moving her fingers nervously and occasionally moaning. Again she altered her attitude and rocked her form to and fro, uttering the while "Oh, my Johnnie! Oh, my little children! My poor, dear children! What shall I do? What shall I do?"

These feeble protestations soon ended in silence, giving way to nervous rackings, then to stillness and over the weary round again as before.

The arrival of strangers disturbed her condition at this time, and she insisted upon being taken to see her children and her husband. Accompanied by *The Republic* representative she visited the hospital. The guard having been summoned and the gate opened, she was quietly ushered up to the ward where John Finn and the dying Willie lay. Willie's cot stood close to the entrance way, where the mother could see him upon entering. Mr. Finn was screened off to himself near the east wall. Willie, who was most seriously injured, having a fractured skull, his right cheek bone broken and his lip cut, lay moaning, his head almost enveloped in bloodstained bandages. There were red life-marks upon the pillow and the white linen about.

The mother viewed the child as it lay writhing and held by two attendants. She clasped her hands above her head, and, sinking to her knees by the cot, gave vent to a flood of anguish, such as only a mother's heart must know. It wasn't with tears, nor with loud wailing that she grieved. There was a fullness of sorrow there beyond all tears.

"My Willie! My Willie! My Willie!" was her enfeebled cry. "Oh, my dying child, my poor, poor sick child! Oh, how could he do it?"

Then the very suggestion of intention on the part of her beloved husband flashed upon her as unkind and unjust to him, so sick and delirious near by. Her mind seemed to wander in its endeavor to love all into the fullness of death and give of her motherly pity in proportion. Kneeling by the dying child, bending over the blood-stained lips and feeling the numbered breathings upon her pallid cheeks, she still had heart to moan:

"He didn't mean to. Your father didn't mean to—he loved you all so. Oh, my poor child."

They lifted her from her knees by the side of the cot. They held her, leaning, while she looked love and anguish, a flood o'erpowering, back upon the suffering youth, and then took her to where the father lay. His pillow was unstained by any sign of blood, nor were there crimson spots upon the white linen that bound his wounded neck. The Doctor whispered that he was bordering upon typhoid fever and that now and then his mind wandered. One had thought that the mother's heart had exhausted all its woe over the cot of the child—that grief and love had poured itself out until there was no more. The thought was all misjudgment. It was the heart of a wife that yielded up loving words and gentle caresses to the almost insensible form breathing loud in pain.

The "John, John," almost whispered, was all of love. The "Oh, why did you do it?" was more the query of a wandering mind than of a questioning heart. She pitied and loved him as somehow the unhappy cause and victim of a world of woe.

Finn caught with the weakened, fever-drummed ear the voice of the wife and the question. He did not open his eyes, but rolled and talked as one in a restless sleep. The words as they came were sob broken and tear choked, but they told the story.

"Mary," he moaned, "my Mary. I thought it was heaven. The vision was so beautiful, so bright. It all looked so glorious and I was going. I didn't want to go alone; I couldn't go alone. Oh, Mary, it was bright—so glorious."

"I know, John," came the answer from lips pressed to kiss against the hot, wrinkled forehead; "I know, I know."

There were handkerchiefs in the hands of many as the distracted woman was led away to Johnnie and Mamie and Annie. Over in one corner a pallid patient, slowly recovering from a long illness, placed the edge of a pillow casing to the corners of his eyes and lay back again to rest.

The condition of the others were more of balm to the heart of the mother. They were conscious, not dangerously wounded, and could answer rationally the questions of the mother. By the side of Mamie, in vestments of lace and jingle, ministered a Catholic priest. A lighted candle was there, a cross and a bit of salve for annointing. The reverend father crossed the forehead, lips and limbs of the child with the salve and prayed from his book of prayers. The mother knelt by the bedside and silently joined in the appeal to the Almighty. After several hours of visiting, which was decidedly beneficial and quieting to her distracted senses, she was prevailed upon to leave, assured that all would be much improved by the morrow.

There was a pathetic scene at the City Hospital last night. A mother, who had 24 hours before been mistress of a happy home, presided over by a loving husband and father, and made bright by the prattle of four healthy, rosy children, was watching in dry-eyed sorrow over the wreck of that happy home; a husband delirious and deathly sick; two unconscious children and two acutely suffering little ones—all the victims of a frenzied father's violence.

When a *Republic* reporter was shown by Dr. Marks into the women and children's ward of the City Hospital about 10 o'clock last night, he found there Mrs. John Finn bending over the couch of her little girls. At that moment she kissed little Mamie good night, telling her that her mother must now go the the bedside of poor little Willie, who was very, very sick. The heartbroken mother went to the bedside of little Annie, while an attempt was made to get the story of the tragedy from Mamie.

"Do you know how you were hurt, Mamie?" was asked.

"No; I can't remember."

"What did your papa do to you?"

"I don't know."

"When did you see your papa last?"

"I don't know."

"Where were you when your papa struck you?"

"I don't remember."

"What did he strike you with?"

"I don't remember anything about it."

Here the attempt to get the story of the little one was given up. While seemingly perfectly conscious and coherent the mind of this 7-year-old child was apparently a blank as to all that had happened within the previous 24 hours.

Little Annie, who is but 5 years old, awaked from a light slumber as her mother bent over her and called out:

"Mamma, I want a wet wag; my head aches."

At that moment a voice came from the other cot: "Stay with me a little while longer, Mamma, won't you?"

The mother went to the child and kissed her and then said: "I must go to my poor Willie."

The sorrowful woman stood up and folded her arms and looked from cot to cot. "He was such a good husband and father," she began with utter calmness. "A kinder man never lived." She then went on to relate what she knew of the morning's tragedy.

"The little ones were all up except Johnnie. He said that his head ached and I let him stay in bed. I thought to send him for the doctor for his father, who was sick, and the boy said that he would be able to go in a little while. Oh! if I had only let him! I had given the other little ones their breakfast and the little girls had gone out to play. My poor little Willie was lying on his stomach on the bed alongside of his brother reading the baseball news in the paper when I left them. I thought that he would be company for Johnnie and I left him there. I gave my husband some ice and milk and also some to Johnnie. My husband said that when I was gone he saw the roof of the house float away, and he saw heaven open for him, but he did not want to go without the children. And then—O Lord; it is awful!" and the sorrow-stricken woman could go no further. After a moment she added:

"The boys must have been lying down or they could have gotten away. The little girls must have heard their brothers' cries and ran into the house. It was all done when I came back. If they had only told me that it was dangerous to leave him alone while he had a fever!"

The reporter then went to the bedside of Johnnie, the eldest boy. He was entirely unconscious. A trip was made to some of the other wards, and finally the room was reached in which John Finn, Sr., and little Willie were stretched on cots. The man lay on his back with his hands strapped to the bedstead, as he had shown signs of delirium. A sturdy police officer watched by his side, and the sick man's wife was also there, dividing her attention between her delirious husband and her unconscious, perhaps dying, son. The latter was burning with fever and his breath was coming in gasps. His mutilated face was horrible to look upon. His poor mother came to Dr. Marks as the latter felt the child's pulse and inquired plaintively:

"Will my poor little Willie die?"

"We can't tell; he is very sick," was the response.

The white bandage around John Finn's throat entirely concealed his rather slight wound. His features were intelligent and not peculiar in appearance. He was suffering from a high fever, and, as he had been restless, was being placed under the influence of opiates. The Doctor said that earlier in the evening Finn's hallucination left him and he had realized the full enormity of what he had done. It seemed to trouble him a great deal and soon made him restless and delirious. His wound is not serious.

John Finn is a man 58 years old and a native of Ireland. He has been in America some 50 years and in St. Louis nearly 30 years. When he first came he was a teamster, but later became a streetcar driver on the Chouteau avenue line. The first car that went out of the Chouteau avenue barns when that line was established was driven by Finn. He drove a horse car and afterwards became a motorman on the same line. He was of a careful, saving disposition.

About 14 years ago he married and 12 years ago moved into the house at 2828 Chouteau avenue. Since that time he has bought and paid for the property, laid by payments for six years on 30 shares of Building and Loan stock, and is in excellent financial condition generally. He was known among his friends and neighbors as a peaceful, genial, gentlemanly fellow. To his family, according to his wife, he was exceedingly kind and loved his children dearly. All of them are devoted Catholics. The family is highly respected.

The only conclusion that can be drawn from the facts developed is that Finn was temporarily insane from typhoid fever and not responsible for his action.

Subscribers to *The Republic* who were served by Mr. John Finn will please notify the office at once if the paper is not received promptly. Mr. Meusendieck, the former carrier, has charge of the delivery for the present.

[9 August 1893, pp. 1–2.]

55 - ALMOST A RIOT.

The contest between Jules Wallace, spiritual medium, and J. Alexander McIvor Tyndall, mind-reader and hypnotist, at Hagan Opera House last night, culminated in one of the most dramatic scenes, real or assumed, that was ever witnessed in a public entertainment in this city. If it was premeditated between the principals—and there are those cold-blooded enough to declare that it was—it was a remarkable piece of acting on their part and the execution of the conception must stamp Tyndall and Wallace as the greatest actors of modern times. Starting quietly enough, except for the apparent enmity between the principals, it would have culminated in a riot but for the firm insistence of Mr. O. L. Hagan, owner of the theater, that Wallace leave the stage and that the audience disperse.

The attendance was unusual for the season and the unsystematic character of the advance advertising—a fact that goes to show that many hundreds of people are intensely interested in psychology and allied sciences. Undoubtedly those who firmly believe in spiritual mediums were in a majority; but most of these were quiet, sober people, who would have felt no especial jubilation over the downfall of a man who had declared their medium to be a fraud. On the other hand, there were those present who seemed to sympathize heartily in the pugnacious attitude that Wallace assumed, from the start, and the feeling engendered between these and another large contingent in the audience that apparently wished only to see an honest "show" was what threatened to create trouble. Had Tyndall at the last been physically able to charge what many who sympathized with him charged in his behalf—namely, that Wallace had put him under hypnotic influence at the most critical stage in his performance—there is no doubt that Wallace would have been accommodated with all the trouble he seemed to court. But while Wallace was standing in the center of the stage waving his floral ship and harp, and giving the audience back hiss for hiss and epithet for epithet, poor Tyndall was lying by the stage door gasping, gurgling and groaning, while two skillful physicians, adepts in the treatment of mental and nervous disease, were trying to restore him from a profound cataleptic state. If those who composed the audience paid for excitement and diversion they have no cause to complain that they did not get the worth of their money—there was excitement and to spare.

Hagan's Opera House was quite comfortably filled at 8:20, when the curtain rolled up and disclosed a stage set for a small orchestra. The audience did not seem to take kindly to the appearance of a trio of musicians bearing mandolins and guitar, and who rendered two Spanish airs with tolerable effect. The audience simply endured this prelude. They were evidently of a mind to cheer Wallace when he sidled out from the wings to make his introductory speech. He was a little nervous, but he soon got settled in his professional harness, and told how, last Sunday night, he had been called a fraud and challenged to a public test by Tyndall. He had faced many audiences in this city, given many tests, and never yet failed. He felt sure of being able to convince everyone present that his mediumship was genuine if he were only given fair play. Wallace several times repeated the words "fair play," and seemed to fear that his audience had been packed by Tyndall.

When Tyndall came on he was suffering from evident embarrassment and his introductory speech throughout was hesitating. He admitted that he had called the genuineness of Wallace's alleged spirit manifestations into question; and said that if they were genuine they were the first genuine manifestations he had witnessed in 25 years' experience with so-called spiritual mediums. But he was far more temperate in his speech and manner than Wallace had been, as well as less boastful and pugnacious. Tyndall said that he would take his place in the audience while Wallace was giving his tests, and when the medium had finished he would try to reproduce some of his tests by the process of mind-reading. He did not try to create the impression that Wallace was a fraud, further than in endeavoring to pass off hypnotism and mind-reading for spiritual mediumship. Having thus introduced himself, he retired to one of the boxes on the left side of the house to await the tests that Wallace would furnish.

When Wallace reappeared he was accompanied by the three musicians who had opened the entertainment. The audience began to hiss, as though they expected that some claptrap was intended by this, whereupon Wallace advanced to the footlights and made a testy little speech, in which he said that only two of the brute creation—snakes and geese—were addicted to the habit of hissing, and he hoped that his audience would not sink to the level of either. He sat down near the back of the stage, and while the trio of musicians thrummed a plaintive air, he rubbed his eyes and temples with the tips of his fingers as persons of his profession do when endeavoring to arrive at the clairvoyant state. Presently he arose and the music ceased.

Wallace advanced to the front of the stage and began his performance by appearing to materialize the spirit of "Gladys Lancaster," whose spirit was apparently recognized by a lady in the center section of seats right under Wallace's eye. Wallace read off what purported to be the communication of an affectionate little girl to her parents and grandparents, and at the close on his inquiring whether he had interpreted correctly he was informed that he had. Without comment, further than to thank the ladies and gentlemen who had assisted him, Wallace proceeded to materialize the spirits of a number of persons of both sexes, and apparently widely varying stations in the earth life, as he called it. When he called out "Ross Weder" there was a little shriek from the gallery, and Wallace proceeded to unfold a few chapters of private family history, of no particular interest to the audience, but replete with detail that no one but the one to whom the test was made might be reasonably supposed to know anything about. It may be unfortunate for Mr. Wallace that he materialized this particular wraith at this particular time, but be that as it may, a little byplay was observed here that the public is entitled to have the benefit of. There was a strong suggestion of collusion between the medium and this particular person. The lady occupied a seat one row back from the front seat of the balcony, and she had been accompanied to the theater by Prof. W. R. Colby, the slate-writer, although Colby left his fair charge at the entrance. She was fashionably dressed, a person of fine presence, and would have looked better in a box than in the retired place she occupied. She was the only lady in that part of the house. Presently she was joined by another fashionably dressed lady who had been occupying a box with intimate friends of Wallace, including that gentleman's landlady. When the name of "Ross Woder" was mentioned the lady who had first found her place in the balcony gave a little shriek, covered her face with her hands and heard the unfolding of the tale with apparent great emotion. The part was well played, both by the lady originally addressed and the one who joined her, but there is not the least ground to doubt the previous friendly feeling between the medium and the persons who assisted this "test," though very few in the audience saw anything below the surface.

Mr. Wallace's next test was a hard one. He materialized the spirit of Wash Stevenson and Clarence Wilson, telling a dramatic story in the case of each, and the truth of this was vouched for by Major Charles Osborne, well known as the St. Louis representative of the Western Associated Press, who rose in his place and stated that a letter to which Wallace had referred, and a part of the contents of which he had repeated, had been received only yesterday morning by himself and wife from a relative now attending the Spiritualists' National Convention. This confirmation by a man so well and favorably known as Mr. Osborne sent the Wallace stock up like a well-inflated balloon, and simultaneous with the applause that followed this confirmation a basket of sunflowers came through the box where Tyndall was sitting and was received by Wallace as a matter of course. If he had known it was coming he could not have evinced less surprise.

Wallace went on, giving test after test and telling a variety of stories, not all of them particularly edifying or delicate, but replete with detail, which seemed to be what the audience was hankering for. Wallace now proceeded to give Tyndall a test, reciting facts that the mind-reader admitted were facts, and describing, truthfully, according to Tyndall's own admissions, the grave of Tyndall's mother in Lancashire, England, as well as the home of Tyndall's boyhood. Tyndall said, however, that spiritualism had nothing to do with it, and that when he got a chance upon the stage he would try to explain the processes by which Wallace had reached his alleged results, and to repeat some of his tests by the process of mind-reading.

Medium Wallace kept the stage some time longer with his tests, and then gave place to Tyndall. The latter began his part of the affair by calling for a jury, and experienced much trouble in getting persons willing to act. Finally the following named persons had accepted seats on the stage to act in this capacity: E. L. McDowell, G. Cramer, H. B. Morse, Captain H. R. Whitmore, O. L. Hagan, T. Hostetter and Dr. J. K. Bauduy.

After all preliminaries had been settled, one of the committee went into the audience and after the exercise of great caution, and making a speech in confirmation of his impartiality, picked out a fine-looking gentleman on one of the center aisles, and induced him to stand up before the whole audience. Tyndall was now blindfolded by other members of the committee, and taking the hand of the guide, started nervously forward for the stage steps. Down these he plunged headlong, as though guided by a definite impulse, but his guide faltered at the steps, and in doing so apparently withdrew his attention from the identity of the gentleman whom Tyndall was trying to locate. This caused Tyndall to pull him back upon the stage and a new start was made. Now, one of the phenomena of mind reading manifested itself. In starting back through the house Tyndall took the same course that his guide had taken in locating the subject, and made his stops in exactly the same places. He made two or three guesses without committing himself, but finally pushed through a long tier of seats and laid his hand on the gentleman's head with an air of certainty that was simply inexplicable to those who had followed his actions. He had completed his first test with every appearance of fairness, and the audience proceeded to give him credit.

Tyndall next found, after some hesitation and changing of guides a pin that had been set in the side of a chair on the stage; and before completing this test he asked the committeemen who were assisting to show the chair with the pin in it to the audience. At this there were cries of derision from the audience, but there was no occasion for them, as the whole thing was done noiselessly and without possible hint being conveyed to Tyndall.

Tyndall now, after some trouble, located Dr. Bauduy, who had theoretically murdered a newspaper reporter with a penknife, and also found the "victim," brought him on the stage and showed how the "stabbing" had been done. It was a severe test, but the details which accompanied it almost preclude possibility of conveying information to Tyndall, and certainly no one dreamed of charging collusion on the part of his assistants.

The grand riot, the climax of enthusiasm, the wild division of sentiment, came when Prof. Tyndall concluded the cigar test. That test was an exact duplicate of the one given on Change Wednesday morning, when Tyndall dashed hither and thither through an excited crowd, guided only by the mental inspiration that came through the hand of the guide who had placed the cigar in the mouth of the man to be found. Last night he did the same, only under far more exciting circumstances. By the dozen or more tests of Wallace and his own exciting tests had the crowd been aroused. By the glare of many lights, the vivacity of motion, the constant risings and sittings and by the calling to and fro of the people was the crowd now moved to a condition of tiptoe enthusiasm. The committee of six on the stage were up and moving to and fro, excitedly talking. Newspaper men numbering a dozen, were talking of the tests. Mr. Tyndall, his long, dark hair one wavy mass of disorder, his collar wet and wilted, his clothing in graceful disarray and the sweat standing out in beads on his brow, walked to the stage front and said: "Ladies and gentlemen—my next test will be with a cigar. I propose to find the holder of a cigar which anyone present may take down into the audience and place in anyone's mouth. I will be blindfolded, will take the hand of the person knowing where the man is who sits with the cigar in his mouth and will find him. Will two of the committee please blindfold me?"

Ollie Hagan and Mr. T. Hostetter stepped forward. With them Mr. Tyndall retired to the left dressing-room, where he was duly blindfolded.

While they were preparing Mr. Tyndall, another member of the committee, took a cigar, descended into the parquet and going to a young gentleman sitting in the center of the second orchestra row, asked him to kindly hold the cigar between his lips until Mr. Tyndall came to relieve him. He consented, and someone on the stage called "Ready!"

Then came a very interesting scene. Mr. Tyndall was led out on the stage by a *Republic* representative. He stood as one nervously searching in the dark. His form was slightly stooped, his head pushed forward as though scenting for a trail. His arms and extremities were nervously lax and his long white fingers moved as one might imagine those of a maniac or a murderer to move as they neared the throat of the hapless victim. The man who knew where the cigar was, Mr. Cramer, a gray-haired, middle-aged gentleman, came forward and took Mr. Tyndall's hand. Just as he was about to take it Tyndall jumped, his arm drew back as from an electric shock and he inquired:

"Do you know where the cigar is?"

"I do," said the guide.

"Come with me; think of where it is at the same time," said Tyndall.

The guide or magnet, as the man who knew might be called, acquiesced, and hurried after Tyndall. The search began. Tyndall, blindfolded, led the way. Cramer followed. Tyndall had a tight grip on the wrist of Cramer and seemed to drag him along. Tyndall began queer, exciting movements in different directions, dashing now 2 feet this way and 10 feet that until he finally made a quick dash for the little ladder step that led down into the orchestra circle and thence out in the aisles of the parquet. In going down the steps he slipped and jumped, dragging his "guide" after him. Then began the incomparable hunt, the wandering to and fro that ended so dramatically.

It seems as though something was wrong. With one hand outstretched as though drawing a current of electricity or thought out of the very air, and the other nervously fidgeting with the hand of his follower, Tyndall moved on. To some heads he was attracted, by others seemingly repelled. Now he seemed to have a scent—to know—and so dashed away, drawing his excited attendant after him. Again he seemed to lose the trail and stood as a hound within a trackless field—scenting the ground and the air. At such moments he trembled nervously, worked the fingers of his hands and excitedly brushed his long hair back as if to think. All the time he was depending upon the correct thinking, the concentrated realization on the part of his follower as to just where the cigar was. That individual must have wavered mentally. The excitement of being hurried to and fro in a large audience must have made him forget ever and again the object of all the seeking, the aim of all the nervous thinking, of his leader. If it was not so Tyndall's action stands inexplicable.

At first then, coming down the steps, Cramer must have thought of the smoker near by, for Tyndall seemed to feel his presence. His white hands reached out that way and led him towards it. Then a thought probably came to Cramer about the queerness of it all, the crowd—also most anything but the cigar. Instantly Tyndall stopped as if lost. He moved tremulously, but made for no point. Then Cramer took up the thought of the cigar again. Instantly was Tyndall enlivened. His return was accompanied by a dash that was merely broken by the objects about, and so it went. To regain the proper scent often Tyndall would lead his "thinker" far up the aisle to the rear of the house. As certainly would Cramer say to himself mentally, "This is wrong. He is taking me away." Then Tyndall, finding that his "thinker's" mind was concentrated, would realize that the cigar was down somewhere close to the front, and would return.

His work was, however, fruitless, and he was compelled to give up the hunt with Cramer and call for someone else who knew of the whereabouts of the cigar. The someone came—some young fellow out of the audience. This person seemed possessed of more power of connected thinking, for now Tyndall wandered no more. He did not dash around the outer aisles of the theater, but hovered like a humming bird near that front aisle—near the cigar. The whole test became thrillingly interesting. The audience was on its feet, breathless and leaning forward. There was silence—all but the footfalls of the blinded seeker and his mental guide.

Then came the awful climax—a demon-like contest—a battle of eyes so fire-like, so masterful, so charmful as of a glittering venomous snake that later it all but produced a riot. While Tyndall was hurrying to and fro, Jules Wallace on the stage left the crowd of newspaper men and walked to a chair next to the stage table. Here he sat down unobserved and alone. All eyes centered on the mind-reader moving to and fro before the stage. Then Wallace began to look, to gaze, to stare. His face straightened itself as if one of those professed trances was upon him. His arms straightened out, and he, too, nervously moved his slim fingers. Letting go, the drops of sweat came out on his forehead, and his face grew deathly pale and his eyes increased their vividness. It seemed as though all the fire of his being centered in those eyes. Like the diamond optics of the idol Juggernaut, as the straining, glittering magnets in the head of the cobra, shone those green grey moons from his own forehead and the gaze fell constantly, cat-like, snake-like upon the face and the movements of Tyndall. He was steady, crouching, straining—in reality he was charming, mesmerizing, hypnotizing the mind-reader. So he sat and stared and charmed, but few saw him.

Tyndall below seemed faltering. Now he gained a clew, and darting along the row of chairs stood, as it were, trembling before his victim. The lips of the audience gave vent to a half-smothered cry of gladness and surprise at his success in locating the object. It was then that Tyndall faltered. His hand moved out and waved as a wind-shaken reed before him. It sought that tingling force that should rise up and proclaim the object. Back of him was Wallace and gleaming upon him were the eyes of green that were sapping away the "force" for which the mind-reader sought. The scene was terrific. Then Tyndall drew back the hand, filled with uncertainty and moved on. Once he came; twice, and again a third time, right before the object, the goal of his almost frantic searching, but ever those eyes on the stage were there, shining down upon him like fire-lighted moonstones, and—he failed.

After the third passage past the object he moved south towards the lower proscenium box. As he neared the place he wavered—even staggered. He reached the little stage ladder, placed one foot on it, flung up both arms and fell a dead heap to the floor. As he sank the eyes of Wallace lingered on, glaring demonlike at the place where his form had stood. The battle was over—Tyndall had collapsed.

As he fell, the crowd about rose. From the stage a dozen lookers-on dashed down and from the parquet a hundred ran forward. They gathered about the prostrate form; some brought water, others bottles and clothes. Then arose a crying and a calling. Its burden was "Wallace! Look at Wallace. See his eyes! Watch Wallace. Drive him off the stage. Off! Off! You demon! See his eyes."

In an instant all eyes were upon him—an excellent actor; fakir or a genuine hypnotist and mystic; one of the two—that was the later decision. But they the crowd only saw the stout, Irish build leaning far forward, the white jeweled hands outstretched and moving nervously; the muscles of the face white and tight drawn, but the eyes flashing, drawing, as though seeking to drag forward some unwilling object.

In response to the cries men moved toward Wallace and spoke to him.

Then he came to and straightened up. By this time the audience had judged him most a demon. The crowd despised him and yelled for revenge. They hissed and wailed and groaned. "Get off the stage," yelled one, "Stand aside, you demon!" cried a second. "Out with him! Down with him! Away!" The uproar became tremendous. Men roared and cursed and reached out their clinched fists as Wallace arose and smilingly strolled aside. Then the crowd lifted up Tyndall, bore him on kind shoulders onto the stage and through the stage entrance into the open air. Later a carriage came and removed the prostrate form to the St. James Hotel.

When both medium and mind-reader were off the stage the audience divided itself into factions and took yelling sides with Wallace and Tyndall. They called one another names and cried the names of their temporary favorites. In the midst of the prolonged excitement Wallace came forth again. He was greeted with a mingled storm of hisses and applause. The same wild calls and cheers arose and in its midst there he stood with folded arms, cool, erect, smiling. When urged to withdraw, he said, "No! No!! I'll stay here now," and stay he did. When the crowd stopped yelling he began to talk. As he did so a woman arose and attempted to talk. She stood for a few seconds and at last the crowd listened. She said her name was Fisher, and that Wallace had given her a test. Then she began to speak of the paper she had prepared for him and of her not believing in his work. At that point Wallace interrupted with:

"My good woman—"

"Let her talk!" yelled one.

"D—— you, leave her alone, you scoundrel!" shouted another.

"You fake, let her speak!" yelled a third.

It was no use. The uproar and Wallace's little sentence completed the work. She never completed her story and probably never will, publicly.

Wallace then resumed his speech. He declared that Tyndall had failed. He was about to be greeted with another insane outburst, when the manager ordered the lights out and the whole thrilling affair closed in darkness and disorder.

Mr. Tyndall was taken from the theater to his room at the St. James Hotel, where Drs. J. K. and S. Keating Bauduy of 2808 Olive street at once commenced work on him. He was quickly stripped and the physicians rubbed him and pulled him and applied what they termed counter-hypnotic treatment. Mr. Tyndall continued in the cataleptic state for about an hour, coming to himself at 11:30 p.m. During the hour whenever one of his limbs was moved it would remain in whatever position it was placed—thus when his arm was raised to remove his coat it remained at right angles to his body until placed by his side again. His first words on regaining consciousness were:

"Why does he look at me so?"

When seen by *The Republic* representative at midnight he complained of great weakness and showed it. He also said he had a peculiar feeling in his head and felt feverish. He drank several glasses of iced water and continually asked for more. He was extremely sore from his heavy fall. There is a large bruise at the back of his head and a still larger and more painful bruise on his back at the base of the spine. A gentleman present expressed the greatest wonder that Mr. Tyndall's back was not broken by the fall. He will probably be confined to his room for several days.

Mr. Tyndall was hardly in condition to give any detailed explanation as to the cause of the failure of his last test. He said it was unaccountable to him, as he usually accomplishes it with lightninglike rapidity. He seemed disposed to attribute it to an overstrain as he has not been well for several days. There are others, however, including the gentleman already referred to, who indignantly insist that Wallace's undue influence and his grossly unfair attitude and manner on the stage had an effect on Mr. Tyndall's supersensitive mind. The latter's first words on coming to himself would tend to justify this theory.

[11 August 1893, pp. 1–2.]

56 - THEY MET AND—LUNCHED.

An ominous calm reigned in the hypnoto-telepatho-mesmero-clairvoyant world of St. Louis yesterday, in marked contrast to the tempest that shook it on the night previous. On-lookers watched with bated breath for a renewal of the battle of the psychic giants, but the aforesaid p. g. had decreed otherwise, and instead of bathing the peaceful sward with each other's life blood, as many had feared they would, they hunted each other up and—went to lunch together. First Medium Wallace called at the St. James Hotel to inquire after the health of Mind-reader Tyndall, and then Mind-reader Tyndall went out on the Olive street cable cars and made a friendly division of the door receipts with Medium Wallace.

No challenges are out at the moment of closing the forms.

Mr. Tyndall complained of feeling sore and faint, as the result of his severe trial of the night before; and Mr. Wallace expressed his willingness to go before a notary and swear that he had not hypnotized Tyndall, and that, as far as he was aware, he was not in possession of the hypnotic gift. Mr. Tyndall would not charge that he had been hypnotized by anybody while giving his telepathic tests, but simply said that all of Thursday night, before and after his recovery from the state of hypnotic catalepsy into which he so unexpectedly fell, he was conscious of being under the gaze of a pair of large eyes. But he could not say that they were the eyes of his late opponent. Tyndall, contrary to the fear of all those who saw him fall from the steps of the stage of the theater, seemed but little the worse for the experience except in the particular stated, and he spent most of the day walking about the center of the city, trying to keep his mind off his experience, and to find respite from the whole unpleasant episode. He has telegraphed for his wife, who is now in New York, to meet him in Chicago a few days hence.

It is not impossible that Tyndall and Wallace may arrange another meeting—not to say contest. In the presence of a representative of *The Republic*, Wallace challenged Tyndall to meet him in a similar engagement in any city in the country for $1,000 a side or upward. Tyndall did not say he would accept, and seemed to studiously avoid, while in Wallace's company, any reference to the alleged dispute that had brought them together before the public. The manner in which this challenge was broached and received was not calculated to increase belief in the good faith of the first meeting, although both the principals insist that the meeting was in good faith. Tyndall's speedy recovery from his apparently dangerous catalepsy and Wallace's equally speedy convalescence from the apparently dangerous mood of combativeness in which he was on Thursday night, surprised even their acquaintances and showed them that their enmity was almost wholly professional and that when face to face in private they could communicate upon the plane of friendly equals.

Wallace told a *Republic* reporter that the lady who assisted to increase the excitement in the theater after Tyndall's prostration was one to whom he had accorded a sitting, and who had taken exceptions to some things he had told her respecting her family affairs; and he insisted that her interference on Thursday night was prompted by a desire for revenge. He was at home to social callers, but declined to give any private sittings. In the front yard of the boarding-house where he holds forth were set, conspicuously, the floral offerings which were passed over the footlights to him on Thursday night, and they attracted a great deal of attention, not so much, perhaps, for their beauty, as for the unusual disposition that had been made of them.

Mr. Wallace gave *The Republic* representative an opportunity of calling upon Mrs. Charles Osborne, who permitted her visitors to read the letter from Mrs. Osborne's niece, which letter Wallace outlined from the stage on Thursday night. Mrs. Osborne assured the reporter that Mr. Wallace had not seen the letter up to the time of his interpreting it through alleged spirit power.

Something as to the alleged hypnotic interference of Wallace with Tyndall's experiments is of interest. At the moment when Tyndall was making his desperate, and almost successful efforts to find the young man who held the cigar in his mouth, Wallace was sitting at the rear center of the stage staring, in a peculiar way directly at his opponent. At Wallace's side was one of the jurors, a man named Hostetter, who is a massage operator, and presumably somewhat skilled in hypnotic treatment. The instant Tyndall fell unconscious beside the stage Hostetter shouted: "He has been hypnotized," and immediately turned to Wallace. The latter had not moved from his position, and still stared with frightful intensity toward the spot where

Tyndall had stood last. Hostetter at once made three or four downward passes in front of Wallace's face, saying each time: "Wake up," and after the third or fourth pass Wallace gave a start, seemed for a brief instant dazed, and then ran from the stage. This incident may or may not indicate that Wallace was doing a little hypnotizing on his own account, but it is absolutely true.

The opinion of Dr. Jerome K. Bauduy was sought yesterday as to the net results of the contest between Wallace and Tyndall. It having been asserted that Tyndall was in a hypnotic, as well as cataleptic, condition toward the end of his experiments, and that Wallace had hypnotized him, Dr. Bauduy was asked:

"Was Mr. Tyndall in an ordinary cataleptic trance or paroxysm when you were called to his side in Hagan's Opera House?"

"No; he was in a profound stage of hypnotic catalepsy."

"What do you mean by 'hypnotic catalepsy?'"

"It is the most intensified and developed stage of the hypnotic condition."

"What is your opinion as to the cause of the profoundly developed state which you believe him to have been in?"

"There are two causes which will suffice to explain it. In the first place, the present developments of hypnotic science to my mind incontestably prove that all manifestations of developed mesmeric trance and other varieties of hypnotism, clairvoyance, clairaudience and the subjective mental phenomena of first-class mediums are primarily the result of autohypnotism. In other words, all psychic phenomena, no matter how produced, are the result of the universal law of suggestion, which is invariably present in such conditions. In order to get into the hypnotic condition for the development of all the above mentioned phenomenal mental conditions the operator subjects himself to an autohypnotic process, which may become more and more intensified during the progression of the varying stages of hypnotic developments by his increasing power of hypnotic suggestion. Last night Tyndall performed his clever feats of mind reading by telepathy, or thought transference, in consequence of the hypnotic condition super-induced by his own efforts; and had he not been in that hypnotic state all his efforts at mind reading would have been abortive.

"Secondly, the hypnotic condition in which he deliberately placed himself in order to successfully perform his experiments may have been intensified through the agency of another hypnotizer."

"Then, please state whether, in your opinion, Wallace succeeded by his own individual efforts in intensifying Tyndall's already developed hypnotic condition."

"This is a very difficult question to fairly answer. Of course, such may possibly have been the case, but of the positive correctness of this view no third party can authoritatively state. The reason is obvious. Hypnotism is obtainable through mental influences mutually reciprocal between the hypnotizer and the recipient. And all hypnotic processes pertain to the domain of mental influences, and are more or less allied in character to Nature's great imponderables, not appreciable by the standard of the objective senses of outside witnesses. In other words, to the latter thought transference, telepathy or hypnotic conditions cannot be measured by a sense-standard of appreciation. They are not ponderable, visible, sensible, tangible or auditory in character; therefore cannot be perceived or appreciated by the spectator or witness presented during the hypnotic seance."

"Would Tyndall's declaration that he had been hypnotically influenced by Wallace during the last experiment possess any weight with you—Tyndall's personal honor not being questioned?"

"I am not in a position to affirm or deny his statement, but I certainly think that Mr. Tyndall's statement in this respect is fully entitled to credibility."

"Do you consider that Mr. Tyndall's cataleptic state which terminated the seance was genuine?"

"I am not, of course, infallible in my opinion, but if I have ever witnessed a genuine cataleptic collapse in my life it certainly existed in Mr. Tyndall's case last night—the multiplicity and concurrence of all his symptoms strongly pointing in this direction. My son and myself exhausted all ordinary medical means to restore him to a normal condition, and they all failed, and he was eventually restored to his normal state by the well-known principle in hypnotic science of 'counter suggestion,' which all modern writers on this subject recognize as the most effectual means of restoration from the condition of profound hypnotic catalepsy."

"Do you believe that Wallace's tests were successful?"

"I certainly do; but they, in my opinion, resulted from human intelligence, and not from the extra-mundane influence of disembodied spirits. I think Mr. Wallace has extraordinary hypnotic or mesmeric power, and he is an excellent mind-reader by clairvoyance accomplished through the ordinary laws of telepathy. The man who denies the physical phenomena of spiritism to-day is not entitled to be called a skeptic—he is simply ignorant; and it would be a hopeless task to attempt to enlighten him. But the origin of these phenomena can be accounted for on rational principles, thus removing them from the realm of the supernatural. Modern scientists have an easy way of treating such phenomena, which consists in denying their existence, refusing to investigate. Truly, as Hudson claims, such men would plug their own ears and deny the phenomenon of thunder if they could not account for it by reference to laws with which they are familiar. And such a proceeding would be no more senseless than, at this day, to deny the phenomena of spiritism. In my opinion, however, all the phenomena of spiritism can be accounted for on the ground that living man possesses inherently the power to produce them; and, as Hudson concludes, there is a dynamic force residing somewhere that is capable of moving ponderable objects without physical contact; and that this force, whatever it is, or from whatever source it emanates, possesses intelligence, oftentimes to a remarkable degree. Now this intelligent force either emanates from the spirits of the dead or it does not. If it does not it necessarily follows that it emanates from the living. That this last supposition is the true one is evidenced by many of the characteristics of the intelligence which it manifests, but it would not be appropriate to enter here into the discussion of this question."

[12 August 1893, p. 5.]

57 - BLINDFOLDED HE DROVE.

Alexander G. McIvor Tyndall, the mind reader, executed, blindfolded, last evening one of his most difficult feats—that of driving a victoria through the crowded streets of St. Louis and finding a certain fixed object of which he was previously unaware.

At 2:30 p.m. there gathered in the rotunda of the Southern two well-known local artists, Messrs. Dick Wood and McCord, Dr. J. Keating Bauduy, Mr. Tyndall and *The Republic* spirit editor. Mr. Tyndall made the assertion of being able to drive, blindfolded, through the streets and locate any object, wheresoever placed. The proof of the statement was called for—and Mr. Tyndall ordered a carriage.

While the victoria and pair was being brought the company adjourned to a parlor above and arranged the details. By a toss of pennies *The Republic*'s representative was delegated to watch Mr. Tyndall. Messrs. Bauduy, Wood and McCord stepped into an adjoining room and prepared the details. It was arranged among themselves that the carriage should drive from the Walnut street entrance of the Southern east to Third street, thence one block south to Elm, west to Seventh street, north to Olive, one-half block east to the alley between Sixth and Seventh streets, south through that to Pine, east on Pine to Broadway and south on Broadway to No. 119, where the room of Mr. Wood is located.

In it, on the dresser, stands a head of Alley Sloper, and this, per agreement, Mr. Tyndall was to find. Having arranged the details and fixed them well in mind, the trio returned to the parlor. The spirit editor of *The Republic* was taken aside and told the proposed route. By this time Mr. Tyndall's eyes had been covered with a double bandage of a white and black handkerchief, which all pronounced sufficiently opaque. Then Mr. Wood, whose room was the object sought, agreed to mount the box with Mr. Tyndall and act as his mental guide. The remaining gentlemen of the party took seats in the body of the carriage.

Mr. Tyndall grasped the reins and the exciting drive began. His quick, jerky rush down the stairs and across the sidewalk had attracted the attention of a great number, and a crowd was massed in an instant.

Tyndall drew tight the reins, swung the horses about, and then, perceiving his error, completed the swinging circle and headed the pair in a gallop towards Third street. As he neared the corner of Walnut and Third the occupants of the carriage bent their thoughts upon the course and mentally following their thinking, Mr. Tyndall turned the team south to Elm. In a little while the horses were running a stiff pace west to Seventh street and north to Pine, where an error occurred. Mr. Tyndall drove east into Pine street and north on Sixth to Seventh, but there his guide mentally arranged a course differing slightly from the one previously arranged, and to this thereafter the mind reader closely adhered. At every step of the speedy team's course the people on the streets halted and stared. The blindfolded figure was a curiosity to them all. Men gazed wide-eyed after the disappearing vehicle, women stopped and children ran after it for blocks.

On Olive street the carriage all but collided with an east-bound cable car. On Seventh street it rubbed hubs with a great lumbering truck, and in a dozen other places narrowly escaped collision. Eventually, after much mental excitement on the part of all, Mr. Tyndall turned in on Broadway and drove due south to the number desired. The mind reader during the entire drive was seemingly calm, and it was only his tightened grip on the reins and the muscular tension of his drawn limbs that augured differently.

The final rush came at the furnished room house, No. 119 South Broadway. The building is directly opposite "Tony Faust's" and the room wherein the Alley Sloper head stands dusty and silent on the top of a musty dresser is just back of what would be the front parlor of a regulation flat. Its door is just south of the top of the first stair landing, and its only window looks out on Elm street. The lock of the door is one of the Yale pattern and the key a small, flat piece of nickel, making it quite hard to locate and insert.

The victoria dashed south on Broadway quite rapidly, almost rubbed its polished hubs against a north-bound cable grip, and swung around the corner into Elm street. Here Tyndall abruptly drew up, leaped from the box and dragged his intensely interested satellite after him. He was immediately surrounded as before by a crowd of passers-by, who danced along after him, almost frantic in their efforts to see it all. The strain of his hurried tugging pulled a ring off the right hand of his guide. That individual did not notice it, but Tyndall did. He drew up with that short, nervous jerk and hurriedly mumbled, "I've lost my ring!—no, you have." Delay could not be tolerated, however, and the ring was left to be found by others.

Turning from the search for the ring Tyndall seized the wrist of his guide and half sprang, half ran, towards the southeast corner of Broadway and Elm, turned hurriedly and dashed up the stairway. The gathered crowd did not hesitate to follow. The stairway at that number is tall and dark. Midway in its height the road is half barred by a storm door and above this the shadow is complete. The darkness offered no impediment, however, to the mind reader. His sensitive touch divined all and in a trice he was on the main landing, excitedly fumbling at the lock and knob.

"The key! The key!" he exclaimed. A bunch was handed him. He found the right one and in a moment opened the door. Against the east wall of the room, which at the time was well darkened by the drawn blinds, stood a tall, dark dresser, and on the top a stuffed goose. On the head of his long since spiritualized gooseship rested the head of "Alley Sloper," a gaunt, disfigured face of brown plaster. Towards this dresser hurried the mind reader, passed his hands up and down the front of the dresser, along the door front and finally touched the body of the goose.

"That's enough," said one, feeling the test satisfactory.

"No, higher!" exclaimed the mind reader, and, leaping again, touched the face of Alley Sloper. The test was complete. Everybody was satisfied and Mr. Tyndall was pleased.

[18 August 1893, p. 1.]

58 - HE GOT A RIDE.

Either a most diabolical outrage was yesterday committed upon one of St. Louis' prominent merchants, Mr. Austin M. Nelson, president of the A. M. Nelson Paint Company, or the police of the Third District have been guilty of gross negligence in a matter of serious criminal import. A very serious accusation, by implication at least, was made against Mr. Nelson by officers of the Third District yesterday afternoon, and that gentleman was carted off from the rear of a vacant dwelling at 601 North Levee in a hoodlum wagon, accompanied by an unknown negro girl about 9 years of age. The arrest of Mr. Nelson was the cause of a scene of excitement, and was attended by sensational features. At the Third District Station, where Mr. Nelson was arraigned before Captain Joyce, the latter official saw fit to set him at liberty and discharge the negro girl without taking either her name or address.

The whole exciting incident occurred at 3 o'clock yesterday afternoon in the rear of 601 North Levee. The rear of North Levee street is partially an alley and partially a business street, which the City Directory gives as Commercial street. At that number on North Levee, which lies between Washington avenue and Lucas avenue, a plain, faded two-story brick stands. Just south of it the tunnel passes out into the bridge. South of this tunnel, facing on Washington avenue and with its west wall forming a portion of the Commercial alley line, stands a three-story brick structure that backs close up against the Eads tunnel as though trying to crowd it out. It is very old, very musty and unoccupied, except for the garret-like third floor, which some colored children playing below said was occupied by one Mrs. Clark, colored. The second floor has long been vacant, as well as the ground floor, which has long since been a Levee saloon. The walls of the place are much smoked and dingy, the floor rotten and bulging from damp in places. The entrance to the upper floor is by a covered rear stairway of black rotten wood, which is decidedly dark and filthy. It was on the second floor landing of this stairway that Mr. Nelson was found by Officers Callaghan and McInerny of the Third District. With him was the now untraceable negro girl, 9 years old, who is supposed by some neighbors to live in the vicinity of Sixth and Cerre streets. The two officers named were standing on the Levee, near Lucas avenue, when a stranger came forward and informed them that he had observed a strange man going up the stairway in question in company with a negro girl. He hinted at a monstrous crime and the two officers started to go with him. By the time they reached Commercial street and Lucas avenue Officer Kirhen joined them and the three proceeded towards the dark stairway. The neighborhood in question is a mixture of wholesale houses and dwellings. The class of residents there is decidedly conglomerate and, according to the police, very "hard." The progress of the officers south through Commercial street attracted a crowd that grew to fully 500 people, who somehow had got the idea that a great outrage had been perpetrated and passed the word about until the crowd became a mob following and centering about the bluecoats. When the officers came to the stairway all three entered and soon returned with Mr. Nelson and the girl, the latter carrying a lemon basket. Then some one in the crowd yelled, "Lynch him!" This cry was taken up and repeated, coupled with the assertion, "If it was a nigger, he'd soon be swinging to a lamp post." The excitement was increasing as the crowd swelled, and the situation was looking very serious when the patrol wagon arrived and the two prisoners were hauled away.

Among those who saw the policemen ascend the steps and reappear with Mr. Nelson was John Harrison, a boarder of the St. Louis Hotel, which is near by, at the northeast corner of Main and Lucas avenue. Last evening he said to a *Republic* reporter:

"I saw the policemen bring a man out of that stairway; also a negro girl. People around said the man's name was Nelson. When the policemen got him out in the light one of them said, 'What's your name?' The man was awfully nervous. He fidgeted about and finally pulled out a business card. He said he was president of that company. The officer cursed him and said: 'Well, you come along.' Nelson looked very old and wore a seersucker coat and vest and a straw hat—as I remember."

A number of other people corroborated John Harrison's testimony, namely, John Camien, a tailor at 14 Lucas avenue, and his employes, as well as the employes of other firms, who witnessed the arrest from the rear doors of business houses that open out into Commercial street.

Mrs. Potter, a colored woman, living at 601 North Levee, said that her father had seen the officers bring Nelson from the stairway and had heard the negro child state that she lived near the corner of Sixth and Cerre streets.

Mrs. Potter had seen the policemen and Nelson together at the patrol box near the corner of the Levee and Lucas avenue, and had seen the couple bundled into the patrol wagon. There was a big crowd and considerable excitement.

A *Republic* reporter having gathered these facts proceeded to the Third District Police Station, where Mr. Nelson and the girl had been conveyed. There Captain Joyce was found complacently reading.

"Where is Mr. Nelson?" was asked.

"What Mr. Nelson?" queried the Captain.

"Why, the Austin M. Nelson who was brought in here from the Levee with a negro child."

Captain Joyce gazed thoughtfully away for a moment and then said: "Yes, I believe there was such a man in here."

"Where is he now?"

"Why, I set him free. There was nothing to the case. The man is a prominent business man and can be found any time. There's nothing to the case."

"Didn't the officers charge attempted rape?"

"No, sir."

"Did you question the child any or investigate the case?"

"I heard her story. There's nothing in the case; the officers didn't charge anything especially."

"What was the child's name?"

"I don't know."

"Where does she live?"

"I can't tell. I didn't consider the case worth investigating. You are endeavoring to make a sensation out of nothing."

"Have you made out an official report?"

"Oh, no; there isn't anything to the whole matter. Mr. Nelson is a prominent business man. He couldn't be accused of anything like that."

"How did Mr. Nelson explain his presence in that stairway?"

"He said the girl called him up and wanted a dime. That's all."

Further explanation could not be had of Captain Joyce, nor would he discuss the very remarkable conduct of his officers in forcing such a prominent man as Mr. A. M. Nelson to submit to the ignominy of arrest and a ride through the streets in the patrol wagon, when the case was of such a trivial character that the first glance of the Captain's eagle eye showed him there was "nothing in it."

Later Mr. Nelson was visited at his residence, No. 4055 Delmar avenue. He was out driving, but returned at 8:30 p.m. He wore the seersucker coat and vest and the straw hat described by the people about Lucas and Commercial street. When accosted he was smoking a pipe on his front stoop.

"You were engaged in a rather unpleasant affair this afternoon, Mr. Nelson, were you not?"

"Yes," confidentially drawled Mr. Nelson.

"You were conveyed in a patrol wagon to the Third District, were you not, in company with a negro girl, 9 years old?"

"Yes."

"Will you state how you came to be up the dark stairway in the rear of the store at Washington avenue and Commercial street?"

"Why," said Mr. Nelson, "I was passing by there at 8 o'clock to-day and I met a little colored girl with a basket. She stepped into that doorway and as I passed called me. I didn't know what she wanted and so I went toward her. She went up the stairs and when she got into a dark corner she exposed her person and wanted to know whether I would give her a dime. When I heard this I came right down."

"You had never seen the girl before, had you?"

"No."

"Do you know who sent the policemen after you?"

"No."

Mr. Nelson expressed the fear that if the story was printed someone might misjudge him, but expressed no resentment toward the police for giving him a free ride, but it is not improbable that the action of the officers in the case will be laid before the Police Board in the shape of a complaint, or Captain Joyce may discipline his subordinates, who certainly acted in a very injudicious manner if the case is as plain a one as Captain Joyce seems to consider it.

The Nelson Paint Company occupies a four-story brick structure at Nos. 701 and 703 North Second street. The negro child could not be located in the neighborhood given as her home.

[26 August 1893, pp. 1–2.]

59 - BANDIT PENNOCK.

[Excerpts]

PENNOCK TALKS IN JAIL.

When Pennock was taken to the holdover he was locked up in cell 10, where he stretched himself out on a bench and gave himself up to his thoughts. Pennock, to look at, is an ideal train robber. He is 30 years old, stands 6 feet 2 inches in his stocking feet and weighs 205 pounds. His body has not one ounce of superfluous flesh. His frame is not well knit, however, there being a general appearance of awkwardness. Pennock's face is not a bad one. He has a high forehead, nearly black hair and a straight aquiline nose. His eyes are steely gray and look straight at a person when he is engaged in conversation. He has a dark brown mustache which shades a well-shaped mouth and chin. His hands and feet are abnormally large, tremendous in fact.

Pennock readily admitted being on the train.

"Where did you get on?"

"At Tower Grove Station."

"Where were you going?"

"Sullivan Station, where my mother and two brothers, Mike and George, live.

"They don't live in Sullivan, though, but on a farm four miles southwest. I was going out to pay them a short visit, as I haven't been there for some time."

"Where were you riding on the train?"

"Between the baggage and express cars."

"Was anybody else on there with you?"

"Yes, two tramps, but I paid no attention to them."

"Were they armed?"

"I don't think they were."

"What was the first you knew of the robbery?"

"I did not know anything about it until the train stopped."

"You knew the train was being held up as soon as it stopped, did you?"

"Well, I am a railroad man and when a train stops between stations I know there is something going to happen."

"Don't trains ever stop between stations except when they are being robbed?"

"Not often."

"What did you do when the train stopped?"

"I looked around the car and saw the engineer and fireman and two more

"Pennock in Custody"
(*St. Louis Republic*, 7 September 1893, p. 1).

men. They were walking back to where I was. The engineer and fireman were in front. As soon as I saw them I ran out on the same side as hard as I could go and laid by the fence near the Missouri Pacific tracks. I laid down on the ground."

"What did you run for?"

"I wanted to get out of the way."

"Why didn't you run out on the other side of the car? If you were afraid why did you risk being shot by the robbers by running out on the same side where they were?"

"Well, there were the two tramps on the other side of me, between me and the steps, and I didn't want to bother them."

"You were well armed; why were you afraid of two tramps?"

"Well, I was just afraid, that is all."

"Do you usually carry two guns?"

"Most of the time."

"What do you want with two?"

"I always carry two when I want to. I carry two for the same reason another man carries one."

"Where did you get the guns?"

"I've had them about a year. One I bought on the Levee and the other near Seventh and Walnut in a secondhand store."

"What were you doing with the five extra cartridges and the pillow-case found on you a minute ago?"

"Well, I just had the cartridges in case I needed them, and I was taking the pillow-slip out to bring some apples back from my mother's."

"Do you know Neeley?"

"Yes, I have known him for about a year."

"Did you see him yesterday?"

"No, I haven't seen him for some time."

"Where were you born?"

"In Crawford County in 1863."

"You served a term in the pen once?"

"Yes. I was sent up for two years from Crawford County in 1882 for killing a man named Gilchrist. I did not mean to kill him, but he was overbearing and I hit him over the head with a shovel. I stayed in the pen a year and a half."

"Were you not at one time training to be a pugilist?"

"Yes, I gave Rufus Sharp, the colored pugilist, $50 a year ago to give me lessons. I only took two, and quit without taking the rest."

"What made you quit?"

"Well, I did not have any money to back myself against anybody and I gave it up."

"How long have you been married?"

"One year about."

"What were you doing on the Frisco?"

"Braking on a local freight for Conductor Kline. I laid off last Thursday because I wanted a rest for a few days."

"You are sure you only saw two train robbers?"

"Yes, very sure."

These questions were repeated over and over again to Pennock with the hope that he would confess his crime, but his answers were about the same. He will have a hard time trying to establish his innocence.

TRYING ON THE CLOTHES.

Last night Superintendent Clark of the 'Frisco, Chief Clerk Pettigrew of the office of Superintendent Simpson of the Wells-Fargo Express Company,

J. T. M. Connor, the Wells-Fargo detective, and George Prizer, the messenger who was held up, called at Chief Desmond's office and a long consultation followed. Pennock was brought up from the holdover and introduced into the room. Messenger Prizer, after carefully inspecting him, said he was an exact "ringer" for the man who acted as leader of the robbers. Chief Desmond then had Pennock put on the ulster which was found near the barb-wire fence where he laid, and it fitted him exactly. On the right side of the ulster, near the bottom, was a rent, which was probably torn as the robber tried to get through the fence. The rent looks exactly like it was snagged from a fence barb. The hat found near the ulster also fitted Pennock. Pennock told Chief Desmond that he bought one of the guns from a secondhand store in the rear of the Cupples Building a year ago. On investigation it was found that the store referred to had only been there eight months and so Pennock's first lie was nailed. There is no doubt in the minds of the detectives and those concerned that Pennock is one of the robbers.

Messenger Prizer, when seen last night, told the story of the robbery. He said that the first he knew he heard a knock at the door. Then he heard the engineer say "Open the door." Prizer obeyed the summons and saw five men—the engineer and fireman and the three masked robbers. Two of the bandits had white handkerchiefs over their faces and the other a blue polka dot. The men covered him with revolvers, held in each of their hands, and told him to offer no resistance. The fireman and engineers were told to get in the car and the robbers followed. The spokesman was a man about 6 feet 2. He was the one with the "polka dot" mask. On getting inside he seized the messenger's Winchester and handing it to one of his assistants said to the messenger, "Take that lamp out of there," meaning the bracket, "if you don't want to get burnt up." The messenger obeyed and the leader said: "Have you got anything in there?" The messenger replied that he did not know, as he was ignorant of the combination. The robber then produced a stick of dynamite. This was tied to the bolt of the safe and a fuse attached. The word was given and everybody piled outside. A second later came the explosion. The robbers and victims climbed back inside. The explosion had only blown off the bolt, leaving a hole. Another stick of the explosive was inserted in the hole and touched off. Again the six men went out into the air and the explosion followed. Just at this time the rumble of an approaching train was heard in the rear. The robbers hurried the men inside, but disappointment followed when they saw the last stick of dynamite had only blown the outer plate of the safe door off, leaving the iron-knobbed rivets of the inner plate exposed, but the safe no nearer open so far as the money was concerned than before. The robbers cursed their ill luck and said to the engineer and fireman: "Come, get out of this d——n quick, and get on your engine and clear out before that freight hits you." With this the engineer and fireman leaped from the car and, jumping on the engine, pulled the train out. The robbers ran north toward the barb-wire fence.

In speaking of Pennock, Prizer said he was about the same size as the robber and looked very much like him. In fact Prizer is sure that Pennock is the robber, but not having seen his face cannot positively identify him. The officials and messenger, after being closeted with Chief Desmond, for three hours left the Four Courts. Reisch, Hall, Neeley and Meyers were released at 10 o'clock. Before leaving, their statements were taken by Chief Desmond and will be presented as evidence at the trial.

James Marion Pennock, on whom at present the only apparent hope of solving the mystery of this desperate raid depends, is 30 years old. He is well known among railroad men and does not bear the best reputation. He is said to be of a quarrelsome disposition and admits that he served a term in the penitentiary for manslaughter. He has been married for about a year and lives at 1547 Tower Grove avenue. He has been employed as a brakeman on the Frisco road, running with conductor Klein, but was laid off last Thursday, saying he needed a rest. It is hard to explain his actions on the night of the robbery. As a railroad man it was not necessary for him to beat his way to Sullivan, as he could have ridden in a caboose and probably in one of the passenger coaches of the very train he was on. He admits that he was on the train, and says that when discovered by the conductor and Dr. Bond he was lying face-downward in the weeds near a barbed-wire fence to get out of the way of the robbers, for fear he would be shot.

Engineer Weckerly says that Pennock was the big man who climbed over the cab and that he recognized his voice.

General Superintendent J. R. Wentworth of the Frisco is convinced that the police have the right man.

When captured Pennock's revolvers had all their loads in them, and he had five extra cartridges on his person. When searched at the station a blue handkerchief with white spots—the exact counterpart of the handkerchief found on the spot where Pennock was captured—a white handkerchief and another pillow-case were found on his person. He had no money.

The express and railroad people were loud in their praise of Conductor Carrigan and Dr. Y. H. Bond for the gallant part they took in the affair. When Conductor Carrigan stepped off the car, lantern in hand, to see what was the matter a gruff voice said, "You've come far enough," and a revolver was discharged over his head, evidently to intimidate him. Conductor Carrigan did not retreat to the car for protection, as some papers have stated, but to get a weapon. He went into the car and said: "Ladies and gentlemen the train is held up. Secrete your valuables as fast as you can."

Some of the passengers thought this was a joke, but his serious manner soon convinced them that it was a serious fact. He then went through the train asking everyone if they had a weapon. He failed to procure one until he came to Dr. Bond's party. One of the party gave the conductor a shotgun and Dr. Bond volunteered to accompany him. They jumped off the train determined to confront the robbers, but before they had gone very far the explosion occurred. In another moment or two the noise of the approaching fast freight was heard, the express car was on fire and the engineer pulled out and reached the water tank at Pacific, where the fire was extinguished.

The conductor and Dr. Bond were left on the ground, and the Doctor, instead of hunting ducks on the Gasconade, went robber hunting in the weeds of Sand Cut. They were attracted to the place where Pennock lay by a noise in the grass, and, leveling their guns on him, captured him. It was a very neat piece of work, but the suspected bandit, although heavily armed, could not look into the mouths of two shotguns.

[7 September 1893, pp. 1–2.]

60 - A SPIRITUALIST FRAUD.

Jules Wallace will hold a spiritual test to-night at Cooper's Hall, Thirty-fifth and Franklin ave., at 8 p.m.; positive proof of spirit return; skeptics invited.

In accordance with the above the skeptic was there and *The Republic* obtained indubitable evidence that Jules Wallace is an unmitigated fraud and that his alleged spiritualistic messages are obtained through the most flimsy trickery.

At the appointed hour last night Wallace was at Cooper's Hall, Thirty-fifth street and Franklin avenue, with his store clothes, his diamonds and his assurance. The audience was composed mainly of two classes—fleshy, gum-chewing ladies and thin, cadaverous men, with just enough of curiosity hunters and venerable cranks to give it spice. The latter came to be amused, and spent a rather pleasant evening in curiously examining the devious methods of the forked biological specimen before them—otherwise Wallace.

Wallace's face was sandpapered and oiled for the occasion. His partner, the ponderous blonde from Denver, Mrs. Bicknell, whom he had "developed," sat at a table at the door and wafted a corpulent smile across each shining quarter deposited by suckers, pleasure seekers or investigators. But Wallace kept an eye on the pile, and two other fleshy heaps of femininity sat around to see that nothing got away.

LEFT: "Wallace Is a Fraud" (*St. Louis Republic*, 11 September 1893, p. 3); RIGHT: "I Am the Prettiest Irishman in America" (*St. Louis Republic*, 11 September 1893, p. 3).

The faker was very much engaged to and fro and making side glances with his bovine-catamount eyes to enable him to locate cappers whom he would have use for after a while.

The gaunt and ghostly form of Prof. (?) J. McIvor Tyndall was caged in a back room while the vacuum in the upper story was receiving injections of Wallaceism. There were lots more of his sort schooled and located as they went in.

About the time the audience had gotten tired waiting a spirituelle female, one of the few in the room, fell upon a helpless piano and tortured it egregiously for some minutes, while the abused instrument, cadet-like, tried to get even by torturing the audience.

Wallace, his assurance, his "store close" and his diamonds then came forward. He was going to put his traducers to confusion by proving all that had been published about him in *The Republic* untrue. To do this he introduced Prof. (?) Tyndall.

The latter seemed to have leaked some of the Wallasonian cerebral injection. His defense of Wallace was of a very dubious character.

"A *Republic* reporter asked me," said he, "if I think Mr. Wallace a faker. I said: 'Yes, he is a faker and the most remarkable faker I have ever met.'" After admitting that the interview in *The Republic* was entirely correct Tyndall said that he would stand by all he had said and then left.

Wallace then got up and blew his own horn. He gave a history of himself and said that with a towel he could reproduce Dion Boucicault from start to finish. He then said that he was an honest man, even if he had owed Fred Lucas, secretary to Chief of Police Lawrence Harrigan, $14 for 10 years, and that Lucas was the most tickled man on earth when, in a flush time, he had paid the bill.

Wallace said that he owed small bills to lots of other people. Then he said that he was ready now to pay all bills. He then brought down his fist and shot out his lower jaw as far as its stringency would let him, and announced that the whole published article in Saturday's *Republic* was a lie from beginning to end. He told of several other articles which might have been used in his trade as well as alcohol, and intimated that he could read spirit messages better with them than with the less reliable spirit of corn. He said he predicted that we would not have cholera this year, and could prove it under oath. He did not say whether "it" referred to the prediction or the having of cholera. He was a prophet, or at least the son of a prophet, and it was not always necessary that he should be under the influence of alcohol to testify.

He said that he did not remember certain seances by which he was exposed. He said that Schloss was there and would deny the charges against he and Wallace, but Schloss did not. He said that a certain woman came to him and paid him $2 and got $2 worth of fraud.

He then blew Mrs. Bicknell's horn and poured billingsgate on the reporter who exposed him. He said that the juror's son spoken of in the expose was from Little Rock and had not lived all of his life in St. Louis, and in proof of the fact, dived down into the audience and fished up a cadaverous young man, to all intents and purposes a dummy; said that he would deny, but the fool spoke not.

"When did you come, Madam," said he, addressing, in broad brogue, Mrs. Bicknell. "A week ago last Wednesday," came in a corpulent voice from the rear. He then said the article in the yesterday's *Republic* was an apology, evidently forgetting that a moment before he had called it a lie.

He gave an inventory of himself and gloated over his fraudulent gains. He had a $150 suit, and he turned around to show how "store close" fit him. He had four or five diamonds, worth from $40 to $250 each. He had money in bank and real estate. He stormed and swore and said he was the greatest man in the business. The best looking Irishman on this continent. "I am colossal," said he with an oath, as he straightened up. "When I get my license to marry I will know who will be benefited," and the suckers howled. He then said that he was here to stay and would gull people for the next six months just as of old. His impudence became supreme as his gulls applauded. He introduced Mrs. Hammett, one of the fleshy women at the table, as a Spiritualist from California and she presented a very choice scheme for raising money for a spiritualist institute which, up to date, was simply in her eye. She got a collection, however, after having sung to a squeaky guitar in a flannel voice a pathetic song furnished by a little spirit for the occasion.

While the stout lady collected the cash the spirituelle female tortured the piano, and Wallace joined in in torturing the audience. He sang "Only an Idle Word" with great pathos. The end of each stanza was to the effect that they never came back.

Wallace then got an inspiration. He tackled a gullible-looking, gray-headed man, for whom he had a message from the spirit world. After looking tragic and beating his forehead the medium saw the beautiful spirit of a woman and told a message she had.

The message was of no importance to anyone and it seemed strange that the spirit should take the trouble to come for so slight a thing. Kate Burns and John Williams corresponded and said nothing. The man with the gray head shook it like a pump-handle and said quite correct. "Thanks No. 1, not with envelope and alcohol," said Wallace.

Wallace then struck an attitude before a man looking like the "after" of a patent medicine ad.

"I see a man with a bald head, red mustache and bleared eyes. I see a scene in which he is persuading you that I am a fraud. He took you out to have a drink. Have nothing to do with him." Right here comes in *The Republic's* expose. The man addressed was one Carroll of 918 Lasalle street. He is a friend of Wallace, being with him at various places. He boards at the above number and was talking over Wallace yesterday afternoon with one Van Busen, maliciously described as above by Wallace. Carroll told Wallace the story of the conversation between himself and Van Busen. Wallace repeated it to him and he verified it. But this was not the worst case.

Wallace went into ecstacy, and called loudly that he saw a short, rather stout woman with a white cap. "Who recognizes this spirit? Its name is Grandma French. Who recognizes it? (No answer.) Who recognizes it? It is unladylike and ungentlemanly not to recognize spirits when they come to you." (No response.)

"Here is a dear friend of the family. The spirit says she wants to give him the message and let him take it to the family. He had always been her dear friend when she was on earth and now she wishes to confide in him. She wants him to tell her family that she is happy and hopes they are, etc."

And Wallace went on with colorless rot. The friend of Grandma French was E. F. Carroll, a clerk in the employ of the American Express Company. Carroll's son, Robert Lee Carroll, is a prize fighter and lives in the family descended from Grandma French. Young Carroll was a capper and a bouncer for Wallace in Denver and a close friend of Mrs. Bicknell. Wallace knows all about the family in which he boards. He told Carroll the elder the facts. Carroll the elder was with Wallace yesterday afternoon, told him of Grandma French and was ready last night to spring the fraud on the audience. Carroll here went and got his son and went to the seance and the two saw a representative of the family come in the hall. They gave Wallace the tip, he told the story, but could not locate the victim. *The Republic* learned these details from representatives of the family and can give names and residence place. As the family does not want cheap notoriety, however, *The Republic* withholds the name of the present generation, but they will come forward, if need be, and give evidence to expose the fraud. They are quite as indignant at the Carrolls, who acted as cheap cappers, as they are with Wallace, who sought to reap the benefit. All of the other cases were jobs put up in a similar manner. It is now in order for the investigating public to ostracise the bifurcated fraud who attempts spiritualism.

Wallace tackled Billy Hobbs and was told that the "facts" related were gotten from an individual in the audience whom Hobbs pointed out. Wallace struck another tartar. He went to a young man and gave him a message from a doctor spirit.

"Is that right?" said the medium.

"I do not know as it is," was the response.

With another victim Wallace was five years off as to a date. He had evidently forgotten the story.

The seance ended abruptly, for Wallace saw that his rank impositions were becoming plain even to the deluded brains of his miserable dupes.

[11 September 1893, p. 3.]

61 - HIS OWN STORY.

In a prison cell at the Four Courts, within that dark, gloomy bastile, where ill-garbed, ill-visaged criminals, and an odorous atmosphere are joined, as it were, inseparably, is confined one man who presents a strange contrast to the surroundings. This is John Finn, who a few weeks since startled the city with apparently a most brutal attempt upon the lives of his young and helpless children. John Finn yesterday told a *Republic* reporter his story of the awful deed. It has never been told before. The details of the crime on first vision appeared brutal in the extreme. Apparently the father had risen in the early morning, seized a flatiron and without other motive than that of heartless brutality attempted to beat out the brains of his innocent offspring, four of whom were sleeping near him in cradles and cots. The crime found its fit culmination in the murderer attempting to cut his own throat with a razor. The developments of the case showed many extenuating circumstances.

John Finn lived at 2828 Chouteau avenue in a two-story brick dwelling which was and is his own property. Finn was a newspaper carrier and was quite well situated. His family consisted of himself, wife and four children, named respectively Johnnie, Willie, Mamie and Annie. Johnnie Finn was 13 years old, Willie 11 years, Mamie 7 and Annie 5 years old. Finn had been married 14 years; had lived at 2828 Chouteau avenue for 12 years and worked himself into respectful comfort at least. At the time of the tragedy he had been ill with a kind of bilious fever which was fast changing to typhoid. For two weeks previous to the morning of August 9, when the tragedy occurred, he had been confined to his home, worried with recurring fever of the brain and general disability. On that fatal morning he awoke early. His wife, Mary, had awakened also and heard him complaining of severe pains in his head. At about 8 o'clock she arose and said that she would go for Dr. Jones, who had been attending her husband. While she was preparing to leave Johnnie, the oldest child, awoke and complained of being sick. His mother brought him a glass of milk and then left. The father, who had been wandering about the lower rooms seeking rest, entered the bedroom where all the children were sleeping and lay down on one of the beds. On one of the other beds lay Johnnie and Willie with Mamie stretched at their feet. Little Annie was lying asleep in a cot near by. When Mrs. Finn had gone a little time Finn was seized with a fevered dream.

It seems, according to his fitful tale told later at the City Hospital, that he was greeted by a vision of something indefinitely grand. There was that in it all that called him away from earth and his physical being and beckoned him to regions of rest beyond. In fact, he felt that his death hour should come now. He conceived the idea that it would be loving charity to release his children from earth's troubles, and rising, he entered the kitchen, seized a flatiron from behind the stove and returned to the deadly task. He attacked the children in the order of their age, first striking Johnnie and last Annie. He violently beat them about the head until he was satisfied in his insane frenzy that they were all dead, and then he attacked himself. The result of his assault was that Willie, the brightest of the four, died the next day at the City Hospital, and the remaining trio are still confined in that institution. The two girls, however, will shortly be discharged. Finn himself was held there until Saturday last, when he was transferred to the Four Courts on a warrant sworn out by the police.

The appearance of Finn as he walks the corridors of the jail is a standing argument against any charge of murderous intent which might be placed against him. There is that in his physical make-up, much worn now as it is by long illness and confinement, that argues against any such fiendish shade to it. Though only 58 years old, his scant locks and short growth of beard are tinged with gray. His form is slightly bent, and he walks with a sinking step, due more to his long illness, however, than to his age. His once brown, wrinkled skin is pale and softly gathered in furrows. His eyes look sunken and are of a rather mild blue.

The effect of his continued thought upon the subject of his unintentional deed has worried him into a state of sad nervousness, so that a slight reference to his dead child or his remaining children will cause the tears to flow.

Fearful as his crime was and pitiful to relate, Finn is not a murderer. Long illness had weakened him and temporarily affected his brain. A sudden fever seized him and a ruthless vision prompted him with a glamour that made it seem charity to take the lives of his children. In the last place his general bearing, religious character and kindness to his family during 14 long years of labor and care, as attested to by all who know him, are all against the idea of criminal brutality. A talk with Finn himself is the best proof of his innocence.

Last evening about locking-up time Finn was visited at the Four Courts and interviewed by a *Republic* representative upon his own recollection of the case. When the Warden sent for him he came with a slow, weakly step down the iron staircase from his little pigeonhole cell up on the first balcony row. His eyes wandered inquiringly about the rooms and faintly brightened at the sight of an acquaintance. After a few friendly greetings he was urged to take a seat and then interviewed.

"Are you quite recovered from the effects of your typhoid illness now, do you think?" was asked.

"Yes, sir. I believe I'm quite well, although I feel very weak."

"Is the food here such as would nourish a sick man?"

"I don't know, sir. I'm satisfied, however; such as it is, it's good I believe."

"Your wife visits you quite regularly, does she not?"

"Yes," said Mr. Finn, and his voice became slightly strained as he endeavored to swallow the lump that rose in his throat. The thought of the kind, faithful efforts of his good wife was almost overpowering, so great is his nervous sense of the pain that his act has caused that long-suffering woman.

"While in the City Hospital did you dwell much on the thought of what you had done that Wednesday morning?"

"I didn't think of anything else, sir. Very little."

"Do you remember now just what you did on that morning?"

"Well, you see, sir, I was quite out of my mind, sir, I'm afraid. I was sick with fever and I don't remember just what I did at that time. I remember though when I woke up in the hospital that I had a kind of recollection of what I had done. It seemed more of a dream than anything else. It was just a faint recollection like everything else that occurred that time for a day or two after the deed, but I think it was nearly correct so far as I thought."

"Just tell me, will you, what your thoughts and feelings were on that next day in the hospital after the tragedy?"

"I can remember that I was in pain—a weary feeling—when I first woke up. I heard voices around me and someone crying. I thought my son Johnnie was crying, but I wasn't certain. I believe also that I knew that I was in a hospital, but still doubtful of it. When I came to I began to remember what I had done. Even then it seemed as though I was dreaming something about a dream I had dreamt before. That was, that I had a vision. I felt as though the top of my head had been lifted off, and at the same time a vast vision opened before me. I saw a great open space that I thought was heaven and it was filled with angels, great numbers of them. They were looking at me and motioning me to come to them. I thought I heard voices calling. I wanted to go. It was so grand, so beautiful, that I wanted to go at once, for I was afraid the space would close and they would not wait for me. I thought of my children then. I imagined they would be happy there and I wanted to take them. The only thing I could think of was to kill them and then they could go with me. That's why I got up. I can remember jumping up, that is I remember this dream of mine in the hospital, and of going into the kitchen to get a razor. I tried to cut my throat, and I sank down on the floor. Then all I remember from that on is of someone asking me questions and of hearing my name mentioned."

"Don't you remember taking a flatiron down from the kitchen wall and beating your children with it?"

"No; God have mercy on me, I don't. My poor Willie! he was such a bright boy," and so saying, Mr. Finn's voice weakened as though he would cry.

"You remember that your wife left for a doctor, don't you, on that morning?"

"Yes, that is the last thing I do remember. All the rest, as I said, came to me as a kind of dream in the City Hospital."

"You had always cared for your family quite respectably, had you not, before this happened?"

"I always tried to. I worked on the Chouteau avenue street car line as steady as anyone for years and saved all the money I could. I bought that lot and built that house just so that my family could have a good home. We were always happy and got along very well."

"You are a Catholic in good standing, are you not?"

"I am, sir. I've always attended mass as regularly as my work would permit. When I was a street car conductor I couldn't get off only once in a long while, but when I could I always went to church with my family and attended to my religious duties."

"Your children were being reared in that faith, of course?"

"They were that. A finer lot of children you couldn't have found anywhere. My son Willie was the brightest boy in his class at school, and it was the same with Johnnie. I had very bright children. I tried to give them the best education I could. It was my object to save enough money to keep them in school and give them a good education rather than to save money for them to use after awhile. When I was working on the street car line I didn't have much time to attend to them, but I used to sit up with Johnnie and Willie when they were 5 years old to teach them to read. I wanted them to have a good start when they entered the public schools, and they did."

"How much are you worth financially?"

"I only own the house I live in. That's worth $3,500."

Mr. Finn went on to tell about Willie, the boy who died, claiming that he was the brightest one of all the four children. He said that Willie, though only 11 years old, was in all the classes of schoolmates who were 13 to 15 years old and that the boy often came home laughing at his elder classmates because they could not grasp problems which he readily seemed to understand. Willie was the one whose brain weighed 52 ounces—a most phenomenal weight.

Finn's story of an insane vision receives more value when the statement of Dr. Heine Marks of the City Hospital is taken in conjunction. Dr. Marks said the other day that he did not think Finn was guilty of the shadow of an interest in the case. "The man," said the Doctor, "had a touch of typhoid fever and was out of his mind at the time. He came into the hospital with that disease upon him and suffered afterwards a long siege of it. His actions were those of a man whose mind was suffering a keen remorse that was almost as wearing as the disease he suffered. I believe Finn to be a good, hard-working, honest man, who meant ever so kindly towards his family and who was really the victim of suffering and disease."

Finn in the jail presents a most pitiable sight. Perhaps it is not so pitiable as it is lonesomely mournful. The discouraging air of shadowy crime and untold tales that hangs over it sweeps back temporarily in the presence of poor Finn, whose countenance is so plainly honest and sorrowful. His slow gait and modest, retiring expression chime well with the deep sorrow that hangs over him. From his little cell he looks out upon the motley gathering, not with rebellious feelings, but rather with wonderment and religious sorrow for their degradation. He finds consolation in muttered prayers and religious reflection, that prefers the dark seclusion of his cell to the gray light of the prison promenade. The weight of his unconscious crime bears him down constantly.

The loss of his dead child, the pains of his other children, the suffering of his wife are all additions to his burden.

As Finn concluded his interview and turned, being informed that that was all, he slowly tramped across the wide, resounding floor space, bending his weary step to his shadowy cell. He walked the space, climbed the stair and edged his way to the open door that awaited him before he turned his head to look back. Then stopping for but a moment he looked back towards the reporter, then sinking his head on his breast entered the cell, on which the iron door closed for the night.

[20 September 1893, pp. 1–2.]

62 - WILL WEAR THE MEDAL.

Miss Lizzie Schuble has been adjudged worthy to wear one of *The Republic*'s Bravery Medals, and it will accordingly be presented to her. Miss Schuble is the young girl who was in the car the night young Edgar Fitzwilliam was murdered. Her conduct that night was certainly conspicuously heroic, and has attracted the attention of Chief of Police Harrigan and Fire Chief Lindsay. These gentlemen have addressed to *The Republic* the following letters:

City Editor Republic: Dear Sir—I respectfully suggest that Miss Lizzie Schuble be awarded one of *The Republic*'s gold medals for the conspicuous bravery she displayed on the night of the Fitzwilliam murder in St. Louis County. The account of the affair published by *The Republic* shows that she is a real heroine. Very respectfully,

L. Harrigan,
Chief of Police.

————

City Editor of The Republic: Dear Sir—I am heartily in favor of awarding one of your Bravery Medals to Miss Lizzie Schuble, the young lady who so gallantly went for help when Edgar Fitzwilliam was shot. From the published accounts I am of the opinion that she is justly entitled to the medal. Yours respectfully,

John Lindsay,
Chief of the Fire Department.

————

LEFT: "Edgar Fitzwilliam" (*St. Louis Republic*, 25 September 1893, p. 1); RIGHT: "Miss Schuble" (*St. Louis Republic*, 1 October 1893, p. 1).

The conditions upon which *The Republic*'s Bravery Medal is awarded are set forth in the following notice, which appears daily in the paper:

THE REPUBLIC
WILL GIVE A GOLD MEDAL
Of the Design Shown Below

<table>
<tr><td>THE ST. LOUIS
REPUBLIC
BRAVERY
MEDAL</td><td>AWARDED
TO
————
FOR
CONSPICUOUS
HEROISM.</td></tr>
</table>

To Every Person Who Performs an
Act of Conspicuous Bravery.

————

THE ACT OF HEROISM MAY BE IN
AID OF HIS INDIVIDUAL FELLOW-
MAN OR IN THE GENERAL SERVICE
OF THE PUBLIC.

————

COMMITTEE OF AWARD.
CHIEF HARRIGAN,
St. Louis Police Department.
CHIEF LINDSAY,
St. Louis Fire Department.
—AND—
The Manager of The Republic.

Already the roll of honor is becoming one of rare value, and those who are heroic enough to deserve being added thereto may well be proud. The category of heroic action is wide. Humanity may be served in many and almost mysterious ways, but it is the deed, not the mode, that is awarded. Miss Schuble's action, details of which have been printed, was most notable. The night was gloomily sullen, the district was barren and the situation most unnerving. The four negroes who entered the Midland Branch road car on the night of Edgar Fitzwilliam's last ride were armed desperadoes, with crime-hardened visages and fierce intentions. Their suspicious actions and the subsequent murder were such as would cause the hearts of men even to quail, and yet Miss Schuble, alone in the car with the body of Fitzwilliam, did not lose her courage. She did not sink helpless, an additional victim to the foul and murderous proclivities of the ruffians. Instead, she made good her escape, fleeing through the darkness and across the fields to a human habitation, not to seek aid and refuge for herself, but to find assistance and comfort for another, till then supposed to be alive. Sympathy, not fear, was the marked characteristic of her actions on that night. Her subsequent success and return at the head of a trio of not overconfident men, bearing a lantern to the very resting place of young Fitzwilliam's bleeding form, was only in accordance with the previous display of courage—not more surprising.

Miss Schuble's own words are much the best criterion by which to judge her, and of that night's experience she related to a *Republic* reporter as follows:

"I was coming home from work on the Midland Branch car and Mr. Fitzwilliam was operating the car for Mr. Walden, the absent motorman. At Suter avenue four or five negroes got on board. They were very vicious-looking creatures—so much so that I was badly frightened. Mr. Fitzwilliam opened the front car door and came back to collect the fares. The negroes made no effort to pay, but simply said they had no money and rose up out of their seats. Then they drew revolvers and the lights went out and Mr. Fitzwilliam was shot. I jumped up and ran out the front door and over to a Mr. Cragen's house for help. I roused him out and when he came to the door I told him what had happened.

"I wanted him to come down to the car, but he said he was afraid. Then I asked him to go and call some neighbors, but he said he couldn't leave his wife alone. I asked him if he would lend me a horse so that I could ride off to the neighbors and wake them up, but he said he was afraid the negroes would catch me and take the horse away from me. I didn't know what to do. I spent ever so much time there arguing with him, but he was really scared and wouldn't do anything at all. He had a revolver and I wanted to borrow that, but he wouldn't even lend me that. Then someone came up through the shadow and Cragen was going to shoot. He thought it was the negroes. I told him not to shoot, because I thought it was Ed coming. I thought maybe he might only have been slightly wounded. I called to the stranger coming. I said, 'Is that you, Ed?' but he didn't answer. I called to him again, but received no answer, and he kept coming. I saw who he was in the light. It was John Taylor, and I told him about the shooting. Then he wanted to get Cragen to go, but Cragen wouldn't go. Finally another man, Mr. Cilley, came up, and I borrowed Mr. Cragen's lantern. Then they went back with me, and we found Ed dead, lying with his head just outside the rear car door. After that I don't know what happened. People were sent for, and in a little time a crowd was collected."

"Did you lead the way back to the car with the lantern?"

"Yes."

"Did you first go up and find the body of Ed in the doorway?"

"Yes. The two men, though, were not far away."

Miss Schuble's action since the night of the murder has been most pleasantly consistent with the trend of her story, combining energy and willingness with that calm, courageous fortitude that is the chief characteristic of heroism. She has labored most willingly to revenge the dead. Though kept busy and constantly confronted with untoward scenes of police station misery she has kept her wonted smile and willing energy.

The information that a bravery medal was to be awarded to her was brought to Miss Schuble by a *Republic* representative, and was received with a glad rejoicing that was most pleasant to witness.

"So I'm to receive a medal," she said with a happy laugh. "Well, I'm very thankful, sure. I don't know that I deserve it, but if the gentlemen want to give it to me I'll be very much pleased. I'm sure I thank you ever so much for the information."

Miss Schuble, whose home is near Page avenue and Hanley road, is only 16 years old.

She is small of figure, and dresses very plainly. Her face is not one that poets and artists would rave over as beautiful, but it is a good face, with strong features. Her eyes are gray, wide set, good natured and always merry. Little less than a wreath of dark brown hair enwreathes a high, broad intellectual looking forehead. Her smile, which is winning in its attractiveness, easily shades itself into the drawn, set determination of a negative.

The parted lips show a row of splendidly even white teeth, which really add to the beauty of her smile.

At present Miss Schuble looks fatigued, naturally enough, the bloom of health and rest having temporarily vanished under the long continued strain of excitement.

A shadow of that unconscious determination that beams out so modestly from her gray eyes shows itself in her conversation, especially when the latter trends in ways where sudden decision is necessary. Something of this showed itself in her conversation upon the subject of her motives and impulses of the evening of the 23d which she had with a *Republic* reporter yesterday.

"When you were in the car and the negroes sat opposite you, what did you think?"

"I thought they looked fierce and brutal—just as though they came with some evil intention."

"Did you look at them?"

"I just glanced at them. I wouldn't look at them for a moment steadily. I could see them, though, well enough."

"You didn't feel frightened, or as though you might faint if worst came to worst, did you?"

"I was scared, yes, indeed, I was, but I wouldn't faint. I'm not so frail as all that. I wanted to get up and move to a front seat in the car, but I was afraid those negroes might stop me. Then I decided to sit still."

"When the bullet was fired and Mr. Fitzwilliam fell, you ran out. What was your exact mental conclusion at that moment?"

"It was to get out, I guess. I had Mr. Fitzwilliam in mind, and also the fear that those negroes would follow and shoot me. I thought of help and getting to a house and ever so many things else."

"Well, when you saw that you were safely away from the car, nearing the house you were running to, were you still filled with fear or were you thinking of some way to aid Mr. Fitzwilliam?"

"I was uncertain whether those negroes were following me. I feared they were, but then I was thinking of getting someone and going back."

"You didn't go to the house just to be safe and out of danger?"

"No, indeed. I didn't want to go in the house. I didn't go in, either. What I wanted was someone to go back with me and help Mr. Fitzwilliam if he was alive. Then, too, I wanted to get the neighbors out so that something might be done. I thought the negroes ought to be caught and punished."

"When you returned to the car with the lantern and found Ed dead, with his head outside the door, weren't you unnerved?"

"No. I felt very bad and angry at the negroes, but I didn't feel faint. I thought most that something ought to be done at once to catch the murderers. I would have been willing to get on a horse and ride about to the neighbors and get them out, but I couldn't get a horse. I can ride and I know that country. Night doesn't frighten me."

While the print of some of Miss Schuble's statements might read boastful or vainglorious to those who do not know her, a personal narration of her own impulses and feelings told in her own quaint manner would soon dispel all thought of boastfulness or unwomanly boldness and leave only admiration for the goodness that could combine such courage and outspoken good sense with ability and simplicity of language enough to rob her curious story of all the odor of vanity or self-praise.

[1 October 1893, p. 29.]

63 - BRILLIANT BEYOND COMPARE: THE GLITTERING BALLROOM.

And there lay the hall, broad and wide and high, aflood with the battling gleams of a thousand lights; its long, shrinking corners of shadow aglow with radiance of color such as had not warmed their depths for 12 long moons and more. The great high ceiling, beautified by the oil decoration by strong artistic hands, showed there, in that magnificent splendor of night revelry, all the depth and shadow of noble coloring, all the ingenuity of artful curves and dainty tracings. Nowhere was the beauty less—everywhere seemed it more. Everywhere one could look where "Old Glory," drooping, vied with "Old Union" a-wing, gilded and silvered and milk-hued, with nothing of shadow or night, light fringing the pillared balcony, the high-arched windows and the dome. There each pillar cap was folded about with Union colors, and before it were gathered in graceful groups a handful of flags bearing staffs each of which might have honored the dying gasp of a Savior, leaping high to the crest of the breach, or leading some battle fray through the smoke.

The west wall, like the north, south and east, was festooned with fresh cut sprays of evergreen, hung with orderly grace. At regular periods along the balcony's ridge groups of gathered flags drooped, shading the Union shield and crowned by the arrow-grasping spread of the Union eagle's flight. While all above was fair to behold, so wide and high and colorful, the scene below was rich beyond compare. About a fountain of glistening waters, gleaming through a bower of silver lace work, whose interstices were of evergreen, lay a milky cloth, waxed and tightly drawn, across which the fair dancers were to skip in midnight merriment. Beyond this snowy spread were ranged the tiers upon tiers of orderly seats, looking here like flights of cedar steps and there like pyramid tiers of softest plush.

On the west side of the hall, exactly in the center, was arranged a lace

"The Ballroom at Midnight" (*St. Louis Republic*, 4 October 1893, p. 1).

shaded bower of potted plants and evergreens, within which the musicians of the evening were concealed. There was immense space within this square, well filled with chairs and lights for the artists. Every seat was bended over by a potted palm, and the music stands were kissed by the leaves of the swaying verdure mounted about.

The most delightful feature of the entire preparation was the excellent order of the electric effects. It seemed as though there might be two ceilings of fire, the one directly above the other. Gathered in circular bunches, a full half hundred such were suspended like sky-flung torches in even lines high above the heads of the dancers. A little above these bright constellations hung another tier of fire balls in even rows, but always just above and away, as though of another system. Looking far from the north landing the suspended lights seemed to be more like rows of firelighted arches in a cathedral than the more central suspension of so many shimmering globes.

Everywhere was light, color and gayety. Everywhere the restless eye was greeted by the gleam and glare of suspended globes or the shimmer through lace work and palms of lights concealed. The profusion of flags seemed cloying. The natural magnitude of the vision seemed overpowering. Such lines and curves and mounting piles gave one the impression of being self-created and containing within themselves the matchless glory of their own continuance. To the right and left, east and west, stretched the vast hall, aglimmer and aglow, until the eye found no resting place and the mind no ease. Only then, through wide-arched windows and high flung casements, did the flood of silvery moonlight from without seem peaceful and for once at rest.

THE BALL AT MIDNIGHT.

The grand ball, for which so many anxious hearts have waited, planned and long beat in ecstacy, began beneath the glow of light in view of full 10,000 eyes and none among them all to cast a baneful glance of ill or saddened thought. All through the long evening hours the mass had gathered. Between the solid lines of anxious spectators they stepped, so gay of dress and heart, into the great resplendent hall and now they were to dance. The cloaks of richest fur and softest down had been most softly laid aside. The last dainty touch had been added to the rose-decked hair. The last downy puff had been straightened, the lips compressed and the glance cast direct before, and then that gorgeous tempting line of "fair, well-spoken dames" tripped in, each gayly touching the arm of some most brave and gentle cavalier.

They tripped smiling, and bowed right and left as fair faces of friends and companions beamed for an instant before them in the circling throng. They filled the great floor, crowned the already jeweled palace and filled the waiting tiers of seats. The gallery was crowded, and looking up and around a sea of happy faces greeted every eye. Then came the arrival of the Prophet— he of the silver veil and the mystic glance. He came, his long, snowy beard just glimmering through that sheen of silver. After him his retinue poured, and such a pageant it was as might well honor the majesty of so glorious a potentate. The Orient's splendor seemed lavished in their bright array. Silver, gold, the sea's pure gems and Golconda's jewels were wasted in their robes. They came, two by two, arrayed in shimmering pearl-decked cloth of silks, dancing their slippered feet, all decked with jewels and bearing aloft such crowns of mine-born stones as never yet bedecked a pageant here on earth. They marched about the hall after their sovereign viewing the beautiful gathering womanhood hard by until one would envy them the pleasure of so straight unquivering a glance.

They marched, then broke and chose their partners. Each one went forward to the circle's edge, pointing his finger in charming certainty that there at last sat beaming the certain sharer of his pleasures. Those eyes that glanced and smiled now made him sure that in their depths at last was found his heart's desire. So the gay cavaliers, with the Prophet's leave, chose from the endless throng of beauty their choice and stepped upon the floor.

Never before, even in those old days of Arabia Felix—when the Veiled Khorassan led his mighty host across the rich Valleys of the East—did so knightly a throng choose fairer maids. The cheeks of Yezd or Shiraz never bloomed more fairer than these that graced the ladies of that courtly train. Great India's wines or those of Samian growth never sparkled with more clear radiancy than did the eyes that looked about so modestly to gather in the glory of that throng's strong glance.

While they walked and smiled a courtly throng, from out the bower of silks and palms stole the music of the hour, such soft, mellifluent wine-rich strains that in an instant transformed the gathering into a newer life and gayer throng. Music was in the air, music was in the mind and very heart of that proud gathering, and as though a flood of sunlight had been poured in upon some darkling garden the whole vision brightened and bloomed—a scene worth dreaming of.

The strains swelled louder and more richly clear. The marching to and fro grew each moment more animated. Eyes brightened, smiles dimpled more merrily, roses quivered with dainty nods and jewels gleamed as though with anger toward nature for long ages of sullen earth confinement. Now freed they sparkled their defiance and knew no limit to the power of their sheen. The very air seemed to hang rose perfumed in the expectancy of waiting on that momentary baton-flash which should move the shimmering mass to real life.

With all that flood of light drowning the eyes in its glory; with the air warm and perfumed beyond the power of Edenic bowers or the roses of Bendemeer stream; with life, color, harmony, music—the grand moment came.

There was no sullen stillness, no hanging expectancy as of nature doting and withholding her richest gift.

It came as with a flash, and a roar of music followed that in a moment died down to the soft melodious cadence of finger-swept strings, and the dance was on.

It was on, for the Prophet, silver veiled, leading his evening bride, dashed away with many a graceful step and curve, lifting his arms and snowy veil to bow. It was on with his Orient guard, for Jap and Turk alike, tossing their flowing robes from off their silver-slippered feet, reached out their steel-girt arms and led away with such a song of motion as had not been seen in many a moon. It was on with the Russian knight, fur robed and capped, for he, too, with many a bow and smile, dashed his gray locks aside and, catching the music's grace of movement, grasped his fair partner's tingling finger tips and was lost in the merry maze.

It was on with all the other of that gala company who kept the proud monarch of the East company on his gorgeous pilgrimage, for Arab, Greek and Hindoo, Chinese, Cambodian and Berber with one accord grasped their flowing skirts, clapped tight their scimitars and bowing low with kindling grace dashed off and were no more, but as a part of that rich throng. In that grand hall with its towering dome, where sound magnifies itself so richly that the patter of merry feet becomes music and the sighs and laughter of many become more the wafted echo of Perian bliss the grand pageant moved in all the soulful cadence of a summer song. There in the flood of those golden beams the city's chosen danced, swaying and rocking as though the soul of pleasure were kissing each lip in whispered praise and the heart of song had taken the throne of each one's own that the blood might surge and leap in rhythmic cadence, knowing no weariness, feeling no pain. Away went the gorgeous, smiling throng—merry, blissful, unconscious of all but that there was music and beauty and love. Without, the night's proud orb, queenly resplendent, careened her star-flowered course, flooding the earth with waves of her silvery veil as though to repay in part its grieving absence from the scene.

And on they danced. On through the night and its charms, with the cool breeze wafting its lonely course without until morning came, and radiant with the gaze of dew, the sun awoke and smiled to find the scene still gay and awaiting his presence.

[4 October 1893, pp. 1–2.]

64 - A FAKER'S VICTIM.

The correct name of the young man who was driven into a madhouse through his relations with Jules Wallace, the spiritualistic faker, is Lowell Putnam. He is a young music teacher whose mother resides at 1121 Leonard avenue. As has already been stated in *The Republic* he is now confined in St. Vincent's Asylum. He was known to Wallace as Henry Sanders.

Putnam was a teacher of the mandolin and violin, and has a brother employed by Rice, Stix & Co. He had a large number of pupils, all of whom speak in the highest terms of his ability.

He was the support of his mother and sister.

Until he met Wallace he was healthy, happy and contented. He is now a physical and mental wreck and believes that he possesses supernatural powers.

The difference between the unfortunate lunatic and Wallace, the medium, is that Wallace professes to have power that he knows he does not have, while young Putnam fully believes that he can recall the spirits of the departed dead.

Experts on diseases of the mind say that there are times when the condition of the human brain is such that the most trivial circumstance will cause derangement. Young Putnam must have been in such a condition when he met Wallace.

Mrs. Putnam does not know how her son happened to become acquainted with the "Medium-healer," as Wallace calls himself.

It seems that the young musician first visited Wallace about three months ago. He called merely out of curiosity. In the course of conversation Wallace told him that it would be very easy for him to become a medium. He flattered the young fellow, telling him that he possessed remarkable latent power, which only needed development.

Putnam at first ridiculed the idea and went away, but his vanity overcame his common sense, and the next day he called again. He was not yet in a condition to become a follower of Wallace's teachings, but Wallace gave him a "sitting."

Wallace held Putnam's hands, and from an electric battery concealed in his pocket, sent an electric current through both their bodies.

Wallace is a man of powerful physique; the young music teacher is slightly built and unable to stand a shock of electricity which would scarcely be felt by Wallace.

Being naturally of a fanciful, imaginative turn of mind, the young victim when he felt the tingling sensation caused by the electricity believed that it was due to the wonderful power of Wallace. Having received what he foolishly believed to be an exhibition of Wallace's power he became his blind dupe and visited Wallace regularly.

About five weeks ago Putnam decided to become a medium, and paid Wallace $25 to develop him. The process of development by Wallace's methods is too horrible for detailed description. It began by repeated and powerful shocks of electricity administered by the process already described, and when the young man left Wallace's rooms his nervous system was demoralized and his mind in a condition to believe anything which Wallace might see fit to tell him.

In vain Putnam's mother and sister implored him to cease his visits. He told them he was under Wallace's control and compelled to do whatever Wallace told him.

One evening about two weeks after Wallace commenced to "develop" him, the young musician returned to his home. He was terribly excited. The pupils of his eyes dilated and contracted with alarming rapidity. He was on the border of insanity.

But the wrecking of his bright mind was not yet complete.

Mrs. Putnam observed her son's peculiar actions, and sharply reprimanded him for some exaggerated statements. Later the family retired, but the young man sat before the grate seeing sprites and spirits directed by a satyr with Wallace's features in the embers.

Suddenly a maniacal laugh awakened the sleepers.

There could be no mistaking the horrible sound.

The mother bolted her door and called on her son for protection. She did not dream that young Putnam was the maniac. He went to her room and his eyes flashed one intelligent glance to hers. He attempted to speak, but again that horrible laugh came from his lips and he sank to the floor exhausted.

When consciousness was restored he was hopelessly insane. He declared that he was hypnotized. All sorts of hallucinations and vagaries filled his mind, in all of which Jules Wallace was the principal figure.

Is it a wonder that the agonized mother is bitter in her denunciation of the man whom she regards as more than a murderer?

Is it remarkable that young Putnam's sister wrote the letter received at the Mayor's office denouncing Wallace in the most scathing terms?

Mother and sister believe that Wallace not only robbed them of son and brother, but placed him in the asylum a raving maniac.

———

Mrs. Charles O. Putnam was seen at her home, 1121 Leonard avenue. She is almost broken-hearted because of the calamity which has befallen the family, and it was with difficulty that she related the details of her son's misfortune.

"Neither myself nor any friend of the family has discussed Lowell's case with any one except the physicians," said Mrs. Putnam. "It came upon us so suddenly. There never was a happier family than ours until this villain Wallace dethroned my son's reason and caused his utter ruin.

"Lowell was formerly a salesman, but for the past two years was a music teacher. He had a large number of pupils and was doing well. He was a member of the Pastime Club, and usually took considerable recreation.

"Suddenly he ceased going to his club and commenced to visit Wallace. From that time he was never the same boy again. I do not know what power the man had over him, but it must have been something terrible, for it has robbed me of my boy and put him in a madhouse."

Mrs. Putnam then told the story of Lowell's visits to the medium substantially as related in the foregoing.

"I am positive that my son gave him money," she continued, "but how much I cannot tell. I do not know that he will ever recover. This man Wallace is worse than a murderer, more cowardly than a robber and more villainous than Satan himself.

"Up to this time I have never wished ill to anyone, but I do hope that this man will get his just deserts. I hope that the most terrible torments of the hereafter will be his and that he will never know rest or peace in this life or throughout eternity."

———

Miss Putnam, who wrote the letter to Mayor Walbridge asking him to investigate her brother's case, is a young lady about 19 years of age and is prostrated with grief. She has been trying to find other victims of Jules Wallace, and it is understood she has been successful. She refuses, however, to make their names public at present.

———

When permission was asked last night of the Sister Superior of St. Vincent's Asylum to see Lowell Putnam, the sister said that it was contrary to the institution's rules to allow anyone to visit or communicate with patients without a written order from their parents or guardians.

The Sister Superior, in reply to inquiries, said: "He is much emaciated and as I understand it his mind has been affected by hypnotism. He is tractable, however, and we have hopes that when his constitution has been built up his mental strength will return. He is progressing as well as we could expect.

"There is nothing in his general appearance or actions to indicate insanity, but a close inspection of his eyes clearly shows it. He does not rave, but yields ready obedience to us, and we are encouraged to expect his recovery. It is a rule of the institution not to discuss the names or condition of patients. There have been several here to inquire about Mr. Putnam's condition. I have told them all I consider it proper for me to say about him."

———

As will be remembered Mayor Walbridge recently received an anonymous letter which was published in the Sunday *Republic*, and which stated that Jules Wallace, the self-styled medium and Spiritualist was responsible for the destruction of a happy home and that he had been the means of causing a young man to lose his mind. Jules Wallace denied the charge, but the friends of the young man persist in their story. He was called upon again yesterday and informed that Mrs. Putnam had said that she was positive that her son had given him at least $25 and that she had reason to believe Lowell had given Wallace $15.

"It is false," said Wallace. "The young man to whom I suppose they allude never visited me but once. He wanted me to develop him into a medium, but I refused."

"Why did you refuse?"

"Because he told me he was controlled by the spirit of Abbe Liszt which enabled him to play the mandolin. I asked him to sit down at the piano and demonstrate that he was controlled by the spirit of Liszt, but he would not do so," said Wallace, reiterating the statement.

"Do you know that there are persons in this neighborhood who saw the young man come here regularly?"

"He was never here but once," persisted Wallace.

"Did he expect you to teach him music?"

"No; I do not know one note from another, although I am the author of several songs."

Wallace produced several songs by the well-known composer of variety songs, T. J. Wallace, and audaciously claimed them as his own productions. Various spirits, he said, had assisted in the composition of them.

"Why," he continued, gaining confidence in his own falsehoods, "I can at the present moment invoke any great spirit I choose." He placed his hands over his forehead and eyes, remained in a half-stooping posture and began:

> "O Domine Deus
> Speravi in te,"

repeating the entire prayer of Mary Queen of Scots, made the morning before she was beheaded, which is familiar to almost every schoolboy.

"That," said he, "that is Mary Queen of Scots imploring to be allowed to enter heaven. I hear her voice even now. Is it not beautiful?" he continued, repeating a portion of the euphonious composition. "Is it not more beautiful than any human being could compose? Wait till I translate a portion of it," which he did most barbarously.

With some difficulty he persuaded the celestial central to cut him off from the unfortunate spirit of the Queen and succeeded in getting connection with the spirit of Beethoven. The spirit of the musician was apparently weary, but finally consented to assist a colored woman who had just come up from below, bringing with her a suspicious odor of the kitchen, to play one of his compositions on the piano. How Beethoven could rest or why he did not turn over in his grave during the performance that followed is a mystery.

"I will now invoke the spirit of a famous man and have her play a tune he loved to hear," said the medium. He wrote the name of Abraham Lincoln on a piece of paper, not allowing the colored woman to see it. It was unfortunate for his test that the woman commenced to play "Dixie." Wallace stopped her and did not seem to be embarrassed by the mistake she had made.

"People envy me," said Wallace, "because I always have the price of breakfast, bed and a shave. They are trying to make me leave St. Louis, but I shall stay and live down the lies told about me."

It is alleged that Wallace is now corresponding to go to Brooklyn to give his famous tests, but the society of Spiritualists there wrote to Denver and St. Louis to get his record, and it has been sent on. It is believed that he will journey elsewhere with his tricks and his loyal friend Mrs. Bicknell.

[24 October 1893, p. 1.]

65 - WARRANTS FOR WALLACE.

Two summonses commanding Jules Wallace, the "medium-healer," to appear in court Friday, November 3, and answer to the charges of telling fortunes without a license and of conducting a place of amusement without a license, were issued yesterday at the instance of Charles W. Putnam, whose brother, Lowell Putnam, it is alleged, was made insane by Wallace. The penalty for either of these offenses is a fine of not less than $10 nor more than $300.

Mr. Putnam and his relatives are determined that the case shall be prosecuted with vigor, and have subpoenaed a number of witnesses who were at Cooper's Hall the evening of September 10. This is the date specified in the information charging Wallace with conducting a place of amusement without a license. Chief Lindsay of the Fire Department, Abe Slupsky, ex-Building Commissioner Furlong, James Egan, member of the House of Delegates; Recorder "Billy" Hobbs and J. J. Lane are the witnesses who will testify against Wallace.

Wallace, however, is making preparations to defend himself. He said yesterday that he was in communication with the spirit of the late Judge Normille, and was receiving instructions which would enable him to win his case. He was also in close consultation with the astral bodies of other eminent attorneys, he said, and was confident that he would be victorious.

Wallace declared that with the aid of spirits he would defend the case himself and would employ no attorney on earth. He was determined to stay in St. Louis and would defend all suits brought against him.

It is rumored, nevertheless, that Jules Wallace will close his St. Louis career, at least temporarily. He has packed many of his belongings in boxes and is ready to move at a moment's notice. He has not been placed under bond to appear and answer the charges preferred against him, and it is believed that his departure would not be interrupted if he did not intend to return.

If Wallace is compelled to leave the city at present the ambition of his life will be thwarted.

J. S. Craven, who called himself a "spirit photographer" and Louis Sloss, who is one of Wallace's mediums, have concocted a plan to spring a new religious creed upon their followers. Wallace is the central figure. He is to be in direct communication with Divinity, and has already prepared several revelations which are to be circulated among his chosen flock at the proper time.

Wallace's new plan resembles that of Schweinfurth, the Illinois Christ, whose heaven, at Rockford, Ill., is notorious. Wallace's doctrines are fully

as pernicious as any promulgated by Schweinfurth. They advocate the practice of polygamy, and the female members of the church are to be known as
angels and are to be relied upon to make many converts to the new religion.

There is nothing new in Wallace's theories. They are merely a combina-
tion of the Koran and Schweinfurth's teachings. Wallace believes that if a
Mohammod or Arabian camel driver could found a great religion, Jules
Wallace can also become the head of a religious sect.

The "medium-healer" has not yet boldly proclaimed himself as a prophet.
He has confided to only a few his intentions, but as soon as he has a sufficient number of converts he expects to circulate a number of copies of his
bible. He has followers in Portland, Spokane and Denver and several in St.
Louis.

When he meets a person whom he thinks sufficiently credulous, he at
first claims to be in communication with spirits. Once made to believe that
fact, the possibility of Wallace's being a prophet is easily swallowed.

This plan was told by one of Wallace's friends.

Craven, Louis Sloss and Wallace, it is said, are all acting in concert.
The story told is that Craven secures information to be used by Wallace at
his seances and that Wallace obtains photographs of dead persons which
are reproduced at a photographer's gallery and palmed off as "spirit photographs." Sloss assists both Wallace and Craven and in return they proclaim
him as a medium.

There are many indignant husbands and brothers who are anxious to
prevent their female relatives from visiting Wallace, and the "medium-
healer" receives a large number of threatening letters daily. The climate of
St. Louis is becoming decidedly sultry for him and it is believed that he will
leave the city before the case against him is called for trial.

———

In view of the facts which have recently come to light anent the practices
of Jules Wallace, medium, a great deal of interest is being manifested in the
question as to whether the city authorities will take some steps to rid the
city of him. To learn the intention of the persons in official authority a *Republic* representative called yesterday upon Mayor Walbridge, Chief of Police Harrigan and other officials.

The Mayor said that he had given the letter written to him by the sister
of Lowell Putnam, the latest of Wallace's victims, to the press in the hope
that the facts in the case would be brought to light. The newspapers had
developed the facts, and the Mayor considers that his mission on the matter
is now ended. He says that there is nothing that he can do. Action lies with
the police and the courts.

Charles Putnam, the brother of the unfortunate young man now in the
asylum, called on the mayor some days ago and related to him the disgust-

ing story of Wallace's practices. The Mayor advised the young man to make complaint to the Prosecuting Attorney, and have the destroyer of his brother's mind arrested for immoral practices. The relatives of young Putnam did not wish to father such a prosecution on account of the unpleasant notoriety which it would give them, and the Mayor did not see what else could be done.

Chief Harrigan is not disposed to interfere in the Wallace affair. He says that no law has been violated so far as he knows, and if anybody knows to the contrary let them make formal charges, and they will be investigated.

"In the case of thieves, gamblers and vagrants, do the police not find a way of driving them from the city without any formal charges having been made against them?" was asked of the Chief.

"There are laws that cover these subjects," was the response.

"Is not this man more dangerous than a gambler or a vagrant? Why do you not drive him out?"

"We have no complaints against him."

"Did you not rid the city of a gang of his sort who frequented a certain locality on Broadway? Why do you not dispose of this character in the same way?"

"If all of the disreputable characters in the city were driven out we would have a much smaller population," was the response.

"I repeat," said the Chief, "that I know of no law having been violated. If you do make a complaint and we will look into the matter. You should go and see the Prosecuting Attorney."

The suggestion was complied with and the Chief again seen.

"The Prosecuting Attorney thinks that Mr. Wallace might be arrested for vagrancy on the summons of a police court," was suggested.

"The attorney should read the vagrancy statute," was the response, and the Chief quoted part of the law.

"But the man has no recognized profession."

"He has a boarding-house and money, and that is enough. Why do you not make a complaint against him?"

"As keepers of the peace and order of the city should not the police on their own motion lock up such cases when they become as notorious as the one in question?"

"I say again that I know of no law having been violated, and until a formal complaint is made by a reliable person I will do nothing."

"But in the case of vagrants and gamblers you make it your business to ascertain whether a law has been violated."

"We do not act in the dark." And the interview ended.

Prosecuting Attorney Dierkes said that he would be only too glad to prosecute Wallace if a complaint were made. If the stories told of him were true, he should be disposed of in some way. It would be difficult, the attorney thought, to prove immoral practices, but the man might be reached on the ground of fraud. The attorney thought, too, that he might be prosecuted as a vagrant. Assistant Estep agreed with Mr. Dierkes. The prosecution of Wallace has begun and it is thought that things will be made very hot for him.

[28 October 1893, p. 5.]

66 - WALLACE'S WORK.

The flight of Jules Wallace, the self-styled Prince of Fakers, has left a void in local mediumistic circles which many novices are anxious to fill. It seems also to have left aching voids in the ample bosoms of several fat and more or less fair females of 40 or thereabouts. There was no meeting at Cooper Hall last night, and the faker's rooms at 2661 Olive street were chill and vacant, but a diminished coterie of affinities linger about awaiting the coming of another prophet.

As has long been expected and prophesied, the covert departure of Wallace on last Friday night has unsealed a number of lips and brought to light transactions enough to stock a Zola for several lifetimes. The fat fakir with his inexhaustible mine of lies and wellspring of nerve is being jumped upon with vigor. The jumpers are principally those who knew him during the entire time of his career in this city, both men and women. Not content with jumping on Jules, these men and women are jumping on each other, and several of them are making "revelations" that are entirely unfit for publication; and which, if true, show that certain shining lights in the mediumistic firmament are central figures of a coterie of perverted human beings beside which the "Cleveland Street Gang" of London and the revelations of the *Pall Mall Gazette* pale into insignificance. The worst feature of these revelations is that many worthy people, and even little children, have been led into identifying themselves with some of these fakers and frauds through a sincere belief in Spiritualism as a religion. A *Republic* reporter yesterday uncovered a seething cauldron of past misdeeds, the odor of which, with Wallace as a prime ingredient, was sufficient to cause the closing down tight of the lid. In other words, the moral stench of Wallace's decaying aftermath was too strong to permit much digging.

Mrs. Hill and the other roomers at 2661 Olive street as well as others who associated with Wallace were seen. The stories elicited from these parties involve the honor and prosperity of entire families, and involve such details as, however much glossed over and shielded by marshaled phalanxes of phrases, must nevertheless test the limit of newspaper expression and cause expressions of disgust from all who despise such degradation.

If the police do not do their duty with the imitators and disciples of Wallace who remain in the city, both male and female, these expressions of disgust may change to expressions of indignation; for surely there is great cause.

It appears that Wallace moved into 2661 Olive with much eclat and the usual flow of egotistical palaver which characterized his every move. He took two rooms and prepared his tricks, which, as his ingenuity would have it, required no especial wall cutting or carpentering. A few natural facilities were present, however, which his former landlady, Mrs. Hill, will not now deny that he used. He brought his electric battery with him from which his physical coruscations were produced. It is now related that while exhibiting it one day he dropped the battery and spilled all its spiritualistic fluid upon a new Brussels carpet, ruining it. Then in payment for the damage done he gave promises which were never fulfilled. Jules, as the public has long known, could not keep his mouth closed. That orifice was the physical sewer-vent through which flowed all the rant, braggadocio, ill humor and profanity that made up the most of Wallace's brain. Through it he blabbed, bragged, raved and promised in endless continuity until his hour of departure. He seems to have made little attempt to disguise his real character in the house where he lived.

Anyone could pat him on the back and call him a faker, and Wallace would take it and apparently appreciate it. He made no effort to conceal the fact that he drank. He inaugurated an air of freedom about the place that had not previously been. He brought his friends and intimates to the house, secured them rooms and thus seems to have controlled the sense and liberty of the entire building. This was not all. With his increasing notoriety women came for sittings, and then all sense of the vicious trend of things was lost. The back parlor was filled with female believers. A trance lasted from 10 minutes to two hours behind barred doors, and there was no accounting for anything that was done, for the cloak of "religion" covered it all.

Wallace went further; money was pouring in upon him. He could afford diamonds and jewelry. With his prosperity his characteristics, passive and dominant, became disgustingly apparent. He stacked a cupboard with liquors. He gave seances to women at night, and swore with ill feeling and bad temper in the morning. Sometimes he came in intoxicated and hilarious, making the stillness of a quiet neighborhood resound with his "whoop-las." The man was apparently insane on the subject of his own personality. He seemed actually crazed by his ability to inspire and betray confidence and his general notoriety. Never at a loss for a story, he related his experiences or those of others, claiming them as his own; cried out that all believers in Spiritualism were fools, and rejoiced that St. Louisans were so easily gulled.

In short, if *The Republic* should print in full the details of revelations made yesterday and last night an outraged public sentiment would revolt against it and declare that the immoral chapter should remain untold.

It was to put a stop to all this bestiality and swindling that *The Republic* made the first revelation concerning the great faker's operations, showing Pat Burns, alias Pat Wallace, alias Prof. Jules Wallace, up in his true light. That publication has been followed by others until finally the fraud or freak or both in one has been driven out of town. But he has left an awful stench and many disciples. These, unless driven out, will follow in his footsteps and prey upon the people. The names and games of many of these are known to many people, and it is probable that the truth—or as much of it as can be printed—will be told.

———

It was Mrs. Hill, his landlady, who detailed for a *Republic* reporter yesterday afternoon the facts that make Wallace's career in St. Louis seem so fearful. For fully an hour she talked on Wallace and his doings, the story being actually curtailed and limited by modesty and the inadequacy of English.

"Wallace went away Friday, did he?" said the reporter. "Did he owe you much money?"

"Well, some; yes. He owed me for room rent and a spoiled carpet. He brought a number of young fellows here to room and stood good for them. Most of their rent he paid out of his own pocket, but the rest I lost. He never did pay for the carpet that the battery fluid spoiled, although he said he would."

"How much rent did he owe you?"

"About $60 in all."

"Did Wallace have the room prepared for him when he came here—I mean did he cut holes here and there so as to arrange his paraphernalia?"

"No, he didn't use much paraphernalia. He had lots of tricks, though, and he used to brag over the way he could fool people."

"What was his mode of living here, anyway? Did he have friends, associates and the like?"

"Well, I know more about his mode of living since the papers exposed him than I ever did. I never quite understood Wallace. He was so loud-mouthed and inconsistent. He was good-hearted, free with his money, and all that, but he was so egotistical. Then he was false and cowardly, after all his bragging. I am horrified now that I understand how he carried on here.

Since *The Republic* printed the story about Lowell Putnam I understand what he had so many young men around him for. He always had a crowd of six, and sometimes even more. For some of them he paid room rent and he used to closet himself with them, but as he gave seances I thought nothing of it. I do now, however."

"What has become of Sloss, the San Francisco slatewriter who was here?"

"Oh, he's gone back to Denver. He left 10 days before Wallace. Sloss and Wallace never agreed, but that was on account of Mrs. Bicknell. Mrs. Bicknell hung around here and associated herself with Wallace. Some people thought her his wife. When *The Republic* exposed Wallace and spoke of her Denver career she began to suspect, I think, that Sloss who knew her in Denver, was telling tales outside. She didn't want him in the house and kept telling Wallace stories about him so that Wallace would quarrel with him and drive him out. After the exposure Wallace came in the house and met Sloss. Wallace grabbed him by the throat and threatened to beat him all up, saying all the time that Sloss had given him away. Sloss just begged for mercy, and Wallace cursed and raved about fearfully. A little while afterward when a half dozen of us, along with Sloss, were in the parlor Wallace got down on his knees and in that silly dramatic style of his swore that if he could get proof that Sloss ever had a hand in that exposure he would murder him. Someone told him to get up and not act the fool. I believe that Wallace was drunk.

"Wallace, for all his bragging, was a moral coward. He once came in after some trick of his had been told to a friend. He was angry and accused my son of telling the secret to others. My son denied the accusation and Wallace called him a fearful name. Then my son resented the insult and struck Wallace in the eye. Just as soon as this happened Wallace became fearfully frightened and called for someone to help him. Two friends of his were here and they held my son while Wallace hollered: 'Keep him off! Keep him off! Don't let him disfigure my face!' Then he went inside his room and didn't come out for 24 hours for fear my son would injure him. About that time he did come out and begged my boy's pardon, which he received. He was really all bluff, for the moment anyone stood their ground and re-sisted him he gave up."

"What were his relations with his visitors? Do you know?"

"Well, they were not right in many respects. He had a number of women friends who seemed deeply interested in him. Mrs. Bicknell was one of them and there were several others. I know that Mrs. Bicknell's relations were not what they should have been. Another woman who came here fre-quently acted very strangefully. She came here very often, sometimes twice and three times a day. I don't know whether it was to receive sitting, or treatment for sickness, but one day last July shortly after Wallace returned from Chicago, my daughter accidentally opened the door of Wallace's private office, or seance-room. This woman was in the room with Wallace alone. She was partially disrobed and in a compromising position."

Mrs. Hill related in detail some most astounding facts about this occurrence.

Continuing, Mrs. Hill said:

"I cannot tell all that I now understand about Wallace's position here. I realize that his associates, male and female, were of his own stripe; much lower even than scarlet women. His moral nature must have been strangely perverted or else he could not have gathered about him such a band of young persons, whom he was physically wrecking in his endeavors to make them mediums. When I spoke of them, thinking, as I did, that they were friends who were in hard luck and were imposing upon his charitable nature, he said yes, they were. Sometimes he would complain of being compelled to assist so many of them, and then, when I told him that he was too good-hearted and that he ought to leave them to take care of themselves, he would quit talking at once or change the subject. Some of these were miserable-looking fellows. I suppose his mediumistic training was wrecking them."

In reference to the statement of Mrs. Hill that Wallace kept several young men about him it was learned that he had use for them. He paid their board and gave them a little pin money, but it was they who made his money for him. He made them his slaves, subject to his beck. When a stranger applied to him for spiritualistic help he would get his name and address, and put him off for a day or perhaps for an hour or two. He would at once send his cappers to grocery and drug stores in the vicinity of the address to see what gossip could be picked up. A number of more or less reliable pointers could be gotten in this way, and with these for a foundation the "medium" could get up a plausible story quite acceptable to the victim. This was one of the many ways in which he worked his gulls. When not actively engaged he circulated among the gossip mongers of the town and got as many idlers as possible "on his staff."

His business was most prosperous. He developed fully 100 persons at $50 per head. He gave any number of spirit communications at $2 per seance. He had a convenient way of being busy or "out" when he got tired of seeing his victims. Mrs. Hill, who related the above story of his gains, said that he often, after giving a few sittings in a "development" case would substantially refuse to see the victim again. He always got the money in advance and that was all that he cared for. The gulls were afraid to demur, as they feared the unscrupulousness of the "medium."

For a time Wallace courted newspaper criticism, for he thought it would advertise his business, but after the specific disclosures in *The Republic*, his landlady said he seemed to lose heart. He once said to his landlady on the departure of Lowell Putnam from his rooms: "That man is as crazy as a loon, and he will go off and say that I did it and I will get some more advertising."

This air of braggadocio all left him when Mrs. Hill told him that he would have to find rooms elsewhere. He said that if he was driven out of there no one else would rent him rooms, and that he could and would disprove the ugly charges which she had then heard. When Mrs. Hill confronted him a second time he said that he was going away next week, and that it would not be worth while to make him change. He went sooner than he expected to.

Many of Wallace's victims were young women and young men whose parents or relatives did not know of their foolishness, or wives whose husbands—many of them solid, sensible business men—were entirely ignorant of what their wives were doing. On these, of course, Wallace had a clutch that they could not shake off.

Information came to *The Republic* that one Mrs. Mayhew could give some exceedingly interesting information concerning Wallace's operations. It was reported that she was a "full-fledged" medium who had been developed by Wallace. It was further reported that Mrs. Mayhew—who was formerly Mrs. Montell—had a little daughter who had been utilized in Wallace's spook show as the spirit.

Mrs. Mayhew was out last night when a reporter called, but her little daughter, Miss Carrie, the reputed spook, said that her mother would be in in a few minutes. Directly Mrs. Mayhew appeared on the scene full of cordiality and vivacity. She is very brunette with very small and very sharp eyes, not the sort of looking person one would pick out for a gull. Her velvet hat with its stiff jaunty feather sat saucily on her head and her grey plaid gown fitted her to a nicety.

"I have disclosures to make," she began, "which would make interesting reading, but if they were published to-morrow as coming from me, my life would not be worth that," and she snapped her fingers dramatically. "There are vampires in this city—men who are taking the very life blood out of their victims—and I could expose them let me tell you. I am a full-fledged medium. I have been investigating Spiritualism all of my life, and Jules Wallace is the first medium who would undertake to develop me. I paid my money for Spiritualism, and I learned it all. Do I look like a fool? I would not pay a nickel for all the rest of the Spiritualism in the United States. I have been attending seances and paying for Spiritualism for 10 years, but I am done. I know it all now. I did not make the investment for fun, and I will make money out of it. Wallace gave me what I wanted. He said that he would make a medium out of me, and he did. He told the tricks of the trade, and I can use my own judgment to apply them. He is not to blame if people are too dumb to find things out.

"I owe Wallace something and I am going to find him. No, it is not money, it is not a debt of gratitude. I want to square myself with him," and Mrs. Mayhew looked quite mysterious.

"Oh, you are going to join Wallace?" suggested the reporter.

"No; I am just going to find him if I can. Let me tell you something," and Mrs. Mayhew looked quite impressive.

"I came here without money and he cured my child, who was suffering from St. Vitus' dance, and he did not charge me a cent. I paid for my 'developing,' but still I want to square myself with Wallace. Yes, I know where he is. He is not far off, but he is not in the city. He has not gone to New York. He will not go to Mrs. Bicknell. By the way, Mrs. Bicknell is Wallace's wife. She was married to him last summer.

"No, I never helped Wallace at his seances. Oh, no, I was never a spook. That is absurd. Honest to God, my little girl never acted as a spook. I am telling you this on my honor. What is the penalty if one was caught playing spook? Would it all fall on the medium? I thought that they could be prosecuted for getting money under false pretenses.

"Wallace is to be back here soon. He will be back this week, but I do not know at what number he will locate. I know that he will be back.

"I am going to make money out of Spiritualism. I am from Baltimore and my husband is a theatrical man. He knew Wallace at Honolulu, at San Francisco and Denver, but he was not the man who made the cabinet and fixed up the rooms for Wallace in the last named place. I have a photograph of Wallace which I got from my husband. My husband was a stage carpenter, an honest, hard-working man. He was not intimate with Wallace."

Mrs. Mayhew then spent some time in praising Wallace and in telling how very simple the profession of "medium" is when one understands it. One can get up a spirit bureau of information with a small code of instructions and a still smaller cash capital.

"By the way, Mrs. Mayhew, speaking of vampires, do you think Wallace among the number?"

"Oh, I do not know. There is a woman coming from Chicago in a few days to work this town, and won't I rip her up the back? I intend to rip Spiritualism up the back. That is why I learned it. This woman I speak of is an unmitigated fraud."

"How about other spiritualistic mediums?"

Mrs. Mayhew put her finger to her nose and winked the other eye. She started and ran on on all conceivable subjects, being all the while very wise and very noncommittal. She says that she is not living where she is now, simply stopping, and her main object is to get out of there and out of St.

Louis as soon as possible. She said first that she was going to get out to-morrow morning, and then seemed sorry for saying it and took it back. According to her own story she will have an opportunity to square herself with Wallace before many days.

Mrs. Mayhew had a friend with her, whom she called Mrs. Wilkins, who is also imbued with the medium craze and was ready to swear by what her friend said. From the tone of their conversation they consider playing medium a praiseworthy fake. She wanted to make terms before telling her sensation which would not leave her life worth a dramatic snap.

Concerning Jules Wallace's departure from the city quite an interesting and somewhat graphic picture is painted by one of his dupes, who was cognizant of his intention to depart and who was present part of the time during preparations. No less than five "ladies" and probably several more aided and abetted the fellow—at least to the extent of giving him advice and extending their sympathy at his escaping the clutches of the law. It cannot be stated with absolute accuracy that all of these women knew that the man was at that time a subject of a police court summons and was supposably being searched for by officers instructed to take him into custody. All of them, however, did know that he had been exposed as a fraud and an arrant knave and that he was making preparations to leave the city to escape the consequences of his evil doing. According to the story of one of these women, who insists that she had no idea she was doing any wrong, but now admits that she was most gloriously duped, she dropped into Wallace's rooms for the purpose of "sitting for development." She found there at the time three or four others, all of whom she had met at different times at Wallace's seances or sittings, and she soon saw there was something out of the ordinary going on. Wallace was bustling about the room getting his goods and chattels together and chatting with the women. The informant remarked with some surprise, "Why, Mr. Wallace is going away," to which one of the others replied:

"Yes; what else can he do?"

Then there ensued a general conversation, in which Wallace assumed the role of the poor persecuted pet of all those present, and they in turn condoled with and tried to console him.

One of them suggested that he might remain in the city and just keep quiet until the storm had blown over. This idea did not, however, strike Wallace very favorably, and the other women took his view of the case. They all advised him to get out of town as quickly as possible, to avoid arrest on the summons that had been issued for him, but are said to have exacted from him a promise to return again. One of the women present is said to have even gone so far as to boast of her "pull" with Chief Harrigan and to promise Wallace entire immunity if he would just stay away from town long enough to let the newspapers drop him.

Mrs. Hill, Wallace's landlady, was asked last night if she knew where he was. She replied:

"I do not. He packed up his things and left last Friday. He said nothing to me until the last hour, when he came out and remarked 'I'm off.' There were a number of people in the house. Four or five women came in to console him and see him safely away. He had been, so he said, downtown to square up a few small accounts with the newspapers. They did not know I guess that he was wanted by the police. That night he left and Mrs. Bicknell's son went to the depot with him. He says that Wallace was badly frightened; kept in the shadow and talked about being unable to avoid arrest. Where he went I haven't the slightest idea."

Mrs. Walsh of 2346 Chestnut street, who was once one of Wallace's most ardent followers, said last night that she knew Wallace to be a fraud and a scoundrel. She also said that many persons who attended the seances were robbed of their jewelry.

"I was one of Wallace's dupes," said Mrs. Walsh, "and I paid him $50 to develop me as an independent slate writer. I found that Wallace could not assist me in any way.

"Among those who attended the seances was Mrs. Fagerty, wife of the Postmaster at East St. Louis. She wore several valuable diamonds and during one of the seances she missed a diamond necklace which she valued very highly. She quietly told Wallace about it and he actually made the poor woman believe that her dead daughter's spirit had taken it.

"'But my dead daughter was not a thief,' remonstrated Mrs. Fagerty.

"'Hush, you must not speak of thieves in the presence of spirits,' said Wallace. 'The diamonds have only been dematerialized for your daughter's use, and as soon as she is through with them they will be returned.'

"Mrs. Fagerty was satisfied with this explanation. When she came to the next seance she fully expected to have the necklace restored to her, but instead of that two diamond rings were stolen from her and she was informed that her daughter needed more jewelry for some celestial function which was soon to come off and when that was over all the jewelry would be returned. At the next seance Mrs. Fagerty lost the only remaining ring, and she strenuously objected to giving it all to her daughter's spirit. A row was imminent, but Wallace quieted her by explaining that she would get her jewelry back as soon as he could communicate with the spirit of her daughter. Besides the loss of her jewelry Mrs. Fagerty is out $50, which she paid Wallace to develop her."

"How were those robberies accomplished?"

"Of course I did not see the jewelry taken, but I am positive that the persons whom Wallace employed as confederates took the diamonds. Mrs. Mayhew of 2319 Olive street, her daughter Carrie and others were assisting Wallace. Carrie Mayhew is a bright little girl only 12 years of age and frequently had to be whipped before she would consent to take part in these seances. She was frequently slapped by Wallace and her mother never made any objection. The child seems to have known that she was doing wrong and would not take part except under compulsion.

"Carrie Mayhew's duties were to creep around in the dark and when a person called for a certain spirit she would tap their knee either two or three times, according to the answer to be given. Twice meant 'yes,' and three taps meant 'no.' It was given out at the beginning of each seance that nobody was to resist a spirit, and when Mrs. Fagerty felt someone removing her necklace she did not resist because she believed it to be her dead daughter's spirit.

"Yes, there were other victims. Here is one right here," continued Mrs. Walsh, introducing a lady as Mrs. Clark, who declined to give her residence.

"I only wish Wallace would come back," said Mrs. Clark. "I would like to hammer him. I paid Wallace $50, too, and I was very foolish for doing it. At the second seance I attended an attempt was made to get this necklace," she said, indicating a handsome diamond necklace which she wore; "but I refused to let the spirits, as they are called, have the jewelry. Some one then grabbed my throat and tore my dress. I jumped to my feet and was about to scream when the spirits disappeared and the lights were turned up. Wallace said to me, when I was going away that night: 'Do not wear diamonds at seances, Mrs. Clark, because the spirits might dematerialize them.' I always kept them out of sight after that and the spirits did not molest them.

"Wallace told me that the spirit of my little girl, who died not long ago, wanted a doll. I bought six dolls, all together, and took them to the seances. I am told that Mrs. Mayhew has all but one of them in her room and that she gave the other one to Mrs. Walsh, and here it is."

The doll was produced in evidence.

"At another time the spirit, which I am convinced was little Carrie Mayhew, felt to see if I had my diamonds on, and discovering that I had not she asked me in a confidential whisper to buy her a diamond 'just like ma's.' I began to be convinced that the whole thing was a fraud and wished that I had my money back.

"Wallace must have made a small fortune while he was in St. Louis. I have seen as many as 40 persons at one seance. Letter Carrier Wood was a regular attendant and I understand he paid Wallace $50, as did almost everyone else who attended the seances, and had it to pay."

Mrs. Clark also declared that she thought Mrs. Mayhew had the missing jewelry, and said she would advise all persons who lost money and jewelry at the seances to have a warrant sworn out and prosecute the case. She said that she knew of persons who were only too anxious to prosecute Wallace if he should ever dare to return.

There is one man in St. Louis whose implicit faith in the powers of Jules Wallace cost him $50, for which he has the receipt.

This gentleman is so deeply interested in the missing "medium-healer" that, unless the two warrants now out find him, a warrant for obtaining money under false pretenses will be sworn out and the efficacy of a criminal charge tried.

The gentleman is very chary of his name just at present, but says it will soon appear in a large, round hand at the bottom of an affidavit.

This man who is minus $50 was—and is—a believer in Spiritualism. He became a follower of Wallace and paid him $50, in installments of $25, and has receipts for the money, though he says that it was not the habit of the medium to give receipts. He further alleges that there are 20 persons, to his personal knowledge, who have been defrauded of money and valuables by Wallace.

This one-time dupe says that he has learned all of Wallace's tricks and, with confederates, can give as good seances and "manifestations" as the original.

The "spirits" are material and some of them were named. For instance, Wallace, being an excellent actor, took several parts. At times he was an Indian. With this part went a heavy tread, grunts, an "Ugh! Ugh!" occasionally and an unintelligible jabber.

"Mrs. Murphy," or her spirit, seems to have been a regular visitant. Her greeting, "How are yez all this evenin'?" was always answered by the circle sitting in darkness with "Good evening, Mrs. Murphy."

Wallace was Mrs. Murphy.

Wallace is said to have seated his followers in a circle, having near him his confederates. The lights were then extinguished and all joined hands. Wallace then warned them that if the circle was broken or anyone attempted to seize a spirit such rash person would be promptly knocked on the head by one of the spirit Indians, for which astral sandbagging the medium disclaimed all responsibility.

Incidentally it is said that Wallace always carried a "billy."

The money was taken from those of whom Wallace would make mediums. He took all he could get. He had a sliding scale. He discovered "powers" in all who came to him, and the money was the consideration for developing the "powers."

[30 October 1893, pp. 1–2.]

67 - MYSTERY OF A MURDER.

Alexander McClelland, a prominent farmer of Marion County, Illinois, disappeared with his 20-year-old son, Oscar, in the summer or fall of 1881. He left behind him four sons and a divorced wife, who had given birth to a girl child by him only a year before. The McClelland boys remained about the old home until circumstances forced them to relinquish it.

Twelve years elapsed after McClelland's disappearance, when on Tuesday, November 7, last, two workingmen employed by R. S. Tate, the present owner of the McClelland farm, to clean out an old stock pond discovered the skeleton of a man staked and stone-weighted to the bottom of the slimy pool, where it had been for years. Three days later another skeleton was found buried in a similar manner, 30 feet west of the resting place of the first, in the center of the pond.

The community was immediately aroused as never before in all its history and suspicion was directed toward the sons of the missing McClelland.

The skulls bore marks of a violent death and instruments for such purpose were found near by—a pick and hoe.

The investigation by the Coroner has not yet been concluded, but the testimony so far lies only in the direction of the immediate relatives of the family, who are endeavoring to clear themselves of suspicion and may perhaps accomplish their purpose.

As yet no one has been legally censured.

A tale of murder and concealment that 12 long years have failed to weaken its dread terror; a disappearance so strange that the whole population of a county and State are moved by more than a common interest, is what at present excites Marion County of Illinois with a kind of quivering wildfire justice that calls for legal vengeance upon the murderers of Squire Alexander McClelland and his 20-year-old son, Oscar.

In the triangular center of three rural towns, Odin, Sandoval and Centralia, Ill., the farmers are whispering and arguing, while hundreds of idlers flock to the inquest center (Centralia) and discuss the deed and its perpetrators and their blinding of justice for so many weary years.

Squire Alexander McClelland was 12 years ago a prosperous farmer, a Justice of the Peace and a well-known old settler of Marion County. He was the father of 12 children during his matrimonial career, covering 40 years and the lives of two wives. At the time of his disappearance five of the children were still living. He was respected and well related.

During the summer and fall of 1881 people heard Squire McClelland say he was going West. People saw him last in the harvesting season of June–July, 1881, and heard of him last in October–November, 1881. Then he disappeared.

"House Where the McClelland Boys Lived" (*St. Louis Republic*, 19 November 1893, p. 9).

"The Skeletons as Found" (*St. Louis Republic*, 19 November 1893, p. 9).

An entire community had all but forgotten his existence until a stock pond on the old homestead was cleaned about 10 days ago and two skeletons unearthed.

Were the skeletons exhumed those of the long missing Squire and his 20-year-old son?

That was the absorbing question.

On Tuesday evening, November 7 last, two employes of R. E. Tate, the present owner and occupant of what is known as the old McClelland homestead, were digging about a recently drained stock pond with a view of widening and deepening it for future use.

The old McClelland homestead, where, 12 years ago, Squire McClelland and his four sons resided, is nearly centrally situated between the towns of Odin, Sandoval and Centralia, being within three or four miles of either place.

At the time of Squire McClelland's prosperous existence his farm swept its limits broad and wide over 600 acres of timbered and arable land, and he controlled a grist mill of no mean proportions nor slight patronage. Its limits were bounded by strong fences. His house and storage structures were models of convenience and durability, and his fields were in a state of excellent cultivation. Besides all of this he had a large stock of cattle and hogs and five able, willing sons to assist him in the direction of his comfortable and growing possessions.

Years before, in the early stage of his farming career, when first the stock-raising idea took possession of him, he excavated, about a quarter of a mile north of his house, a wide and long stock pond, where the fattening cattle might find a wading and drinking place the year round.

It is to be surmised that at the digging no omen of the fate which should stretch him face upwards, stone-weighted and chain-staked, butchered and rotting at the bottom of its slimy depths, ever crossed the vision of his striding prosperity.

Since 12 years ago, or about 1881, when the Squire and his son Oscar disappeared, great ruin had come upon the old lands and the stock pond had become so filled with the accumulation of mud and filth that it stood practically useless.

When the present owner, Richard E. Tate, took hold of the place he began a system of improvements and repairs, which included the building of a new house and storage barns, the reparation of fences and the cleaning, widening and deepening of the old stock pond.

This latter work began on Saturday, November 4, last. Two men were set to work. They were Henry Sanders, who lives close to the old farm, and Robert Poke, whose house is not much farther away. The men drained the water and began digging and hauling the mud away. The work continued uninterruptedly until Tuesday, November 7.

On that afternoon Sanders and Poke, while scraping the bottom of the pond, uncovered the skeleton of a man laying under about a foot of sediment formed since the body was laid to rest.

The men were using scrapers and the first portion of the body they struck was the skull. At regular spaces from the head to the feet cross stakes were found, standing sentinels over the whitened bones, as though to prevent their rising and stalking abroad, veritable ghoul avengers of their own foul death. Beneath these stakes, crossed, sawbuck-fashion, were piled on the wasted form great blocks of stone aggregating in weight hundreds of pounds.

The uncovering continued, and the ghastly find developed peculiar circumstances that since has caused no end of excited and open comment.

Mr. Tate was immediately called, and he in turn sent word to the authorities at Centralia and Sandoval, from which places a crowd of curious spectators soon arrived.

An examination was begun, which showed that there was no flesh visible on any part of the skeleton, except a fibrous substance at the roots of the hair. An old pair of trousers, colored and rotted with the slime of years, were found stretched across the fleshless knees. An old pocket-book, in a fair state of preservation, but with nothing in it, was also discovered near the head, which lay face upwards to the west, exactly in the center of the pond.

It was thought from a jagged rent in the left temple bone of the skull that the man had been murdered, but the deed was placed at 20 or more years before.

Later the suggestion concerning Squire Alex. McClelland's absence came up and many immediately suggested that it might be his murdered remains.

The news of the discovery spread rapidly to the limits of the county. Investigation was called for and soon the shadowy hand of suspicion began to point in the direction of Alexander McClelland's relatives.

People began to inquire where the man's sons were and why they did not come forward.

Old-time acquaintances declared that by certain marks on the body they were able to say that it was that of Alexander McClelland.

Foremost among these was C. M. Welsh, an old resident and friend of the Squire's, who lives at present one mile northeast of Sandoval. He recognized the hair and the heavy eyebrow protrusions, as well as certain other marks.

A. J. Matthews, McClelland's son-in-law, and one whom the old Squire had assisted to start upon a successful marriage career by a donation of 25 acres of land and some money, was first of all the relatives to reach the old farm after the discovery of the skeleton. Upon seeing the old purse he declared that it was exactly the same as one McClelland always carried.

In the pursuance of natural public curiosity the relatives of the long missing McClelland were visited. Some of these said that Alex. senior was at present in Old Mexico, but the assurance only tended to increase the general mistrust and to lead people to believe that the skeleton found was that of the missing man.

Coroner J. H. Aiken of Marion County came down from Salem, the county seat, to Centralia on Thursday, November 9, and empaneled a jury. He brought along with him Dr. Downey of Sandoval, who is an expert in matters pertaining to physiological identification, and held a partial investigation. The work was not satisfactory and that evening the jury was dismissed with instructions to convene on the following Monday morning at the old McClelland homestead near the pond, when the investigation would be continued. In the meantime subpoenas were issued for nearly every man and woman within 10 miles around who knew anything of the family relations and troubles of the missing McClelland.

During this time little or nothing was said of Oscar McClelland, the missing son of Squire McClelland, who disappeared about the same time.

During the preliminary hearing of Thursday, November 9, some of the evidence presented diverged widely. There was a marked difference as to the length of time the pond had been upon the McClelland farm.

Harry McClelland said that the pond had not been there to exceed seven or eight years.

A. M. Jarvis testified that he swam in it when he was a boy, and that was over 20 years before.

The doctor and Coroner then for the first time agreed that the bones had been under the waters of the stock pond for at least 10 or 12 years.

Before Monday, November 13, had rolled around another astonishing piece of evidence had been added to the celebrated case.

On Friday, November 10, the day following the first Coroner's investigation, Henry Sanders and Robert Poke, the two excavators at the pond, unearthed a second skeleton 30 feet west of where the first one had been found. Its head was also crushed and lay face down to the west, staked over and weighted as the other had been with heavy rocks, supposed to have come from a neighboring railroad trestle built 12 years before.

The news of the discovery of a second skeleton came as a decree of fate destined to corroborate the publicly expressed opinion that young Oscar McClelland had been murdered with his father. The skeleton, when examined by physicians, was pronounced that of a young man.

The father and son, after 12 long years of absence, were accounted for. The manner of their discovery was actually looked upon as a kind of providential intervention ordering the dead men to return and by the horror of their bleached and burdened bones to force from the lips of their slayers the story of the terrible crime.

Matters soon took a legal shape and the pond was made the object of renewed and especial labor. An old cistern near the McClelland house on the farm was ordered excavated for the body of Miss Gertrude, an adopted daughter of the Squire and Mrs. McClelland (now Mrs. Glick of Central City, Ill.), which was supposed to be buried there, dealt with perhaps as the others had been.

This action of the Coroner showed the trend of the general feeling at the time.

It seemed as though the entire population of the county was flocking to the scene and that everyone was pointing at John and Oliver McClelland as being the murderers of their father and brother. Meanwhile the Coroner adjourned the investigation until yesterday to await developments and the arrival of witnesses.

At the Monday inquest Dr. W. A. J. Delancey, David Coffee, H. C. McClelland (cousin to the missing Squire), C. M. Welch (an intimate friend), Mrs. Nodine, Dr. E. Broomeer and John A., Oliver J. and Otto McClelland (the Squire's resident sons) all went on the stand to testify.

The teeth of the older skeleton were introduced as evidence that the remains were those of the Squire. He had filled teeth corresponding to those of the skeleton. The hair and the general appearance were testified to as being that of Alex. McClelland.

The sons swore to the departure of their parent and brother. Also to the good feeling prevailing in the family at the time of their departure, as well as the general impossibility of the skeletons having aught in connection with the missing man and his son.

John A., the eldest living son, testified that he had received letters from his father as late as 1883, but had not preserved them.

C. M. Welsh testified that he had once heard A. J. Matthews, the Squire's son-in-law, say that he had received a letter from his father-in-law, but it was not to be found.

This testimony Mr. Matthews stoutly pronounced false. He asserted that Welsh's testimony was prompted by a long-standing grudge.

Only one thing stands blazing, torch-like, out of all the surrounding gloom of uncertain suspicion, and that is that the two skeletons found are those of murdered men. Whether they are father and son is another question, and whether they are McClelland and son still another.

True, they were found on the McClelland farm, and the stones piled upon them were from a neighboring trestle built 12 years ago, or about the time the father and son disappeared.

The stakes that pinned their unfortunate bodies down to the slime beneath the muddy waters of the pond are pieces of wood that came from machinery and fences about the farm.

If an enemy of local habitation, a man who had longed for an opportunity to do away with the missing men, he would not have taken the lives of his victims and then proceeded deliberately to bury them upon the land of their nearest relatives, within a stone's throw of their old home and their nearest kin.

It might have been done, but the very men suspected, John A. and Oliver McClelland, admit that it would not be a plausible nor a sensible view to take of the matter.

The proposition thus narrowed down was presented to the two sons mentioned and they were asked whether it was not reasonable to suppose that the person or persons who committed the fearful crime were well acquainted, in fact absolutely familiar with the conditions and environments of the old McClelland homestead.

They answered yes. It was reasonable to suppose so. Yet they could not venture the opinion as a certainty.

They went further, and admitted that the stones and the stake came from the place pointed out by the Coroner's investigation, and that the bodies had probably been buried in the pond at night, but they stop there and go no further.

The possibility of any one transporting two bodies at night to their farm and the pond in question, not over a stone's throw from where they were, self-admitted, sleeping or waking at the time, does not seem improbable. In fact they insist that since the bodies have been found there they must have come there by some such method of which they knew nothing.

It is such conversation and such vented opinion as this that causes the entire community, with, of course, some exceptions, to eye the boys with marked and certain suspicion.

The whole talk about Centralia, Sandoval and Odin, where they are so well known, is condensed in the queries as to why the boys were not present at the pond when they knew that two bodies were being removed under such strange circumstances, and why they constantly and persistently fight the idea that the skeletons now locked up in two plain wooden cases at Centralia could possibly be the remains of their long missing father and younger brother.

Pinned right down to a plain question, such as "Do you stand here and assert that these two skeletons could not by any possible means be those of your father and brother?" John A., Oliver J. and Otto, the three boys, will answer that they do not.

The Marion County public look upon these facts as being almost absolute proof positive of the guilt of the boys, insisting that such cold-blooded indifference cannot possibly mean anything else.

All Marion County knows by this time that when old Squire McClelland disappeared he was on the high road to poverty and financial wreck. His style of pioneer intelligence had become almost worthless in the light of the modern art of money-making, and the old stock-raising system was in that county fast becoming obsolete.

Besides he was getting well along in years at the time—57 exactly—and had more than once ventured the remark, even to those that are at present endeavoring to prove him murdered, that he could not ever expect to retrieve his lost fortune. Along with this fact comes the other that more than once both he and Oscar had said that they were going West.

Old Grandmother Elethes Martin, who lives near the old McClelland homestead, remembers that in 1881 Oscar came by her house and shook hands with her, bidding her good-by and saying that he was going away. It was about this time that he disappeared, and Grandma Martin's remembrance is not to be questioned even though she is 83 years old for her memory is clear on other salient points.

Next in order come the statements of ever so many close neighbors and old acquaintances, who assert and insist that the boys, especially John A. and Oliver, the two suspected, were always good, steady, hard-working, honest fellows, who remained at home and worked almost like slaves to maintain the falling prestige and financial standing of their parent. It was, so many assert, never known that old Squire McClelland ever had a favorite son, as Oscar has been termed. If anyone was a favorite, say they, it must have been John A., now suspected, and not Oscar, for John A. was the eldest and the most faithful.

At the time that McClelland disappeared no one knew that he had come into the possession of any sum of money. If he had there was not the evidence of property sold or traded to confirm it. The old gentleman was in financial straits. Everybody seems to know this. McClelland's death is not laid to any desire on the part of the sons to obtain money, but rather to some internal family dispute.

Since the disappearance of the twain, in 1881, the remaining boys of the family have led respectable and hard-working lives, and have been out of the reach of ordinary reproach. They did not leave the country nor forsake the old farm until they were forced to by an untoward combination of unkind circumstances. When they did leave they went to work in the vicinity, laboring as diligently as the next one, and kept this record up for 12 long years. They have paid their debts, retained their friends and made no especial enemies. It is only the present strange circumstance that has aroused the public feeling of suspicion and distrust that follows them now wherever they go.

Perhaps no family in all Southern Illinois was better known than this of the McClellands. The old Squire so long missing was at the time of his disappearance a Justice of the Peace at Central City, and had been for many years. Geo. W. McClelland, one of his first cousins, is at present one of Marion County's three Road Commissioners, and has held other offices in the past. W. C. McClelland, another cousin, is at present a School Trustee of Odin Township, and has held other positions in the past. The latter gentlemen are well known and rank as two of the most prosperous and thorough business men that the county possesses.

A. J. Matthews, who has been accused in several ways by outsiders of having aided in bringing about the death of the missing men, is an ex-school trustee of Odin Township and one of the wide-awake politicians of the county.

W. Scott Matthews, his brother-in-law, is ex-Sheriff of the county, having served a term previous to the present incumbent, and now is a well-known lawyer of Kinmundy, Ill.

L. C. Matthews, a third brother, living at Sandoval, was formerly a Justice of the Peace for 12 years, and is now Postmaster of Sandoval, as well as one of its wealthiest residents.

Wm. A. Matthews, a fourth brother, is also quite wealthy, and holds the position of Supervisor of Odin Township.

For their long residence, position, record of honesty and personal wealth all the gentlemen in question are held in the highest estimation.

What brings them into the matter at all is the fact that A. J. Matthews, the son-in-law of old Alex. McClelland, has been accused of complicity. While a direct assertion on this point has never been made to his face he is aware of the charges going the rounds and is most anxious to assist in the unraveling.

When the old stock pond on the McClelland farm began to be drained Mr. Matthews heard of it and was an interested spectator as the work progressed. It was said that when his first wife, who was the daughter of the old Squire, died, she had made a death-bed confession to a Mrs. Martin of that neighborhood. This confession was supposed to have contained charges against the sons of McClelland. It was also hinted that Matthews had in his possession certain papers and letters which would show a condition of money transactions at the time of the Squire's disappearance which would prove that the Squire had money and some property which John A. and the other boys desired.

The papers were looked over by *The Republic's* representative at the home of Mr. Matthews and it was found that they referred to the transfer of some six acres of land which Oscar, the missing son, had disposed of in 1879, no money being involved in the case. Besides this, Coroner Aiken said that the papers had been offered him, and that he would take possession of them in due time.

It is these charges that deeply worry the Matthews family, not so much from the fear of any untoward consequences, but rather from the general stain of suspicion that may linger.

In the office of the R. E. Tate Livery Stable at Centralia, the two suspected brothers, John A. and Oliver, 41 and 34 years old respectively, were met by *The Republic* emissary. The two men had been earnestly solicited for a public statement and came in response.

John A. looked all that so many had described him, a queer, nervous, good natured fellow, slightly troubled with an impediment of speech, but withal strong of build. His attitude was that of deep thought perhaps of nervous reflection, and when his eyes sought a certain object and rested there they seemed to linger, as though he found it hard to cease looking.

"You two are suspected of murdering your father and brother," was the opening remark. "You both declare your innocence and also that the skeletons found are not those of your relatives. Now, how do you know?"

"How do we know?" answered John. "Well, father went away in 1881. I heard from him in 1883 the last time. They say the skeletons have been buried 12 years, so I think that they have nothing in common with my relatives."

"You saw your father last in 1881 and heard from him last in 1883?"

"Yes."

"Well, how do you know that he isn't dead then?"

"I don't know."

"What makes you fight the idea of these skeletons being those of your relatives?"

"I'm not fighting the idea, only I don't believe the bones are those of my relatives. I haven't any proof."

"They were buried on your farm and in your pond. How did they come there?"

"I'm sure I don't know; I can't tell. Somebody was evidently murdered and placed there, but who I can't tell."

"Did you ever have any trouble with your father?"

"Never."

"Have you lived in Centralia ever since his disappearance?"

"Yes, I'm working here now in the Centralia car shops."

"Aren't you anxious to have this matter cleared up?"

"Yes; indeed, as much as anyone, yet I'm not worried over the matter, because I feel that both father and Oscar are still alive."

To all of this Oliver had been nodding and agreeing, so that further questioning was useless. At present Oliver is employed on the Illinois Central, and runs into Centralia every few days. Both declared that the only reason that they had not gone to the farm when the skeletons were exhumed was simply because they had not heard of the matter. When they did hear of it they went.

Otto, the youngest son, 24 years old, was also found in Centralia. At first he seemed disinclined to discuss the matter, but being informed of the general trend of the charges made a few answers.

"When did you last see your father?" was asked.

"Some time in the summer of 1881."

"Was he living on the farm with you at that time?"

"No; the old house burned down in 1879 and father went to live at Central City. He shifted about though from time to time and stayed in Springfield for awhile."

"Did he come and bid you good-by when he left?"

"No."

"You merely heard of his going, then?"

"That was all."

"Was there ever any difficulty between the boys and your father previous to his departure?"

"No."

"Was Oscar his favorite son?"

"I never knew that he had a favorite son. He was all that a father could be, I think. If anyone, he liked John a little the best. We all got along splendidly."

"You have been living here ever since?"

"Yes; I've been working around the country here and on the Illinois Central ever since."

"You have seen the bodies taken up, haven't you?"

"Yes."

"Are they the remains of your parent and your brother?"

"I think not. I haven't any reason for believing they are the remains of my relatives, because I don't think that my father is dead. I believe he is down in Mexico somewhere."

"How do you account for the presence of those two skeletons in that pond?"

"I can't account for them. Two men were probably killed and put there."

"Do you think that anyone could have brought two bodies to the old farm, day or night, and buried them without some one of you perceiving it or hearing of it?"

"Do I think so? I can't think anything else. Those bones are nothing to us, and as we didn't kill anyone, why, they must have been put there. We heard nothing of the matter, so we can't account for them. I'm not fighting the idea that the bones found are those of my father and my brother, but I haven't any reason to think so. I may later, but of course it will have to be proved."

A. J. Matthews, son-in-law of the missing Alexander McClelland, who has been unpleasantly mentioned in connection with the affair, responded freely to all questions propounded to him.

"Many persons seem to think you are in a measure implicated. What have you to say?"

"Well," said Mr. Matthews, "the Lord knows I have nothing to do in the case. I am a son-in-law. My first wife, who died five years ago, was Mc-Clelland's daughter. I was under obligations to the old gentleman, for he first gave me my start in life."

"You have seen the two skeletons. Whose are they?"

"I don't know. I'm sure I can't tell. I don't say that they are not the remains of Mr. McClelland and his son, but I don't think so. I can't offer any explanation as to how the bodies could come on the farm that way, but I don't believe that the boys ever had a hand in the matter. If they had it would surprise me, for I always considered the boys the very best of fellows. They worked hard for the old gentleman and they worked for me occasionally. I always found them faithful. There's suspicion directed against me. I don't know why, but I suppose I have enemies. Now, I don't know a single thing about this case. I saw Squire McClelland last about the latter part of June or the early part of July, 1881. I had heard him say he was going away. Along about November of the same year I heard that he had gone, but I didn't think much of it, as he had been saying that for some time. I heard that Oscar had gone along and that didn't surprise me. Oscar worked for me in 1880, I think, and I have some papers here of his that relate to a small sale of land. I never opened them until this thing came up, but goodness knows I'm willing to turn them over to the Coroner. They don't bear on the case. That statement of Welch's about my having received a letter or having said so is absolutely false. He doesn't like me and that's the sole cause of it. Now some people are saying that my first wife made a deathbed confession, but there is absolutely nothing in that. I'll name you the people who attended her in her last illness and you can go to see them. They can tell you about that matter. Some people said that when I heard that the old pond was being excavated I went over to the farm and watched the work as though I suspected strange developments. Now, as a matter of fact, I never went near the place until the first skeleton was taken out, then I hitched up and went right over. I expected to find the boys there, and some people are holding it up against them because they didn't seem to manifest any interest in the find. Now I know the boys didn't hear anything about the case until they were subpoenaed."

"Do you scout the idea that the two bodies in question are those of McClelland, Sr., and his son Oscar?"

"Not at all. If it is, I want to know it. No one is more anxious for justice than I am in this matter, but I don't believe those two skeletons are the father and son. I have no reason to think so."

"Do you believe that anyone could have killed the two men and buried them in that pond without the relatives on the farm knowing something about it?"

"It does look improbable. What else can I believe, though? It has either been done that way, or the bodies are not those of old McClelland and son, or the boys are guilty, and I don't believe they are."

"You have known John A. a long time? Do you think he could have had a hand in the affair?"

"I don't believe John did. I have known him too long. He's too good-hearted and too kind. He has always been a little queer in his make-up, but not in a way to cause anyone to dislike him. John's always been nervous and reserved. That's why people suspect him now. I can't imagine any reason why the boys should have made away with their father, but if they did I'm just as anxious as you are that they should be found out and prosecuted.

"No," concluded Mr. Matthews, "I never could believe it of the boys."

The most direct testimony obtained which has not yet been presented to the Coroner developed in an interview with Mrs. Elethes Martin, 83 years old, who lives close by the old McClelland homestead. Mrs. Martin stated in detail:

"I knew the McClelland family well, but never heard of any trouble among the members of it. I know that in 1881 Mr. McClelland and Oscar disappeared, but I was not surprised, because both of them had told me they were going away. I saw Alex. McClelland in the spring of 1881 last. I saw Oscar in the fall, I believe, or late summer of 1881. He came up and shook me by the hand and said good-by. He said he was going out West and might not come back for some time. I never saw him after that. Oscar was my favorite boy, and he came especially to tell me."

John Martin, the son of Mrs. Elethes Martin, when asked as to what he knew of the matter declared he knew nothing. Later he spoke of the family relations of old Mr. McClelland as being pleasant, and said:

"I know the boys well. All of them are honest, hard-working fellows, who have always tried their best to get along well. Things went wrong though and they've been shoved down some. I don't know anything about those skeletons, but I don't believe John A. or Oliver had a hand in that murder. I never will believe that John A. had a hand in it until I hear it from his own lips," with which Mr. Martin wheeled about and disappeared into the house.

Probably the most important clew that has yet come to light was furnished by Nunn Deadmond of the McClelland neighborhood. To *The Republic* emissary Mr. Deadmond related a conversation that took place between himself and Henry Martin, whose statement precedes this.

Mr. Deadmond said that he was subpoenaed in the McClelland inquest on Monday, November 13, and that in the witness-room at Centralia he found Henry Martin, who had also been subpoenaed. Mr. Deadmond is somewhat hard of hearing, and yet he says that Martin struck up a conversation with him while others were listening and soon turned upon the McClelland case.

"I was sitting in one corner of the room," said Mr. Deadmond, "when Martin came up to me and said, 'I'm called in this case as a witness and I'm afraid to go on the stand. I'm afraid if I go on the stand that I'll break down and tell all I know and that would create a sensation. I don't like to testify against the boys.' I asked him what he knew and he said: 'Well, I'll tell you; I can go and put my hand upon the murderers of old McClelland and his son at a minute's notice. The persons that killed him are right here in Centralia and don't intend to run away.'

"'Somebody did murder the two then, did they?' I said, and he answered: 'Yes, and that's why I hate to go on the stand. I'm afraid that I'll break down. I don't want to if I can help it, but when they get a man on the stand, why, it is hard to hold out.'

"I said, 'Don't you want to tell the truth?' and he said, 'Well, I don't want to hurt anybody, and especially the boys, so if I could hold out I would.'"

Mr. Deadmond was not certain whether or not Martin was drunk at the time. He knew that Martin drank some, but did not think he was intoxicated. Martin seemed very nervous and talked in a loud voice.

John S. Harvey was present and heard him. Mr. Harvey when seen asserted that he knew nothing of the case whatsoever.

C. M. Welch of one mile north of Sandoval, had some interesting information to give on the subject of Alexander McClelland's disappearance.

Mr. Welch was the one who testified to the identity of the oldest skeleton as being that of Squire McClelland before the Coroner. He also testified that A. J. Matthews, the Squire's son-in-law, had once spoken of having received a letter from the Squire, and then when asked for it said that it could not be found. Mr. Welch said:

"I knew the Squire for the past 25 years or more. We were good friends and I visited him often. Once he waited on me when I was sick with the fever, and I always found him good-hearted and upright. He wasn't, in my opinion, going to the dogs very fast, as some of these people say, although he certainly was a little unfortunate."

"When did you see him last?"

"Some time in 1881, I think. I traveled back and forth between New York and here those days, and it was on my return from the last trip that I learned from his relatives that he had gone. I heard him mention his intention of going West once or twice, and I thought he meant it."

"Did you see the skeletons taken out of the pond?"

"Yes."

"Do you know who they were in life?"

"I think they were the bodies of the old Squire and his son Oscar. I believe they were murdered and placed there. When the oldest skeleton was taken up I examined it. I found some hair on the spot where he was taken up and it was of a sandy gray color. In life that was the color of the Squire's hair. I noticed the heavy protrusion of bone where the eyebrow should have been, and in life I knew 'Squire McClelland's eyebrows always stood out heavy. Everyone remarked his heavy eyebrows. I saw the stakes and I know they came from old machinery about the place. The stones that weighed him down were from a neighboring trestle bridge that was built in 1881 near the place."

"Do you believe that his sons murdered him?"

"I don't know. I'm not certain. I know this, though: Ever since 1881 I have always considered the sons somewhat reserved upon the subject. I used to inquire after the old man. I wanted to know whether they ever heard from him. John A. said once that he had heard from him occasionally, but he couldn't produce the letters.

"One time I was visiting A. J. Matthews. I think some time in 1882. We were talking about McClelland, and I asked Mrs. Matthews whether she ever heard from him. She said yes, and I asked to see the letter. Mr. Matthews jumped up and walked out of the room. In about a minute he came back and said 'What's become of that letter? I can't find it.' The matter ended in the letter not being found, but I had my suspicions at the time and I thought Matthews acted strangely. I never knew of any reason for quarrels between the father and sons, and I don't know that there were any."

[19 November 1893, p. 9.]

68 - ZYTHUM'S EXHILARATION.

"Let me at him! What do you want to hold me for? Let me at him, I say. I feel like a 3x sausage machine ready for chopping mincemeat."

"Keep quiet," exclaimed the football editor in company with a chorus of a dozen other friends of Russ Samuels.

"I won't keep quiet," answered Mr. Samuels. "Don't you believe for one palpitating minute that I'll keep quiet. I'm hotter than a four-pronged purgatory fork, and I won't cool down. Let me loose!"

"For the love of champagne, Mr. Samuels," argued the football editor, "don't let this football game excite you so. You are perfectly cantankerous in your attitude this morning."

"Cantankerous, young man," exclaimed Mr. Samuels. "Cantankerous; I'm more. I'm ophiophagous in my cravings. What I want is blood!"

"Dear, dear," exclaimed the football editor, shocked at the turn Mr. Samuels had taken, "but what does ophiophagous mean?"

"Mean, sir?" sneered Mr. Samuels. "Mean? Subjects of the great Lobengula, King of the Matabeles! Here is a football editor who doesn't know what ophiophagous means. Now, by my halidom, this is droll. Ophiophagous means, sir, literally, snake-eating, but has degenerated into a common exchange expression for a fierce bear-killing feeling."

"Well, I swan," murmured the football editor, taking out his diary. "I'll make a note of it."

"Do," said Mr. Samuels. "And I will say, further, that my oppugnation to these Builders is—is——"

"What's oppugnation?" questioned the football editor.

"Shades of a grasshopper's grandpa!" groaned Mr. Samuels. "Oppugnation! Oppugnation! Why, in opposition, of course. You compel me, sir, to be absolutely commonplace."

"I know," said the football editor, "but commonplace is pretty good when it's English. We don't mind it around the office at all. Please go on."

"I will, sir; I will," said Mr. Samuels. "All my life I have been going on. I will go on now. Fear not; I shall not falter."

"I thought," whispered the officeboy, "that he was going to say 'I shall not falter—the ground.' It 'ud have been a goak, then, wouldn't it?"

"Yes," said the football editor, "but, hearken!"

"I have been," continued Mr. Samuels, "a yeanling and a doe. Gayly have I frisked upon the peaceful hills of commercial prosperity, and as gayly ate of the delicate herbage of business margins until now. Opsympathy was not mine and the silver cup, overflowing with the zythum of youthful vigor, I drained to the very dregs."

"What's a yeanling and where does opsympathy come in? Who is Zythum, anyhow?" were the next questions of the football editor.

"Well, well," said Mr. Samuels, his belligerent attitude more and more succumbing to the influence of these gentle appeals to his literary sense, "I never quite did in all my life; I really never. You astonish me with the very intensity of your opaqueness. A yeanling is a lamb or a kid."

"Then you say you are kidlike in your nature," asserted the football editor.

"Well, yes, in the more antiquated sense of the word——"

"Goatlike," smiled the football editor, blandly.

"Goatlike, nothing," harshly commented Mr. Samuels. "What has the antiquated sense of a kidlike nature got to do with a goat?"

"Well, isn't an antiquated kid a goat?"

"No, sir; no."

"Billy goat," corrected the football editor.

"How dare you, sir," exclaimed Mr. Samuels. "Nothing of the kind, sir, absolutely nothing. You don't understand. I said I have been a yeanling in the antiquated sense—the olden sense, the doelike sense."

"Oh, doe," corrected the football editor, "certainly. I grasp it now."

"Hope you do. Now let us proceed. Opsympathy means education acquired late in life. I may say you are opsympathetic, your knowledge of it has been acquired late in life. As for zythum, that is an ancient malt beverage that is said to have been very excellent, indeed. It was slightly reddish in hue and sharp of taste. Pythagoras relates that at the feast of Prozyudicatorium he drank 16 beakers and became slightly intoxicated."

"How did that silver cup overflowing with zythum that you drained to the dregs the other day taste?"

"I never tasted any."

"But you said you did."

"Who?"

"Why, you."

"Never," said Mr. Samuels.

"Didn't you say, 'and the silver cup of youthful vigor have I drained to the very dregs,' not over 10 minutes ago?"

"Of course, I did."

"Then what makes you say you didn't drink it?"

"I don't say it."

"But you do."

"Who do?"

"You do."

"Oh, come! that's figurative. I'm speaking in a metaphorical sense; using a figure of speech."

"Don't you believe it," said the football editor, seeing that Mr. Samuels had by this time forgotten his wrath over the conduct of the builders. "You can't hornswaggle me. You've been drinking zythum, and I'm going to write you up."

"But my dear fellow——" pleaded Mr. Samuels.

"Don't dear fellow me," archly persisted the football editor. "If zythum could make Pythagoras drunk at the feast of Prozyudicatorium it could make you also at the St. Louis Club. You can't fool me."

"But, my good man," pleaded Mr. Samuels. "Reason! Think! All figurative, every word. All metaphor, every line. You understand."

"Don't you try to muzzle the press. You've gone and done it, now you take the consequences. This is a serious matter, and we'll look into it."

The countenance of Mr. Samuels was a study. He had started out with a threatening harangue about how he felt like a sausage machine about to make mincemeat of Mr. Ittner, a prominent builder and football champion. He was just preparing to leave his office, that he might proceed to swab up the sidewalk and bruise the air with the form of Mr. Ittner, who had said that he could not play full back with a stone wall for a shield, but he changed. His literary knowledge betrayed him. The mountain of his anger had melted. Before the silvery cup of zythum had he succumbed.

———

The joint committee of the Builders' and Merchants' exchanges met yesterday afternoon to make further arrangements about the charity football game to be played on Saturday at Sportsman's Park. It was decided that the captains of the respective elevens should choose the umpires and that the umpires should choose the referee. The builders made another demand for tickets, and from reports from other sources it is expected that at least 20,000 tickets in all will be sold, which would yield $5,000.

President Baker of the Builders' Exchange has donated a trophy football, to be played for each year by representatives of these two organizations.

The Builders' Exchange team will meet to-day at the exchange at 5 o'clock to receive their uniforms.

Messrs. Steele of the Merchants' and Henry Fairback of the Builders' eleven were appointed to see the Mayor to-day and request that he declare Saturday afternoon a half-holiday that as many city employes as desire may see the game and also out of respect to the philanthropic character of the game.

The foot race for a gold medal, to be given by the Mermod-Jaccard Jewelry Company, between Russ. Samuels and Albert A. Aal and Phil Hacquette will be started promptly at 2:30 o'clock. The football game will begin at 3 p.m.

The competing teams have applied for good seats at the Exposition Music Hall charity benefit next Saturday night, which seats they expect to pay for out of their own pockets, no matter what shall be the issue of the game.

[3 January 1894, p. 10.]

69 - UNDER THE WHEELS.

While Antoinette Edenborn, 15 years old, was riding on her horse on Park avenue, between Iowa and California avenues, yesterday a few minutes after noon, horse and rider were struck by the Lindell red line electric car No. 25 and both were killed.

The girl's mangled remains are at Eberle & Keys' undertaking establishment, where they are being prepared for burial.

James Harrold, the motorman, was taken by an officer to the Fifth District Police Station, where he made a statement of the accident. He was then released without bond. The car was delayed about an hour, and the line was blocked. The cars had not recovered their schedule time and relative distances at a late hour last night.

Another motorman was put in charge of the car, but Charles Sweeney, the conductor, was not taken into custody, and he remained at his post.

Antoinette Edenborn was the daughter of Wm. Edenborn, president of the Consolidated Steel and Wire Co., and resided with her parents at 2017 Park avenue.

Miss Edenborn was fond of horseback riding, and almost every day was seen in the vicinity of her home mounted upon her handsome black horse.

Yesterday, a short time after noon, she rode out to a trysting place where she was to meet some school friends from the female department of Washington University. About 3 o'clock she was upon her way home, going east on Park avenue. Between Iowa and California avenues an electric car came up beside her. The horse was accustomed to cars and trotted along, evidently wishing to keep in the lead of the great red monster.

A piledriver near the middle of the block was puffing and groaning in its laborious task, preparing the foundations of a new building. The horse became frightened and jumped over upon the track in front of the car.

In the next moment of agonizing suspense the doomed girl frantically tugged at the bridle rein, endeavoring to guide her steed from the approaching car, which rolled on with gathered momentum from the descent of the hill. The frightened horse would not obey, and the iron platform struck him with terrific force, despite the motorman's application of the brake. The animal was thrown forward and his mistress was thrown under the wheels.

When the car came to a stop the body of the girl was lying upon the stones of the street, without life, and so mangled as to be all but unrecognizable. The wheels had passed entirely across the body, almost severing it at the waist. She was also badly cut about the head.

A crowd quickly gathered and was not dispersed until the police removed the remains to the undertaking establishment.

Mr. Edenborn was summoned from his place of business to his home. There the fate of his daughter was told him, and his grief was pitiful. When seen, later, he was inclined to be bitter against the street car company and the motorman, but this was more directly the result of his great loss and his grief. He said that he knew little of the manner of his daughter's death, and that little he had learned from a friend, who in turn had his information from eyewitnesses.

Charles Sweeney, conductor upon the fatal car, was still at his post when seen by a reporter. He refused at first to talk of the accident, but finally said:

"The girl was riding along beside the car and a short distance in advance. For some reason her horse got in front of the car and the motorman, James Harrold, stopped it as quickly as I ever knew it to be stopped; but there was too little room, and in a second the whole thing was over. We were going at the usual rate of speed and did not have many passengers.

"Harrold is a careful man, and I think that he did everything he could to avoid the trouble. After it was over he was a very sick man. He sat down on the platform of the car and was too weak to move. I don't believe that he will ever have the nerve to run a car again. I just stayed on the car and have not been molested by the officers, and I don't expect to be."

Motorman Harrold was accompanied by a police officer to the Fifth District Police Station and there made his statement of the tragedy. Upon this statement and the absence of a complaining witness Harrold was allowed to go to his home, which none of the street car officials were able to designate.

The manager of the Lindell Company gave his version of the accident, with little or no variation from the accounts secured elsewhere. He also added that the company stood prepared to give any bond which might be required for the freedom of its two employes whom they regard as entirely free from blame.

The keeper of a livery stable in the block where the girl was killed, and other citizens of Park avenue, assert that the cars upon that thoroughfare are run too fast for the safety of the public and express the hope that the dreadful lesson of yesterday will result in more careful regulations on the part of the street railway company.

[6 January 1894, p. 1.]

70 - AT A ROPE'S END.

Sam Welsor's sands of life have run out. With the streaming rays of the early morning sun the hangman's cap will shut out the light from his eyes, and in the strangling grasp of the encircling noose he will pass into the great unknown. Between the hours of 6 and 7 o'clock this morning the last solemn march will occur to the scaffold, from where his broken body will be carried to the Morgue.

In cell 46, on the first floor of the City Jail, where he was placed Wednesday morning, the condemned murderer spent last night. The long hours intervening between the night and the morning were spent in such recreations as the perturbed fancy of the doomed man might suggest. His every wish was obeyed and every remark noted. He was agreed with in all

"Sam Welsor"
(*St. Louis Republic*,
12 January 1894, p. 1).

things and consoled, though in that obvious manner that was probably more harassing than soothing. Outside his cell tramped through the solemn hours of the night the death watch, James Dunn and Charley James, from 6 to 12 p.m.; Thomas Skidmore, Ed Giener and Joe Hatton from 12 to 6 a.m.

They listened to the words of the prisoner and were for the time his friends. His jokes, some sarcastic, some filled with that aching fear that hides itself in jest, were their food for laughter, and never by sign or word did they refer to the approaching doom.

The murderer was, to all appearances, calm; those about expressed it as being "game." When he smiled they said he did it to hide his fear; when he frowned it was counted bravado. If he chose to eat of the excellent fare spread for him he was counted heedless, and in all things he was marked as one shamming—hiding the truth 'neath a mask.

At different periods between 6 and 12 p.m. the prisoner chose to walk, and, accompanied by a deputy, he plodded back and forth at a most wearying gait, talking and jesting the while. Some insinuated that he was endeavoring to wear out the faithful guardsman, but it was more than probable that his own wild thoughts needed companionship in spirited movements of the flesh.

Towards evening he sent for Tom Wand, the liveryman and undertaker, an old acquaintance. When Wand came and spoke to him he livened up and began an animated conversation about his funeral arrangements.

"I want you, Wand," he said, "to take charge of my body. I want a nice burial; the best you can give me."

"Who is going to pay me?" queried Wand.

"Oh, that's all right," answered the prisoner. "I'll give you my note, payable 30 days after date with 7 per cent interest. That will do, won't it?"

"Yes," answered Wand, who had but jested in the first place.

"I figure," said Welsor, "that it's to cost $150. I want a fine casket and five carriages at least, if not more. I hope you'll see that I get them."

"Yes."

"I want the best, now; do you hear? Nothing cheap; the very best."

Mr. Wand agreed and then the prisoner entered into details and arranged all things to suit his own fancy. However, his wishes, even in this, will be obeyed. Friends have contributed $500 for these arrangements and his wishes will be fulfilled. A fine casket will be his and eight carriages besides. The funeral occurs Sunday morning from Wand's establishment.

Between 5 and 6 o'clock last evening Pete Morrissey, the well-known saloon-keeper, called to bid Welsor good-by.

"Good-by, old man," said Morrissey. "It is probably the last time I'll see you on earth."

"No, it isn't," answered Welsor. "You'll see me again. Some time, when a crap game is running over at your place and Lee Burning is ringing in some of his horse dice, I'll come back. I'll be there and Jack Looney will be with me."

The companion referred to has long been dead.

Outside of these peculiar bursts of strange speculation Welsor talked a great deal, but always in a way that betokened affection. He impressed one as being more "game" than fearless. He welcomed his friends, but avoided newspaper conversation. He wanted no reporters and insisted on having them debarred.

For some reason or other he seemed to detest notoriety. When a reporter approached he invariably sought refuge in his cell and, seeking its darkest corner, gathered himself up on his cot and feigned sleep.

There was only one wish of all his desires that was not granted him yesterday. He asked to be shaved, but, fearing that he might grasp the razor and wound himself, he was refused. All else was given him, and the one refusal appeared to pass quickly from his mind. At 12 o'clock midnight he had not changed in his demeanor, and, still waking, conversed freely with his guards.

Sam Welsor, at 3 o'clock this morning, was chatting to his guards—the death watch—and was to all outward appearances the most cheerful of the four. At times he was more than cheerful, and his jests had a genuine ring.

He asked for a can of oysters at midnight. These were brought him and a plentiful supply of cigars was kept on hand. Welsor prepared a game of checkers and challenged Deputy Tom Skidmore to a contest. The challenge was accepted and for an hour the game was played with varying turns of fortune.

But Welsor won. It was his last battle before he should meet the great Arch enemy. In the final contest certainty of defeat awaited him. But in the game of checkers he had a chance and he played as though the loss of a King was to him more than the loss of life.

The game was finished at 2:15. Welsor, laughing, "guyed" Deputy Skidmore, but declined to give him revenge. He had had enough of checkers.

The can of oysters had been untouched during the game, but now Welsor attacked the bivalves and speedily finished them. Then, lighting a cigar, he threw his feet up against the iron grating, tilted back his chair and seemed to be enjoying himself.

It was noticed that for the space of two minutes he gazed through the grating and that the smile gradually gave way to a sterner look until his lips were tight-drawn and his face was haggard. But a word from one of his guards roused him and from that time until 3 o'clock Welsor maintained his part of a general conversation, in which death had no part.

The crime for which Sam Welsor is to be executed was the murder of Clementina Manning, August 4, 1890. Neither murderer nor victim could lay claim to good social ties.

Eight years before the tragedy Sam Welsor, the bartender, met Clementina Manning in a St. Louis brothel. Welsor's position in life made him a fit associate for the woman. For five years they lived together. Their life was frequently interrupted with quarrels. At the end of that time Welsor tired of his association with the woman. They parted. Welsor went to St. Paul some time afterwards and continued in his vocation of bartender. A few months before the murder the Goddess of Fortune smiled on Clementina. A lottery ticket proved lucky. She won $5,000. With the little fortune she proclaimed to her associates that she intended to lead a good life. Bidding them farewell she went to live with her sister at 1014 Walnut street. She was then 30 years old.

News of the fortune gained by his former mistress reached Welsor in St. Paul. He returned to St. Louis determined to compel her to share the money with him. He got a position in a saloon where he formerly worked at Sixth and Elm streets. Three days before he killed Clementina he met her on the street and, he claims, she agreed to go buggy riding with him the following Monday, but the facts do not bear this statement out. Promptly on the morning set for the ride Welsor, armed with a revolver, drove up to the door behind a spirited horse. He passed into the house and, a few moments later, Mollie Green, Clementina's sister, walked out of the house with a bucket, on her way to a neighboring saloon for beer. The murderous instinct in Welsor was crafty. He wanted to make no botch of the job. He had sent Mrs. Green out in order that his act should not be interrupted. He did not care for the consequences. What he wanted was to kill.

The sound of the footsteps of Mrs. Green had hardly died away when the neighborhood was thrown into a panic by the sound of five pistol shots in rapid succession. Immediately following the shots the murderer issued from the door, the evidence of his guilt, a smoking revolver, tightly clinched in his hand. He ran to the buggy and was in the act of escaping in it when Sergeant Shoemaker turned the corner and running hastily to him ordered that he stop. Welsor accompanied the officer to the station. His victim, Clementina Manning, was dying. Three of the five shots fired had entered her body. The other two sped wide of their mark. One of the bullets entered the left breast, after passing through the fleshy portion of the arm. This was the fatal wound. Another passed through the hips and lodged in the abdominal cavity. The third entered the right thigh. Physicians were summoned, but she was past human aid.

Before she died Welsor was taken before her to be identified. She was speechless from the time her sister found her on the bed in a pool of blood. She looked up and saw Welsor in charge of an officer. She nodded her head and a faint smile crossed her face. Three hours from the time she was shot a gasp proclaimed her end.

To the police Welsor told his side of the crime. He said that he had gone to take her riding according to agreement, and that he sent Mrs. Green out for some beer. While she was gone Clementina called him a terrible name. This insult he wiped out by slaying her. The true reason of the murder came out afterwards. On the night that Welsor met his victim he told her that he had a chance to buy a saloon in St. Paul for $1,500 and requested her to advance him that sum and take up her old life with him. She refused, saying she wanted to lead a good life. Welsor, angered by her refusal, planned and executed the crime.

After the crime Welsor was bound over to the Grand Jury, indicted, and after several continuances the case went to trial in the Criminal Court before the late Judge Normile, October 15, 1891, over one year after the tragedy. The trial lasted two days. Nearly half a hundred witnesses were examined. Charles T. Noland, Welsor's counsel, made an effort to prove Welsor insane, and many witnesses were examined to this end. They were men who had known Welsor when he kept bar at Sixth and Elm streets. The testimony of these witnesses tended to show that Welsor claimed to be a "hoodoo," and they told stories of his peculiarities. Notwithstanding this on the following day, October 16, 1891, the jury brought in a verdict of guilty of murder in the first degree. On October 20 a motion for a new trial was filed. Welsor was sentenced to hang according to the verdict February 16, 1892. The motion for a new trial was overruled, and an appeal was taken to the Supreme Court. A supersedeas was granted to December 15, 1893. On December 9, 1893, the mandate of the Supreme Court was handed down affirming the judgment of the lower court. The case was then taken to the Supreme Court in banc, with the same result. Governor Stone granted a stay of execution from December 15, 1893, until January 12, 1894. The death warrant was delivered to Sheriff Patrick Staed December 13 last.

The last execution that took place in St. Louis was that of Henry Henson, a native of Denmark. On August 13, 1891, he paid the death penalty for the atrocious murder of his wife, Ida, on Christmas Day in 1888. Henson had only been married to the woman a little less than three months when the deed was committed.

Prior to their marriage his wife was the proprietor of a boarding-house at 405 South Second street. She was a hard working woman. Henson was of a jealous disposition and made life a burden to her. Her every movement was closely watched by him. He was especially jealous of a crippled peddler who boarded at the house, to whom his wife was civil.

On the day of the murder Henson came home just as the cripple was leaving the house. Henson found his wife and her son, by a former husband, sitting in a room together. He immediately accused her of infidelity, and she resented the insult. He went out of the room, and for the time the matter was forgotten.

Shortly afterwards he returned, and, walking around back of his wife, drew a revolver, and placing it to her head, sent a bullet crashing through her brain. At his trial, February 2, 1889, the jury was out just 35 minutes when a verdict of murder in the first degree was returned. He was sentenced to be hanged July 2; but the case was taken to the Supreme Court, necessitating a stay of execution until August 13, when he was executed.

Perhaps no execution ever created more interest than that of Hugh Mottram Brooks, alias Walter H. Lennox Maxwell, the murderer of Arthur Preller. He was hanged, together with Henry Langraff, on August 10, 1888. Langraff was executed for the murder of his sweetheart, Lena Deitsch, in Carondelet.

The crime committed by Maxwell was one of the most sensational in the history of the country. It was on Easter Sunday in 1885 that Maxwell murdered his friend and companion, Preller, in the Southern Hotel. He forced the body into a trunk and left the country.

The next hanging prior to the one above was that of Alfred Blunt, a negro. He paid the death penalty June 24, 1887, for the murder of his wife some time before.

Sam Welsor possesses all the characteristics of a crank. In appearance, however, there is in him no indication of mental weakness. He looks and talks like any ordinary man of limited education. It is in Welsor's acts that his crankiness shows itself.

As a "Voodoo" Welsor, though a white man, is entitled to the name of past grand master. This bent of his did not take the turn it usually does in people who believe in such things. Instead of carrying the feet of defunct rabbits around his person, Welsor procured dismembered portions of human bodies. To him these grewsome relics constituted the elixir of life. Through their aid the tongue of his calumniator and the arm of his enemy were paralyzed. Where Welsor got the horrible idea is not known. As a bartender in a saloon at Sixth and Elm streets for years Welsor was thrown into daily contact with medical students, janitors and physicians from the old Missouri Medical College around the corner.

Through some means, Welsor gained access to the dissecting room of the college. The horrible sights of dead bodies, dissected legs and arms were too much for a mind like his.

He immediately developed a weakness for such scenes and would gloat over a dead body like a ghoul or vampire. His next step was to collect portions of the bodies and surreptitiously carry them away.

These he guarded as if they were jewels of inestimable value. To him a human ear became a Kohinoor—a portion of the nose a moonstone. Each portion obtained by him became in his eyes a cure for all ills; a balm of Gilead. By performing certain mystic signs and incantations while holding these dreadful relics in his hands he was placed in his diseased imagination outside the pale of law.

His especial delight was to see an enemy, either imaginary or in fact, before him. His "voodoo" instinct then was uppermost. When the enemy called for a drink, Welsor the drink mixer became Welsor the enemy slayer. He would fix the drink in a glass and would stir the mixture behind the bar with a dead man's finger. When the liquid passed down the palate of the customer, Welsor felt safe. He never afterwards looked on the man as other than a friend. The magic spell of the dead finger made friends of all. None could withstand it.

At times he was also known to cut small particles from human ears and mash them up with lemons in cocktails.

[12 January 1894, pp. 1–2.]

71 - THE HANGING OF WELSOR.

Sam Welsor, the convicted murderer of Clementine Manning, was hanged yesterday morning a few minutes after 8 o'clock, in the jail yard of the Four Courts.

The condemned man was resolute, hiding the inward terror behind a restless expression of countenance. His last walk was quick and decisive. His last remarks were few and so cursory as to be astonishing—merely a comment on the weather and a command to go ahead.

A great crowd assembled as early as 6 o'clock about the Four Courts. It was an unruly throng and miserably handled. At 7:30 a.m. the jail yard was invaded and prepared. At 7:45 the scaffold was in order and the witnessing crowd immense.

At 8 o'clock the death cortege left the cell, and at 8:04 Welsor had just fallen, hardly quivering in the tightening grasp of the noose.

Sheriff Staed accompanied Welsor from the cell to the scaffold, holding his arms, bound as they were, the entire distance. Deputies Skidmore, Geiner, Hatton and James completed the grewsome procession.

On the scaffold Sheriff White of Illinois and Sheriff Staed officiated. Deputies Skidmore, Geiner and Hatton assisted, Hatton cutting the cord that controlled the trap.

There were no religious ceremonies and no gallows oration.

Sheriff White adjusted the black cap and the noose, as well as crooked the thumb that meant "cut."

A squad of policemen guarded the place. Drs. Marks, Frank, Kingsbury and Neville examined the suspended body, agreeing upon the death moment.

At 8:22 Sheriff White ordered the rope cut and the body was immediately transferred to the Morgue. The autopsy developed that Welsor had died of strangulation. He was unconscious and free of pain the moment the trap fell.

All the night Welsor remained awake. About 1 o'clock in the morning he took a bath. Then donning new underclothing and a new pair of trousers he announced his intention of remaining up the few remaining hours that intervened between him and the last sleep.

The night was spent in chatting with his guards, the death watch, Deputy Sheriffs Skidmore, Geiner, Hatton, James and Kickham, and in pacing the bull ring with nervous, rapid strides, a deputy on either side. At midnight Welsor expressed a desire for oysters, and they were brought to him in bulk. Plates were provided and Welsor served the oysters to his guardians, eating a goodly share of them himself with evident relish. He drank whisky and beer at intervals during the night and morning, but did not drink much. He said he would not go upon the scaffold in an intoxicated condition. He wanted to meet his death like a man.

The conversation during the night was made up for the most part of stories and reminiscences. Welsor never avoided an allusion to his fate. When someone was mentioned who was dead Welsor laughingly promised the deputies to remember them to the boys "over there." His Bible and a volume of Burns' poems were lying on a table. Welsor occasionally picked up the Bible and read for a few minutes. Then the forced gayety gave way to silence, and there came into his eyes a strained, anxious look that betokened a realization that his life was about to end. These times of sober thought were followed by a tramp up and down the bull ring in the rapid, nervous walk of one to whom physical exertion was a relief from a mental strain.

Welsor had been told that he would be hanged at 7:30 o'clock. He asked the time at frequent intervals and expressed the wish that the hours would pass faster. He gave his clothing and personal effects to Frank Moore, now in the penitentiary. His Bible was verbally willed to Charles Wisdom, one of the negroes charged with the murder of Edward Drexel.

At 3 o'clock in the morning there were few persons in the Four Courts Building outside the jail door except newspaper men and officials. At 6 o'clock the corridor before and on each side of the jail door was filled with a dense mass of humanity. Ticket holders and those who had no tickets, but who hoped to get in by some means, were indiscriminately mixed. The crush at the jail door became terrible as those in the rear tried to crowd forward. A squad of police attempted to clear a space about the door. It soon became apparent that if the door was not thrown open there would be no possibility of preventing all from entering. The newspaper men were taken into the jail by a private way. At 7:30 the corridor was cleared and the crowd sent to the Twelfth street gate, where the ticket holders were admitted to the jail yard. Here they stood in the cold morning air, shivering through the half hour that elapsed before the execution.

Welsor prepared for his death at 5:30 o'clock. He had been sitting in trousers and vest, the latter thrown over his undershirt. He donned a white shirt and a turn-down collar, arranging his black bow tie with care and frequently asking one of the deputies if he looked all right. He seemed anxious about his appearance and spent considerable time brushing away imaginary specks of dust with a whisk broom.

A few minutes after 7 o'clock Welsor began jesting with a nervous gayety, more marked than during the previous hours. He told his guards to "give him a lift" over the scaffold bridge, and then, becoming suddenly grave, earnestly said that he hoped to die like a man. He feared that he would break down at the last minute. To test his nerves he held his hand outstretched before him. It was steady and he laughed as though reassured. When 7:30 had passed Welsor was greatly disappointed and urged his guards to hurry the arrangements along.

When Sheriff Staed entered, a few minutes before 8 o'clock, Welsor welcomed him eagerly.

"Never mind reading the death warrant," he said. "It will be wasting time."

"All right, Sam," replied the Sheriff. The others then withdrew, and in a few minutes Sheriff Staed and Welsor emerged from the cell, the latter with his arms bound at his sides.

The death march was begun immediately. Sheriff Staed placed his right arm about Welsor's shoulders. Two officers went before to clear the way; then came Welsor and the Sheriff, and behind them were deputies, policemen and the others.

Welsor's face was ghastly in its pallor, but there was a smile upon his lips, which did not leave them until he stood upon the trap. He was hurried through the storeroom between two lines of police, through the jail door, into the yard, across the bridge to the gallows. That same set smile was on his face as he came from the gas-lighted jail into the sunlight, and his eyes stared straight before him, seeing what—no man knows, but certainly not taking cognizance of the crowd nor the surroundings.

When Welsor bade his guards good-by in the jail he expressed regret that Hedgpeth had not set him right about the attempted escape. He denied all connection with it.

Long before 5 o'clock the crowd which came to see Welsor die gathered in the corridors of the Four Courts and surged around the jail door. Each moment swelled the number until at 6 o'clock fully 200 people were packed under the large stairway. For an hour and a half they impatiently waited. A few gained entrance to the jail yard, and stood shivering in the early dawn. At 6:30 the crowd in the corridor was sent to the Twelfth street entrance of the yard. Those then in the yard numbered fully 500. The police arrangements in the corridor were exceedingly poor.

On the housetops surrounding the jail men and boys stood with straining eyes to catch a glimpse of the execution. A telegraph pole near the wall afforded a vantage place for half a dozen men who climbed amongst the net work of wires, craning their necks in the direction of the gallows.

The short walk from the jail door to the bridge which led to the scaffold was kept open by officers, but on either side the people formed solid walls of humanity between which Welsor would be compelled to march.

"I wonder if he will die game?" queried a beardless youth.

"He has been drinking all night," said another.

"No. He is perfectly sober," said a third, "and will die game."

When the deputies came out to arrange for the hanging the operations were watched with feverish interest.

"That rope is strong enough to do the work," remarked one who had not taken his eyes from the scaffold from the time the deputies began their work.

Presently the word was given that the death march had begun, and Welsor would shortly appear. He did so in a few seconds, and from the time he came through the door until the execution was over the silence was oppressive. The spectators kept their eyes fastened upon Welsor. If a word was spoken it was in a whisper.

The easy bearing of the prisoner was the subject of admiration by the onlookers. When he was standing upon the trap before the cap was adjusted the rope was left carelessly dangling about him and brushed against his right cheek. For once only the smile left Welsor's face and a look of irritation passed over it. A shudder crept through the assembly, and expressions of outrage were heard in low tones at the lack of regard for the condemned man's feelings.

"It's a shame," said several. "He ought not to have seen the rope at all, much less to have it brushing his face."

When the cap was drawn over Welsor's head and the trap was sprung a rush was made for the gallows. Those who had been standing upon the embankment jumped into the area and started forward. The police quickly formed a cordon around the scaffold, clasping hands so as to make an impassable barrier.

The spectators watched the swinging body until life was extinct. When it was cut down another rush was made for the Morgue. Scores of boys and men then clambered upon the scaffold and began hacking at the rope.

Into the Morgue door the crowd pushed and shoved, but the large force of police kept them back and only a few gained entrance and they were quickly excluded.

In 15 minutes after the body was lowered the yard was clear and the grim gallows was alone.

[List of observers' names omitted.]

As the gray dawn of the east brightened into morning the rumbling noise of the city, the first throbs of the great metropolitan heart, came distantly to the ear, and the jail took on new life. Deputies and keepers began to arrive. The rusty screechings of iron, the bolting and unbolting, where chains were used, added to the now broken solemnity and gave the watchers food for thought. By 7:30 o'clock quite a crowd had collected within and a large one without. Sheriff Staed, with his assistants, and Sheriff White of Illinois, who was experienced in the hangman's craft, arrived and passed through the fatal doorway to the scaffold. The wooden bridge from the jail walk to the gallows floor was put down and the hempen cord brought out. The Sheriff and his assistants gathered on the platform and examined the trap so that its workings might be sure. They viewed the rusted hinges, the iron catches and all, while about them watched the idlers.

The moments seemed to linger so, except when one thought of the prisoner inside, whose life tide was ebbing.

Sheriff White took the rope and arranged it in the iron circlets above on the cross beam. Knot after knot was made until it should be secure, and then the Sheriff tried its strength with his own weight. They practiced with the drop and pronounced it sound and sure.

By 7:40 the court yard was all but filled. Dozens of officers were scattered about and lined up along where the unfortunate was to pass. Officers were at the scaffold's base and on its floor, while everywhere were newspaper men, mingled with the crowd and the keepers.

Moment after moment slipped past until it lacked but a few moments of 8. Then someone whispered that 8 sharp was the hour, and the word went round. Interest rose to a breathless pitch. All faces turned to the shadowy doorway in expectancy. Someone came out and whispered "They're coming."

With the word the tramp, tramp, tramp of marching guards was heard, and men mounted tip-toe to see. Another moment the sound was at the door.

"Clear the way!" It was an officer commanding.

With this sound Welsor stood on the threshold. It was only for an instant that his white, tight-drawn countenance appeared, framed in that somber molding. His companion guard, Sheriff Staed, kept his step and was leading him on. Now he glanced up and beheld the crowd.

At the gallows top he rested while Sheriff White gave the commands. One deputy was to be at each catch, one at the spring. Once again he looked out upon the anxious, silent mass before him. They were staring at him. Perhaps he noted that many were on tip-toe and craning their necks. Maybe he saw the housetops lined and the telegraph poles heavy with them. Perhaps faces were everywhere in reeling uncertainty, none definite, but all filled with the same cold, unfeeling curiosity. If he did no expression occurred to prove it. His face was set and his glance cast down. Only by the nervous moving of the fingers could one guess the inner conflict.

A stir of the multitude or perhaps the chill morning air caused him to shiver, and he murmured that it was cold. Then the old relapse came, and again he was braving it out.

The Sheriff placed a tobacco box square in the center of the trap and said: "Stand on this, please," to which Welsor answered by movement, but no word.

Once upon the box, the guards began fastening the cords about his knees, for his arms had been bound while in the jail. He was now squarely facing the mass beyond for the last time. They were looking at him. He scorned them with that same indifferent disregard. He would not look at them. When the Sheriff asked:

"Have you anything to say?" he simply answered: "Go ahead!"

Sheriff White had the noose in his hand. A deputy held the black cap. When the cords below were tight the former said: "Bring me the cap."

Again there was a stir outside—one of those many tremulous quivers that had passed over the gaping crowd. They seemed to wonder why he did not move and cry out. Why he stood biting his lip as though scorning the delay.

The cap was lifted by Sheriff White and spread out. The victim could hear its rustle, but did not turn. A few thought he would glance up, if only to see the crowd, the city or the day. Nothing of the world seemed worth a last glance to him, not even the sunlight. What so many expected he would not do he did—died without looking.

Down over his eyes came the cap and a moment later he felt the noose. It lay on his shoulders and then tightened under his left ear. They were pulling on it and he was to drop in a moment.

He could hear the scratching as they twisted the catches. They were stepping aside and the crowd was murmuring.

It was 8:07 1/2 a.m. and the time was up. Deputy Hatton had advanced and, stooping, cut short the life and speculations as easy as he cut the cord. The trap fell with a bang.

With a ghastly swish and uncanny creak the body dropped downward and brought up with a straining sound, then hung motionless, lifeless, with no tremor, no sigh.

The slipnoose had not failed. From the ear to the spine it had twisted with flesh-ripping force, but had not broken. The neck was not disjointed, and though the form breathed there was inanity and repose.

For a moment the clamorous crowd was still.

Doctors gathered about and caught the strain of the victim's last pulsations. It was 8:07 1/2 when he fell, and 8:16 1/2 before they called him dead.

When all was over, Korzendorfer, the Morgue Keeper, brought a rolling bier, and, with the command of the Sheriff to "cut the rope," the body was lowered and carried into the Morgue.

Welsor was for once and for all irretrievably dead.

The drop fell at 8:07 1/2. Nine minutes later Welsor was pronounced dead. The physicians in attendance were Dr. C. A. Frank, Dr. Heine Marks, Superintendent of the City Hospital, Dr. W. V. Kingsbury, Dr. A. W. Fleming, Dr. Brasford Lewis and Dr. E. C. Neville. Dr. Frank seized the pulse on the right side and Dr. Marks on the left. The first minute Welsor's pulse beat 80, and the next minute dropped to 78. At the end of four and one-half minutes the pulse registered 71. After the third minute the pulse grew weak and fluttering and so continued until six minutes had elapsed, then ceased beating. The physicians placed their ears to Welsor's breast to determine the action of the heart.

Welsor only struggled twice—once shortly after he fell the muscles of his body contracted, his knees drew up and straightened out. At the end of two and one-half minutes the body went through a similar convulsion, but much weaker than the first.

Morgue Keeper Henry Korzendorfer and his assistant, George A. Thompson, placed under the scaffold a truck, and at 8:22 the body was cut down and taken to the Morgue and transferred to a marble slab.

When the black cap was removed the only marks of violence was a livid scar extending around the dead man's neck and a hemorrhage in the left eye caused the lid to bulge out. Small streams of blood trickled from both nose and mouth. The brain was pronounced normal by the physicians.

Dr. Frank cut two incisions, one on each side down the spinal cord in the back of the neck, exposing the backbone. The neck was not broken. The only thing discoverable was a fracture of the small bone just below the Adam's apple.

The physicians announced that death had been painless.

The hemorrhage in the brain caused unconsciousness and death was the result of strangulation.

The body was washed and Thomas Wand, the liveryman, Welsor's friend, was notified. At 11:15 a.m. the body was removed to Sixth and Clark avenue, from which place the funeral will take place Sunday afternoon at 3 o'clock.

In Welsor's inside vest pocket a slip of note paper was found containing a list of names written in ink. The list is supposed to be of friends Welsor wished to invite to his funeral.

[List of names omitted.]

[13 January 1894, p. 5.]

72 - THE CHINESE IN ST. LOUIS.

Within the confines of St. Louis at present there are about 1,000 Chinese. Within the same confines there are nearly half as many laundries operated by Chinamen. The public is familiar with the Chinese laundry and the Chinese method of labor. It knows how they toil, is fully aware of their manner of clothing themselves and has read endless accounts of what they eat or are supposed to eat. Dissertations on social life in China, like that on the discovery of roast pig by Lamb, are common library familiarities, and the movements of the denizens of Chinatown at the Golden Gate have been recorded and re-recorded.

St. Louis has no Chinatown and no specific Chinese quarter. The red and white signs one can stumble across almost anywhere between De Hodiamont and East St. Louis. She has no high-class opium-joint abominations and no progressive Chinese emporium to which upper tendom pays homage and money at one and the same time. She has, however, what it is difficult elsewhere to find—a Chinese rendezvous. In this rendezvous, restaurants, lounging and smoking rooms, a few Chinese families and general sociability prevail; and more, this rendezvous has the patronage and good will of the entire Chinese element in this city.

When a St. Louis Chinaman wishes to "blow himself" he takes the requisite cash and saunters down that portion of South Eighth street lying between Walnut and Market streets. Here he finds every opportunity to dispose of his week's wages or profits, or, perhaps, his laundry—for laundries have been lost and won in this block. Sundays and Mondays are days off in the laundry business. At noon Sundays all the laundries in the city are closed for the day, and in a short time the different car lines begin dropping Chinamen by ones and twos in the vicinity of Eighth and Market streets. Some straggle around on foot, and by 2 o'clock, it is safe to say,

"In the Chinese Restaurant" (*St. Louis Republic*, 14 January 1894, p. 15).

there are several hundred Mongolians in this block enjoying themselves in a way peculiarly Chinese. The crowd shifts and changes all afternoon and evening, but never grows less. As fast as one sporty John "goes broke" at the game of fan-tan another takes his place, and the broken one stoically gazes on while the winner keeps on winning and the loser drops out.

The more pretentious of the resorts in this neighborhood have restaurants as side issues, a meal partaken at one of which will form the subject of a later discussion. The more pretentious keepers of these more pretentious resorts have wives and oblique-eyed babies, who are occasionally permitted to disport themselves, clad in the tiniest little blue frocks, on the front steps of the paternal dwelling. It is usually when the morning sun is streaming its genial rays into Eighth street that these little codgers may be seen, and then for a not over-lengthy period. John has discovered "lat Melicans" are deeply interested in these queer little babies and are entirely too fond of stopping to enjoy their company.

Besides this social quarter with its homes and resorts; besides the widely scattered array of red sign laundries and occasional Chinese stores, there is a feature, not so much social as dependent thereon, which possesses interest to a degree. This latter is nothing more nor less than a Chinese grave-

"In the Chinese Barber Shop" (*St. Louis Republic*, 14 January 1894, p. 15).

"Chinese Cemetery" (*St. Louis Republic*, 14 January 1894, p. 15).

yard, and as such deserves distinct, if not honorable, mention. Those who have ever studied the heathen Chinee and his history, either social, political or religious, know too much of him to credit the statement of the presence of a Chinese-American graveyard in St. Louis. Yet with some modifications this statement is true, as will be duly detailed. Perhaps it is more of an American graveyard, with the Chinese element as a dependent feature, and perhaps the Mongolian end is more of a way-station resting place en route to China; but, nevertheless, it is a Chinese graveyard, and a very interesting one at that. They are resting there awaiting that auspicious moment when fate and fortune shall decree that their bones shall be removed to that celestial haven of which Wingrave Cook so aptly wrote:

"A land where the roses have no fragrance and the women no petticoats; where the laborer has no Sabbath and the Magistrate no sense of honor; where the needle points to the south and the sign of being puzzled is to scratch the antipodes of the head; where the place of honor is on the left hand and the seat of intellect in the stomach; where to take off your hat is an insolent gesture and to wear white garments is to put yourself in mourning," namely, China.

———

SUNDAY AT FIVE.

———

Of the restaurants it was said above that usually they were mere attachments to the more pretentious resorts on South Eighth street. At 19 South Eighth street the order is reversed and the restaurant becomes the chief attraction. Cold lunch may be had at any hour, or hot lunch cooked to order, but the regular table d'hote is not announced until 5 o'clock p.m.

A visit to this restaurant at midday disclosed proprietor, cook and waiter sitting in the front room chatting, smoking and tea drinking.

"Wat you want?" inquired the proprietor as the visitor entered.

He was informed that a Chinese dinner was the thing desired.

"No can get him," he replied, while the cook and waiter gazed blandly on.

As the proprietor of an eating-house this Mongolian was certainly unique. On each side of his face were straggling black hairs, vainly endeavoring to resemble whiskers. But his upper lip fared better and held the roots of a long, drooping mustache, which appeared to be his greatest pride and his brothers' greatest envy. A double-breasted coat of thick goods and store pattern compassed his body, while his legs were encased in a pair of woolen trousers. The toes of his bare feet were thrust into the regulation Chinese footwear. The heel of the right shoe, hanging down from a leg crossed over, beat a rhythmic tatoo on the board floor as he repeated, "No can get him."

A letter of introduction from a Chinese friend in another city, written in Chinese characters on a narrow strip of paper and addressed to all good Chinamen whom it might concern, was tendered. Of course, they all read it, then jabbered away, grinned and reread it, laughing aloud as the proprietor volunteered the information that the letter described the bearer to be a "Velly glood man."

"Come a Sunday. Got glood dinner Sunday. Come a flive clock; bling flend."

Sunday at 5, the investigator with a "flend," turning the corner at Seventh and Market streets, encountered a Chinaman who looked carelessly at them and turned his eyes again up Seventh street. At Eighth and Market a similar experience was had, and from that corner, strung out in all four directions, could be seen solitary Chinamen standing on the corners doing nothing apparently.

"Bung Loo?" said the friend.

"Fan Tan," corrected the investigator.

At the alley on Eighth street between Market and Walnut streets, were stationed two robust-looking heathens, and in the first doorway beyond an almond-eyed Celestial stood against the wall in an attitude altogether too alert for mere pleasure.

A red paper sign pasted in the doorway marks No. 15. Up three rickety old steps and the hand is on the knob.

When the newspaper man and friend entered, the place was comfortably filled. A table was secured which favored a good view of the room and its occupants, as well as leaving the eye free to wander through an open doorway to the inner room and kitchen beyond. Those who were eating glanced up, and seeing no cause for alarm dipped their chop sticks deeper into the rice, and with the bowl to their lips crammed the steaming cereal down their throats. The sight was truly alarming. Then came the waiter, bowing and smiling, and in a sing-song fashion chanting. "Hollo! Wat you want?"

"Dinner."

"Wat you like?"

"What have you got?"

"Chicken, duck, pork, rice and China dish."

"Bring it all but the pork."

"How muchee you want to pay?"

"How much does it cost?"

"Chicken, 35 cents; duck, 35 cents; China dish, 40 cents; odder tings, nutting—tea nutting."

"Let it all come."

"You likee chop stick? Maybe likee flawk?"

The handling of a chop stick would have been a more laborious task than writing with a pencil three feet long. Accordingly the chop sticks were declined.

The first dish set on the bare table was no larger than a silver dollar and contained a tiny dab of mustard in a spoonful of oil. Three dishes of like size followed, one containing pepper jam, the other meat sauces. Tea was served in bowls, and was delicious. The duck, likewise the chicken, was halved, then sliced crosswise after the manner of bologna sausage, and served on round decorated plates. One bowl of chicken soup comprised the same order for two, which was served with dainty little spoons of chinaware, decorated in unmistakable heathen design. Rice, steaming hot, was brought in bowls, while the mysterious China dish completed the spread. This dish was wonderful, awe-inspiring, and yet toothsome. It was served in a dish, half bowl, half platter. Around the platter like edge were carefully placed bits of something which looked like wet piecrust and tasted like smoked fish. The way they stuck out around the edges suggested decoration of lettuce, parsley and water cress. The arrangement of the whole affair inspired visions of hot salad. Celery, giblets, onions, seaweed that looked like dulse, and some peculiar and totally foreign grains resembling barley, went to make up this steaming-hot mass.

The cautious manner in which these delicacies were investigated by the visiting friends no doubt afforded much amusement of the habitues of the place, and gave rise to more than one unchristian joke, rich in hidden force, for they laughed, chatted and cast good-natured glances, full of meaning from one to the other, and then at the strangers.

At the next table sat two Chinamen, evidently winners, with all that the bill of fare called for spread out before them. Their positions were grotesque. The one sat with half-closed eyes, his head resting on his hand, lazily fishing from out the soup a bit of meat, dipping it into the miniature dish of mustard and oil, thence to the pepper-jam, thence to the sauce, from which point he leisurely conveyed it to his mouth. The other, squatted on the chair seat, knees tucked under his chin, jabbering and grimacing, was forcing hot rice down his capacious maw.

Over in the darkest corner sat one evidently a loser. Occasionally he paused and gazed wistfully into the blank wall. Others were eating, drinking and smoking, the while chattering away like school girls.

When the tea gave out the temporarily embarrassed individual immediately repaired to a mammoth tin teapot, kept continuously steeping, filled his bowl and returned to the feast.

Chinese eating is a novelty with a limit. The strangers reached theirs and tendered a bill in payment. The correct change was returned and a quarter shoved to the waiter.

"What you want?" was asked.

"Nothing; keep it."

"You give him me?"

"Yes."

"What for?"

Here was a puzzler, to be sure. How could the glorious privilege of promiscuous tipping be explained to this meek-eyed Mongolian?

"Ask me something easy," returned the giver, "but keep the money."

"Tankee! tankee!" exclaimed the heathen, and straightway the coin disappeared among the folds of his voluminous jacket.

The contents of a small glass case screwed against the wall, above the ever-steeping teapot, aroused the friends' curiosity. The upper shelf contained a quantity of the famous birds' nests, which these people esteem so highly as a stock for their world-renowned delicacy, birds' nest soup. The lower shelves held candy, which was discovered to be a very fair quality of the peanut variety, differing from the American product in that the candy proper was neither of sugar nor molasses, but some glutinous mixture. This, in addition to peanuts, was sprinkled with a little seed akin to millet. An invitation to smoke was declined with thanks.

Then the waiter said "Chang lar," which is the correct Chinese mode of bidding adieu, and the visitors departed.

It was learned through a friendly heathen that such a thing as a Chinese barber shop existed in St. Louis, and that its location was 21 South Eighth street. This place was visited, but the two Celestials who were in charge retreated step by step, as the visitor advanced, until when the latter had seated himself on a convenient three-legged stool, the Celestials had disappeared through a rear door. In the little time before their return it was observed that the room was dirty, almost bare of furniture and entirely lacking anything which to the visitor would betoken a barber shop. Several small packages and bundles, some of them broken, aroused suspicion of opium and its use, and cigarettes were profusely in evidence. There was also one instrument which might be a razor, or it might not. The preponderance of evidence, after a critical examination, was in favor of the negative.

When the proprietors returned they had with them an interpreter who inquired what was wanted. No, the American could not have a shave nor a hair-cut; didn't know what a shampoo might be, but he couldn't have that, either. They had nothing which they desired to exchange for coin of the realm; good day.

And the visitor was gazing at the outside of the door of No. 21.

Passing the shop a day later, a Mongolian was seen seated in the chair and submitting to the manipulations of his brother-heathen tonsorial artist. But the view was across a street and through a begrimed window and was altogether unsatisfactory.

A TEMPORARY BURIAL.

Aside from the social Chinese circle, away from the mundane influences of South Eighth street and the entire local laundry element, lies a small strip of ground just now strewn with the seared leaves of a dead year, where, after all the strifes and strugglings that make up this earthly career, even the heathen Celestial must lay down his burden and enter upon the sleep of eternity. It is a spot pleasant enough in its environment, graced by a vista of sloping woodlands and blessed by nature's own rich ornamentation of forest and glade, where sunlight and shadow play at hide and seek through the long summer time, but it is woefully lacking in one thing. To the laboring exile from his blessed kingdom, the local laundryman, it is not in China, and not to be there is not to be at all. Yet it stands as a Chinese graveyard, where at present some 17 are buried, and will continue as such until the Six Companies see fit to complete the letter of their contract and return the bones of the sleepers to the blessing of their native soil.

Wesleyan Cemetery, which stands in a 10-acre field at the junction of Olive and Hanley roads, seven miles west of the Courthouse, is very pretty, though not over large nor populated with the remains of the wealthier class of citizens. Only a little over four acres of its entire surface is occupied by the graves of the dead, and at the present rate of burial no call will be had for more space. It is this place in the far southwest corner, covering a small space of ground, that the Chinese of St. Louis have fixed upon as their burial ground, and it is here that at one time 22 Celestials lay peacefully at rest.

Their names are all registered in the cemetery record, Hong Sing, Wah Chi Lee, May Lin Foo, Sam Wo, Foo Gee Chin, Wah Lung and a long list of such meaningless translations that are drearily void of interest. They were buried at different times, covering a period of nearly nine years now, and though time elapses, they are all destined to have their bones exhumed and transplanted in that more sacred soil which is where the other half live.

They all came from China to make their fortunes. All, very probably, bound themselves by contract to the great Chinese Six Companies, which furnished them with transportation and the guarantee that either their living selves or their bones shall be returned to their native sod. Once here they struggled along, saved considerable money, then sickened and died, and are now buried at the Wesleyan. May Lin Foo, whose grave is marked by a very plain board, covered with daubed characters, came all the way from the far distant sea of stars in Western China, while Sam Wo came from the populous coast above Hong Kong. The others were reared similarly in the populous coast cities of their native country, and belonged undoubtedly to that underdog strata of Chinese society commonly designated "Coolies."

Two years ago six of the 22 dead at Wesleyan were taken up. Two Chinamen, according to the sexton, appeared on the ground, digged up the bones, and building a fire, baked them dry. Then they scraped them, and, packing them tight in brown paper parcels, labeled them and departed. Since that time, however, no removals have occurred, although it has been said that a few more are soon to depart.

William Schmieder, sexton and general keeper of the graveyard, knows a bit of local Chinese history that cannot be discovered elsewhere. He has been the gravedigger at the Wesleyan Cemetery for years, and remembers distinctly the arrivals and departures of the Chinese dead from the first to the last. The "goings on" of the living friends of the dead Celestials over their graves—as he called their mournings—are to him of little interest.

One dreary afternoon not long since, when the dull, leaden sky overhead threatened rain, this unobtrusive denizen of Wesleyan was found raking a huge pile of searbrown leaves from the grass and paths preparatory to making a good riddance bonfire of them. He was asked how many Chinese were buried there. He thought that 18 or 20 was about the right number.

Of their burial ceremonies the keeper said:

"They come out here in carriages, sometimes as many as 19 or 20 of them. They have the corpse in a coffin and rough box stowed away in a hearse, just like Americans. That's about all they do have like Americans. One of them will sit on the hearse with the driver, or in the first carriage, and drop little bits of white paper with holes in them all along the road. I always receive notice beforehand that they are coming, and so I have the grave ready. They'll drive in and take out the coffin. Then they always have a bottle with them that holds some kind of liquor and a little bit of china cup that holds about two thimblefuls. One of them will take the cup and pour it full of liquor. Then he'll go and kneel down about six feet away from the foot of the grave and begin mumbling something. At the same time he'll have the china cup between his thumbs before him and he'll keep swaying it up and down and crosswise until all at once he pours it around on the ground. Then he'll take the empty cup and go through the same motions. Everybody takes a turn doing this until all of them have blessed the grave. Then they throw the cup and bottle down alongside.

"Then I put the coffin down and when I begin to throw on the dirt they passes crackers around to one another and begin to eat. Some of them throw a bit of rice in the grave, another scatters the pieces of paper around, and another cuts the head off one or two chickens that they bring, and throw them in the grave. When the grave is filled they go away."

Schmieder says that revelries occur twice a year and sometimes oftener. Chinamen come and bring various offerings which they place on the graves. A peculiar kind of small, highly decorated waxen wafer, shaped Roman candlewise of the Fourth of July stripe is always brought. Two of these are lighted and stuck in the earth at the foot of the grave. Whether they burn a moment or not matters little, as the form seems only to require that they be lighted. Food, such as rice and chicken, and wine in cups are placed upon the mounds when these visits occur. Incantations of a moderately solemn nature are gone through with, while the whole ceremony is wound up with a most energetic fusillade of revolvers over the graves of the dead. Schmieder says that he is certain they shoot over the graves to frighten away the evil spirits supposed to linger about them at times. Schmieder, however, cannot be counted as absolute authority on the subject of the Chinese ritual.

THE LONE MOURNER.

When a rich Chinaman dies the burial service at Wesleyan is more imposing. A large party of Chinamen usually accompanies the casket and bears offerings of a more interesting nature. Music is not wanting, nor yet a plentiful array of flags and candles, which are thrown about the open grave.

Some five years since, when Wah Chi Len was buried, two bands discoursed music at his graveside and a half dozen of his country's flags drooped their silken folds upon the sod and decayed upon his casket's breast with the lapse of time. Bowls of fine china filled with choice food offerings were left upon his grave, and at regular periods thereafter friends came to decorate his resting-place after the manner described. One of the peculiarities of these after mournings is that none of the graves surrounding the especial one visited is forgotten. In scattering their offerings they scatter them over all, and in firing across the grave they fire over all.

Once, relates Schmieder, there came two travelers to St. Louis from their distant flower land, Chan Wo and Hoo Li Ging by name, who, upon arriving here, were taken suddenly ill and died. It so happened that although both men were well to do they had no relatives, nor perhaps any especial friends, in the city to look after their remains. Accordingly the ceremony that witnessed their caskets placed beneath the sod was short and without much ado. Two very plain boards were placed at their heads and at their feet burned several candles, which, decaying, were never replaced. No visitors came to seek their resting-place. Only in the ceremonies held at the graves of others were they included and bits of the wide-flung rice fell to their lot, more in charity than sorrow.

So they rested, seemingly forgotten, far from the sacred soil of their countrymen, and none wept their absence. It is now somewhat over two years since there entered one day the Wesleyan gate a traveler from the banks of the river of golden sands, who came in search of two brothers who had died away from home. He had with him a small scroll on which were printed a number of Chinese characters. Of Schmieder he desired that he be shown the graves of his countrymen buried there, which was accordingly done. Arrived at the spot where there were then some 22 Chinese buried, he moved from one head board to another, inspecting the inscriptions on each and comparing them with those of his scroll, until he came to the head boards over the graves of Chan Wo and Hoo Li Ging. Here he stopped and, going six feet distant from the foot of each, knelt down, poured a fluid from a vial into a thimble glass and, scattering its contents over the grave, offered prayer to the particular providence of his worship. With his actions the sexton was most deeply impressed for he relates that he felt certain that here was one out of all the mourners who had visited the graves who really felt and did not feign grief.

The stranger departed, but came regularly thereafter for some three months, when he ordered the caskets exhumed and had the remains shipped to China. The keeper says that all the others usually came in company, talked and chatted around the sacred earth without apparent sign of sorrow, until he had really been led to believe that the ritual they executed excluded sorrowful manifestations of whatever kind. Be this as it may, the grief of the stranger was genuine.

[14 January 1894, p. 15.]

73 - THIS CALLS FOR HEMP.

Special to The Republic.

Manchester, Mo., Jan. 16—Two criminal assaults committed by the same brute in less than one hour, one victim being colored and one white, is the awful record of crime in this vicinity to-day.

About 3 o'clock this afternoon a worthless negro character named John Buchner, an ex-convict who has only been out of the Jefferson City Penitentiary a short time, where he served a term of three years for criminal assault upon a young colored school teacher named Mary Weaver, started out with the determination to make a new record for fiendish brutality.

Arming himself with a double-barreled shotgun, he left his home, about two miles south of Valley Park, and started out in quest of victims.

He first met Mrs. Al Mungo, the wife of a respectable colored farmer. It seems as though a presentiment of what was to occur came over the poor woman, for as soon as the fiend saluted her she told him she was in a hurry to get home to her sick baby, and to please not detain her.

This was not in accord with the demon's plans, however, and he boldly made an indecent proposal to her. Still hoping to escape, the poor woman begged to be allowed to hasten home, promising faithfully to say nothing of his proposal.

All of this was, however, to no purpose. Clubbing his gun the brute knocked her down and dragged her some 30 yards off the road into some timber and there accomplished his purpose.

After leaving Mrs. Mungo, Buchner went to his home, which is on the farm of Mr. William R. Harrison, the father of his second victim. After carefully prospecting about the place for a while and discovering that none of the Harrison family were at home save Miss Allie, a beautiful and accomplished young lady of about 19 years, he determined to make her his second victim.

He waited and watched until he saw her go into an out building, and then swooped down upon her. Forcing the lock off the door, he entered the building. Then a fearful and nearly a death struggle ensued. The poor frightened girl battled with all the strength of desperation, while the black fiend, all the time threatening to kill her if she did not desist in her efforts, scratched and pounded her almost into insensibility.

Persons who saw the room after the struggle declared that it looked like a slaughter-house.

Blood, bits of clothing and tufts of the poor girl's hair were all over the room.

The young lady's parents deny that the negro accomplished his purpose here, but if he did not it was only because he was so exhausted from his terrible struggle that he could scarcely crawl home. After the brute left his second victim she managed to crawl to the home of a neighbor and there related her awful experience. The negro went directly to his home.

Immediately after the alarm was given a horseman was sent at once to Manchester, where a warrant was procured for the negro's arrest. Armed with this, and with a dozen or more mounted men, all armed to the teeth, Constable Schumacher started in hot pursuit. Arriving at Valley Park, this posse was re-enforced by 15 or 20 more and they all started for the negro's home.

After detailing his force to guard all the exits, the Constable walked up to the door and demanded admittance. One of the members of the family opened the door and there sat the demon.

When he saw who it was after him the darky made a break for an inner room, where his loaded gun was hanging, but the ominous click of the Constable's revolver stopped him.

Had he attempted an escape he certainly would have been filled with buckshot, as every avenue was guarded.

Securing his man, the Constable started for Manchester, being met at Valley Park by your reporter.

Here a feeble attempt was made at lynching, but the crowd lacked the nerve, and, whipping up his horse, the officer successfully ran the gauntlet of 20 or more armed men, who but five minutes before declared their firm determination to "string him."

Arriving at Manchester the negro was taken before Squire Hofstetter, and in default of $1,000 bond was committed to the Clayton Jail.

The Constable was afraid to a start to-night, as a large and frenzied mob gathered, vowing to have the fiend's life. Should a mob be organized at Valley Park and come here before this mob disperses, the chances are that the Coroner will have a job by daylight.

At midnight mounted men are galloping up and down the road, and to add to the seriousness of the situation the colored people have gathered in considerable numbers, and evidently intend to resent an attempt at a lynching.

The negro acknowledged to your reporter that he had accomplished his purpose with Mrs. Mungo, but will not talk about Miss Harrison.

[17 January 1894, p. 1.]

74 - TEN-FOOT DROP.

They lynched him.

That is the way the people of St. Louis County dealt with John Buckner.

They tied one end of a rope around his neck, tied the other end to a bridge timber, and gave him a 10 foot drop.

John Buckner was the negro who, as detailed exclusively in yesterday's Republic, assaulted Mrs. Al Mungo, a colored woman, and attempted to assault Miss Alice Harrison, a young white lady.

At 4:30 o'clock yesterday morning, 12 hours after the commission of the crimes, John Buckner paid the penalty, according to the Coroner's verdict, "death from hanging at the hands of persons unknown."

The scene of the criminal's last moments was upon the planks of the second span of the Meramec River wagon bridge, about 200 yards west of Valley Park on the Hawkins road. Every arrangement for his demise had been prepared. A crowd of masked men surged about his rope-bound form, while a few chosen leaders forced him forward to his horrible fate. They asked him no questions and demanded no explanations. He was guilty, they knew it and barely offered him the courtesy of a few last words.

Bound by rope and bruised by a long, rough journey of four miles from Manchester to Valley Park, the criminal was too frightened and dismayed to quite fully realize that his hour had come and that death was before him. His thick, brutish lips were sealed with the more than crouching brute fear. The faces which he saw about him were set with the determination of masked fury. None were among the throng who discountenanced the proceedings. All were anxious that his crimes should be atoned for, and that speedily.

In the crisp atmosphere of a bright dawn strong arms lifted the struggling form over the adjoining railing. They held a moment there to see that the noose about his throat was sound and secure. The knot at the span's arm was again examined, and then, with a half whispered "all right" from the leader, the form was tossed downward to the end of the noose. His stout burly form was more than a guarantee for the surety of his death.

With a swish and a plunge his great hulking body strained at the cord. The bones of the neck yielded, and with a few frantic struggles, a few short lung-straining gasps the body ceased its movements and hung lifeless. There was quiet exultation then in the watchful faces about. After assuring themselves that death was stiffening the form below the watchers turned and departed from whence they had come.

Buckner's crime had been an awful one. It included the third of a similar nature and proved that his character was that of a brute. Swinging so in the cool morning breeze, with the river's bright waters rippling merrily over innumerable pebbles below, the administrators of such summary justice were fully assured that at least he would not further disturb the peace of their pleasant homes. The scenes of the night previous to the tragic enactment of unwritten moral law were fully as appalling as the tragic climax itself. Never before had the residents of Valley Park, Manchester and the surrounding territory evinced any desire to intercept the ordinary course of justice. They had lived along in peace, taken the illegalities of men as they came, with the assurance that ordinary legal processes would fully avenge them. Yesterday however, and the night before, the calm was broken. Justice could not be waited for, and Buckner's death was the outcropping of such anxious fury as knew no bounds and process other than that of speed.

The crime or crimes were committed Tuesday afternoon in the immediate neighborhood of Buckner's home, which is fully three and a half miles west of Valley Park. There, with his parents, three brothers and one sister, he lived on the Harrison estate, part of which farm his father worked on shares. The Buckner family, with the exception of the dead man, was fairly respected and considered good enough. William H. Harrison, the owner of the farms, whose daughter, Allie, was assaulted by Buckner, considered the family character sufficiently good to permit of their remaining on his place. A little farther along on the Hawkins road, about two and a half miles south of Valley Park, lived Buckner's uncle and aunt, where last evening the stiffened corpse lay, awaiting the interment it will receive to-day. Through the broken panes of a miserable log window the pale, cloud-broken moonlight cast its sheen and shadow on the gaunt form of the dead, while near it, in a dark corner, wept the mother of the erring boy alone.

Not more than a stone's throw from this log cabin stands the cabin of his first victim, Mrs. Al Mungo, who lay sick and suffering from the fearful wounds he inflicted upon her. Not far from the dead man's home, on the same farm, stands the residence of Mr. Harrison where, too, lay his injured daughter, suffering severely from the injuries she had received. In the distance, lighted by the pleasant moonlight, could be seen the crest of the hill where not only the present assaults, but the previous one of Buckner on Miss Weaver nearly five years before were committed, and in a neighboring valley lies the small Baptist meeting-house and the cemetery, where to-day Buckner will be interred.

The details of the dead man's deeds are already familiar. But 18 months released from the Jefferson City Penitentiary, he chose to permit his brutish passions to once more overcome him. During all the period since the time of release he had remained away from Valley Park. St. Louis had been his residence and odd jobs about the city furnished his livelihood.

Two weeks ago, however, he returned to his father's house and spent his time loafing about the neighborhood. He did nothing other than to hunt and hang about the Valley Park alehouses.

Tuesday afternoon his instincts took a new turn. About 2 o'clock that afternoon he took a shotgun belonging to his father, presumably to hunt, and strolled towards Valley Park along the Hawkins road.

On his way he passed the cabin of Mrs. Mungo, but she was not in. Continuing along the road he came to the identical spot where he had assaulted Miss Weaver. Here he met Mrs. Mungo. It seems that Buckner was thoroughly bent upon the execution of his crime. The woman saw it and endeavored to pass without stopping. The villain would not have it that way and barred the roadway with his presence, at the same time greeting her. Being accosted she endeavored to avoid the dilemma by pleading haste and the illness of a child; neither this nor other pleas secured her passage.

Buckner divulged his object by brutally insulting the woman. It was then that Mrs. Mungo pleaded and begged for mercy. She went further and, falling on her knees, implored the obdurate criminal to forego his fiendish purpose, but without avail. Insisting upon gratifying his desires, he seized her, and for many minutes they engaged in a struggle that was abusive and almost deathlike. The woman fought with all the strength that she possessed, but was finally overcome and thrown to the ground.

Then Buckner dragged the torn, bleeding, half-senseless form into the neighboring brush and carried out his purpose. Leaving the woman in a semi-conscious condition, he retraced his steps toward his home. Arrived there, he crossed the land to the residence of Mr. Harrison and found that gentleman out. All of the family were away except the pretty 19-year-old daughter Allie, who was working about the place. Buckner had revived his criminal purpose once more and now contemplated an assault upon the innocent girl.

He hung about the place unobserved and waited until the young woman visited one of the outhouses of the place. The moment she had entered Buckner made his appearance and demanded admittance. This was refused and he forced an entrance.

With her there, once inside, he renewed the fiendish struggle that had characterized his assault upon Mrs. Mungo. Her cries and exertions were of no avail. Although she gave fierce resistance, he beat and threatened her, finally succeeding in forcing her to the ground.

For some unknown reason, which has not yet developed, the villain failed to complete his purpose. The struggles of the girl were perhaps telling upon his strength or some noise may have distracted his purpose with the fear of detection. At any rate he desisted and departed, leaving the girl in a fainting condition and so weak as to be barely able to crawl.

Again he returned to his home, and, strange to say, remained there, unconcealed, nor yet attempting flight.

Both victims of his strength succeeded in giving the alarm. When Mr. Harrison, the father of his last victim, returned home he was astounded with the fearful intelligence. Barely remaining long enough to bemoan the fearful catastrophe that had befallen his child, he left his farm in his shirt sleeves to seek the nearest Justice of the Peace.

That person was F. J. Hofstetter of Manchester and the distance of seven and a half miles Mr. Harrison traveled alone, informing people along the way. He left in his trail squads of speculating citizens who pitied his condition and talked of the summary justice that was so soon to be administered.

At Manchester Mr. Harrison found Squire Hofstetter and saw the warrant placed in Constable Nick Schumacher's hands. That individual started at once for Buckner's home in company with the father. No one attempted to accompany these two from Manchester. The news had spread and excitement was fast growing.

At Valley Park, however, the men who had brooded over Harrison's wrongs and had meantime heard of the first assault on Mrs. Mungo decided to accompany the Constable and help seize the negro.

About 9 o'clock at night the posse arrived at Buckner's home. He was inside, and realized with the resounding knocks that trouble had come. He rose from his chair. When the door swung open he recognized the form of Schumacher, whose "I want you," caused him to start.

At once the criminal endeavored to secure the shotgun he had carried earlier in the day, but that move was seconded by the frosty glitter of the moonlight upon Schumacher's leveled pistol.

"Make a move and I'll shoot," said the latter.

Buckner did not move. Instead he weakened and simulated innocence with an inquiry as to what was wanted.

"You're wanted, you ——— ———," was the answer.

They gathered around him then and placed him under arrest. Handcuffs were produced and the criminal's hands were bound. Then he was rudely forced through the doorway and helped into the cart in which the Constable had come.

Then Buckner's farewell ride began.

It was moonlight, ever so clear and beautiful. The rough roadway was lighted up with the peaceful glimmer and sheen, making the faces of captive and guardsmen perfectly visible. The three and a half miles to Valley Park were soon traversed, over the same wagon bridge, the identical iron beam from which a few hours later the prisoner was to swing lifeless. Across the bridge in the village they found citizens awake and stirring. The news had brought many out and gathered them about the taverns. While passing some of the guard dropped back. They mingled with the crowd and gave the particulars of the arrest. A few moments more and someone from the crowd cried:

"Hev you got him?"

"Yes," called back Schumacher.

"Hold on, then," came the command, to which the Constable answered by whipping his horse and leaving the crowd some distance behind.

The crowd was not to be robbed of its prey so easily, however. Several men swung into their saddles again and took up the chase. Not far along the road they caught up with the cart and dogged its tracks into Manchester. In the village the prisoner was hauled into 'Squire Hofstetter's office, where he was held in the sum of $1,000 bond.

During this legal process a crowd of a hundred men—large for so small a hamlet—gathered about the door and clamored for justice. Several entered and took it upon themselves to ask the prisoner questions. At first he denied any knowledge of the assault, but his answers, impelled by fright, entrapped him.

"You were out hunting," said one. "Did you catch any game?"

"No, sir," answered Buckner.

"Then where did you get this blood on your clothes? Did it come from Mrs. Mungo or Miss Harrison?"

"I didn't do anything to Miss Harrison," was Buckner's reply. The questioners smiled and jested over the answer and accused the villain in fierce language of his crimes. He only blanched and stammered, but said little more. It was noticed by the authorities that the crowd outside was becoming entirely too large and demonstrative not to bode evil. Lynching was feared and voices demanding it were listened to through the doorway. Men outside were hooting and yelling, and working off that hasty frenzy that afterwards accomplished the death.

Revolvers were constantly fired and a veritable bedlam seemed inaugurated in the ordinarily quiet lanes of the village. Counsel was held in secret and a plan of campaign was formulated. A scheme to get him out was discussed, but the size of the throng without proved too much of a barrier. It was then decided to place the fellow, bound, in the cellar below and place two armed constables on duty. This was done and thereafter began the long night watch without.

The crowd without studied and suggested plans. They intended hurrying him to a convenient telegraph pole and stringing him aloft, but that plan was not executed. Those who were yelling and shooting lacked nerve. Besides, in the Squire's office were several determined men, men with revolvers and who would fight. They received each fresh outburst with caution to be calm and expressions of severe determination as regards their particular duties.

It all meant business and the crowd knew it. They hung about and at 11:30 p.m. some resorted to a new strategy. Some masks were secured and handkerchiefs utilized. With their faces concealed the crowd felt more courageous and began creating more and more disturbance. They swarmed about Hofstetter's door and several advanced, pounding upon the portals. To this Schumacher responded. When his face appeared the ringleaders shouted:

"We want that nigger. Give him to us or we will break in and take him."

"No you won't," was the answer. "We are to protect him. I know you fellows, and if any attempt is made now you'll get in trouble. You'd better let up." The answer was received with jeers of derision. The crowd surged only more strongly and pounded against the rear entrance. In the shadow below, Buckner lay shivering, speculating upon the momentary consequences of his crime. The temporary effect was excellent, however, for not long after 12 o'clock the mob reduced in size. The shooting and yelling ceased and a large number of persons dispersed to their homes. At 1 a.m. all were gone save a few stragglers and these only lingered in the shadow.

The quiet was not a harbinger of peace by any means. It was merely the lull which boded the later storm. In reality, a portion of the crowd was watching, and another portion had taken the advice of some counselor and departed for Valley Park, where certain courageous characters were to be secured and enlisted in the dire service. Who were secured is not known, but certain it is that the call at Valley Park brought a crowd. Well-known doorways were rapped at, whispered commands were given, horses were saddled and masks fastened on, after which, one by one, the persons repaired to the roadway north of the town and began the journey to Manchester. A wagon was brought along and a rope, indicating that this time they meant to complete the object of their pilgrimage.

The peace of Buckner in his cellar dungeon, though welcome, was not of long duration. At 3:30 the party arrived from Valley Park and joined its forces with the silent watchers about. No delay was had from that time on. A leader had been chosen and advanced rapidly at the head of the closely pressing throng to the door. Gun barrels were used as knockers, and no sooner had the door opened than, without parley of words, the mob pushed in. There was no resistance. The guards were merely shoved aside and told to hold their tongues. Lanterns were brought to the front, while the crowd surged downstairs into the cellar. In one corner, hugging the wall and the shadow, lay Buckner.

"Come out, you black devil!" commanded one, at the same time poking a light in his face and rudely jerking him forward. The negro's answer was a plea for mercy. "Don't kill me, boss."

"Here he is now; bind him, will you?" urged the leader. Someone had a rope, another held the light, and within a moment the criminal's limbs were bound solidly together. They turned then and bundled him up the stairs. They fairly dragged him on his back, so great was the rough enthusiasm to have him out.

It was dark outside. The moon had sunk, and only by the dull, yellow flames of lanterns bobbing numerously about could the negro's lineaments be distinguished. Those who saw him declare that the sight was such as to linger forever. His face was distorted with all the fear of a hunted beast. The eyes rolled wildly and great beads of sweat gathered on his forehead. Instead of pleading the miserable fellow began wailing more like an animal than a human being. It mattered little though, his agony. No one listened to him.

Like so much weight he was flung into a wagon, and it is believed his cries were silenced with a blow. The men then vaulted into saddles and began their march to Valley Park. On the way, it is asserted, the Meramec bridge idea was voiced and at once accepted. No delay was had in getting there. The rough wagon road was jumbled over at a great rate, while the groans of the prisoner were mocked with the jeering purpose of his angry captors.

By 4:30 o'clock a.m. the cavalcade reached Valley Park and hurried through it to the bridge beyond. There the wagon halted, and while men fastened the rope to the bridge others dragged the helpless form of the black from the sawdust of the wagon bed and adjusted the noose. Without words—perhaps with but little consciousness—the criminal was swung off, frantically struggling to the last at the end of the rope. When the sun broke upon the horizon Wednesday morning Buckner hung lifeless.

All the morning a crowd of idlers surveyed the remains, and only at noon did Coroner Hoffstetter arrive with the jury and ordered the corpse lowered. It was removed to one of the neighboring stores where the legal form was gone through with, and at 2 o'clock a verdict was returned.

It read: "We, the jury, find that John Buckner came to his death at the hands of a person or persons unknown to the jury."

Then the corpse was taken to the cabin of John Buckner, his uncle, on Hawkins road, from where to-day it will be removed for burial.

The home of Miss Harrison, as well as the cabin of Mrs. Mungo, were visited last evening by a Republic reporter. Both women were found in a somewhat improved condition, it being the opinion that within a few days they would be about.

[18 January 1894, pp. 1–2.]

75 - AT THE THEATRES.

[Excerpts]

Paul Dresser, the famous writer of songs, will appear in St. Louis this week in the somewhat familiar play, to state the case mildly, "The Danger Signal." Dresser is a clever, interesting comedian on the stage and a pleasant, companionable fellow off it. He is more prominently before the world as a writer of songs than as an actor, although he is capable on the boards at that.

Within the present decade Mr. Dresser has flooded the country with ballads that have become famous. Some of the familiarly known ones are "Only to See Mother's Face Once Again," "The Convict and the Bird," "The Pardon Came Too Late," and a good many others that are equally popular.

In his songs the author has touched upon a vast variety of homely subjects; scenes and incidents dear to every lover of home—dearer still to those who have experienced the realities of which he sings. All of his ballads have a vein of simple melody which causes one to wonder why the strains instead of being broken were not continued and set to poetic effusions of length, that they might be preserved among the popular classics of musical literature. The melancholy fact remains that they have not. "The Outcast's Grave," "Mother Told Me So" and "The Letter That Never Came" have come and gone. The simple strains that moved an entire nation to tuneful sympathy are little more now than a remembrance. It is only in instances that the motives of several of the songs live, these being preserved as a part of current newspaper literature. It is here, by the way, that one of Mr. Dresser's characteristics enters in.

Nearly every one of his songs have at one time or another invited inquiry as to the motive. "What made him write that?" has frequently been asked. "What moved him to compose such a weird piece as 'Only a Stranger'?" His own answer is "facts." The motive is gained from life. What he writes he has witnessed and felt, having laughed or cried over the reality. To this he attributes the success of his pieces.

In some cities of the Union he draws an audience of personal acquaintances. In the southern part of Indiana, where his priestly studies were conducted at St. Meinrad's, and later his minstrel escapades occurred, in company with Wizard Oil, an organ and a yellow dog, his audience becomes one of interested relatives and friends.

Realizing that he understands his own comic aptabilities best he has planned a farce comedy of his own, writing it to suit his peculiar qualities. In this, which he calls "The Green Goods Man," he will appear next year as a star. In St. Louis Mr. Dresser is well known, and draws by his personality a high class of patronage.

$$* \qquad * \qquad *$$

Here is a pathetic story of an incident in the career of Mr. Dresser and the bearing that it had on one of his best-known songs. Two years ago in Chicago he had a part in "A Tin Soldier." On the previous Saturday, while playing in a one-night stand, he received a telegram announcing the sudden death of his mother in a far-off city. On Sunday she was buried, and on Monday afternoon the bereaved actor was making the whole audience laugh at his sallies. Everybody said, "Isn't he funny?" and none recked of the pain tugging at his heart strings. Between the afternoon and evening performance he sat idly thrumming the keys of a piano, thinking of his mother, not noticing what he was playing. In a half conscious way he evolved a tune—a sad, mournful tune, in keeping with his thoughts. He framed words to the melody, and in an hour he had composed the words and music of his most beautiful and successful song. It is called "Only to See Mother's Face Again."

[28 January 1894, p. 11.]

7ʊ - NEWS OF THE THEATERS.

[Excerpt]

HAVLIN'S—"THE DANGER SIGNAL."

Railroad paraphernalia, tanks, wires, live engines and Paul Dresser appeared conglomerately yesterday afternoon and evening at Havlin's in De Mille's railroad play, "The Danger Signal." The interpretation yesterday was excellent, even better, perhaps, than that of last year, the cast having been strengthened in a number of instances. In it Paul Dresser shines as the star, taking the part of Putzels with hilarious effect. Mr. Dresser's work yesterday was vastly appreciated by the large audience in attendance. His funny songs and off-hand drollery were accepted with momentary bursts of applause. His listeners seemed to wait on him, and the recalls were numerous. By ordinary computation Mr. Dresser's part should be minor, but his comicalities have dislocated the solar arrangement of the piece and swung him into the star place. The remainder of the cast was excellent.

At Havlin's to-night Acting Manager Jones and Doorkeeper Knapp will have a benefit. The boy holding a lucky ticket will be presented with a suit of clothes.

[29 January 1894, p. 2.]

77 - AT THE THEATRES.

[Excerpt]

GOSSIP OF THE STAGE.

Paul Dresser was the plumber in Hoyt's "A Tin Soldier" for two years, and in those days he was somewhat addicted to drink, a habit, by the way, that he has thrown to the winds. On one occasion Mr. Hoyt visited the company and found Dresser and two or three other prominent members of the company in an exceedingly hilarious condition.

"See here, boys," he said, in his peculiar Vermont voice, "I believe that it would be a good idea for us to go out of the show business and start a distillery."

[4 February 1894, p. 14.]

78 - PLAIN MURDER.

Those who believe in fate—in the certainty of that indefinable power, surer though less swift than human hands, that pursues and drags down from its rest and security iniquity and wrong doing of every kind—will be interested in the story of Louisa Miner, who now languishes in prison for the murder of her husband.

Since 6 o'clock yesterday morning, when, pierced with a bullet wound, her husband fell dying, while she sank upon the floor near by with the smoking revolver still in her hand, Louisa Miner has sat behind the iron grating of a dismal cell and pondered over the history of her life.

Yesterday morning she quarreled with her husband, John Miner, in her rooms at 910 Morgan street. He threatened to beat her, as he had often done before, and in attempting to carry out his threat he was killed. The pistol had been lying on the sewing machine all night long, placed there by Mrs. Miner in the fear of midnight robbers, who are not infrequent visitors to residents of the locality in question. The sight of its loaded presence was instantly transformed into the purpose of protection, perhaps of vengeance, that so momentarily flashed into her mind with the passing of his threat.

The life, the environment, the intellectual attainment, were all conducive to the quarrel and the crime. There were the plain, miserably furnished rooms ever before the woman's eye, with the certainty of their continuance, if not their deterioration, in the future. There were the facts and the memory with both of several long, wretched years spent in company. Years filled to the brim with degradation, poverty and ill feeling until it looked as though anything would be welcome for a change. There lived the memory of quarrels, oaths, brutal blows and pain, until it burned in the brain, even though deadened to pain as hers was.

The story of what, to those whose footsteps have always wandered by the rose-bordered path of uprightness, purity and truth, would appear swinish passions and affections, were in their minds and upon their lips, when the quarrel whitened to frenzy's heat. Infidelity was charged. With the exchange of slurs passion grew until almost murder was in the heart of one, and preservation, even at the expense of a life, was the sole passion of the other.

It was then that John Miner leaped from his miserable bed with an imprecation and a threat, and it was then that Louisa Miner reached for the resting weapon and warned him of his danger.

A quarrel, a blow, a struggle for possession of the weapon, a shot and John Miner lay dying on the floor.

It was this that Louisa Miner brooded over last night alone in her prison cell.

The room occupied by the pair is more than dingy. The tragedy, following the accusation by the wife that Miner had been intimate with another woman, brought Tom McHugh, who was sleeping in an adjoining room, to the scene. He ran to the door just in time to see the fatal shot fired. He immediately procured the services of Dr. Gallagher, but before the latter's arrival John Miner was dead.

The police were called and Officers Dietring and Sloan responded.

Mrs. Miner was arrested and taken to the Third District Station to await the action of the Coroner.

The body of Miner was removed to the Morgue.

During this excitement and death, a 2 1/2 months' old baby lay soundly sleeping in a crib near by. It is an adopted child, only recently taken to the now desolate home.

The revolver was a Smith & Wesson. The day before Mrs. Miner borrowed it from Miss Emma Lewis, saying that she wanted it for protection against burglars.

The dead man was 26 years old and has been in the employ of the St. Louis Transfer Company.

Mrs. Miner is about 31 years old. In her face one can see traces of a purely physical comeliness that has long since disappeared. A flabby, unsightly strength of constitution has come, displacing beauty of form and feature. It is only in the momentary sparks of the recollection of something better that one sees the former woman as distinguished from the wreck of to-day. Yet this woman is the daughter-in-law by a former marriage of ex-Judge Kyte of Springfield, Mo., and once possessed moderate means, as well as a respectable position in society.

When seen last evening through the bars of her cell Louisa Miner told the story of the shooting without the faintest trace of emotion. She said she shot her husband in self-defense, feeling that if she did not kill him he would have killed her.

After the marriage four years ago they went to housekeeping at 912 St. Charles street, and from there moved to 18 South Eighth street. At this number, one year after their marriage, Mrs. Miner says her trouble began. A young woman of the name of Flora Ward came to live with them. Mrs. Miner suspected her husband of undue intimacy with the girl and accused him of it. This caused the first fight, and resulted in John Miner leaving his home with the young woman, returning only at long intervals when he wanted money. As often as he came so often did trouble ensue. The couple finally came into great disrepute, which compelled them to change their name to Meyers in order to raise money on their furniture.

Two years ago Mrs. Miner, advised by her attorneys, Messrs. Martin & Bass, brought suit for divorce on the grounds of desertion and failure to support. When the papers were served on Miner he threatened to burn them up and told his wife that she could never have any other name but his own as long as she lived. Mrs. Miner finally received the papers again, but withdrew the suit on Miner's faithful promise to do better. Miner failed in his promise and on January 1 last the wife filed suit, which is still pending in the Circuit Court. Since that time, according to the woman, Miner forced his presence and attentions upon her, refusing to live away from her, but still kept up his relations with Flora Ward.

A short time ago he went to work and Mrs. Miner went to Peoria and started a boarding-house there. What little money she had, however, she lost, and returned to this city three weeks ago, taking up her residence at 910 Morgan street, where she intended to keep boarders. During her absence from the city she learned that Miner continued his relations with Flora Ward. Last Sunday evening he came home a few moments after she had borrowed the revolver from Lillie Lewis and began to quarrel with her. This quarrel ended, as had many others, in a severe beating for her. The difference was finally smoothed over and the night passed in company.

In the morning, shortly before 6 o'clock, Mrs. Miner told her husband that he ought to go to Mrs. Long's, on Eighth and Walnut streets, and get his clothes out of Flora Ward's room. She says she spoke good humoredly, but that Miner received her advice with anger.

Jumping out of bed Miner exclaimed with an oath: "Keep your mouth shut or I'll teach you to stop talking about me," and ran towards her.

It was then that Mrs. Miner edged to the sewing machine, seized the revolver and waited. Miner, perceiving the weapon, caught hold of the muzzle saying, "You'll never remember drawing another revolver on me."

Then she answered: "Jack, let me go; I'll not hurt you," but his reply was a blow with his fist on her right cheek.

In endeavoring to dodge this latter Mrs. Miner tripped and fell, dragging her husband after her. The struggle for possession of the weapon continued even there. Mrs. Miner then resorted to the last means and pulled the trigger. At that moment the muzzle of the pistol lay close to Miner's heart. She then awaited the coming of the police and departed with them.

In a bureau drawer in the room was found the petition for a divorce, brought in April, 1892, by Martin & Bass. The petition alleges that the couple were married November 18, 1890, and lived together until January, 1892. Mrs. Miner alleges that two days after the marriage Miner struck her several times. Then followed the details of cruelty extending through a period of two years.

Mrs. Miner was born in Franklin County, Missouri. She was a widow when she married Miner, her first husband's name being Kyte. She has a 16-year-old son in the city, who visited her last night.

Miner was formerly a member of the Fire Department, and lost his position through drunkenness.

In Clinton, Mo., where Mrs. Miner was born her father was a well-to-do farmer. When he died his widow came to St. Louis and married again. Louisa remained in Clinton, working out at the age of 11 years. When her mother moved from St. Louis to Springfield, Mo., Louisa went there. She met the son of ex-Judge Kyte of that city and married him. Later he died and she returned with their only child, a boy, to this city. Here five years ago she met Miner, who was then a watchman in Kensington Garden. The two became intimate, and lived together one year before their marriage.

During this year Miner was twice suspected of murder, once for that of a man by the name of Brennan, who was shot near Union avenue and the Kensington Garden road. A second time he was eyed suspiciously when Annie Weiss, a young woman from Jefferson City, was dragged in the weeds near the Kensington Garden entrance and murdered. Both times Miner was strangely connected with the circumstances, but always came out of it uncensured.

Mrs. Miner denies knowledge of the crime, but will not say that Miner was not guilty.

Flora Ward, the cause of the tragedy, is an inmate of the immoral resort of Mattie Wilson at Tenth and Walnut streets. When told of the death of Miner she expressed no signs of emotion. The inquest will be held by Deputy Coroner Rohlfing Wednesday morning.

[7 November 1893, p. 1.]

79 - WHISKY DID IT.

The big door at the Third District Police Station opened and Hans Pozzinski was thrown into the cell. A pretty Polish woman came timidly into the station-house and said that she was his wife. She knew he was drunk and that his face was disfigured by ugly cuts and bruises received in a disgraceful brawl, yet she loved him. She was an humble Polish woman, but she had a loving heart. The big Sergeant led her to the cell, but she could not arouse him from his drunken stupor. She hastened away from the station-house with tears flowing down her cheeks and her bosom heaving with convulsive sobs.

Two hours later the pretty Polish woman again came timidly into the station-house and put a number of foreign coins on the counter. They were all she had and she had not exchanged them for American money because she wanted to save them. Doubtfully the big police Sergeant counted them and decided that they were equivalent to $25, enough for the bond of the drunken man slumbering in the cell. Hans was led out and the face of the woman was transfigured with the glory of a great joy. She held his arm as he reeled along the street and pleaded with him, but her only answer was a curse.

The garish light of a saloon sign attracted the man's attention and he refused to go farther. She pleaded with him; then she implored and prayed to him. The great hulking brute drew back his big fist and struck her in the face. She fell limp and bleeding on the slushy pavement. He started away, leaving her lying there, but a policeman caught him by the shoulder and took him back to jail. The woman struggled to her feet and without casting one glance at the disappearing forms of the patrolman and her husband, hurried to her home. An hour later she handed the big Sergeant a letter with queer Polish characters on the envelope. Silently she left the station, without asking to see the man she had called husband. Out into the noisy streets, without one friend on this side of the great sea, the woman with her cherished hopes blasted went without one word of farewell except the few crisp words contained in the letter.

Yesterday morning the husband was released from jail. He went to his home, but it was deserted. All the forenoon he searched for his wife.

Later in the day the patrol wagon was called to an immoral house on North Eighth street. It was a case of disturbance of the peace, and the Polander was the disturber. He was sober, but there was the despairing look of an animal at bay in his glistening eyes. The complaining witness, who followed him to the station and preferred a charge of assault and battery against him, was the same pretty Polish woman who had come to bail him out the night before.

Dressed in tinsel and tawdry finery, she laughed as the man appealed to her, and the harsh echoes of that laughter were a knell to future hope. The big door opened and Hans Pozzinski was thrown into the cell. The woman made a grimace at the Sergeant and then flitted out. She was Polish, but she was proud, and she no longer had a heart.

[19 February 1894, p. 8.]

Toledo Blade

With the night police force out on duty with the day service men, and crowds lining the various streets along which the Toledo Electric Street Railroad cars travel, the strike assumed pretentious proportions to-day.

The company's transfer office at Madison and Summit streets, was crowded by "scab" applicants for positions, though a great crowd of idle strikers lingered outside and talked over the situation, having at the same time an eye to business, should any develop. Along the line the Robison family and managers conducted the cars with a few wayworn emigrants who had sorrowfully drifted in, and miserably assisted the company in holding its own. There was a slump in the egg market, also, owing to certain precocious merchants who had reveled in an enormous sale of eggs at a moderate profit, and accordingly brought down the price. The stale variety were at a premium, however, and brought as high as 11 cents along Canton avenue near the barns. In fact, several huge chalk signs were exposed conveying the information that desirable quantities were on hand.

At other points, mud and chunks of dry clay were used. Several solid pieces were donated to C. R. Herbert, the able Robison manager. His tile has been caved in and decorated. The strikers were sarcastic. They developed a facetiousness that added great scornful weight to their every remark when addressed to the temporary employes, who are filling their rightful places.

"No negotiations have been opened between the Robisons and the men," said President Mahon, of the International union, to The Blade to-day. "The men are out, and are offering no interference in running cars. We are law-abiding citizens, and have acted as such ever since the trouble began.

"We certainly all recognize the authority of the law, and shall abide by it. The restraining order of Judge Lemmon we recognize and honor. Any violation of that order will certainly not be countenanced by the union. Still we have rights as peaceable citizens, and are not to be bluffed out of them.

"We are willing and ready at any time to submit the matter to a local arbitration committee or to the state board. We believe that our cause is just, and we will endeavor to secure our rights."

The statement in the injunction that President Mahon came here of his own free will to incite the men and stir up dissension is vigorously denied by the employes. By a unanimous vote of the union President Mahon was summoned to Toledo.

M. F. Bittner, of 1003 Summit street, to-day sent three boxes of cigars to the committee for distribution among the men who are out. George Tait, the well-known Adams street baker, sent four baskets of lunch to the "boys" watching at the Canton avenue barns this morning. The baskets were called for, and offers made to refill them.

Free cots have also been furnished the men stationed there. The women, too, are distributing popcorn for the men to eat while on their watch.

Several business men have made proffers of money to the men, but this has been refused at present for the reason that the men are yet in good shape. The boys of the Consolidated lines, however, will on Monday contribute $3 each to the support of the striking men.

Although trouble in connection with the strike is not considered imminent, Chief Raitz has prepared for any emergency that may spring up. The entire night squad is on duty, and ready for detail. Ten were dispatched in the patrol wagon from the central station at 10 o'clock this morning to drive away the mob at the corner of Summit and Adams streets. Eight men are constantly on duty at the Canton avenue barns, and the men on their beats are instructed to be vigilantly on the outlook for outbreaks from thoughtless spectators.

At 3:30 yesterday afternoon Detective Manley arrested Edward L. Scott for the alleged grounding of wires. Deputy Ernsthausen left his home at 6:30 to issue bail bond for $200, and Scott was released. This morning the case against him was continued to March 28th.

Of the four cars that sallied so bravely forth and trailed over the route at breakneck speed regardless of passengers or profits, No. 19 was one. C. R. Herbert, the husky and able manager, stood on the front platform of this with the door open behind him, guaranteeing a mode of defensive shelter, should such be necessary. On the rear platform, minding the trolley bar, stood Allen J. Andrews, one of the "scab" conductors, who held his place and his job per the order of his employer in front. The car began its pilgrimage around at 8:30 a.m., and was still going in the same direction at 12:30 noon, little the worse except for shied eggs and heaped up anathemas. During the entire forenoon few persons entered the car or sought to part with a nickel for the sake of such excitement as the thing offered. A few venturesome citizens, however, did try it along with several officials. There was a charming looking lady of about 28, who had all the perquisites about her of a dashing widow, who climbed on at Monroe street, and rode a few delicious blocks. Later there came a very fat gentleman who puffed and smiled, and said he would "be blessed if them strikers could scare him." However, his anxious attitude told a different story, for he watched the passing territory with almost an eagle eye, so fearful was he of a well directed brick or a handsome egg, generously donated from without. A Catholic priest happened along on Michigan avenue near Adams, and hailed the car with a

gold-headed cane. He, too, ensconced himself comfortably in the rear portion of the car, and looked boldly out. However, to a Blade representative
he admitted that a berth under the seat would be an excellent haven in case
of a brick storm or a soft egg simoon.

As the morning proceeded and nothing of import happened, Mr. Herbert
and Mr. Andrews grew less apprehensive, and looked about. They even
went so far as to jest with passengers and make inquiries as to the strength
of feeling among the watching strikers without. About 10 a.m. as Mr. Herbert was so discussing, passing along Canton avenue, an artful and saga-
cious citizen greeted him with the first missile of the day. It was an egg, and
lingered in large gobs about the brim of his black slouch hat.

The sight of the egg remaining seems to have been an inspiration to
others for the car had not gone two more blocks before another bystander
shied a chunk of mud and took Mr. Herbert square upon the crown of his
hat. It hurt, and he said so—to himself. He danced around a moment, expressed himself as much disgusted and then endeavored to make the best of
it. In this he had some assistance, for Mr. Andrews was hit not long after by
a similar chunk of mud, and left to feel his wound in much wrath. There
were discouraging incidents, however, without number. People were inclined to yell "scab" and "don't you want to earn a dollar" along Summit
street. Every conductor of a passing car and motorman took the opportunity
as a good one and called out some stinging greeting, that was bitter enough
to make most any one wince. They often went further, however, and cast
corn or beans at their object. In addition the crews of cars ahead, belonging
to other lines, often slowed up and fairly crawled along, making the Robison car to travel slow and thus receive the benefit of whatever jeering and
hooting might be going on around.

Number 19 fared well. Of course Conductor Andrews was nervous and
unsophisticated, and of course Motorman Herbert was consequently irritable
and out of humor. Once Conductor Andrews forgot to watch the trolley bar
and then twice and so on, into many times, when Motorman Herbert got warm
under the collar. It was on Monroe street the trolley bar jumped the wire,
while Conductor Andrews was inside collecting the darling widow's fare.

"I say," wailed out Motorman Herbert, "gol darn the gol-darned luck!
Are you going to watch that trolley bar?"

"Scab!" yelled some one from without, "want a dollar?"

In the excitement of the moment Conductor Andrews dropped his change
on the floor, and retired to readjust the trolley. The darling widow opened
her eyes wide in astonishment and said, "My, oh!"

Motorman Herbert simply looked back and said "Damn," turning in
time to speed the car on its way once more.

After 10 a.m. there was trouble with the register. Some one had trifled
with its affections, apparently. It didn't work. Up to that hour 23 fares had

been registered, but there it stopped short. Worst of all, Conductor Andrews did not notice it. Whenever any one climbed on, he collected and rang up. The bell rang as usual, but indicated nothing. Finally a passenger called:

"What's ailing your register?"

"Nothing."

"It doesn't ring up."

"Don't, hey? The bell rings."

"Well, try it for yourself. It hasn't moved the last five fares."

On the strength of this, Andrews tried it and found that a count was not made, which left his fares collected at his own able discretion in accounting for.

So it went all morning, one misery after another piling up until life on the line seemed nothing but discouragements multiplied. All idea of time was abandoned. Trips were made just as fast as possible, the idea being simply to keep the cars moving. Cars 29, 31 and 37 were also operated, but with no more grace or satisfaction than came to the lot of 19.

At a little after 10 o'clock Robison Car No. 11 crashed around the corner of Adams and Summit streets and into the side of a Consolidated car moving north. The corner was instantly swarming with people, shouting and jeering at the clumsy work of a "scab." The motorman, dripping with rotten eggs, the shells of which stuck to his clothes and hung from his hair, abandoned his dilapidated car and disappeared from sight. The crowd undertook to release the imprisoned Consolidated car. Twenty strong arms lifted No. 11 from the track and laid it in the Adams street gutter. By this time, three thousand people had gathered along Summit and Adams, and crowded around the corner. They ran over the abandoned car, sounded the gongs and hooted at its filthy condition.

Chief Raitz appeared and attempted to clear the streets. He managed to clear a few inches, when the patrol wagon, with seven stalwart bluecoats, dashed upon the scene. Then there was a scattering, and a lone woman with a baby carriage was the only person within an area of 200 feet.

David Robison, jr., pale and covered with dust, his hat pulled sidewise over his eyes and his pants rolled up, appeared. He turned to his forsaken property and looked it over. He mounted the motorman's platform, and the crowd yelled "Scab!" from a distance. Chief Raitz called the police and attempted to place the car on the tracks. David Robison tugged and pushed and lifted with them. He did not say anything. He looked tired, and his delicate hands did not seem formidable. The crowd laughed and Mr. Robison and the policemen still tugged and lifted. The car was finally rolled into position, and Mr. Robison held the trolley in while his superintendent manipulated the motor, running No. 11 back to the barns.

The car was returned to the barn at 10:30, and was received with cheers by the bystanders.

"You'd better get some oats and coax the car out again!" yelled one.

"How many fares did you ring up?" cried another.

"There was no swing crew to-day; so Uncle David put away his car for dinner," was the explanation given by one of the men for abandoning the car.

The bombardment of mud balls begun at 8:30 when "Jim" Robison mounted the platform of a belt line car and drove it out of the barn. "Dick" Momy, whom the boys say has been "fired" three times off the Robison car, held the trolley rope behind. A shower of mud balls and a little guying by the men standing near was all the objection raised to the movement of the cars. No violence was attempted by any of the street car employes and a large part of the jeering was done by sympathizers of the men. The first car was followed by a second with Superintendent Herbert as motorman. A stranger held the trolley rope behind. The third car carried Superintendent Adler as conductor and Will Robison at the motor, and the fourth a pick-up named Dick Snitchiker at the motor and David Robison, jr., while two strangers operated the trolley on the third and fourth cars.

As the last car disappeared in a cloud of dust the men settled back to watch the next movement of the Robisons. Nothing was done until an hour later. The cars sped on down town and a crowd collected at the corner of Woodruff and Canton avenue to see the first car as it completed its circuit around the belt.

On its arrival it was met with jeering and a volley of mud balls by the boys. There were very few street car men at this place at all. The crowd remained and as each car came around the belt the yelling continued.

At 9:30 o'clock James Robison took the sixth car out of the barn. On the platform with him were a stranger and Patrolman Olmns, while Transfer Agent Wagner operated the trolley rope. The men looked on the movement of this car and suffered in silence. Scarcely a word was spoken. The firm countenances of the men were fierce for a moment. There was a severe mental struggle and then the faces assumed the same determined air. The feelings must be restrained; there must be no violence; the law must be obeyed.

At 10 o'clock the patrol wagon from the Lagrange street sub-station dashed up to the barns.

A squad of police under Sergeant Ed. Kimes alighted to assist the force by Sergeant Robison, already on duty. As everything was quiet at the barns three of the men were detailed to watch the crowd at the corner of Canton and Woodruff avenues.

[24 March 1894, pp. 1, 6.]

81 - NO UNION MEN NEED APPLY TO THE ROBISON COMPANY FOR WORK.

There was much discretion used at the transfer office of the Robison company at Summit and Madison streets, where train crews were being hired. Union men were not wanted. They could not secure a place for love or money. Applicants were closely questioned as to their affiliations on this score, and their labor sentiments generally. Non-resident laborers were wanted, experience not being necessary.

T. H. Dreiser, of the Wood County Herald, applied at the office about noon and requested of the recruiting manager in charge nothing less than a job. That individual leaned back in his chair and surveyed the applicant leisurely, after which he condescended to remark:

"Where you from?"

"St. Louis."

"Want a place, eh?"

"Yes, sir."

"Ever run a car?"

"Endless numbers of them."

"Union man?"

"Yes."

"We don't want you."

"But I don't belong to the union here."

"That doesn't make any difference. You're a union man. Your ideas run that way. We don't want you. I couldn't hire you anyhow. The company wouldn't allow it."

"Would you take me if I wasn't a union man?"

"Oh, perhaps. If you looked all right we might. It's too late now, though. We don't want you."

[24 March 1894, p. 6.]

82 - WAR OF WORDS.

Shortly after noon Jim Robison, acting as a motor man, in charge of a Robison line belt car, received a very liberal "joshing" from a crowd of several hundred men who had congregated at the corner of Monroe and Summit streets. Robison, being unacquainted with the methods of the switches, turned the wrong point, and instead of going up Monroe street, as he had intended, turned toward the river. The speed of the car was considerable, and several persons narrowly escaped being run over. The jeers and hoots of the crowd badly rattled Jim, and when he succeeded in stopping the car, it had cleared the sidewalk. On advice of a police sergeant, Jim attempted to get his car out, and did so after considerable difficulty.

The presence of eight sturdy policemen and a sergeant kept the crowd from offering personal violence to the scab or his employer, but they took their fill of shouting and calling "scab!"

[24 March 1894, p. 6.]

83 - CARS WILL BE WITHDRAWN.

The large crowds that gathered on Summit street to-day caused merchants to grow apprehensive that an attempt might be made by some to loot the stores.

"When it grows dark," said Chief Raitz, "it would be no trick at all with three or four thousand people on the streets for sneaks to get into and rob the stores. I have talked to Mr. Robison, and he has agreed to take in his cars at dusk. We will have our hands full dispensing incipient crowds and quarrels to-night."

[24 March 1894, p. 6.]

84 - AS IF IN OLD TOLEDO.

As if it were an ancient castle in old Toledo, for years bound by a Moorish spell, but suddenly released and exhibiting to astonished eyes treasures before unseen, Trinity church is the marvel and delight of spectators to-day.

Behind its cold stone walls shine a hundred brilliant lights, and the faint sound of voices is heard.

As the doors open, an aeolian harp sounds its weird welcome, and the bold visitor is confronted by heaps of choicest bric-a-brac, rich tapestries that adorn the walls, an endless collection of the rarest pictures, and treasures of the city.

Every household has robbed its cabinets of the best and its cupboards of the oldest.

Trinity church must be redecorated, and it is for this purpose that one of the finest exhibitions of pictures, vases and curios of all kinds, a bazaar of all things desirable, and a daily lunch, for three days, has been prepared.

Never in the city's history has there been such a collection. Among a thousand interesting pieces is a bed warmer, 150 years old, loaned by Mrs. Henry Tracy; an Indian war bonnet, by Mrs. A. T. Babbitt; remarkable embroideries, by Mrs. Geo. Emerson; Mexican drawn work in table clothes and doylies, by Mrs. T. H. Bowman; 19 beermugs of every fantastic shape, by Miss Bockee; a Japanese bed spread, by Mrs. E. Pearsons, of New York.

In the center of the room stands a table with a tall glass case, in which stand three remarkable vases, and two jewel boxes, such as are not often seen. There is among them one crown Lambetta, by Mrs. Warren Colburn; and two Sevres, by N. H. Swayne and Mrs. F. Welsh. The Dresden jewel boxes were loaned by Mrs. W. A. Gosline and Mrs. Charles Reynolds.

There are studies, impressions, fancies, marines and pencilings of delightful merit. A few excellent tile colorings are not wanting, one porcelain dinner picture being of exceeding value and great age. Some of the water colorings are from the brush of renowned artists, and several of the smaller oils are real masters.

Last night the collection was shown off to great advantage because of the position and clearness of the lighting. The managers put themselves to the trouble of stringing the ceilings of the rooms with squares of incandescent bulbs close to the walls, so that the pictures might have the benefit of slanting rays. More helpful still were the tasteful ornamentation of corners, doorways and windows, all of which were hidden or beguiled by exhibits of pottery and china, or better still, were completely hidden by cloths of silk and hand workmanship imported, and of great value.

A rare collection of Japanese vases may be seen and a plenitude of oddities in relics and ancient workmanship seldom brought so conspicuously together. One collection of 19 ancient and very handsome porcelain beer mugs, the property of Mrs. Roff, are of surpassing interest of course. The most convenient feature of all, however, is a printed catalogue.

The gallery last evening was fairly crowded after 8, and was graced by the wealth and fashion of the city. More, the bazaars were handsomely patronized and many pieces of bric-a-brac disposed of, as well as numerous laces and gems of needle work.

To-day there will be the same order, only that there will be neither dinner nor supper—a lunch being served throughout the day instead. The bazaars will be duly replenished and the last three days of the affair made as interesting as was the first.

By the numbering of the paintings it has been possible to determine the generous donators who range in the order of numbers of paintings exhibited somewhat as follows:

[List of names omitted.]

It was decided this afternoon to continue the exhibition until Friday night and perhaps longer.

[28 March 1894, p. 7.]

Clebeland Leader

85 - M'DOUGALL'S DREAM.

A number of years ago a short, heavily-built man entered the Weddell House and inscribed his name on the register. He was assigned to a room, and there, in the presence of several vessel owners of the city, he exhibited the model of a boat which was new and wonderful in design. The new theories which were said to be embodied in the design had met with skepticism and unbelief elsewhere, and the ideas involved were slow in finding advocates. But the patience and perseverance of their inventor triumphed and "McDougall's Dream" became in time a solid and heavily remunerative fact. The company in which Captain Alexander McDougall is interested has built thirty-seven whalebacks since four years ago, representing an aggregate value of four millions of dollars, and the strange craft of which he is the father ply on both salt and fresh water. The captain was at the Weddell House yesterday for a short time, on his way to the West. In speaking of the outlook for the season, he said: "So far as I can see, the situation has not changed materially since some time ago. It appears to be a 'starvation season,' when the boats will run just to keep running and not because they are making any money. There is considerably less grain in the country than there was last year, and what little is moving the railroads are butting each other's heads open to get. I guess they are all carrying at a loss. When the fall comes the vessel men at least will be as poor as when the spring opened."

It was reported some time ago that Captain McDougall had gone to Washington to invite President Cleveland to take a trip up the lake as the guest of the vessel men. In answer to a query on this point he replied: "I do not know anything about that matter. Mr. Hill, of the Northern Steamship Line, I was told, went to see the President, but what came of it I do not know. I do know that he visited the President, for I saw him as he was coming out of the door, but I never heard what passed between the two."

[20 April 1894, p. 3.]

Pittsburg Dispatch

Thomas B. Reed, soon after the return from the drive in the afternoon, received a reporter for *The Dispatch* in his room in the Monongahela House. He was preparing for the affair of the evening, and had not many minutes to spare.

He is a very tall man when you are close to him. At a distance his width and "heft" are such that he does not look very tall; but when you stand beside him his more than six feet of height are all in evidence. He is a physical as well as a mental giant.

Mr. Reed did not desire to discuss the Coxey movement. He said: "I do not wish to talk about Coxey and I wish nobody else would. It is too serious a subject. As an evidence of the general unrest of the people, the Coxey movement is ominous. Unfortunately, the people in power in Washington do not seem to appreciate its significance."

He was asked what were the chances for the defeat of the Wilson bill in the Senate. He replied:

"There is still a reasonable hope of its defeat, and every energy on the part of the people of the United States ought to be directed to that end. It seems to be the general opinion of all persons well qualified to judge that, if the bill could be defeated, notwithstanding the great shock which the country has already received, business would resume at least its prosperous condition. I have little doubt of it myself, if the death of the bill could be speedy."

"What," he was asked, "will be the probable result of the Congressional elections this fall?"

"In my judgment," Mr. Reed replied, "the people are longing to get an opportunity to reiterate the judgment which was expressed in Pennsylvania, New York and New Jersey.

"All over the Northern States at every election where they have had an opportunity to express their wishes they have had but one voice."

"Do you anticipate general Republican victories this fall?"

"It looks as if we must carry the next time. Of course it is a terrible handicap to have a solid South against us."

Mr. Reed said he knew of no new proposition for free silver coinage likely to be brought forward at this session. There had been some talk in committee about a second bill for the coinage of the silver seigniorage, to meet the objections of the President in his veto message, but Mr. Reed had no idea whether this bill would be presented at the present session or not.

[28 April 1894, p. 9.]

87 - HOSPITAL VIOLET DAY.

Yesterday was violet day at one of the hospitals. It was not so named, but, for the first time, violets came in quantity. Along with the such flooding sunshine as there was, the morning awakened to the patients most pleasantly, and caused many a weary sufferer to turn, blink and bless the great Creator for another May Day of life, reviving beauty and delicious warmth.

Many asked to be lifted up and braced with pillows, more wanted to be near the open casements, through which could be viewed the emerald brilliancy of the verdure, and all the stronger begged leave, and in rolling chairs betook themselves to the large open, whitewashed court, where the shade was on one wall and the sunshine on the other.

True, no verdure waved about them there, or lifted its paean of incensed song to the skies, but the blue was overhead and violets were shown from jars in some of the ward windows above, so that all was not so bare.

When everything seemed dreamiest, the hour most blessed, when the attendants, pattering across the cool brick pavement, clattered their shoes in musical time, the left door opened, and poor Fintz was borne out on a bier.

Poor Fintz! He had suffered so long and moaned so weakly in pain that very morning before the sunlight came, and then, when it did, when its earliest rays slipped through the drawn blinds and checkered the floor with odd cross beams of gold, Fintz grew worse.

When the light shone bright he coughed blood, and when all the patients had been arranged by windows, or wheeled to the court below, long-suffering Fintz died.

He bent from the pillow to the porcelain basin, and parted his pale lips for one more gush of heart blood when he fell back weariedly, opened his wide, hollow eyes to the sunbeams and died. Even while they were yet strained the glassiness crept into them, and the watching attendant closed the lids. Then the loosened jaw was bound shut, the arms folded and the body wrapt in rough linen. As the attendants pushed the bier along the ward aisle all the brightened sufferers turned from the violets and casements to sigh "poor Fintz!" They still were happy, for they were convalescent.

But out in the open court, when the door opened, all saw the white linen bound burden and Magnoni ceased his jesting. Little Magnoni had been amusing himself with many a droll impersonation on this his first day of outdoor convalescence. Little Magnoni! Everybody liked him and called him the jolly Italian. Sick and pale as he was, he made them laugh, for when they asked him, "How do you like America, Magnoni?" he invariably answered:

"Ah, ga! 'Leven-a months here, 'leven-a months sick," which sounded very funny, even to Magnoni. When he landed in New York eleven months ago, he was taken sick, and since then had been all but dying. But when Fintz came out Magnoni was not saying that. Rather he was imitating the telephone in the next ward.

That telephone had been a sad source of woe to him during his fever. He had heard it ring and whirr and talk, and although he could not understand English had learned to repeat the sounds until any American patient could recognize them. What Magnoni heard, what he was telling was

"B-r-r-r, bing, bing! Hello! Yaas! —— —— Hospital! Yaas! Goodby!" which was all he had ever learned. But it was what had happened every day repeatedly, and not one of his bandaged, pale visaged hearers but did not smile as Magnoni's face executed the various muscular movements supposed to represent the meaning of the words repeated. When Fintz's corpse was pushed past, he ceased. The sunshine was fair, the air delicious, the humor so contagious that poor Fintz's body seemed out of place, an intrusion, and Magnoni felt so, but all he said was, "Goodby, poor fell—, I may come next," which was as much of a prayer as ever had been offered for any departed soul in all the world.

Then the bier rolled on, the deadhouse door opened, and upon one of the cold, drear shelves poor Fintz was stowed, tagged and written upon like any other baggage, to await a claimant; or a potters' grave.

Yet, while the door was still open, the patients in the court had resumed their jovial conversation, and everyone was as happy as though Fintz had never been.

Through all the hallways and open doors inside there wafted the odor of violets. Some kind-hearted soul, or club of souls, had donated a market basketful. They came in a dark rich purple mass, exhaling invisible clouds of perfume that purified the atmosphere. Before their joyous breath the acrid fumes of medicine fled, and left the dry aired chambers fresh and sweet. When the roses were brought and separate bunches sent to every bedside, when many pale hands had feverishly clutched at the delicious harbinger of health and strength, and all the window casements shown ornate with these floral tributes, the clear bright day had really first been inaugurated. It was only then that the manifold charms of life broke in upon the sick-pained senses of the sufferers, and, as through the Ayesha Pool of these flower voices, all the glory of health and rampant vivacity returned in memory until the morning was one of radiant beauty, indeed, and to the sick ones the fairest one of many. Magnoni thought so, and so did Tim O'Hara, whose No. 16 feet had been working nervously before him on the footrest of his chair. Tim said the "Top o' the mornin'" to everyone, even the physician-in-chief, and for once condescended to glare at his ancient German enemy Von Spiegel, whose daughter auspiciously brought him a German pipe to cheer along in his recovery from a broken leg, and remark, "I think violets be fine."

"Yah," answered Von Spiegel, and forthwith blew all his other opinions aloft in a cloud of smoke, which enveloped him completely.

But Violet Day was the day of all, and although poor Fintz had passed away, the others still rejoiced. In the court yard they laughed and jested, rolled their chairs about with the changing shade and listened to Magnoni. That estimable Italian humorist wound up his outdoor recreation with a deep souled soliloquy, worth all the chattered sympathy of the day.

As he rolled his chair in through the ward door toward evening, he glanced back toward the deadhouse door to sigh "poor Fintz."

[12 May 1894, p. 2.]

88 - AFTER THE RAIN STORM.

Pittsburg never experienced a more delicious sensation or breathed a cooler breath than it did yesterday for one short hour, between 4 and 5 p.m., after the rain. It had been so hot—so awful hot! The air seemed heavy and thick. Enough of it could not be gulped in at once to give the straining lungs relief.

'Squire McKelvey in Allegheny, observed it, and said it was "turrible." 'Squire Donovan, of Pittsburg, said the Weather Bureau must be "verrikt," which 'Squire Brinker translated for the benefit of other suffering mortals as meaning foolish. All men stigmatized it as dreadful, and after the chill brightness of Thursday night, when the stars towards morning gleamed frosty and the night air penetrated coldly to the skin, it did not seem paradoxical.

But after the rain came and departed nature was mollified. The colors of things became so much brighter; the air so much purer; the sky, rifted with gorgeous shreds of blue, so much more colorful and heavenly than before. All the bright paints upon buildings contrasted more strongly; the granite paving stones were drenched so clean and white; the green verdure of the steep hillsides in every direction brightened so much fairer to the eye than ever before.

Then there were the many spires towering refreshed in the sunlight, and the winding stretches of park land, bejeweled with pagodas and flower houses, lying broad in the bars of sunlight, that playfully chased each other to and fro between the jagged apertures of the dark storm mantle.

Fairest and freshest of all were the rivers, winding brightly along, framed in by the green clad hills and shore festooning, and spanned by the lightsome archwork of the many bridges, so oddly placed at distances along their length. They flowed so peacefully, so full revived by the gamboling streams from the hills and the highways. Here they swept along in curves of sheenful silver beneath the slanting rays of the sunlight; there in somber hues of purple turned brown, where the solid dark mass of clouds lowered and shut out the light. Everywhere, along their shores, clung white steamers and rested dark barges in mirthful contrast, with here and there a moving one splashing the cool waters as it slowly plowed its way against the tide.

No housetop but what was not darker and more cleanly, no grass plat but what was made a brighter green, no tower or spire but seemed more clearly outlined to the eye, after the northwest phalanx of blackened rain drops bore down upon the city with the sudden breeze, and broke and pattered over all.

But the glory of it was not to be had in Smithfield or Federal streets. Fifth avenue could not show it, nor Ohio street. One had to climb out of these hurrying thoroughfares and ascend to the neighboring hill crests before the full reality of it broke like a gorgeous dream, and pictured every delight to the eye with vividness multiplied.

There all the beauty of the valley about the forks cleared itself to the eye in subdued colors, and every local point of interest declared itself with a voice of outline and brightness, whose quality was little if not resonant and certain.

From Mt. Washington St. Paul's spires seemed still to glisten with the trickling drops that had so lately fallen. The proud head of the Court House tower still dripped the water from its pea-green slate. Black old Trinity, fringed about with its elms and grass plot, seemed more peaceful than ever, and its few moss-grown gravestones satisfied to totter upright another hundred years.

The dear Old City Hall, with its scrubby little window trees in front, its clock tower and endless quota of sparrows, was not to be scoffed at. If it really is not handsome, its contour blended that way, and to the naked eye it added a charm to its corner, as much as any other structure elsewhere.

In Allegheny, the monument and Carnegie Library seemed actually framed in the neighboring green of the park, and the steep decline of Seminary Hill to the rear. That steep's clustering foliage looked like weighty clouds of mist turned green, and now of a sudden floated down to envelop the hilltop and rain emeralds upon its sides. There was Schenley Park to see, resembling a huge green rug cast out to dust, with a few specks of flower houses and small pavilions clinging to it that the housemaid's broom had not swept off, and Allegheny Park, grasping, octopus-like, whole blocks and frail white streets in its winding grip, as though it chose to dress itself and wear them all for ornaments on its rather public, and certainly thoroughly traversed, bosom.

Yet they were all damp and cool, with the rain drops peeping from every leaf and sunlight stealing across them, their beauty adding not a little to the already luxuriant wealth of color.

During that hour the white-drenched streets revealed the spider's web of metropolitan life. Along them crept and fluttered the umbrelled mass of humans, all caught in the meshes of the great human fly-trap, and compelled to stay there willy-nilly or struggle loose with the loss of life or strength and hurry away into some other web, some other fly-trap, there to work and struggle just as before.

An opera glass easily revealed the pedestrians ascending Wylie avenue toward the reservoir or those who followed the Perrysville road toward the summit. Far up and down the Monongahela and Ohio the smallest of little craft were apparent wherever they decked the bright waters in motion or rocked lazily fast to their moorings.

To be sure it all lasted only an hour. In scarcely any time at all to speak of, the clouds had gathered again "for keeps," and people "histed" their rain-shields. Then the mist and the showers came between all eyes and all prospects, leaving the vantage grounds the dreariest places of all. Pittsburg was enveloped and remained so until the twilight swapped places with the mist.

When Mr. Starly, Mrs. Loboard's siderical constituent, jocosely inquired for the "baken swine" at supper last evening, he took occasion to add that he thought it was lovely "weathaw." He did this in a spirit of positive raillery, for he counted the changing clouds, the occasional showers and rapidly cooling atmosphere as disagreeable. Mrs. Loboard said she thought so, too, but then her acquiescence was mercenary. Neither of them had been to Mt. Washington's crest, nor to any other hilltop that day. On the contrary when rain began to pour, Mrs. Loboard had shut the windows and exclaimed "Gracious!" so she could not tell whether the day was lovely or not. However, the hour cannot be questioned.

In addition, there are other considerations besides "lovely." Somewhere there may have been fevered brows suffering in close chambers, where the humid morning atmosphere brought further weakness. Somewhere, in the

East End or the West, or any end at all, there may have been pallid countenances and weak, violet lips, dry with the lowering heat abounding, to whom the rain came refreshingly, and the purified coolness of the air brought rest and even slumber. On many a quiet hillside near at hand white gravestones clustered and grassy mounds swelled solemnly side by side. Here and there lay a new one, still mournful and mourned, with the sense of severed years.

To these, whose only ornament was the emerald sod, the cooling drops brought life and brightness, making the grass to grow with added tenderness and to shine with even more of that soothing significance that typifies eternal peace—the life after sorrow, after pain and sickness and death.

[19 May 1894, p. 2.]

89 - REAPERS IN THE FIELDS.

The whirr of the reaper is heard in the land—land of receding hills hereabouts and farther West, land of the level and abundant prairie. Those who have not heard should ride far out to the end of any street car line and walk into the woodland a small way. Then, when they are least expecting, will come the drone of distant reaper machinery, blended softly, however, and scarcely distinguishable from a hundred other woodland echoes.

This is the season of nature's most generous offerings to man. It is now that the whole temperate zone witnesses the fruit of the chill winter, the rainy spring and the dry summer. Pittsburg, as a humble portion, may likewise distend her optics and behold. For yesterday over our neighboring hillsides the lumbering machinery of the farm was toiling. Great, strong-boned men, with dark tanned faces and wide straw hats, were following after gathering in their arms the swaths of fallen grain, as yellow as Golconda's gold, and binding it into sheaves. Some carried them forward and made square heaps of their luxuriant burden, while others labored at a distance making of the humble piles symmetrical, conical roofed stacks, that dotted the shorn field into a miniature city of golden savage tepees.

There was no gainsaying the beauty of the scene. Its inspiration was infectious, at 200 yards, in the shade. Bucolic idyls of the most rhythmic cadence involuntarily crept upon the mind, and those mythic divinities of the forest and stream, of the woodland shadows and sunlit-glades, were mysteriously real for once, however fleeting and evanescent they might prove, with the interruption of so modern and so mundane an exclamation as "gee-haw!" Even these oft repeated calls of earnest non-poetic guidance could scarce rob the scene of its dreamy influence.

To be frank and explicit, yesterday was so fine a day, as of itself to create thoughts of a rather dreamy and ethereal character. Nature's smiles were far too abundant and crept over too many exquisite landscape views. The hilltops were too fair in their paler and brighter shades of green not to excite the finer sensibilities. Then where wide-open spaces broke to the eye between them, and far in the distance, over the modest swelling of a lesser mound, one saw fields of yellow, framed in forests and hedges of emerald, there was no controverting the impression. It was one of nature's own resonant requests to lay aside care and linger awhile in rest.

From every hand out of those cultured fields came the murmur of the reaper. One might have gone miles and miles, clambered upon flying trains and sped through endless acres and tiny villages, only to hear at unerring intervals the dull bumble drone creeping through trees and the solitude from where farmers drove and reaped and sheafed and stacked the staff of the world, its wheat.

There were many at work wherever the warm sunshine lighted upon this great grain belt that begins here and extends with the Ohio and Missouri far into the very snow-capped teeth of the Rockies. It was a day out of the nation's saving period, though no Saturnian feast marks the garnerers' progress nor rejoices in the approaching fall, with its overladen bins and bursting granaries. Yet the world and the crop editors depend upon them.

It took ancient Canaan and old undeclined Rome to celebrate such proceedings as those of yesterday. Romulus and Remus were more endued with the sense of what really brings greatest peace and comfort to the world's children. They marked the period by inspiriting revelry, and did other things that make interesting reading. Accordingly there remains an opening for a true wail upon the decline of ancient systems in general.

Some of the most pleasant harvesting views were to be had far down the Ohio, past Davis Island, on either side. The pastoral views were splendid, and several attracted the skill of a kodak fiend, who perched himself on various promontories and pressed the button with much ardor. Those time-tried spectacles of Maud Mullers and Boaz and Ruth weren't present to greet him. No one came by swaying a sickle or the later scythe, but in the distance, just at noon, a "vision" of a farmer's daughter did come out upon the small lawn surrounding the house and rang the farm bell that surmounted the crest of a post after the fashion of a poised crow ready to take flight.

Though the bell did not fly away, the sounds did. With their first mellow passing all movements of toil were suspended. Sheaves were lazily carried to the nearest mound and dropped. The heavy reaper ceased to whirr and hum. The tired horses pointed their ears as "Whoa!" greeted them and heavy buckles were loosened. Farm hands cut crosswise at an earnest gait over the field and joined together again about an entirely problematical washpan which could not be distinguished for the crowd. Within five minutes after the fair daughter had pulled the rope, not a laboring soul was visible. The little dining room in the small white cottage among the trees contained them all.

Then for once the noonday stillness was verified. The very birds seemed to have gone out to lunch. Those soothing murmurs that seem to rise at other periods of the day from the wind breaking through the heavy foliage of the trees, fled as though by command. Down by the river's brink Irving's "straw" floated lazily round and round in a small, still pool. The distant whistle of a passing train sounded strangely loud, and a lone wagon rumbling up the dusty hillside proved an almost intolerable intrusion. Nature was taking her hour off and lying down somewhere, undoubtedly resting in the shade.

During the long afternoon the reaping progressed rapidly enough. The square patch of remaining grain, whose long, slender stems were constantly rolling billow-like with every breath of air, grew less and less. Noisily the red iron reaper rolled about and about, cutting away yard after yard, until only a small space was left. The driver found himself constantly calling and tugging at his lines to get the weary team about the sharp and frequent turns. Thoughts of the supper table and the calling bell were more and more evinced by the relaxing energies of the workers.

From the home chimney curled aloft the smoke of an evening fire, and across the sloping land stretched the long shadows of the tree-crowned hills, behind which the warm sun had hid. Those more plaintive carolings of birds enriched the shadows and made the distant tinkerings of the cattle bells seem doubly musical.

When the shadows lengthened far and wide into one, and all the varied sounds mingled in that rich evening volubility that seems born of the knowledge of approaching rest, when the air grew balmy and cool and nature's soothing dews spread about the square patch of golden stalks was no more. Across the field from the clustered village of sheaves loitered the harvesters and their horses. A playful dog danced on before and out of the low white doorway came a maiden. Then the bell rang—making the story of labor and rest, struggle and comfort, patriotism and home, complete and beautiful.

[6 July 1894, p. 2.]

90 - ODD SCRAPS OF MELODY.

Music, as a numerous quality, is very prevalent in Pittsburg just at present. Not the music hall music, nor the classic recital music, but a kind of dodging, fearful, fleeting, yellow dog kind of music that no one really knows, completely, but everyone knows in fact. That's "scrap" music.

Our community allows no street musicians of the mendicant order. An ordinance says nay, and when one appears he is forthwith pursued into the indefinite hence. Accordingly, there are no Italians with hand-organs and monkeys. No gutter-band, its individuality crowned with the giant form of a Dutch cap, can approach the unsuspecting store-front from any direction and drive away trade. The cripple with his little organ, crouching at the edge of a street corner pavement, is conspicuous alone for his absence.

There is, however, the man who sells penny whistles and the other man who vends that anomaly of musical, or rather unmusical inventions, the wooden hand-calliope. Everyone has seen him, with his market basket and plain cedar wares. There are about ten little reeds fastened together, with which, running to and fro across his lip, French harp fashion, he manages to make everybody within a mile know of his approach. In this connection come the French harps themselves, and the jews-harp, and the able cornet, and others.

But lip music is what is more apparent. Those evanescent bits of tune that everybody picks up from just hearing them. They are countless in variety, but soon become contagious. When the popular song is "on" the era of "scrap" music has been temporarily submerged.

In following the bent of life in this city just at present, each one is regaled by a few things. If it is not an occasional shower, or an invitation to a companionable lunch in some quiet and cool restaurant, it's the satisfaction of being where one may stand on one leg in the shade of the all-too-warm buildings, and escape for a few moments the crowd and dust and sun.

The best element, then largely agreeable and all pervading, is scraps of music. In this is not included whole songs or classic strains of any kind except as they come floating to the ear, mere wisps that bespeak the original whole, now passed and entirely problematical. For instance, some rainy morning, even in this month of July, the air may be chilly, and some one may be caught in exceedingly inappropriate garments for such weather. While doing a disagreeable errand into a more disagreeable neighborhood, there will be a door standing open, or window, and out will float a scrap of music. It may be only a droning, disconnected tune, as bad in its relation to those exquisite strains that soothe as doggerel is to the polished lines of

Paradise Lost, and yet it's something. The man in the rain, with his coat collar up and his spirits away down, will feel the influence, and weave out of the wisp a heart song of his own. It may bring merry or wistful feelings, summoning with a flash a train of thoughts and pictures, in which are included everything that is comforting and luxurious, and from which is excluded everything that pertains to a chill, miserable, disagreeable man in the rain.

There are other scraps. They come to the penniless wanderer whose clothes look shabby and feel worse; who has been wandering from show window to show window looking at fine, sharp-pointed, yellow shoes and velvet lined cases of glittering diamonds, which he can but look at, and all at once from the most unfortunate of all places in the world for him, a lunchroom, comes another scrap in passing.

Strange, it may be the parting scene in that most melancholy of operas, "Cavalleria Rusticana," to which dreamy strains hundreds are eating pie and drinking hot coffee. Or it may be so lively an air as Robyn's Mexican Schottische, and the penniless one, whose sensibilities have been lacerated all day by the sharp points of the unattainable shoes, is forthwith reminded of some other more agreeable situation, wherein the scrap was heard. His heart was at ease then, his body at rest, and the returning thought that now he is a wanderer makes the situation rather bitter.

Everybody is not penniless, however. To them the music scraps are somewhat like blossoming flowers in blue China vases set upon neighboring window ledges—pretty. They hear small strains creeping up and out, and from above and down, and from before and again over their shoulders. When it is a human voice it means that someone is light-hearted, if only for a moment. On the street everyone is in a measure light-hearted, because they are forgetful.

People sing and hum and whistle. Men lean against telegraph poles in gay suits and whistle the grievances of the "Fatal Wedding," with a light abandon that is enigmatical. The "Dead March in Saul" is hummed for fun. "After the Ball," at one time before its age made it offensive and disreputable, had its broken-hearted significance utilized to lighten the cares and fears of perhaps nearly all the 65,000,000 people who try to live in the United States. And this is just one in a million, for the airs of the land are as the sands of the sea. One wonders what becomes of them all.

At night time tunes float out upon Pittsburg's evening air like bats. With the cessation of toil begins the murmurings of song. On their way home men with tin buckets go hobbling along all wrapt in their own thoughts singing softly to themselves. On the street cars, where the crowd causes modesty to hush itself, people sing under their breath. Others take advantage of the rattle of the wheels to hum their favorite air and often being carried away by their belief in the sweetness of the melody sing carelessly and so louder than the noise which brings facetious glances from their neighbors and flushes of blood to their own cheeks. It's apparently bad form to sing aloud anywhere in public and yet no item in Mrs. Grundy's code is more frequently disregarded.

One gets a scrap of song mingled with the crash of machinery in the great steel mills. On the Southside last evening near the Point bridge the wide doors of a steel belt mill flamed with the light of a dozen blazing rollers. Great lengths of thin rolled steel wound in and out like fiery serpents.

Flinging the blazing ropes from side to side, with a pair of huge tongs, the sweating "taker" loudly voiced "Sweet By and By," being no doubt the most congenial companion his weary thoughts could summon.

Everywhere the idle pedestrian is recalled to himself. In one place an aged Chinese, at the bottom of a pair of dilapidated stairs, amuses himself with the most doleful of Oriental concoctions, a one-stringed instrument. This libel on the adored violin squeaks consecutive discords and has caused the immigration of all the respectable rats in the neighborhood. In another place the tuneless piano yields up air-bruising versions of "Sweet Marie," which, were it not for such false representations, would bid fair to live as one out of a thousand. Out in the East End real melody in a hundred forms steals through the soft curtains and out over the shadowy lawn, causing one to dream of all the places where one wishes but cannot be. And that bringing the realization that we cannot have any of the things we want makes the music wistful and wholly sad.

The finest bits of "scrap" music are the wedding bits, where the arched doorways of the churches stand wide and the flood of wedding march symphony rolls forth for a short space; where the carriages are numerous and the garments soft and white and fleecy and gay. The saddest bits of music are the requiem strains, where the solemn organ rolls its lonely song of the soul high into wide, dark arches, and across sad, draped forms of kneeling mourners—when the coffin stretches solemnly before the altar on the bier.

[7 July 1894, p. 3.]

91 - FENCED OFF THE EARTH.

There is a place out on Second avenue near the Eliza Furnace, where a community of 40 families live between an inaccessible hill and an insurmountable fence, and are consequently unhappy. As a fact they cannot

LEFT: "The Milkman in His Whistling Act" (*Pittsburg Dispatch*, 19 July 1894, p. 3); RIGHT: "This Is the Man Who Responded" (*Pittsburg Dispatch*, 19 July 1894, p. 3).

climb the hill, nor can they walk round it, and neither can they climb the fence nor walk round it. Both hill and fence begin at a stream and end at a stone wall.

And these 40 families, living in their metropolitan solitude, are face to face with a world of inconvenience, for no one can get to them, nor can they get to anyone, and day by day they are living along awaiting the coming of that magic dissolvent, the modern injunction. All this sounds much like a Black forest fairy tale, but hear the story.

Along Second avenue travels in this Sahara weather the iceman every day, and when he comes to the 40 houses where the 40 families live, between the high hill and the high fence, he whistles, and one from each house of each of the 40 families comes out and gets the minute chunk of coolness that is now sold for many shekels, and lifts it over the high fence with a rope-lowered basket and goes in again.

And when the groceryman comes along with his groceries he whistles, also, and again the residents come out. And the milkman comes and they come out, and the mailman whistles likewise and they come out, and, in fact, they have all become so used to coming out when anyone whistles they are out most of the time. All of which is very distressing in the present deluge of sunshine.

But a sudden feature is that of the engine whistle which is mistaken frequently for the iceman, and the small boy whistle which is mistaken for the milkman, the passerby whistle which is often mistaken for the iceman and milkman put together, and many other forms of the necessary whistles that come to these people of necessity in their fence-bound life. Such is honestly the condition of the 40 families on Second avenue opposite the Eliza Furnace between the high hill and the high fence to-day.

Those who read the papers about ten days ago will remember that 20 families on Second avenue, owning 20 lots, signed a petition for an injunction by which the Baltimore and Ohio Railroad might be restrained from building a fence in front of their property and thus cutting them off from access to the world. Anyone who strolls out Second avenue will see that h~!? of what should be the street is occupied by the double track of the Baltimore and Ohio, and in places this track is built higher than the street and rests on a wall-bound bed. Through this wall at regular intervals have been cut little niches for small stairways by which people living on the hillside above the tracks may cross over and climb down into the street, where the car line runs.

But the niche staircase where the wall is, and the wooden steps where the wall is not, are now useless. People living above the track and the somewhat steep hillside are supposed not to want to come down to the street car line, or if they do they are supposed to fly over the tracks, for a high fence, signifying as much, has been constructed on the right side of the track nearest the hill, which has neither gate nor stile, and which will shortly have a barbed wire crown and a surplus of notices stating that anyone climbing over the fence or defacing it will be prosecuted to the full extent of the law and fined $8.

And furthermore the people on the hillside are not supposed to eat because the groceryman has no right to cross over the tracks and hand anything over the fence, for that would be defacing the same. Nor has the milkman nor the mailman, nor any other man whatsoever, because any man is just the same as one man, and not unlike the mailman in anything but occupation. As for getting in food, any other way than over the fence is sheer fallacy and utterly impossible. The hill above is too high and too steep and barred with fences and high rocks so much that the idea of letting down any problematical baskets of provisions to the wall-bound inhabitants is not thinkable. Those 40 families are supposed to adopt the Mexican frog idea of subsistence, air being the only thing not cut off.

It follows that the condition of the 40 families is growing extremely interesting. The injunction asked for has not injuncted any as yet. The fence is daily growing more complete in its frowning despotism, and the rough face of the hillside seems to grin with hard satisfaction as it looks upon the predicament of the children of its bosom.

People passing along the avenue stop and wonder. They look at the fence and then at the dry brown houses, stuck tight to some narrow ledge above, with a flight of stairs that leads down toward the fence, and they immediately presuppose a tunnel somewhere, leading under the tracks, and, not finding it, they again look at the houses, while visions of balloons and air-machines, of toboggan slides and parachute drops flit to and fro across their comprehension.

It is evident to them that some unforeseen process must be in vogue by which the hillside community confers with the outside world. They can see women sewing in doorways above and children playing in groups and men smoking occasionally on the front step of an evening and they prescribe some mental scheme for the comfort and accessibility of it all, but they are mistaken. Those citizens are actually and wholly cut off.

They can't get in or out, except they climb the fence and break the law or begin a slow process of tunneling. For the latter the most are not wealthy enough.

Into this fastness a *Dispatch* representative ventured yesterday, facing the extreme peril of arrest, or doubtful honor of being taken for a railroad official. He climbed the fence and scaled the hillside and inquired "why?" promiscuously. No one seemed to know. The railroad company had suddenly secured an idea somewhere, and the idea secured the fence. They began on an afternoon two weeks since, and nailed up board after board, shutting off the hill's visions and turning the minds of the residents to the more etherial forms of locomotion.

No notice was served, no signs put up. Nothing was said about the lives of the little children who belong to the families, and who sometimes cross the double tracks where the engines are. The only information vouchsafed the interested watchers of the curious work was that the company knew what it was about. Then came the application for the injunction.

And now the encompassed residents are staving mad. They frown down upon the obstruction even more than the hillside frowns on them. They do not want any high board fence nor any barbed wire obstruction on the top, as it were, to boot. They want ingress and egress and such other forms of getting around so badly that they are becoming aggressive. They want the privilege of the milkman restored, and are prone to inquire "why are we shut off from the bland smile of the mailman? Why?" and so it looks as if a real old delightful Second avenue rumpus is now in progress of construction.

The Baltimore and Ohio says nothing but saws more wood for its fence. It proceeds calmly in its work of concocting hair-raising admonitions and diabolical threats calculated to stop anything but a railroad train from passing. Signs inflicting penalties all the way from $8 to $1,000 are being hung up and the attention of the residents is appealed to by huge hands, whose forefingers point blandly upward to the sky. Yet the residents remain contentious and declare that they will not be further fettered. So the war is now on.

Some of the residents told the most distressing tales. Jesse Erdley, of 1155 Second, complained bitterly and recounted points wherein the fence stands a lawless imposition. The street, he said, had been paid for by the taxpayers whose property fronts it. It is now kept in repair by them. The government has the privilege of entrance to each house that fronts it and the right of way. Yet all of these things are overridden and the rights of the owners trampled upon because the company wants its tracks left inviolate. So the residents propose to do something desperate.

A look at the situation really does reveal the astonishing. The most ingenious caprice could not have contrived a more thorough way of annoying the wicked than does the great board fence annoy the good people of Eliza Furnace district.

[19 July 1894, p. 3.]

92 - WITH THE NAMELESS DEAD.

Among the countless hollows of the hills which go to make up portions of the beautiful scenery about Pittsburg are many that are ornamented with the tombstones of the dead. They rise and fall, do these cultured mounds, made inviting by sod and flowers and trees, and restful by birds and sunlight, benches and white marble pillars; and friends of the friends who sleep in them forever have named them cemeteries.

They have called them Allegheny and Uniondale, Highwood and St. Mary's, and one and all are exceedingly fair to see. But there is one where the friendless sleep and the erring lie buried, and this one has no beautiful name and no loving ones to watch over it. Their abiding hollow is uncultured and their graves are forgotten. Most of them are irreclaimably lost. That is the potter's field and one may see it at all times in Highwood, out toward Bellevue.

On one of the hillsides there stands a round wooden cross amid a vacant stretch of broken rocks. The wind and the rain of summer, spring and fall beat upon it. The snows of winter fall about it and make all nature white and frozen pure, but no vestige of the fleecy mantle clings to it, because of the wind and the storm. Day after day it stands bleak, black and desolate, a fitting emblem of the barren lives about, wasted as sparks are wasted on the night wind. Such is the county burying ground.

No keeper watches over it especially. No visitors walk among its barren paths. Those who lie there came tagged and written upon from the river's slime and the garret's discouraging want, victims of the same unerring forces that make beautiful the neighboring mausoleums, and place flowers where weeds grew, and hedges where brush and thorns barred the progress at every step. These sleepers are the potter's brood, the children of God and the country, who have gone down from out the beauties of life and laid their heads to rest, where the righteous walk with pity and from which the hard-hearted turn with scorn. They are the unknowns and the suicides.

And one can see it all and feel it all for a ride on the car, but one doesn't. It's as powerful in its effect as are the night scenes along the Monongahela, only it brings a dread to some minds and a loathing to others, and to still more it makes life sad and discouraging and accordingly few go. And this perhaps, also, is well.

For people cannot think of death all the time. There would be little of real pleasure in life if they did. It's blessed not to be able to feel the desolateness of that mound of the future, which shall be one's own and over which the elements shall sweep in their varying moods, as though we had never been. All graveyards go to seed like weeds. It's a question of time only, until people forget where they were.

This one of Allegheny county at Highwood is a lonely place. It's only one side of a hollow, but the trees are dead and the weeds are numerous. There are no flowers and no lawn. Most of it has not even grass, being broken pieces of sandstone thrown out from the graves. Between these stray pieces weeds have sprung up and concealed the numbers upon the rotting boards. There are no claimants. An inquirer for any lost victim has not come upon the scene in six months past.

There are fresh arrivals, though, constantly. Yesterday two graves lay open, having been dug on the order of the Coroner. They were covered over with a few old boards, and the odor from the damp earth below was moldy. A large heap of sand and rocks lay at the side of each. The dead branch of a tree hung over one. Dry, scraggy weeds clustered about the other. To-day the sexton will come with the yellow pine box and lower it. A new pine shingle will be driven into the ground and then the unknown will certainly have reached the end of his woes. No one will pursue him there.

Every newcomer is buried that way. The stony level covers them all. No ornaments dignify their rest. It's dryness and barrenness for each and forgetfulness. Away in other States and countries relatives and friends may credit them with homes and happiness. They may be dreamed of some-where, as strong and successful. Yet the wind knows better. The weeds that rustle over them, the dry stones and branches, the rain, clouds and sunlight all know that their lives were failures and that hope had long since com-pletely fled.

The mutations of time do not seem to have mutated the loneliness, for-sakenness of these places any, nor has the burial procedure improved much. In the first potter's field, near ancient Jerusalem, which was a pot-ter's field in reality, having been hollowed out by molders of clay and for-saken when there was no more clay to mold, they buried the plague-stricken and the lifeless unclean. Those 30 pieces of silver that bought Jesus went to buy that desolate abode of the poor which travelers look on nowadays with awe. It was about the most barren-looking district in all Canaan, and all other potter's fields seem to partake of the same quality. They're discourag-ing enough to encourage misery-loving crows to come and dwell in them. Some crows live out in this one at Highwood.

And the change from beautiful to disagreeable comes to one with a jolt after leaving any portion of the neighboring hillsides. Standing among the weeds and low head-boards one can look away into the distance over the decay and see green fields. Hillsides shine with all the warm life of summer and dark-foliaged trees sigh in the breeze. There are flowers slightly bloom-ing near by and red benches scattered beneath the shade, but not here. If strangers come to view, they do it standing. If they wish to linger an hour it is uncomfortably alone. Gravel paths will not do to sit upon and thorns and weeds are not sod.

Twenty years have passed in which this village of unknowns has been brought together and made one. Society seems to have shaken off these weakenings slowly. The rivers have been slow in yielding up their discour-aged burdens, the garrets have moldered their victims none too fast. All but a few of the murderers have been cared for, and these few are here. Sev-enty-one, 72, 73, 74 are no worse than 1, 2, 3 or 4 in the long list of 100 graves numbered in that order, for no one can tell now their names or deeds. They are left to the poetic of mind and the curious to wonder over and speculate upon. No others come to look or grieve, no others note the barrenness. The flowerless and weed-grown waste can excite nothing but wonder. And the poetic is "to wonder," just as genius is "to work out."

In many parts of Highwood yesterday bereaved relatives were strolling. Quite a number could be seen bending over graves, and toward evening, one or two, more affectionate than the others, still lingered to weep. They were not near the paupers' section. Yet that place at evening is not so bad in all its meanness, and at night, when the shadows have covered up its rough exterior, it is even pretty. For then stars are out, and the lamps gleam like will-o'-the-wisp from distant hillsides. The trees murmur and the hollow lies dimly apparent, a dreamy waste, far more inviting than the frosty white specters of tombstones that seem to move about in the distance. Like their folly and crime-laden souls, their very graves need to be hidden in shadow that others may look and not be disturbed.

[23 July 1894, p. 3.]

93 - SOME DABBLING IN BOOKS.

Who does not want to be literary in taste, or, if there are those who do not want to be literary, who does not want to be thought literary? There wouldn't be many clean negative hands held up in Pittsburg this morning if that were the proposition before the public.

The desire to discuss men and nations, to speak familiarly of P. Vergilius Maro as "Old Virgil," and add that he was a bully old jolt, is innate. People do these things because it's counted the highest attainment outside of war time or election campaigns.

"Young man," any old dusty-coated lawyer along Smithfield street is apt to say, if you stand long enough, "young man, have you ever read Dr. Whately?"

You say, "Oh, yes, you've glanced into him a little," and then comes the statement, "Well, I'll tell you, he was a brainy old cuss, wasn't he?" You fix your lips in position to say that he was an able writer of much tentative acumen, when the lounging old desecrator goes on with, "but Berkeley was a heap slicker in his way. I like Berkeley. Say, did you ever read Don Quixote?"

Yes, you've read Don Quixote.

"That's a pretty fine book, isn't it?"

But the lounging desecrator is sure to wind himself tight to the laughing-stock of a little literary string he tied to his leg. He will never go beyond the labels of philosophy or history. Like a dragon fly he buzzes from label to label. Dante will be called "great;" Milton, "slick;" Voltaire, "away up in G," and so on through the long roster of fame.

When you inquire after the essence of any particular issue advanced in any of the list, or want to know what became of so and so in "Romala or the Decline and Fall," after the close of the LXVI. chapter you finish the discussion. George Gould's yacht race is then good enough to talk about. Even the tariff bill will serve as a loop hole. It's anything to get away from the discursive end of the hundred sublime titles spoken of.

The streets are filled with literary aspirants. It's the simplest thing in the world to pick up a literary discussion. It can be opened with a shoveler in a sewer, if the moment of idleness is seized upon. The busiest merchant will lay aside his accounts for an elucidation of his favorite novel.

In opening the argument the only way to do is to appeal to vanity. The sentence, "say, old man," (if the sayee happens to be a friend) "have you read 'Ships That Pass in the Night!'" or, "will you tell me what kind of book that 'Do do' is," is the surest way to succeed. It lends a feeling of homage to the sayee. He feels that he is looked upon as an authority in literary circles, and from thence onward all is as smooth as the proverbially "greased electricity." No trouble to sweep over the plain of literature then, full charge.

Quotations will be forthcoming in the most distorted and unrecognizable shape imaginable. Verses will be flung loose upon the yielding atmosphere. Paragraphs of saddest strains from Chaucer to Will Carleton and thoughts from Bacon to Carl Browne will be jumbled until the cultivated tympanum aches with its weight of misinterpretations. When relief is afforded by escape, the mercantile aspirant will joyously count threes and fives by the hour, hugging the eminence to which his culture has lifted him.

Beside the street car drivers who regale one with the English versions of Socrates, and the policemen who have dived into Adam Smith and David Hume, there are the work-a-day pessimists, who see literary decline in everything since the Christian era. Most of these are romantic bridge-tenders or sentimental toll gatherers. They appear in the forms of watchmen at railroad crossings, and night keepers of large buildings. Somewhere in a little stogy room, where they manage to crowd in a chair and a wall stove, they have paper copies of almost every scientific frippery of the past 600 years, and from the learning of these they draw dissatisfaction and pessimism.

"Don't talk to me about literature, young man," is the usual run of their pedantic disgust. "There haven't been any poets since Homer; not a one. Why, haven't I been reading some these 30 years now or more. Don't you talk to me."

"But don't you think there's one other good writer?"

"Not a one, not a blessed one. All dead. All died before Christ. Do you mean to tell me any ever wrote like Homer—not a bit of it. Think you can make me imagine that there's anything equals that massive old Greek hexameter. Bosh! Pshaw, young man, pshaw! That's all I've got to say. Simply pshaw! I've been reading literature come now these 30 odd years."

So it goes. There's no convincing these hard-shell literary aspirants. There's no invading the field of the toll-gatherer and the watchman. The office building janitor stands alone in his supreme magnificence of literary dogmatism.

Some of them seem to really have had earnest bonus, at one time or another, of literary success. They may have had a few little harbingers of literary talent published, and coming athwart some later obstacle have been turned aside into the almost unbelievable channels, where they now pause, pause, pause, between small duties—and vegetate.

It is no effort for many of them to prove their claims to quondam talent. It's no stretch of effort to have them go into some miserable, dusty drawer and fish out a badly scribbled scrap of writing that was a part, or should have been, of some pretentious effort at composition. They have them to show, just as the beggars and the blind have sometimes a poem, the emanation of years of constant mumbling, which they sell for the charity of 3 or 5 cents bestowed.

One son of Erin, a watchman at a local railroad crossing, claims once to have been a scholar and more, a lover. In his dusty little hut he still reads Bacon, but never writes. Somewhere, before he wrecked himself by drink and entered the hidden lane where he now dozes out his existence, he had a pretty sweetheart whom he never gained. Her loss is the secret of his soul, only he once loved to scribble messages to her that were never sent. Some of these he still has, one in particular, written on the poorest, soiled yellow paper imaginable.

It read: "So I think of you ever so often, and hear and see you say (in my thinking) a thousand and one dear little things. They're all old. They're all what has been, but they are so much more than nothing at all to me, who am alone. When I'm tired and most weary I like them to come to me. I like to call on them to be my last companion before slumber. I like to dream that you are over me, a pale, misty, silvery-pure Mary, bending soft and low to lay your fingers on my hair, to touch my tired cheek, to smile, to kiss me once and once again, until I doze and dream, and am not. So I wish I might die—I often wish it."

Even at his age he does not count this folly.

[14 August 1894, p. 3.]

94 - SNAP SHOTS AT PLEASURE.

"On a lovely summer morning, in 1823," begins the not always average novel, "a man about 50 years of age was riding along a mountainous road, skirting in places a bright scampering brook, which leads to a large village in the neighborhood of"—it might be Yonkers near the Catskills, or Tucson in Arizona.

Such openings then go on to describe the rare beauties of scenery whose features are no less rare than impressive, and wind up, usually, with the arrival of another horseman whose life, purposes and sentiments are as much at cross with the man about 50 years, as are their two journeys in passing each other by.

But yesterday evening (and a lovely summer evening it was) quite a number of men might have been seen perambulating the mountainous roads that lead into this large city of Pittsburg, each one the principal figure in his own life's drama, but not apt to meet another horseman who would ever trouble him in any other way than that of wishing him a pleasant good evening.

From 1823 to 1829 were great years for gentlemen of 50, getting tangled up in story. Like some years replete with meteoric disturbances, causing showers of rather flinty sidereal messengers, that period was perhaps replete with fine literary disturbances which have since showered so many old gentlemen, brigands, et cetera, upon a long wearied and exhausted public in the form of literary introductions.

Just what the gentlemen mentioned as perambulating were about in each particular instance yesterday can not be taken up as the subject matter of this article. It ought to suffice the busy readers to know that they were out, and so fortunate as to be away from a very (thanks to the weather bureau) dry and not over comfortable mountain metropolis like Greater Pittsburg.

Perhaps some of them had been down to the seashore, where, having tired themselves into a state of perennial lassitude, they returned home to recuperate amid the beauties of their own habitations. Perhaps they, like many another, had but once to get away from their wearying surroundings and knock around among the effete monarchs of the outer world, to find that Pittsburg and Allegheny county aren't so eternally wearying after all.

It was some such sentiment as this, born of foreign conviviality no doubt, that made them stroll out yesterday into the admirable haunts of the jaybird and woodpecker, and lose themselves in the silence of the abundant ravines, where only coolness and the monopoly oil wells flourish. They were resting and no one could criticise them for it.

If there was one there were seven Allegheny politicians out fishing. The City Hall over there pined drearily without them. If there was one there were ten Pittsburg merchants out scraping around with a "Flobert" and lunch bag looking for small birds. If there was one there were 50 small storekeepers drifting around with a robust wife and a half dozen blooming-cheeked, tow-headed children looking for elderberries to make wine, and cat-tail rushes to ornament the shadowy corners of the never-to-be-invaded front parlor. Most of the latter had express wagons covered with high spring seats and a small beer keg trimmed with green vines of a maliciously tempting character. The poor family horse was the only one not in on the delights.

If those family horses could have been interviewed late last night, just after the Siebenthalers, or eight or nine thalers, got home, what a tale of woe they would have related.

"Say!" Just hearken the family nag a moment. "Say! come in! Shove me over that hay, will you? I've had a pull for your mane to-day. Took that whole family out, and would you believe it! they drove me 25 miles with all the children on and a keg of beer. Don't talk to me about day-outings. I know. I thought two or three times they were going to stay and look at the scenery a minute, but, huh! they fooled me. The gabble back there died down and I actually believed they were impressed. Impressed, nothing! Why that would have been a rest for me. I'm not sarcastic, but there's no danger of my ever getting a rest."

Let us softly close the barn door. Poor ring-boned Fritz is tired. We will drop in another time with a friendly measure of oats.

How those horsemen and German families and politicians did enjoy themselves wandering around, fishing, elderberry gathering, cat-tail rush-snipping along the quiet edges of the rivers. How those elderberry bushes did cluster and yield fragrant odor from the warm ledges of the hillsides. How still the water ran! How rare! oh how rare! were the nibbles at the over-weighted bait hooks. The latter was truly the most entrancing feature.

Though all the landscapes nestling within these foothills of the Alle-ghenies have a family likeness, the region which abounds hereabouts offers to the eye a diversity of ground, a mellowness of slope, a changefulness of light and shadow, which may be sought elsewhere in vain. Along our dear Allegheny and Monongahela, stretching north for a time, along the Ohio, the valleys widening suddenly yield to view an irregular carpet of verdure, which, despite the drouth seems most by a miracle of nature to be kept ever fresh and tender to the eye.

Sometimes an iron mill shows its humble buildings and dark stacks pic-turesquely placed among the trees, that from a distance seem to encroach upon it, while before flows the quiet river glistening as calmly as some broad and moving mirror.

Farther still gleam the hilltops and still more distant darkle the valleys, always green, always changeful and fair. In some particularly restful spot, where the roadway winds down between damp-hewn walls into some rugged uncut gully, the air is cool, the songsters plentiful. The fragrance of elder and shrubs blends here with creeping vines and swaying poplars, mingled in places with the resinous pine.

Still richer, come the mysterious perfumes of a hilly region, embodying, as it were, the deepest and sweetest secrets of nature, and breathing aro-matic airs which stimulate old memories, as secrets are wont to do. A few clouds flash lazily above in the serene blue, a few birds wing silently, swiftly by, afar off; a few cowbells come dimly tinkling from almost nowhere to the ear. So much makes the summer evening here—made yesterday.

This is what brought the horsemen out at evening, the fisherman out at noon. This, with the elderberries and the cat-tail rushes, is what induced the German family into a day's outing. This is what made the family grocery horse complain.

The ingrain Pittsburger cannot find it at Atlantic City. Such peace does not flourish near the sea. One has got to come home.

[18 August 1894, p. 3.]

95 - NOW THE PILL DOCTRINE!

W̶e now have the man with the pill doctrine. The man with the microbe-killer mania is also here. Hand in hand they have come upon us in our tariff weighted vale of tears, to point out the foolishness of being miserable, and the utter idiocy of being sick. Hand in hand they bear the double-dyed banner of amalgamated happiness. There is no gainsaying them.

The world heretofore has been divided between the man pessimistic and the man optimistic. Between them they have flung us from the depths of despair to giddy heights of champagne hilarity. They have in turn pointed out that we are at once where we can read the Inferno gate inscription by looking up, and at the same moment knock pearls off the gates ajar, if we only had our little hatchet. Great heretofore has been the power of this opto-pessimo duumvirate. Their days, however, include at present only a few more pages in the sarsaparilla almanac. At last we are about to be freed.

This most Hesperian turn of affairs has come simultaneously with the pill doctrine. The prophet of this latter is strong. He is healthy. He is the personification of the more genial individual in the "before and after" sign. Three meals a day are his delight. Nine hours' sleep catch him exactly. A gentle reference to a possible joke is plenteous humor for him. All things are pleasant, all things well.

His equal half is the man with the microbe mania. If you are blue he knows why. You do not take microbe killer. If you are grim, he knows why; you have never known that your overtaxed vitals need nothing so much as a daily bath in that bacilli annihilator. Your appreciation of Rudyard Kipling is all the fault of your stomach; take microbe killer and, presto! it vanishes. These are the men who have come to chase the opto-pessimo combination far into the unperceivable non-reality. They are the lords of the reigning hour.

Glad ought all Pittsburgers to be with the presentation of this intelligence. Wreathed should their faces be in space-rate smiles, such as qualify our latest stock of campaign photos. Well we know the disagreeableness of the native pill, but that will vanish.

From childhood's contentious hour all have been pursued by the sugar-coated buckshot. The green seal and the red, the gentle purgative pellet and the dusty-looking combinations of circular Buchu have stuck in our throats many a time. When we held them up how small, how mild, how blandly persuasive they looked. All we had to do (they seemed to say) was to put them away back near the larynx, where the tongue swivels, and kind of duck our head down and drink a little water and they were gone. But we never believed them.

Instead, there was mistrust in our eye. We knew better. When they got firmly nestled on our larynx we couldn't complacently duck. They were comfortably resting and would not move. Gallons of water might pass that way and drown us standing. They remained intact. This we knew.

Once started they were like the upper cut of this literary prize fight. The pill in "Before's" hand shows how small they were. Mr. "After" on the other side illustrates how we felt. A giraffe's neck could not compare with ours in length as that pill went down. It found more angles! more nooks to rest in!! more curves to wind in and out of!!! All the time it was stopping to converse with the minute molecules that it met out promenading. An ostrich egg or a football did not near approximate its size.

That is why the pill doctrine may now seem premature, but, anyhow, its presentation can do no harm. Its prophet lays all to the liver. If that is brown and sear, if it is morose and immovable, we are given to attempting to read Browning and thinking we are doing it. Says the prophet: "Man, what's the use talking. Don't I know. Didn't I write poetry before I found out what was the matter with my liver. Didn't I go around hunting beautiful scenery and thinking I felt wistful. Didn't I lay around by babbling brooks and other things and feel sad. Why, I came mighty near reading Carlyle! You can't tell me anything."

"But—" you indefinitely murmur.

"But, nothing," answers the pill prophet. "All your liver; all torpidness; all needs cleaning! Here you are walking around, cynical, studying languages, reading philosophy, enjoying allegories. That's your liver. I did it. Studied socialism, hypnotism, theosophy, even read Ibsen. Look at me. I've got pills in my pocket, health in my face. Strong, light-hearted, good-natured. I'm normal again and read E. P. Roe and Dora Thorne. There's literature that's natural. That's anti-bad liver literature."

If you are the cynical man, the student, the lover of political philosophy and Spencerian individualism, you turn away to crash into the microbe man.

"Where are you going?" says he.

"Home; I've got the blues."

"I knew it. Been brooding again. Too much literature. Too much striving after the unattainable. You're getting to be like that fellow that was in the ship that passed in the night. Jones was telling me about him. Always disagreeable. Now you see if you'd have taken microbe killer you wouldn't be that way."

"Oh, I'm not sick," you say. "I don't need microbe killer."

"Yes, you do. You just think you don't. How can you tell?"

"Oh, pshaw!"

"Oh, pshaw, now. That's the way to disregard all new truths. Just say oh, pshaw! Microbe killer will run all those bacilli out. It'll make 'em move. Tone you up. Do like me. Keep a barrel of it in the house. I drink it instead of water. Bathe my eyes in it. It chases the bacilli away and makes me feel better. Snuff it up my nose, makes me scent clearer. Those bacilli take all the odor to themselves. Put it in my ear and I hear like a long-distance telephone. Great, old man, great! Try it once, and you won't be reading all that gloomy scientific rot any more."

For peace you agree. The liver and stomach you acknowledge. Microbe fluid and pills you will adopt very soon; only peace, now, for the hour. When you get away you feel like an Arab at Rome. You want the pill prophet and the microbe fraud to preach their doctrines among themselves. Nature is good enough. When she is glad, you will be. When she is sad, then you will be sad also.

[20 August 1894, p. 3.]

96 - SURVIVAL OF UNFITTEST.

My Allegheny friend, Prof. Y. Zayker, has a new theory. It is a Northside product, pure and simple. He calls it the "dwindling hypothesis."

The title conveys, perhaps, a poor idea of the nature of the professor's pet, but one who becomes acquainted with the subject will admit that the name fits like the bark on a beech tree. In any event, the professor is eager to explain. I met him yesterday and he told me all about it. He thus spoke:

"Charlie Darwin's notion about things getting better all the time is a fine notion, and the way it has caught on, seeing there is nothing in it, beats anything in my time. Folks take to it just because it flatters the breed. It tells them that they are better than anything before them, and that they are getting better all the time, like old lager. But Charlie has the thing just wrong end to, and the facts prove it. Like Alf Wallace, Tom Huxley and a good many other smart fellows, I was pretty much taken with the notion when Charlie first sprung it, more than 30 years ago.

LEFT: "Jumbo and His Ancient Ancestor" (*Pittsburg Dispatch*, 24 August 1894, p. 3);
RIGHT: "Cholly and the Giant of the Rhone" (*Pittsburg Dispatch*, 24 August 1894, p. 3).

"Some time after that I was up in New York State and saw the skeletons of six mastodons taken out of an old peat-bed. That set me to thinking why all those big animals had died off and the smaller ones were left. My friend, after a good deal of thinking, I came to a conclusion.

"That conclusion is this, that the inhabitants of this earth, instead of growing all the time greater and better, are steadily becoming smaller and meaner.

"Think how much bigger the animals used to be. This very State of Pennsylvania, thousands of years ago, even away in the distant past before Allegheny began to wrestle with the water question, was the favorite romping ground of monsters that would make an elephant look like a dime museum dwarf. There's the Meuse lizard, 75 feet long, a genuine sea serpent! The head alone was over five feet long, as long as two flour barrels placed end to end. Twenty skeletons of that monster have been found along the Delaware valley and around Delaware bay. The woods must have been full of them. Why, 20 of them would be over a quarter of a mile long! They were given a Dutch name because the first ones were found over in Holland, time of the Revolution. At that time in this country we weren't digging up bones. We were planting them. But we've done well in the digging line since. Where can you find a lizard like that nowadays! One of them could wear the whole 400 of New York for holiday bangles. You see the lizards are degenerated.

"Then there was the Stout Lizard, found in New Jersey 33 years ago. It was 25 feet long and stood up on its hind legs like a kangaroo or a Kansas Congressman. He beat all the 'tigers' you can find out at Whitehall or anywhere in this neck of the woods. I'm rather glad I wasn't living just about that time.

"There is a fine example of the degeneration of animals in the armadillo. That animal is only three feet long now, but he used to be 14 feet, unless his bones have grown immensely since they were planted down in Peixoto's country.

"One of the most terrible of ancient creatures, the winged lizard, was 25 feet across the wings. From the number of skeletons found the air must have been full of them. Just think of a flying dragon of that size! The largest condors are only 12 feet across the wings.

"Even our elephant is a dwindled brute. The mammoths and mastodons that used to wander around in the primeval forests of Snowden and Moon townships, but are all dead thousands of years ago, were something worth talking about. The mammoth had tusks 12 feet long, and the mastodon was a still larger animal. They did not confine themselves to Asia and Africa, as their puny successors do, but occupied Europe and America in great droves. Out in the Rocky Mountain region there were immense rhinoceroses bigger than Barnum ever dreamed about, and in Kansas and Nebraska they find the bones of tigers many times more terrible than any that now live in the jungles of India. They were more terrible in that prairie country than a dozen conventions of Populists with their whiskers.

"The deer tribe has fallen away. The great Irish elk was 11 feet across the horns, and in India there was a kind of moose nearly as big as an elephant. We know, too, that the cave bear, and the cave hyena were twice as large as their descendants.

"Then look at the birds. There used to be a monster ostrich in Madagascar that held his head 18 feet above the ground. The tallest ostrich now is a child beside that old fellow. In New Zealand, not so many centuries ago, there lived the moa, a bird 10 to 12 feet high. One species had toe bones almost rivaling those of the elephant. To a gentleman like that I take off my hat.

"They tell us, however, that even the big moa led a hobo's life in his time, for Australia was inhabited by a gigantic bird of prey called the Harpagornis, which could carry off even the moa. That old fellow must have been the Roc that we read about in Dave Henderson's wonderful classic, 'Sinbad.' You know, I think there is a great deal of truth in the old stories about gigantic birds and dragons. There used to be ostriches in Texas larger than are now to be found anywhere. You know what a rail is like? Well, there used to be a rail in the island of Mauritius that stood six feet high.

"Now, the fact is, the whole animal kingdom has been dwindling down to very small potatoes. Beasts are getting smaller and smaller all the time. The buffalo is about played out. The dodo has disappeared in late years. After awhile there won't be any elephants. The big fellows are always picked at and worried to death by the little fellows. The result is the survival of the unfittest.

"Even the trees used to be much larger than they are in our time. The giant trees of California are the last of the Mohicans, in the tree line.

"Man has been dwindling just the same as everything else. All the old authors tell us that giants once peopled the earth. How big they were we cannot imagine. The Bible itself assures us in the most serious manner that before the flood the world was full of giants.

"I don't believe Moses was joking when he wrote that. Goliath was simply a relic, the last rose of summer, run over his time, and he was killed by a little squirt of a fellow with a pebble.

"The ancient Latin authors tell us of the digging up of the bones of an Italian giant 300 feet long. Don't be surprised. It is likely that long, long ago, men were bigger than that. There is plenty of talk about giants in the old Greek and Norse mythology. There is too much smoke for no fire. Something over 400 years ago the Rhone changed its course one season, and in the sand of the old bed there was exposed to view the bones of a man who had been 30 feet tall. Mind you, he was a recent infant. Three hundred years ago a giant 19 feet long was digged up at Lucerne, Switzerland.

"Did you ever read the Book of Daniel? Well, it tells you there about a dream that old King Neb had. He was very strong in the dream line. Seemed to do it just for the purpose of teasing his fortune tellers and having an excuse to cut off their heads. I agree with him that they are a nuisance. In this particular dream he saw a giant statue, with a head of gold, shoulders and arms of silver, stomach and thighs of brass, legs of iron and feet of iron and clay mixed. Now Daniel told Neb it was just that way man was going, and I think Daniel had a good bit of sense. The race is going from bad to worse steadily. We are getting smaller and meaner all the time. I tell you, my boy, we are down to the toes now, down to the toes. Pretty soon there won't be anything left but the nail parings."

[24 August 1894, p. 3.]

97 - THE LAST FLY OF FLY TIME.

We are almost face to face with the last of the flies. That halcyon period in which dissevered wings ornament the strong and fluid oleomargarine and broken and extracted legs float woefully on the surface of our steaming mocha and java is almost past. Fly time, with all its glory of traps and deep laid ruses to ensnare the winged pest, is all but over. A few breaths of chill north wind have done for us what barrels of vinegar and tons of brown paper; what bolts of sugared and poisoned fly paper and triple netted fly traps have not—i.e. brought us face to face with the last of the flies.

And as we see him stiff, dull and rheumatic, his miserable legs clinging feebly to the wall; as we raise the family broom over our head and twist our spine circular wise in an effort to come down upon him with one fell swoop and even as unto a thousand of bricks, we pause, for we feel like saying: "Oh you villain! Oh you despicable and measly coward! Now we have got you where we can get even. All summer long you have tormented us. All through the dog days you have sat upon our brow, and when we chased you off you have come back. You have risen each morning before us and sat upon our nose. You have gathered your companions and paraded along the ceiling and the window sill with a bass drum, just to disturb our slumbers. You have even called in your disreputable neighbor, the blue bottle, and told him to go on and 'whoop it up' for us. Now, by the Great Horn Spoon, we will pay you up."

"Aha!" we feel like continuing as the chill air from an opening door almost shakes him from his hopeless position, "Aha! you are not the same fly, aren't you? Oh, you driveling, shivering coward! You are one of him just the same. Now that you are alone at our mercy, you imagine you will whine us out of a few more hours of life so you can crawl over and die in our soup, but you won't. We will fool you. You think you will possibly live long enough to heroicly spoil our pate de foie gras. Well, we shall see." Smish! Bang!! "Now, then, take that," and as we predicted we have utterly squelched the last of the flies.

If we will just keep our thoughts off the woes of the recent summer, we shall have some cause for rejoicing. Everyone knows we were abused. Everyone knows that as we stand wrathful and broom in hand before the last specimen on this wall, that we have just cause for our ire. The fly tribe has heaped countless indignities upon us. Its members have harassed us until we would have given our kingdom come for revenge. Our house has been a buzzing resort for leisurely and opulent blue bottles. They have joined us in everything.

But still we have some cause for rejoicing. All we have to do is not to recollect that Mr. Fly swung with us in our backyard hammock. When we went on our vacation he went along. As we fished upon the waters of the hidden woodland stream he sat upon our face and chatted pleasantly with the sociable dragon fly. When we carried home our trout he sat upon its glassy eye, calmly speculating upon the probable chances of its resuscitation. When we carried our grip to the return train he perched upon our collar and enjoyed the scenery while we busied ourselves trying to encompass his death. This is what we do not want to remember.

We know that the fly is a suicide by inheritance. Unnatural and untimely death is his delight. This has been a source of our regret. He seems born with an innate desire to depart from this mortal vale in agony. Desperate methods tickle him. The more he can shock the sensibilities of the dining public the better he feels.

If defeated in matters of slight moment he is apt to settle down on the table board and twit his wings as he morosely speculates. Chased from the sugar bowl, while pursuing his daily task of earning a competence, he says, "Aw, what's the use of trying? Every hand is against me. Fly paper is at every turn. They even poison the jam to rob me of life. I'll die!" Accordingly he climbs up onto the vinegar jug, and looking down, says, "Ah, beautiful vinegar, how calm, how placid are thy depths, placid and acid. Beneath thy surface is eternal peace. Farewell! vain world, farewell!" and in he dives, head first.

Chased from the cake dish, he immediately becomes despondent. "Terrible!" he sighs, "terrible! To be thus ruthlessly pursued from the cake. There is nothing left in the world for me now—nothing but blessed death." Looking, he spies the gravy and exclaims: "Ah, beautiful gravy. How delightful! How scalding! In a moment will I bathe my tired wings in your sputtering depths," and in he goes, while Mary removes the dish.

Not always is it grief that so prompts him. Not always the being robbed of sugar and cake. Pure admiration of the beautiful and sometimes absolute gluttony arouses the suicidal mania. Steaming coffee, sparkling wine, odorous beef arouses his remarkable propensity to commit suicide. Sometimes the sight of a crowded board, filled with all culinary delicacies, turns his brain. He grows delirious and in a moment of enthouasia topples off into something and ceases to exist.

We can understand his feelings. Hungry, from a long night's vigil, kept to disturb the man who was dying for a little sleep, he comes upon the steaming coffee bowl of the early merchant. "Ah, beautiful coffee. Just my chance. What is better than coffee? Nothing." Cocking his eye over the rim he exclaims "there is my chance. Never again may I have an opportunity to bathe in such Java and at the same time upset such a gorgeous appetite as my friend here has. All flydom will sing my praise," and in another instant he dives in and sinks from view. This is tragic.

Again it is the sight of so much. "Such opulence! Such abundance! Who could believe? Oh! this is too good. Life after this would be useless. One long round of miserable pickings with the thought of so much good gone before. No, I will not try it. I will not go along compelled to remember that once I had so much. I will just make merry here and eat my fill. I shall roll in bread, wade knee deep in delicious butter, dip my wings in the cherry jam, stride over the beefsteak and then lay me down peacefully upon the cake dish and expire." When the meal is finished we find the promise verified. His wings dipped in jam and peacefully folded upon his back, his eyes loosened by hot coffee, his knees marked with butter and beef and crumbs, we find him quietly resting beneath a mass of fruit slices, a clear example of the suicidal glutton.

This is what we do not want to remember. This is what, as we wield the weapon of death upon this morning, we want to overlook. We want to think of the fly tribe as have played in hard luck all summer long and then our joy in mutilating the last one will be keen and fiendish. We can look upon ourselves as ghoulish and heinously cruel.

The abstemious fly should be our thought. The fly against whom every screen door was shut and every fan was turned. The winged outcast who ever found the sugar lid down, the vinegar bottle corked, the cake dish covered, the pie dishes screened. The poor, forlorn outcast who singed his wings in merely approaching the beef, burned his toes in merely reconnoitering the pudding, crippling himself for life by accidentally lighting upon the butter. The miserable insect who was pursued by the housewife, poisoned by the flypaper trust, fooled by the rat poison, eaten by the yawning lye cup. How sad!

No, we will take that back. We can't be hypocritical. We are not sad. We are delighted at the thought. It was good for him, all too good. More horrible tortures would be contrived if only our genius permitted. Some system of wholesale slaughter would be to the point. "Oh!" we say. "Oh! for the man with an idea in this case." For instance, the summer frost maker. If we could only have a weather bureau that would be a weather bureau—that would send a 30 degrees below zero frost each summer morning devastating the whole fly race. If the frost would only damage the fly crop alone and leave the fruit for our own blighting touch. Then would the millennium have come—but we rave.

All we can be is content with this morning. All we can delight in is that winter occasionally rolls round and freezes out the worst of Pharoah's ten nuisances. The fly on the wall, shivering and alone, is all we can rejoice over, but we can do that—and slay him.

[3 October 1894, p. 3.]

98 - GENERAL BOOTH SAYS FAREWELL.

Salvation's latest and greatest call was at the New Grand Opera House last evening, where, from 6:30 until 10 o'clock, fully 3,000 people sang and prayed and enthused over one of the most typical sermons that an audience could wish to hear. It was General William Booth's last evening in Pittsburg and his last appearance, for he announced that he could not hope to ever be able to come again.

It was a great crowd and a religious one in its sentiment, for every new word of fiery exhortation that was used was received with a visible movement from gallery to pit. People crowded the aisles of the balcony and lined the walls of the farthest recesses of the great gallery, from whence came audible murmurs whenever some new plea was sent ringing upward.

One remarkable feature connected with the great gathering was the presence of a number of women well known in police circles.

A great crowd was on the stage. All the local officers of the army, the Salvation band and a score of hallelujah lassies were seated back of the rostrum. General Booth, Commander Ballington Booth, Major Lawley, Major Halpin, Captain Milan, Ensign Harris, Captain Herald and wife, and Captain Groome and wife were among the most conspicuous.

It took a full half hour for the immense crowd to come in and be seated. Fifth avenue for a block was crowded with people, and about the foyer of the theater there was a crushing mass. When the door opened there was a genuine rush which filled the parquet in a little over three minutes.

When General Booth came on the stand with Commander Ballington someone called for a cheer and a veritable yell went up. Then the General took charge in an easy, friendly manner and said that the best way to open a Salvation meeting was to do so with a song. "We're Traveling Home," he said, was quite easy. Anyone could sing it, even if he didn't know the tune. Anyhow, he said, everyone could come in on the chorus with grand enthusiasm. Here an old gentleman shouted certainly, that was the idea exactly.

The song was given with great enthusiasm, after which General Booth called upon Captain Milan to lead in prayer. That beautiful-voiced singer rose and led in a prayer that seemed to enthuse the most casual of the great audience. His voice was soft and musical, and as he drew picture after picture of the victims of sin going down to ruin, a torrent of cries of "Oh, yes," "Help us, Oh Lord," and the like broke forth. Just as the last words of the prayer concluded, Major Lawley began to sing in a low voice, "When the Pearly Gates Unfold."

The effect was wonderful and as voice after voice joined softly in until the whole audience was singing, the instruments of the musicians took up the strain and added to the truly striking picture.

The power of the entire situation was of course in General Booth. His striking figure reclining for a few opening moments attracted much attention, and put the meeting in a spirit for the stirring words that followed, which with songs and prayers brought some 15 persons to the mourners' bench. He leaned back, with his hands folded across his knees, looking steadily upward toward the painted vault above.

There was no change in his garb. It was the same long blue soldier's coat, the red blouse without a collar, the striped trousers and inwoven letter S at each shoulder, which he proudly wore.

During his rest, while apparently lost in superior meditation, his fingers twitched nervously and one foot tapped rapidly and ceaselessly upon the floor. His was a striking figure, and although there is little of what any one would call real harmony in his voice, his whole personality made up for it. There is harmony in his movements, in his complete abandon of all his physical energy to the harmonious emphasis of his words. He made a powerful impression and there were hundreds of handkerchiefs drying eyes before he concluded.

While the audience-song, led by Captain Milan, was still filling the far recesses of the great theater the voice of Major Lawley dropped from melody to prayer and asked the people to come and get saved. Appeal after appeal was thrown aloft with all the passion of sincerity and elicited, as before, astonishing results in the way of fervid cries from seemingly every part of the audience.

Something rich in the way of religious effect was produced when at the close of this prayer without any announcement, Major Lawley changed off into a solo of his own composition, "Hear the Savior Knocking" with a lone guitar accompaniment. The captain's voice is also rich and soft and filling the hall as it did with one lone strain of plaintive melody, the idea of sorrow and sentiment it cast over the situation cannot be well described.

Ballington Booth then announced that a collection would be taken up to aid Salvation work in America and the chink of silver filled the room, making quite a pleasant accompaniment to a third verse of "Hear the Savior Knocking" which was entoned.

General Booth then read from the 17th chapter of Luke's Gospel, 20th verse, which recounted the effect of flood in the time of Noah, and of the fire and brimstone in the time of Lot, at Sodom and Gomorrah. He applied them to the certainty of eternal justice coming some day, when none could escape. For the text of his evening address he took Luke 17:32, "Remember Lot's Wife." He said:

"People often come to me and want to know what they shall do to be religious, to pray in earnest. Some of these people can't pray, some can't feel about their soul and its welfare. They can't realize anything concerning heaven, hell, Christ and His mercy. They want to be saved. They want to pray but they can't."

"To these I would say go and think. Put away the novel, the newspaper, the ordinary events of the day and retire and ponder. Study over these and before many hours I believe an understanding will come to your heart and you will adore the truth of the Divine God's presence and your lips will rejoice in the words of prayer."

He then took up the story of the city of Sodom and Lot's wife which he described quite graphically. It was evident, he said, that the city was prosperous, for luxury usually produced the kind of wickedness for which the place was destroyed. His description of Abraham interceding with the God of Israel for a sparing of the city was simply a marvel of nervous enthusiasm. His voice rose to a strength of penetration which might have almost been called musical. His body swayed not slowly but with a rapidity of bowing and head-shaking which added wonderfully to the brilliancy of the story.

Sometimes he walked to the foot of the stage saying, "Don't you believe it? don't you believe it?" and then his voice would rise almost to a shriek as he added: "Oh, Christians, you must! you must! you must!" Now it was his voice rising degree after degree, until it was a wild song of enthusiasm, and then it was a dying away, slowly and soft, until one could scarcely hear.

Again his hands lay quietly on his back, as though he was calm. Such moments he only walked; walked, walked, walked, the fingers at his back clinching and unclinching with the restless nervousness of a maniac. All at once the power of his argument would seize him. All at once the fire of belief came to him and loose fell the hands. Up they rose and swayed. Then he walked, bowed, shook, threw his hands aloft, while his gray locks fell about his forehead and his eyes sparkled with the wild brilliancy of truth. His words fairly sprang in the air, cracked and rattled with pyrotechnic effect, while his hands smashed together with emphasis. "Oh!" he would shout, "I see it all! I see it all!"

Again it was a half-circle move in which he turned squarely around. Then a long sweep with his arms that indicated the range of the whole universe. Lastly it was a long "Oh" in which the power of his lungs was exhausted in making it linger until it died away in a soft whisper.

"Oh, I hope," he cried, "that I may be spared many days to preach this story. I want to preach it. I will. I would that I had a high mountain to cry out from this beautiful word and its abiding generosity."

God, he said, was generous to Abraham. He promised that if ten righteous persons could be found he would not destroy the cities. Then when

Abraham went and found that not even ten were there he despaired and asked for mercy. The Lord came to him and told him to gather his relatives who were there and leave.

With this General Booth branched out into another wonderful word picture of the flight. It was fully adequate to the wonder of the actual fact. His description of the hesitation of Lot at leaving wealth and luxury, his home, his friends, his possessions, while the night was yet clear and the stars aloft shone brightly, with no sign of the approaching rain of fire and stone, was simply marvelous.

The doubt of Lot's wife, her protestations and misgivings, and finally her fatal glance backward, were gems of oratory that none who heard will ever easily forget. The whole scope of the ancient condition of the doomed city seemed to be in his mental grasp, and he handled it with power that was simply massive.

As he closed he asked Major Lawley to take the meeting for a few minutes. The Major asked that everybody bow their heads in prayer, and, while this attitude was being maintained, a call for repentant sinners to come forward was made. While the argument for this was continued, a number of the Salvation lassies passed along the aisles pleading with those whom they chose to ask to come to the mourners' bench. They began to come, first two from the left of the parquet circle. They were led by Salvation lassies, of whom there were fully a dozen in the aisles. Then came a number of others, and, by the close of the meeting, fully 15 had taken their places at the mourners' bench.

Throughout the entire evening a kind of enthusiasm was stirred. It was an atmosphere of religion induced by the wonderful praying and singing qualities of the leaders. Major Lawley, Major Halpin and General Booth took turns at praying, in strong, fervid attitudes which caused many to give way to demonstrations which, while admirable, were rather curious. Scarcely anyone left the meeting, and at the close the stage dressing-rooms were packed with persons anxious to have a last look at the wonderful quintette of workers who had exhorted so effectively.

[12 November 1894, pp. 1–2.]

99 - TALKS AT A BANQUET.

Andrew Carnegie's views on Pittsburg and her people and libraries, his opinions of wealth and its responsibilities and what he proposes to do with his own wealth were given last night.

The occasion was a dinner at the Duquesne Club, given by Mr. Carnegie to the members of the Board of Trustees of the Carnegie Free Library. Many things, important and interesting, were said by Mr. Carnegie and others, and it was an affair long to be remembered by those present.

In addition to the members of the Board of Trustees the only persons present were Mr. Carnegie and E. M. Bigelow, Director of the Department of Public Works. The members of the Board present were: W. N. Frew, George A. Macbeth, Andrew Mellon, E. M. Ferguson, Robert Pitcairn, H. K. Porter, David McCargo, James F. Hudson, J. McM. King, W. A. Magee, Mayor B. McKenna, Dr. W. A. McKelvey, H. P. Ford and Thomas G. McClure. The absent members were H. C. Frick, George L. Holliday, Smith W. Shannon and John S. Lambie.

A fine dinner was served. Mr. Carnegie presided at one end of the table and Mr. Frew at the other. After the dinner had been served, Mr. Frew proposed the health of Mr. Carnegie.

Mr. Carnegie responded with a speech in which he said he had been so delighted with what he had seen on his visit to the city on this occasion that he wanted to take this opportunity to express his thanks and his pleasure at the way in which the work of the board had been carried on, as far as it had gone. He said that in visiting the library building he had been very much pleased with the chaste and unostentatious architecture of the exterior, but on inspecting the interior he was even more delighted with the perfection of its arrangements. He said he saw in the progress that had been made the best promise that the work would be carried on so as to make it an unqualified public benefit.

During his visit he had been especially delighted to learn of the public interest taken in the location of the branch libraries and to hear that the people in the various parts of the city were applying for the location of district libraries. It was especially auspicious, as he deemed it, that in various cases free sites had been offered. In his visit here he had seen more of the progress of Pittsburg, and was amazed at the steadiness and magnitude of its growth. He referred with a great deal of pleasure to the Phipps Conservatory and the parks, saying they were unexampled instances of progress.

Referring to the future of the city, he said that, coming as he did from other places, he had expected to find evidences of depression, but was delighted to perceive, as he had, the signs of prosperity and strength. But he recognized in this the quality that was characteristic of Pittsburg. He had been through panics before, and had observed that after the storm had cleared away and when the rivals of this city had been blown out of sight, the good old ship, Pittsburg, was to be seen keeping steadily on her course.

In closing he said that this had been the happiest visit he had paid to Pittsburg since he had transferred his residence to New York. He could say that as he took pleasure in meeting the proof that, as he had left his business interests in the hands of partners especially qualified to carry them forward to success, so he found an equal pleasure in perceiving that the library enterprise was in the hands of a body especially suited to secure for it the highest usefulness.

Following Mr. Carnegie, informal remarks were made by various members of the board, most of them bearing upon the subjects arising with regard to the organization of the library. Nothing whatever was done in the way of making a decision on any of the points discussed, but the view advanced by Mr. Carnegie and generally coincided in by other speakers, was that in order to permit the work to be done in the best manner, the opening of the building would hardly take place before next fall.

Robert Pitcairn and David McCargo, who started life together with Mr. Carnegie as telegraph boys, were among the speakers called upon. Mr. Pitcairn in his remarks recalled the fact that 43 years ago a telegraph boy, without $5 to his name, announced that he was going to accomplish three things in life. One was that he would become one of the iron kings of the United States. Another was that he would provide his mother with every luxury that money could afford. The third was that he would build, not only for his native town in Scotland, but for the city of Pittsburg, public libraries. Mr. Pitcairn held it up as a remarkable example of success in life, that Andrew Carnegie, starting out without money or influence, had by unconquerable patience, industry and perseverance, set these objects before him and, after accomplishing them all, had won the admiration of the world by the lavishness with which he devoted his wealth to public uses. He differed with Mr. Carnegie on one point, as it was a Scotchman's privilege to do.

Mr. Carnegie was in the habit of giving advice to young men on how to succeed in life, but Mr. Pitcairn thought that that was something like Sandow, the strong man, telling little shriveled up men how to make themselves strong. The young men should be told that it was necessary in order to win Andrew Carnegie's success to have the brains, energy and unconquerable pluck of Andrew Carnegie.

Mr. McCargo, as the other early associate of Mr. Carnegie, spoke somewhat in the same strain. He referred to the fact that it was natural for men who had started from poverty and accrued wealth to cling to their money, but Mr. Carnegie exhibited the exceptional quality of devoting all his wealth to the highest public good, in advancing popular education, and this Mr. McCargo held up as a record of true greatness.

These remarks called forth from Mr. Carnegie the closing speech of the evening. He said he could listen to such eulogistic remarks from the old friends of his boyhood, but since they had been made he thought it fit to state his real views. So far as the gift of money from himself was concerned, he did not regard it as anything at all. He illustrated it by saying that after the first donation had been made public, he met a leading citizen of New

York who offered his hand in congratulation to Mr. Carnegie for having made the gift.

Mr. Carnegie said: "No, I will receive no congratulations for having given $1,000,000, but if you wish to shake hands with me on having secured some $40,000 a year in perpetuity from the city of Pittsburg for the support of public libraries, then I will be very glad to receive your hand in congratulation."

The speaker went on to state his theory of life. He said he would divide the men who had the force and energy to make an impression upon the world into three classes. The first class was inspired by the ambition to make money. That he declared to be the lowest and most commonplace of ambitions. He recognized that the men who are led by this ambition to carry on commerce and industry were much more useful to society than the men without force to accomplish anything, but still he placed the ambition merely to secure wealth among the lowest and most sordid of motives.

The second class was inspired by the desire for fame. The men who would scale the topmost heights or explore the deepest depths in order that they might win reputation and honors were actuated by a higher motive than the accumulation of money. Perugini, when he had decorated the town hall for a stipend of two measures of meal, did not care for money so long as he could live, but was seeking the reward of fame. Still this ambition was a vain and emphatic one.

The third class, which Mr. Carnegie believed to be increasing in the world, undertook to accomplish the same things, but did not care either for the accumulation of wealth or what people said of them, so that they were assured that what they accomplished was for the good of their fellow man and their country.

He said he recognized, as he said all of his hearers must, the impracticability of the schemes of the Socialists, but he believed that the time was coming when true success in life would be recognized as consisting neither of wealth nor of fame, but of having been useful to mankind, and that it would not be long until it would be held to be a disgrace for a man to die rich.

Continuing, he said that many men excused themselves for keeping their money to themselves by saying they did it for their children, but that was as false a motive as the other. He said that anyone can look about him and see that wealth, left to the sons of rich men, did them no good. A moderate provision for a man's family was within the limit of duty, but beyond that, the speaker asserted, the excuse of a man for accumulating wealth for his children was really the same selfishness as that of accumulating wealth for himself.

With reference to the remarks concerning himself he said he had never valued the wealth that he had gained. He had valued success in his industrial enterprises, had delighted in carrying them forward and conquering obstacles, and would still take pleasure, if circumstances should require, in successful conflict with the difficulties of business; but the money thus gained he regarded as only valuable to him as he could make it valuable to his fellowmen.

When he should die, he declared, it would not be found that he left any money behind him. He did not want to leave investments in stocks and securities, but rather to leave obligations to support public benefits beyond the resources of his estate in ready money, and which would have to be met from his interests in industrial enterprises.

He closed by saying that the money he had given was nothing, and that what people said about him was nothing to him, so that he knew that what he had secured was for the benefit of the working, intelligent and aspiring masses.

The Chairman, Mr. Frew, said at the close of Mr. Carnegie's remarks, of which the above is a mere synopsis, he thought the gentlemen present would agree that nothing need be added in the way of instructive oratory.

The evening was therefore concluded, in deference to the Scotch origin of Mr. Carnegie and some of his most intimate friends, by those present joining in the song of "Auld Lang Syne."

[21 November 1894, p. 2.]

100 - EDUCATING A GHOST.

A party of developed mediums from Allegheny and Pittsburg met last night in the haunted house on the old Brighton road, near High bridge, Bellevue, to ascertain the nature and identity of the spirit that stalks there at nights. By 8:30 the mediums had gathered, though the night was anything but agreeable for such an uncanny investigation.

The rain, hail, thunder and dark clouds of the day made the conditions very favorable to bring the spirit out, so that the ladies and gentlemen of the circle were not disappointed in the supernatural manifestation. One who was present describes the feeling as akin to the dark melancholy and weirdness borne in the brain of Poe and thrown about the House of Usher.

For many nights, at different times during the past, mysterious rappings and strange sounds have been heard in the building, so that it was difficult to rent the house. It was taken possession of by a "trance medium," well known to the prominent Spiritualists of the city. There were spirit rappings without mediums.

The circle being formed, the light was extinguished, a pleasant song was sung to produce harmony, and the seance commenced. Suddenly the clairvoyants, who see spirits, saw the spirit of an old lady come into the circle, grasp one of the women and throw her to the floor. This was repeated on another lady, and then the spirit tried to make its escape. A prominent lady clairvoyant of Allegheny followed the wraith by the glow peculiar to the earth-bound spirit, down into the cellar, but lost it. She was suddenly startled in the darkness by the sound of footsteps back of her on the steps, but saw nothing.

None of the party had followed her. She then felt a tap on the shoulder and a breath of wind, as if the spirit was hurrying past. She rushed up the stairs, but found the circle in conversation with other spirits who had come there as "controls" for the medium.

Nothing definite was learned concerning the name of the ghost haunting the place, other than it is an old woman who is yet bound to the earth and cannot get away. It is said she lived there some time ago, and keeps around her old haunts as a place she loves. It is said to be the purpose of the Allegheny mediums to educate the spirit that she may be enabled to leave her conditions. Earth-bound spirits are, as the name implies, bound here.

The rappings kept up during the trance state of some of the other mediums, but ceased when the light was turned up. A circle will meet at the old house at stated times to enable the spirit to get out of her trouble. After that time prominent spiritualists say the house will not be haunted. This is a new and unprecedented move in the annals of spiritualism, to educate a disembodied spirit to better its condition, and cease frightening the ones unfamiliar with spirit methods.

[18 May 1894, p. 7.]

101 - ELOPERS CAPTURED.

John Aston and Mrs. Lida A. Sloops, of Bagdad, near Freeport, were locked up in Allegheny last night. They are both young, good looking and well dressed. They had been arrested at McDonald on charges made by S. H. Sloop, the woman's husband.

Sloop is a coal miner, and works for the Western Pennsylvania Coal Company. Until two weeks ago he and his wife kept a boarding house at Bagdad, a small mining town. Among the boarders was Aston, who succeeded in winning the affections of the boarding mistress. One day, while Mr. Sloop was at work, Aston and Mrs. Sloop packed up a lot of household goods, and, taking $160 of Sloop's money, left for parts unknown.

A week ago Sloop learned the runaways were at McDonald, Pa., living as man and wife. He entered suit and their arrest followed.

When brought to the Allegheny lockup last night the elopers were handcuffed together. This is unusual in handling women and caused much surprise among the front office force. The couple were taken to Freeport on the 11 o'clock train last night by Constable Kerr.

[25 August 1894, p. 7.]

102 - USED A HORSEWHIP.

The very unusual spectacle of an outraged wife applying vigorously a rawhide whip across the face and shoulders of a rival for her husband's affections was witnessed in Allegheny yesterday afternoon and caused no end of excitement. The affair occurred on Federal street at 3 o'clock and the row lasted fully ten minutes. A large crowd gathered, yet no arrests were made. Both women were strangers in the neighborhood and were unknown to those who were eye-witnesses of the scene.

From all that could be learned the woman who was the victim has recently been keeping company with the husband of the woman who applied the whip, and this coming to the latter's ears, she decided to administer punishment. The name of the wife was mentioned during the whipping. She is a resident of the Hill section, while the other woman whose name could not be learned lives on the Northside.

The whipper resorted to a little strategy to get a meeting with her rival, and she addressed her a note purporting to be from her husband and asking the other to meet her at the corner of Lacock and Federal street. Shortly before that time, the wife, accompanied by a lady friend, went to Allegheny and purchased a whip at a store on Federal street, which she had hid under her seal-skin sacque. She then proceeded to the place of meeting, and had just arrived when the rival appeared. The wife accosted her at once, and accused her of enticing her husband away from home. This the woman attempted to deny, and in a very few minutes the pair were punching each other with their fists in vigorous style. The wife suddenly remembered the whip, and started to apply it across the face and shoulders of her rival, striking her at least a dozen blows and causing her to scream with pain.

The woman then broke away and ran into a store, whither she was followed by the wife, who again applied the whip with such force as to raise large welts across the face. At each blow the woman cried out: "Please stop and allow me to explain," and the reply she received was another blow, and an indignant cry of "You can't explain. You enticed my husband from his home."

One of the clerks in the store went to the rescue, and succeeded in stopping the irate woman from administering further punishment. By this time the street was crowded with people, and the clerk, to spare the women humiliation, allowed them to depart through a rear door. They quickly disappeared. Both were well dressed.

[20 November 1894, p. 2.]

New York World

103 - BETTER TENEMENTS WANTED.

"How to Improve Tenement-House Life" was the subject of discussion at a meeting of the Tenth Assembly District Good Government Club last night, at No. 9 St. Mark's place. President E. D. Page presided. Edward Marshall, Secretary of the Tenement-House Commission, said: "During the last year or so an important change has come over the tenement-houses of this city. Before then the presence of disorderly women in the tenements was almost unknown, but now—and you may do your own figuring as to the cause—they are full of them. The moral effect upon the children and young people in those tenements is most deplorable."

Mr. Marshall gave figures to show that certain portions of New York were more densely populated than any other part of the earth, and that in some tenement-houses the rental per square foot of floor surface was greater than in the rich Navarro apartments in Fifty-ninth street.

President Wilson, of the Health Board, advocated more health inspectors, free baths, water on every floor, more light and air, no overcrowding, small parks wherever possible and electric lights and asphalt paving in the tenement districts.

Walter S. Ufford, of the University Settlement Society, thought that all tenement-house owners and their agents should be held responsible for the cleanliness of the halls, stairways and yards and should be compelled to furnish ample receptacles for garbage and ashes. John P. Faure, of St. John's Guild, spoke of the necessity and importance of more and better bathing facilities.

The club adopted resolutions urging that the Lexow committee continue its work and extend it to all departments of the city government. President Page denounced any interference with this programme by "the officious Mr. Platt" or anybody else.

[13 December 1894, p. 3.]

104 - MRS. MORIARITY KNOCKS OUT HEALY.

M rs. Healy lives with her husband in a highly cosmopolitan tenement at No. 411 East Twenty-ninth street. Saturday Healy brought home his earnings and began to prepare for Sunday. This involved the production of a small can, which was "worked" thirty times before 6 a.m. yesterday morning. In a rest between two pilgrimages with the can Healy recalled that Mrs. Moriarity, on the second floor, in conjunction with Mrs. Dugan, of the third floor, and Mrs. Cafferty, of the fourth floor, had formed an offensive alliance against him one month before and had almost succeeded in having him ejected. In elevating each individual pail to his own domicile he took good care to inform these three arch-conspirators, who were endeavoring to sleep within, that he knew what they were.

Mrs. Dugan and Mrs. Cafferty said nothing and sawed somnolent wood all night long. Mrs. Moriarity did the same until 5 a.m., when she proceeded upstairs, entered Mr. Healy's rooms, dragged him summarily forth and beat him black and blue. She also threatened him with subsequent annihilation. Healy groaned forth his sorrow, but no sooner had she departed than he picked a quarrel with Mrs. Healy for standing by and seeing him thus severely chastised. Mrs. Healy is said to have replied with scant respect, when he up and kicked her forehead in in a very ungallant manner.

Mrs. Healy was taken to Bellevue Hospital, when it was found that her left frontal bone was broken. But as she had little taste for the higher forms of medical science, she departed without having the bone set.

[24 December 1894, p. 7.]

105 - TAKEN TO POTTER'S FIELD.

E mma Williams, young in years but old in experience, was a daughter of the slums.

For many months she had lived, the only woman in a strange company, in a windowless attic in what was once a fine mansion at No. 171 Thompson street. In the wretched apartment are a stove and several cots, occupied at night by the men members of the community.

Nicolo Alettiero, a white-faced little old man, was known as Emma's protector. Alettiero never did any work.

The woman had been dying of consumption for months. She went to the New York Hospital for treatment for a month last summer. After that she lay on her cot and had no doctor.

A policeman at her own request notified the Department of Charities and Correction of her condition the day after New Year's. A sick wagon was sent to convey her to the Charity Hospital. She refused at the last minute to leave Nicolo Alettiero.

Emma died on Jan. 15. Alettiero informed Policeman Brooks, who reported the case at the Mercer Street Station, whence a message was sent to the Coroner's office.

The Coroner was very busy, and he forgot all about poor Emma Williams. The neighbors, some of whom are already ill, complained to the police about it late yesterday and a second notice was sent to the Coroner.

A permit for removing the body was finally sent to the Morgue, and late last night, and none too soon, some men, who did not remove their hats, nailed up Emma Williams's wasted body in a pine box and took it away to the Potter's Field.

Nicolo Alettiero and his companions watched the proceedings with expressionless faces.

[18 January 1895, p. 14.]

106 - DID HE BLOW OUT THE GAS?

A shabbily dressed man who was without an overcoat registered as John Smith on Thursday night at the Bryant Park Hotel, No. 660 Sixth avenue, and was assigned to a bedroom. The hotel porter, John Meyer, detected gas escaping from the room yesterday and burst open the door. Smith was lying dead on the bed. In his pocket was a Knight of Labor card, with the names of C. O'Neill, of Yonkers, N.Y., and Paul Vaderok; also a slip of paper bearing the name of Michael Coback, No. 15 Centre street, McKeesport, Pa. The body was taken to the Morgue. The hotel people think that it was an accident.

[16 February 1895, p. 3.]

Theodore Dreiser's career as a newspaper reporter began in Chicago in June 1892, two months before his twenty-first birthday, and ended in New York in 1895—probably in March—when he was twenty-three. He had had a year at Indiana University in 1889–90, which was intellectually quickening but which made him feel socially inadequate. He was convinced that if he were to get ahead in the world it would have to be through some channel more direct than college—what exactly he did not know.

He returned to Chicago, where his family then lived, and worked at a succession of trivial jobs: as a real-estate agent, as the driver of a laundry wagon, as a bill collector for installment firms that sold cheap home furnishings to the poor. He was not paid much, but he was exposed daily to the colorful and turbulent street life of Chicago. What he saw awoke an urge to describe the world in which he found himself.

The death of his mother in November 1890 affected him profoundly. This was his first intimate encounter with death, and it gave him an enduring sense of the brevity of life. It also whetted his desire to secure as many of life's gifts as he could while there was time. Newspaper work, he concluded, would give him the chance to express himself and to gain fame and money as well.

For two or three years Dreiser had been a reader of "Sharps and Flats," Eugene Field's column in the *Chicago Daily News*. Admiring Field's realistic comments on city life, he "seethed to express" himself in the same way.[1] In the hope of becoming a reporter like Field or his fellow Chicagoans Brand Whitlock, George Ade, and Finley Peter Dunne, Dreiser began on his own to practice writing descriptions of events he had witnessed—accidents, shootings, fires—and, concluding that his versions were at least as good as those that got printed, he started to make the rounds of the leading newspapers. When he found that the editors had no time for a greenhorn, he laid siege to the *Daily Globe*, assuming that, as the city's smallest paper, it would be less particular about whom it hired. The short-lived *Globe* (1887–93) was a shabby operation. A morning paper running to an average of only eight pages an issue, it was poorly printed and crudely illustrated. Its owner was Michael Cassius McDonald, a rich, out-of-office Democratic politician, who published it to promote his own interests and to attack those of his Republican foes.

Every day Dreiser would turn up at the *Globe*, hoping to get a chance to cover a story and prove his worth. Invariably he would be told that there was nothing for him at the moment but that something might turn up. In his doggedness he became an office familiar. At last Harry Gissell, the editorial writer, made a curious proposal: if young Dreiser would peddle a novel Gissell had written, he could have a tryout as a reporter when the next job opened. Dreiser worked hard at this somewhat distasteful task and was paid off by being hired temporarily to help cover the June 1892 Democratic national convention. By pure luck he got a tip that the party powers were meeting privately to agree to hand the nomination to Grover Cleveland. With this advance information on the biggest story of the convention, he enabled the *Globe*, which "did not subscribe to the general news service . . . being too poor," not exactly to scoop its rivals but at least to keep abreast of them (chap. 11).

John Maxwell, the paper's cynical but kind-hearted copy editor, had taken a liking to the young cub and now showed him how to put his story into readable form. Then he persuaded the other editors to hire Dreiser as a regular fifteen-dollar-a-week reporter. Through the rest of the summer Dreiser gained some of the knowledge and experience essential to a reporter. Though he does not identify much of what he wrote during this period, one can assume that he covered routine news. He learned to satisfy the requirements of a city editor, and he developed a knack for ferreting out and writing the kinds of feature stories that 1890s newspapers and their readers fancied. In *Newspaper Days* he would remember:

> Journalism, even in Chicago, was still in that curious discursive stage, which loved long-winded yarns upon almost any topic. Nearly all news stories apparently were padded to make more of them, especially as to color and romance than they really deserved. . . . All specials were being written in imitation of the great novelists, particularly the then late Charles Dickens . . . who was the beau ideal of all newspapermen and editors and I presume magazine special writers. . . . The city editors wanted not so much bare facts, as became the rule later, as feature stories—color . . . romance—and although I did not myself see it clearly at the time I was their man. Write?—why I could write reams on any topic, once I discovered that I could write at all. [Chap. 12]

Working in this vein, he composed a graphic sketch of Chicago's vilest slum (No. 2), which won Maxwell's grudging praise: "Well, I think you're nutty but I believe you're a writer just the same. They ought to let you do more Sunday specials" (chap. 12).

Sometime that summer, probably late in July, the *Globe* hired a new city editor who was to have a significant influence on Dreiser's career. John T. McEnnis, once an admired St. Louis journalist, now on the downward slide of alcoholism, recognized Dreiser's gifts and urged him to find a berth on a better newspaper. McEnnis recommended his own former paper, the *St. Louis Globe-Democrat*, because its famed editor-in-chief, Joseph B. McCullagh, liked to develop and promote young talent.

Meanwhile, in the early fall, Dreiser was assigned to expose a chain of crooked auction shops that, with the benign indifference of the police, specialized in fleecing naive newcomers to the city. The object, of course, was to enable the *Globe* to embarrass the Republican administration, but for Dreiser it was a chance to do an impressive job on a difficult assignment. His articles (Nos. 4–6), together with his gathering of numerous man-in-the-street interviews for a visiting *Globe-Democrat* reporter who was a friend of McEnnis's, won him a job offer from McCullagh at a salary of twenty dollars a week. The job was to begin the first week of November.[2] Feeling as though life were going to do wonderful things for him, Dreiser quickly accepted the offer, even though it meant severing ties with his family and, what was more difficult, with a girl he was all but engaged to marry.

The *Globe-Democrat*, Republican in politics despite its name, was the most prestigious and prosperous morning paper in St. Louis. Under McCullagh's leadership it had expanded its national and foreign coverage by using wire services far more extensively than its rivals and had introduced several popular and innovative departments. Its thorough coverage of the states adjoining Missouri made it the most widely read paper in the central Mississippi Valley and in the Southwest. Housed in a new, elegantly appointed office building, the *Globe-Democrat* had on its staff some of the sharpest, most able reporters in the city. It also employed highly talented illustrators, who worked in the city's best-equipped art department, and its issues were printed on the most modern equipment available. Its daily edition ran to twelve pages and to sixteen on Saturday; its Sunday edition, thick with illustrated feature stories, profusely detailed society news, serialized fiction, humorous material, and a great quantity of advertising, often exceeded forty pages.

As was customary for a new man on a big-city paper, Dreiser was given a police precinct for a regular beat. Every day he reported to the station of the tough Third District, where he checked for news of neighborhood crimes, arrests, fires, and accidents. Along with his regular reporting, he was told to provide copy for the daily column "Heard in the Corridors." That regular feature consisted of comments or stories gleaned from passersby encountered in the city's hotels (Nos. 27–32). Dreiser, who had demonstrated his flair for interviewing while in Chicago, had no difficulty in gathering material—real or invented. He received no extra pay for this assignment, but it often gave the embryonic novelist a chance to try his hand at something resembling fiction.

Dreiser may have expected that McCullagh would tutor him, but he found that the famed editor preferred to remain aloof from his staff. Though he always refers to McCullagh reverently in *Newspaper Days*, their actual contacts appear to have been few and brief. Practical guidance seems to have come instead from Hugh Hartung, a likable, sympathetic copy editor. Daily assignments were issued by the curt city editor, Tobias Mitchell, to whom Dreiser took an instant dislike.

The editorial staff must have been satisfied with its new reporter's ability to grasp details and weave them effectively into stories, for he was early assigned to do a long Sunday feature on the new depot (No. 8) and one on the waterworks extension. Other indications of his value to the paper were his frequent assignments to interview visiting celebrities like Henry Watterson, the editor of the Louisville *Courier-Journal* (No. 9), and Annie Besant, the leading exponent of theosophy (No. 10), as well as such local celebrities as Ed Butler, the powerful Democratic boss (No. 16), after whom Dreiser would model one of his most memorable characters, Edward Malia Butler of *The Financier*.

Just as luck had given him a boost at the *Chicago Globe* when he had stumbled onto the news of Cleveland's forthcoming nomination, so at the *Globe-Democrat* his status was improved purely by chance when he got a tip on a train fire and explosion in a nearby Illinois town (Nos. 11 and 12). This gave his paper a major scoop. So pleased was McCullagh that he summoned Dreiser to his office and gave him a twenty-dollar bonus and a five-dollar raise.

Emboldened, Dreiser approached McCullagh a few days later about the position of drama critic, which had fallen open. He wanted the job because his literary interests—stimulated by an association with some young St. Louis bohemians—had now turned to play writing. McCullagh gave the position to the inexperienced Dreiser without hesitation, perhaps because his paper—unlike its chief rival, the *Republic*—never made much of theatrical doings. To Dreiser, however, it was an important step up; he now saw himself at the threshold of an exciting career, about to enter a "wonderworld. . . . To be a real dramatic critic—think of it—a person of weight and authority in this perfect realm!" (chap. 31).

His dreams of glory came to nothing. Some of the most accomplished actors and actresses of the day performed in St. Louis during this period, but Dreiser's critical discernment was so immature that he had little of worth to say in his notices. Furthermore, the paper gave him scant opportunity to improve his skill. Mitchell's attitude seems to have been that if Dreiser wanted to review plays, he had to do it in addition to his regular duties.

Dreiser's critical naïveté and the demands of other assignments were, in fact, the cause of his abrupt departure from the *Globe-Democrat* a few months later, at the end of April 1893, after two faked reviews (see the notes for Nos. 39 and 42) had exposed McCullagh to ridicule by rival papers.

Dreiser was so certain that he would be fired after his second blunder, and so ashamed to have embarrassed his chief, that he wrote him a short apologetic note and never returned to work. He was convinced that he had lost his chance for a brilliant career: "Alas, for all my fine dreams, my great future, my standing in this man's eyes and on this paper!" (chap. 35).

He brooded alone for several days until the need to earn money—enough at least to get out of St. Louis—drove him to apply for a job with the *Republic*, in his eyes a very demeaning step down. The *Republic* had a prestigious history, tracing its descent from the first English-language newspaper published west of the Mississippi, but its plant, located in an old business district, was now run-down, its offices were shabby, and its equipment was worn. Though it carried on a running circulation battle with the *Globe-Democrat*, its format was not as trim and eye-catching, its coverage of national and international news not as thorough, and its departments not as innovative.

On the other hand, it gave more prominence to city news, always printing important local stories in detail on the front page. (The *Globe-Democrat*, by contrast, ran city news on pages 3 and 4.) The *Republic* played up sensation and scandal, and its accounts of local events made livelier reading than the more restrained versions in the *Globe-Democrat*. A story to which McCullagh's paper might give a half-column on a back page was often front-page news in the *Republic*. The papers were political rivals as well: the *Republic* was strongly pro-Democratic, although it regularly excoriated machine politicians and the bossism of Democrat Ed Butler.

The guiding spirit at the city desk was the forceful, eccentric Harry B. Wandell, whom Dreiser describes as a quintessential yellow journalist. Widely read, with tastes that ran to realistic fiction, Wandell frequently exhorted his reporters to emulate Balzac and Zola. "He was at once a small and yet a large man mentally—wise and incisive in many ways—petty and even venomous in others—a man to coddle and placate should you chance to find yourself beholden to him—one to avoid if you were not, but on the whole a man above the average in ability. . . . He then had the reputation of being one of the best city editors in the city" (chap. 36).

After giving Dreiser a trial assignment, Wandell hired him at eighteen dollars a week and assigned him again to the Third District. Dreiser never had more than a few small raises during his ten months with this paper, but his claim that he came to be regarded as a star reporter is sustained by the number and importance of the stories he was given to cover. The *Republic* gave him good opportunities to develop his skills. He was allowed to spread himself, as the length of many of his stories demonstrates. Wandell gave him the most difficult assignments with the injunction: "Write it all up. . . . Write a good, strong introduction for it, you know—all the facts in the first paragraph and then go on and tell your story. You can have as much space

as you want for that—a column, column and a half—or two, just as it runs"
(chap. 36).

Dreiser's usefulness to the paper is evidenced by the range of events he covered: murders, a major fire, the opening of a new railroad route, train robberies and wrecks, a lynching and an execution, a Sunday-school convention, and a society ball. He also turned out descriptions of slum life, exposés of confidence men, and portrayals of colorful St. Louisans.

Dreiser was versatile. Told by Wandell to write a series of humorous articles to publicize a charity baseball game, Dreiser handled the assignment to everyone's satisfaction, even though a flair for humor—as he was quick to admit—was one gift he had been denied. What he did, one gathers, was adapt for his reports some of the venerable comic routines he had seen in variety shows. Though breezy and sophomoric, the articles were a hit and won Dreiser some local fame.

As a reward he was given the task of squiring a group of young St. Louis schoolteachers, winners of the paper's popularity contest, to the Columbian Exposition at the 1893 Chicago World's Fair. All he had to do was write up their adventures, and then he could enjoy himself at the fair. As it turned out, the mission was fraught with future significance, for one of these teachers, Sara Osborne White, was in a few years to become his wife. In fact it was largely as a consequence of his deepening attachment to her that he at last left the *Republic* and St. Louis to try for better things.

Despite Dreiser's proven value to the paper, the management was reluctant to raise his salary. He knew that he could not support a wife on a little more than twenty dollars a week, so he decided to investigate a fellow reporter's scheme to purchase jointly a small rural newspaper in northwestern Ohio. His employers now offered him a raise and even the chance to do some editorial writing, but they were too late. On 4 March 1894, at the age of twenty-two, with a small nest egg and a letter of introduction from the *Republic*, he left St. Louis half-decided to become a country editor.

Once he had sized up the situation in Weston, Ohio, the slow-moving community in which the newspaper was located, Dreiser concluded that such a career was not for him. The equipment was in poor repair and would require a heavy outlay of money to be put into working order. The leading citizens showed small interest in having a newspaper and gave little promise of advertising support. So Dreiser parted from his friend and went on to investigate the prospects in nearby Toledo.

Inquiring at the *Toledo Blade*, he met Arthur Henry, the city editor, who several years later would play a key role in the composition of *Sister Carrie*. The two struck up an instant friendship, but Henry could give him only one-shot assignments to cover a traction strike and a society art show (Nos. 80–84). With a promise from Henry of a full-time job if one opened up soon, Dreiser moved on.

His exact whereabouts during most of April are not clear. Perhaps he swung back to St. Louis to visit Sara White, for a second letter of introduction from the *Republic* suggests that he was again in the city on 2 April. From the 16th to the 22d he was apparently in Cleveland, peddling his services to the *Leader,* which took brief pieces at space rate (No. 85). But Cleveland had little to offer; to Dreiser it was only another dull industrial city controlled by the rich. Buffalo, where he went next, was a lesser Cleveland, so he turned to Pittsburgh. With its glistening rivers and many bridges, its fiery mills and polyglot population, Pittsburgh seemed to be enchantingly different from any metropolis he had seen so far: "a city for a realist to work and dream in" (chap. 68). Here he received a friendly reception from Harry Gaither, the city editor of the *Pittsburg Dispatch,* a thriving Republican morning paper (whose masthead reflects the former spelling of the city's name). In a few days, he was taken on at twenty-five dollars a week.

Dreiser was immediately set straight about the rigidly limited areas to which a Pittsburgh paper was expected to confine itself. This city seethed with social discontent and labor strife, and there were starker contrasts here between the rich and the poor than he had yet seen. Nonetheless, no word critical of the established order was to be printed.

> "We don't touch on labor conditions here except through our labor man," [Gaither] told me, "and he knows what to say. . . . There's nothing to be said about the rich or religion, except in a favorable sense. They're all right in so far as we know. We don't touch on scandals in high life. The big steel men here just about own this place so we can't. . . . Some papers out West and down in New York, I know, go in for sensationalism but we don't. I'd rather have some simple little feature if I could, a story about some old fellow with eccentric habits of some kind than any of these scandals or tragedies any time. Of course we do cover them when we have to but we have to be mighty careful what we say." [Chap. 72]

The efforts of the working class to improve its lot through political agitation, if touched on at all, were disparaged or satirized. When reformers and radicals like Jacob Coxey or Johann Most came to town, they were invariably ridiculed.

As his regular beat, Dreiser was given the city hall and general hospital and police station of Allegheny, an adjoining community, known today as Northside. His daily rounds took little time, so he was often free to browse in the Allegheny public library. Here he began to read Balzac's novels and then the essays of Thomas Henry Huxley, John Tyndall, and Herbert Spencer—works that brought on a crisis of belief and left permanently shaken the religious faith that had been inculcated by the Catholic teachings of his childhood. These readings led him reluctantly to the conclusion that, in the total scheme of things, the individual counts for nothing:

> Up to this time there had been a blazing and unchecked desire to get on, and the feeling that in doing so we did get somewhere. Now in its place was the definite conviction that spiritually one got nowhere, that there was no hereafter, that one lived and had his being because he had to and that it was of no import, no more so than that of any bug or rat. Of his ideals, his struggles, deprivations, sorrows as well as joys, it could only be said that they were chemic compulsions, something which for some inexplicable but unimportant reason responded to and resulted from the hope of pleasure and the fear of pain. He was a mechanism, undevised and uncreated, and a badly and carelessly driven one at that. [Chap. 85]

At this time the *Dispatch* was running a daily column of light, semi-humorous commentary on topics of local interest to which Dreiser submitted a sample sketch about patients in the Allegheny General Hospital (No. 87). The sketch was well received, and he continued to make occasional contributions. These pieces (Nos. 87–97) contain some of the most mature writing he had yet done; though sentimental, they reveal a thoughtful, reflective response to his world, a sensitivity to sights, sounds, and colors, a compassion for the poor, the sorrowful, the victims of injustice. They hint also at his private ideas about the apparent lack of meaning in life and are sometimes pervaded by a gloomy, funereal tone that he feared the editor would dislike.

Dreiser sent some of these articles to his brother Paul, by then an established songwriter and comic actor in New York. When Dreiser visited him later, at the end of July or in early August, the high-spirited Paul urged him to move to New York, where he could surely get a good job on a paper: "Wait'll you're here a little while, Sport. You'll be like every one else. There'll be just one place—New York" (chap. 79). The effect of such talk and of the city's allure was to fix in Dreiser the ambition to count for something here. Back in Pittsburgh he began setting aside all the money he could from his salary in order to sustain himself while he was getting established in New York. Toward the end of November, having amassed $240, he set out to make a place for himself in the most fiercely competitive newspaper system in the country.

His resolve almost misgave him when he began to apply at such formidable institutions as the *Herald*, the *World*, and the *Sun*. The winter weather, cold and wet, did little for a self-confidence badly shaken by brassy office boys who were told to turn away all job seekers with an unequivocal "No vacancy." Faced with a similar situation a little over two years before, he had laid siege to Chicago's poorest paper, the *Globe*; now he decided to make an all-out assault on New York's best, the *World*. Plucking up courage, he pushed past the outraged office boys and into the crowded city room, where, somehow, he made a favorable impression on Arthur Brisbane, one of Joseph Pulitzer's brightest columnists. Brisbane told the city editor to give Dreiser a job.

It looked as if the young reporter might be about to repeat his pattern of success at other papers, but the atmosphere at the *World* was unlike any he had known before. In this milieu his earlier newspaper triumphs seemed small-town stuff. Here everyone worked in the spirit of ferocious competitiveness fostered by Pulitzer himself. If Dreiser were to retain his foothold, he would have to prove himself immediately, for the *World* was quick to replace the unsatisfactory. If he were to write feature stories here, he would have to compete with nationally known writers like James Creelman, David Graham Phillips, George Cary Eggleston, and Nellie Bly.

Also dismaying was the fact that he had not been hired at a regular salary but at space rates. For any story of his that was printed he would be paid thirty-three cents a column inch, with a supplemental fifty cents an hour for the time spent on legwork. Worse yet was his discovery that substantial stories were hardly ever given to space-raters. The few promising tips that came his way during his first weeks were either dead ends or were so slight that it would have taken more ingenuity and audacity than he could muster to puff them into something sensational. Soon a "crushing sense of incompetence and general inefficiency" settled upon him (chap. 89).

His morale sagged lower when, apparently still at space rate, he was given the rounds of Bellevue Hospital, a nearby police station, the city morgue, and various wards of the New York Charities Department—places where each day he faced "as disagreeable and depressing a series of scenes as it is possible for a human being to witness" (chap. 91). More appalling still was the heartless exploitation of the helpless by the very people who were supposed to protect them—doctors, police, city officials. The world Dreiser viewed during the winter of 1894–95 was so squalid, pathetic, and tragic that he became wholly disenchanted with the role of reporter.

In truth, the *World* was wasting Dreiser's talents by giving him such dreary assignments, for he was by now a skilled reporter, not a mere footslogging newsgatherer. Given more encouragement he might have written interpretive articles or editorials that the *World* could have used. (Indeed, only a few months later he would be writing such things regularly as the editor of *Ev'ry Month*, the magazine issued by his brother Paul's music-publishing house.) To add to his frustration, when he did manage to dredge a promising story out of the "messy and heartless world" of his daily round (chap. 89), he was usually told to hand the facts over to someone who would rewrite them, someone on regular salary. He complained to his editor one day and was told bluntly that the paper did not consider him to be of much use. It seemed better to quit the newspaper game and to pursue some other line of writing, perhaps for magazines. First, however, Dreiser took his

troubles to Brisbane, who counseled him to try the *Sun,* which was known
as a good school for young reporters. Dreiser applied there, but to no avail.
Finally, probably in early March 1895, he left the *World,* vowing never
again to earn his living as a reporter.[3]

What were the consequences of two-and-a-half years of newspaper writing to Dreiser? It is tempting to look through his articles for sources of the
later fiction: to infer that Nos. 17 and 18, for example, are the germ of *The
Hand of the Potter;* to recognize Nos. 73 and 74 as the source of "Nigger
Jeff"; to catch in No. 106 an intimation of Hurstwood's final gesture of
despair. But this early work did more than provide material for Dreiser's
mature fiction. These few years gave him a close look at levels of society,
kinds of experience, types of Americans that he could not have obtained in
any other line of work. What he observed darkened his outlook. It made
him see the overwhelming power wielded by big money in its own behalf,
the prevalence of corruption in places of authority, and the possibilities of
failure and tragedy in ordinary life. *Newspaper Days* registers the memory
of Dreiser's shock at these revelations. Repeatedly he refers in the book to
the distance between the rich and the poor and to the disparities between
sanctioned social values and actual everyday behavior. Being a reporter
gave Dreiser more awareness of the ugly realities of urban life than was
possessed by any other young American novelist of the 1890s, with the possible exception of Stephen Crane.

Dreiser's failure as a reporter may have been fortunate, for if he had
succeeded in the tough world of New York journalism, his inevitable over-
exposure to human misery might have turned him into the kind of case-
hardened cynic so often found among his fellow reporters. And although
newspaper work left him embittered toward the American press, at least it
convinced him that he was going to be a writer. His brief tenure as a reporter compelled him to look for more nearly literary ways of practicing his
calling. The seasoning effect of newspaper work must also be considered:
the many articles, the hundreds of thousands of words, habituated him to
the business of putting facts, ideas, and impressions on paper. As a young
man with literary ambitions, he did not merely think about being a writer—
he wrote. By his twenty-fourth birthday he had acquired a professional
competence for a broad range of journalistic writing.

Working for newspapers, Dreiser learned most of the writer's basic craft.
Later, in the process of making his own novels, he would discover for himself much about the composition of long fiction, but in learning how to
satisfy copy editors he acquired fundamental concepts of narrative art that
would serve him well throughout his career. Good writing, he came to recognize, must first of all be informative. Editors who insisted upon the mar-
shaling of facts made him see that details give body to a story. Editors who
demanded "color" trained him to be selective, to look for particularly vivid

and atmospheric elements. And the need to address an undifferentiated audience compelled him to write simply and clearly, yet with dramatic appeal.

The need to turn out large quantities of copy on demand may also have had harmful results. Newspaper work may have given Dreiser the not altogether salutary conviction that he could write well on any subject and, perhaps, the notion that anything he wrote could be shaped by an editor into something worth reading. Working under the constant pressure of deadlines did not beget a self-critical commitment to style. Unswerving attention to the who, what, when, where, and why develops a concern for accuracy, but not for the well-chosen word.

Despite such side effects, the newspaper was still virtually the only writing school available in the 1890s to young people who had literary ambitions. It was a good school, for the job of making readable news stories out of raw data is not unlike the novelist's task of transmuting reality into fiction. Although his newspaper days convinced Dreiser that he himself was not to be a journalist, he could still recommend newspaper work to aspiring writers. To one such apprentice, some thirty years later, he wrote:

> The value of a thorough knowledge of the fundamental principles of journalism, to a person seriously considering the avocation of writing, cannot be overemphasized. A journalist sees many aspects of life and finds his experiences in that field a valuable adjunct to the correct expression of thought.[4]

NOTES

1. Chap. 1 of *Newspaper Days*. All quotations from *Newspaper Days* are taken from the forthcoming Pennsylvania Dreiser Edition and will hereafter be cited parenthetically by chapter numbers in the text.

2. In the manuscript of *Newspaper Days*, Dreiser asserts that he arrived in St. Louis in the *middle* of November, though the 1922 printed version simply says, "The time was November, 1892" (p. 88). The termination of the series of articles on the fake auction shops by 26 October suggests strongly that he actually went to St. Louis on Sunday, 30 October.

3. An early March date is suggested by the appearance (on 8 March 1895 in the New York *World*, p. 12, col. 2) of "Doubtless Susie Martin's Skull," which of all the news items printed from January through April comes closest to being about "a missing girl whose body was found at the morgue." When Dreiser was compelled to turn this story over to a rewrite man, he finally decided to quit being a reporter.

4. To Dwight Sidney Gaffney, 22 May 1927. Dreiser Collection, University of Pennsylvania Library.

HISTORICAL NOTES

Notes are supplied here for passages in the text that are in need of explanation. Included are identifications of unfamiliar persons, places, and events as well as definitions of obscure terms or phrases. Brief identifications are supplied of several now-forgotten celebrities and of several no longer familiar catch phrases. Figures of the past whose names are still generally known have not been identified, for example, Grover Cleveland, William McKinley, Herbert Spencer, and John L. Sullivan. Unfamiliar allusions to and quotations from poems, plays, and old popular songs have been identified. Follow-up developments for certain stories have been indicated when the newspapers themselves reveal these details within the span of Dreiser's employment. A few unidentifiable names and inexplicable terms are allowed to stand, usually without comment: for example, Wingrave Cook (No. 72), T. J. Wallace (No. 64), life-marks (No. 54), and the Mexican frog idea (No. 91). Each note begins with a page-line reference to the location of the passage in this volume.

The majority of articles included in this volume have been attributed to Dreiser on the basis of references in *Newspaper Days*. Boni and Liveright published a cut-down and expurgated version of this autobiographical volume in 1922 as *A Book about Myself*, a title used through the first six impressions. The seventh impression of 1931 was retitled *Newspaper Days*, the title Dreiser preferred, but the text, printed from the original plates, was unchanged. A new edition of *Newspaper Days*, with cut and expurgated materials restored, is in preparation for the Pennsylvania Dreiser Edition. Rather than refer, in the Historical Notes and the Notes on Attribution, to the 1922 text by page number, I have chosen here to refer by chapter number to the forthcoming Pennsylvania text. Most of the chapters in *Newspaper Days* are relatively brief; this system of reference should not unduly inconvenience the reader. In the notes that follow, *Newspaper Days* is abbreviated as *ND*. Headlines and datelines are counted in assigning page-line references; running heads, centered three-em rules, lines of asterisks, and blank lines are not counted.

SOURCES

The principal sources of information about Dreiser's life used in the preparation of this edition are as follows:

Dreiser, Theodore. *A Traveler at Forty.* New York: Century, 1913.
————. *A Hoosier Holiday.* New York: John Lane, 1916.
————. *Twelve Men.* New York: Boni and Liveright, 1919.
————. *Newspaper Days.* New York: Horace Liveright, 1931.
————. *Dawn.* New York: Horace Liveright, 1931.
Elias, Robert H. *Theodore Dreiser: Apostle of Nature* (1948); emended ed. Ithaca, N.Y.: Cornell Univ. Press, 1970.
Swanberg, W. A. *Dreiser.* New York: Scribner's, 1965.

In addition to the *OED, Webster's Second* and *Third International* dictionaries (hereafter cited as *W2* and *W3*), and various editions of the *Encyclopaedia Britannica,* information in the notes has been drawn from the following reference works:

Barnhart, Clarence L., ed. *The New Century Handbook of English Literature.* Rev. ed. New York: Meredith, 1967.
Bartlett, John. *Familiar Quotations.* 14th ed. Boston: Little, Brown, 1968.
Berrey, Lester V., and Melvin Van Den Berk. *The American Thesaurus of Slang.* 2d ed. New York: Crowell, 1952. Also 1st ed., 1942.
Biographical Directory of the American Congress 1774–1961. Washington, D.C.: GPO, 1961.
Burke, W. J., and Will D. Howe. *American Authors and Books 1640–1940.* New York: Gramercy, 1943.
Claghorn, Charles Eugene. *Biographical Dictionary of American Music.* West Nyack, N.Y.: Parker, 1973.
Cox, James. *Old and New St. Louis.* St. Louis: Central Biographical Publishing, 1894.
Craigie, Sir William A., and James R. Hulbert. *A Dictionary of American English on Historical Principles.* Chicago: Univ. of Chicago Press, 1938–44.
Dictionary of American Biography. New York: Scribner's, 1928–81.
Hartnoll, Phyllis, ed. *The Oxford Companion to the Theatre.* 3d. ed. London: Oxford Univ. Press, 1967.
Herzberg, Max J., et al. *The Reader's Encyclopedia of American Literature.* New York: Crowell, 1962.
Marks, Edward B. *They All Sang: From Tony Pastor to Rudy Vallée.* New York: Viking, 1934.
Mathews, Mitford M. *A Dictionary of Americanisms on Historical Principles.* Chicago: Univ. of Chicago Press, 1951.
The National Cyclopaedia of American Biography. New York: James T. White, 1898–1981.
The New York Times Theater Reviews 1886–1895. New York: New York Times & Arno Press, 1975.
Odell, George C. D. *Annals of the New York Stage.* Vol. 15. New York: Columbia Univ. Press, 1949.
Partridge, Eric. *A Dictionary of Catch Phrases.* New York: Stein and Day, 1977.
————. *A Dictionary of Slang and Unconventional English.* 8th ed. New York: Macmillan, 1984.
Pizer, Donald, Richard W. Dowell, and Frederic E. Rusch. *Theodore Dreiser: A Primary and Secondary Bibliography.* Boston: G. K. Hall, 1975.

Shepard, Leslie A. *Encyclopedia of Occultism and Parapsychology.* Detroit: Gale Research, 1978.

Sobel, Robert, and John Raime, eds. *Biographical Directory of the Governors of the United States.* Westport, Conn.: Meckler Books, 1978.

Webster's Biographical Dictionary. Springfield, Mass.: G. & C. Merriam, 1972.

Wentworth, Harold, and Stuart Berg Flexner, eds. *Dictionary of American Slang.* 2d ed. New York: Crowell, 1975.

Who Was Who in America. Chicago: A. N. Marquis, 1943–81.

Young, William C. *Famous Actors and Actresses of the American Stage.* New York: Bowker, 1975.

1. CLEVELAND AND GRAY THE TICKET.

3.1 The text for this *Globe* item is in a unique file once owned by the Chicago Public Library but now lost. This transcription has been made from a photocopy kindly supplied by Blair F. Bigelow. According to Dreiser, John Maxwell, the *Globe* copy editor, helped him shape this first story by writing "an intelligent introduction" for the piece (*ND*, chap. 11). The persons named were all prominent Democrats of the 1890s. *Leon Abbett* (1836–94) was governor of New Jersey (1883–85 and 1889–93). *Arthur Pue Gorman* (1839–1906) was U.S. senator from Maryland (1881–99 and again from 1903 until his death). *Isaac Pusey Gray* (1828–95) was governor of Indiana (1885–89) and U.S. minister to Mexico (1893–95). *David Bennett Hill* (1843–1910) was governor of New York (1885–91) and U.S. senator (1892–97). *Daniel Wolsey Voorhees* (1827–97) was U.S. representative from Indiana (1861–65, 1869–73, and 1877–97). *William Collins Whitney* (1841–1904) was Grover Cleveland's secretary of the navy (1885–89) as well as one of his close advisers during the 1892 convention. *William Lyne Wilson* (1843–1900) was U.S. senator from Maryland (1883–95) and postmaster general (1895–97).

3.19 The lines in the source text are so badly smudged at this point that they are entirely unreadable. Presumably, however, they state that Whitney indicated that Cleveland had enough votes committed to him to win nomination on the first ballot and that William C. Owen of Kentucky would be named temporary chairman. Such are the facts reported by other newspapers. See, for example, "Watterson Elects His Man" and "Whitney Says One Ballot," *New York Herald*, 21 June 1892, p. 7.

3.31 The vice-presidential nomination went instead to Adlai E. Stevenson (1835–1914), U.S. representative from Illinois (1875–77 and 1879–81). For an account of the issues, rivalries, and personalities of this convention, see Ellis Paxson Oberholtzer, *A History of the United States since the Civil War* (New York: Macmillan, 1937), 5:189–235.

2. CHEYENNE, HAUNT OF MISERY AND CRIME.

5.8 **Cheyenne** "Little Cheyenne had been named for the town in Wyoming, known as the wickedest in the nation while the Northern Pacific Railroad was being built." See Lloyd Wendt and Herman Kogan, *Lords of the Levee* (Garden City, N.Y.: Garden City Publ. Co., 1944), p. 25.

5.17 **Arabians** Hucksters or street vendors, "esp. those who possess a Central European or Middle Eastern cast of countenance" (Wentworth & Flexner).

4. SWINDLERS.

8.34 **cappers** A pitchman's assistants who make false purchases so that real buying will begin; shills. **pluggers** Paid enthusiasts who extol the value of worthless watches to suckers. **jay** One who is easy to dupe, usually someone with a rural or small-town background.

9.30 **fly cops** Detectives or plainclothes police.

9.32 **Gaelic association** On 25 September the police, under a Sunday blue-law edict issued by Mayor Washburne, prevented two teams of the Gaelic Athletic Association from playing a hurling match. See "Execute the Threat," *Chicago Daily Tribune*, 26 September 1892, p. 1.

9.32 **Marlowe opera-house** A theater in Englewood, a south Chicago suburb, which had been pressured by churchgoers and a citizens' committee into not giving Sunday performances. Dreiser's interest in this controversy may have been aroused by the fact that the theatrical company in which his brother Paul was an actor was scheduled to open at the Marlowe in *The Danger Signal* on Sunday, 23 October. See "Curtain Goes Down," *Chicago Daily Tribune*, 22 August 1892, p. 3.

9.33 **Garfield Park** Site of a racetrack that was run by friends of the owner of the *Globe* and that the police, pressured by rival racetrack proprietors, succeeded in closing down; scene the previous 6 September of a sensational raid in which a gambler and two policemen were killed. See "A Bloody Battle," *St. Louis Globe-Democrat*, 7 September 1892, p. 1.

9.37 **Steve Douglas** Stephen A. Douglas, Jr. (1850–1908), son of the famous Illinois senator, formerly city prosecutor and by 1892 the attorney for political rivals of the owner of the *Globe*.

5. FAKES.

12.23 **snap** Something of no value (*W2*).

12.27 **terra cotta** The "official color" of the Columbian Exposition.

6. ARRESTED.

13.19 This experience appears to be the principal basis for an episode Dreiser describes in chap. 14 of *ND:* "In company with a private detective and several times with McEnnis, I personally served warrants of arrest, accompanied the sharpers to police headquarters, where they were immediately released on bail, and then ran to the office to write out my impressions of all I had seen, repeating conversations as near as I could remember, describing uncouth faces and bodies of crooks, police and detectives, and by sly innuendo indicating what a farce and sham the whole seeming interest of the police was."

15.33 The week of 16 October saw the formal dedication of the Columbian Exposition, marked by festivities that attracted large crowds of visitors to Chicago.

7. THE RETURN OF GENIUS.

17.39 "I even essayed a few parables of my own, mild, poetic commentaries on I scarcely recall what, which Maxwell [the *Globe* copyreader] scanned with a suspicious and even scowling eye at first but later deigned to publish, affixing the signature of Carl Dreiser . . . because he had decided to nickname me Carl" (*ND*, chap. 13).

8. GREATEST IN THE WORLD.

26.34 **slay line** Has no meaning as an architectural term. *W3* defines *slay* (also spelled *sley* and *sleigh*) as (1) a weaver's reed and (2) a movable frame in a loom that carries the reed. Perhaps Dreiser learned the term *slay line* from his father, "a weaver by trade" (*Dawn*, p. 4) and is using it here in some metaphorical sense that seemed appropriate to him.

9. MR. WATTERSON ON POLITICS.

32.1 Henry Watterson (1840–1921), of the Louisville *Courier-Journal*, an inveterate Democrat, had applauded his party's 1892 platform but had opposed bitterly the nomination of Grover Cleveland. The other persons named in the inteview were all politically prominent in the 1890s. *Thomas Francis Bayard* (1828–98), U.S. senator from Delaware and secretary of state during Cleveland's first term, was ambassador to Great Britain (1893–97). *John Griffin Carlisle* (1835–1910) of Kentucky served in Congress (1877–93), and as secretary of the treasury (1893–97). *Bourke Cockran* (1854–1923), an influential New York lawyer, politician, and orator, served several terms as U.S. representative from 1887 to 1923. *Patrick Andrew Collins* (1844–1905), U.S. representative from Massachusetts (1883–88), was U.S. consul in London (1893–97). *James Biddle Eustis* (1834–99), Louisiana state senator (1877–79 and 1885–91), was minister to France (1893–97). *David Rowland Francis* (1850–1927) was governor of Missouri (1889–93) and U.S. secretary of the interior (1896–97). *George Gray* (1840–1925) was U.S. senator from Delaware (1885–99). *Isaac Pusey Gray* (1828–95) was governor of Indiana (1885–89) and U.S. minister to Mexico (1893–95). *David Bennett Hill* (1843–1910) was governor of New York (1885–91) and U.S. senator (1892–97). *John Percival Jones* (1829–1912) was U.S. senator from Nevada (1873–1903). *Daniel Scott Lamont* (1851–1901) was Cleveland's private secretary (1885–89) and secretary of war (1893–97). *Edward Murphy, Jr.* (1834–1911), was U.S. senator from New York (1893–99). *Edward John Phelps* (1822–1900) was U.S. minister to Great Britain (1885–89). *William Morris Stewart* (1827–1909) was U.S. senator from Nevada (1864–75 and 1887–1905). *Henry Moore Teller* (1830–1914), U.S. senator from Colorado (1876–82 and 1885–1909), was President Chester Arthur's secretary of the interior (1882–85). *William Collins Whitney* (1841–1904), financier, politician, and sportsman, was one of Cleveland's closest advisers and his secretary of the navy (1885–89). *Edward Oliver Wolcott* (1848–1905) was U.S. senator from Colorado (1889–1901).

32.4   In his lecture, which Dreiser may have attended and reported on, Watterson expressed qualified optimism about the nation's future but warned that the desire for money dominant in most young Americans "could possibly wreck the republic." See "'Money and Morals,'" *St. Louis Globe-Democrat*, 7 January 1893, p. 7.

10. THEOSOPHY AND SPIRITUALISM.

36.2   Annie Besant, *nee* Wood (1847–1933), English theosophist and advocate of Indian home rule; devotee of Madame Blavatsky and president of the Theosophical Society from 1907 until her death.

37.13 *Reincarnation* (1892), one of Mrs. Besant's numerous theosophical studies, had just been published.

11. BURNED TO DEATH.

46.16 In 1892 Nancy Hanks, a trotting horse, covered the mile in the record time of 2.04 minutes.

47.19 Ten additional paragraphs in cols. 1 and 2 of p. 2 have been omitted because they are reports from areas outside Alton and Wann, which Dreiser could not have covered. In chap. 29 of *ND*, Dreiser records that "in my eagerness to give a full, brilliant account I impressed the services of Dick [Wood] himself, who wrote for me such phases of the thing as he had seen." Wood's contribution might have been the five concluding paragraphs reprinted here, for they are separated from the main story by a rule and by the heading "Some of the Witnesses." Contrary to Dreiser's assertion, the *Globe-Democrat* carried no editorial praising itself for its skill "in handling these matters and commiserating the helplessness of the other journals under such trying circumstances."

12. SIXTEEN DEAD.

47.33 The last fatality count given by the *Globe-Democrat* appeared on 6 February 1893: "Thirty-first Death at Alton Junction" (p. 3).

15. AN HYPNOTIC SEANCE.

61.22 The "well-known skeptic" is probably Dick Wood, who came from Bloomington, Ill. See *ND*, chap. 22.

16. MAJ. BANNERMAN EXPLAINS HIS DEFEAT— COL. BUTLER RETIRES FROM POLITICS.

63.26 Chester Harding Krum, a former St. Louis circuit court judge high in the Democratic council, wrote a letter to the party chairman late in the campaign criticizing Bannerman for his unwillingness to be identified with the politicians who had secured the nomination for him. A reporter filched a copy of this letter from Krum's office, and it was printed in the *Globe-Democrat*; see "The Local Campaign," 28 March 1893, p. 1. See also *ND*, chap. 26.

64.6 Marcus Bernheimer, a leader of the German-Jewish Democrats of St. Louis, refused to support Bannerman's candidacy because, he claimed, the party convention had been so rigged that his own campaign for the mayoral nomination had been stifled. He made his view known to the Democratic chairman in a letter that the *Globe-Democrat* printed; see "Last Night's Democratic Rally—A Bombshell from Bernheimer," 26 March 1893, p. 5.

17. A GIRL FRIGHTFULLY OUTRAGED.

66.17 A brief item in the *Globe-Democrat* of 19 April 1893, p. 11, indicates that Schwartzman was sentenced to the penitentiary for seven years for criminally assaulting the girl, whose last name is there given as *Americk*.

22. IRREGULARLY ISSUED.

70.23 **chip basket** A basket for wood chips.

72.32 The only follow-ups to this story are brief items in the *Globe-Democrat* of 8 February 1893, p. 2, and 9 February 1893, p. 9, stating that the coroner had ruled the baby had died naturally of "congestion of the brain" and that Mrs. Daly was missing and sought by the police.

23. KIDNAPED FROM ST. ANN'S.

74.2 A brief follow-up to this story in the *Globe-Democrat* of 9 February 1893, p. 9, indicates that Mrs. Lambkin returned the baby to the asylum after Captain Joyce of the Third District Police Station threatened to arrest her.

24. BREAD WAR IN LITTLE RUSSIA.

74.6 **Carondelet** A suburb in south St. Louis. See Dreiser's brief but pungent description of the Jewish neighborhood of the Third District in chap. 37 of *ND*.

25. SHOT BY A MAD HUSBAND.

76.26 Probably City Hospital is meant rather than the emergency hospital known as the **Dispensary,** because Dr. Heine Marks, the head of City Hospital, is present.

77.38 A brief *Globe-Democrat* follow-up of 23 February 1893, p. 9, relates that Borrman was released on $3,000 bond, that Mrs. Borrman was "getting along nicely" and would recover, and that Reagan "does not blame Borrman, and says he deserved being shot." A short item on p. 5 of the following day's issue notes that Borrman was "Charged with Assault to Kill."

28. [ALBERT JONES]

80.24 **wrapped . . . dreams** See "Thanatopsis," ll. 80–81.

29. [PAUL DRESSER]

81.5 This anecdote appears to be a complete fabrication. There is no corroborative evidence to indicate that Paul ever worked in a powder mill. Probably he was not even in St. Louis at this time. It is more likely that he was touring with his theatrical company, which did not come to the city until the second week of February 1893.

32. [OLNEY WADE]

84.25 **He had drunk himself literally to death. . . .** Aaberg was a former co-worker of Dreiser's in Chicago in the early 1890s (see *Dawn,* pp. 341–46). He was still alive on 19 October 1921 when he wrote Dreiser that he had stopped drinking in 1904 and had not had "a day of trouble of any serious nature since" (Dreiser Collection).

33. THE THEATERS.

85.11 **Paul Dreiser** Perhaps an inadvertent slip of the pen caused Dreiser to use his brother's actual name here. Elsewhere in his newspaper writings he invariably refers to him as Paul Dresser.

85.21 On 1 February 1893 Henry Smith, the alleged ravisher and murderer of a three-year-old white girl, was tortured and blinded with red-hot irons by members of the girl's family before fifteen to twenty thousand onlookers. Then he was burned alive. See "Tortured and Burned," *St. Louis Globe-Democrat,* 2 February 1893, p. 1.

34. THE THEATERS.

86.13 *Le Demi-Monde* (1855), a play by Dumas *fils,* was translated as *The Crust of Society* by Louise Imogen Guiney and adapted for stage production by William Seymour.

86.35 In another brief notice of this play a few days later, Dreiser gave his brother an additional plug, referring to him as "the famous lyric song writer." See "The Theaters," 16 February 1893, p. 4.

35. MISS FAY'S SEANCE.

87.5 Annie Eva Fay was an American medium of international reputation. She performed at the Crystal Palace in London in 1874, and her powers were subjected to scientific examination in England. See *Encyclopedia of Occultism and Parapsychology*.

87.11 Dr. Jerome Keating Bauduy (1842–1914), a prominent St. Louis neurologist, author of *Diseases of the Nervous System* (1892) and other works. See James Cox, *Old and New St. Louis* (1894), pp. 542–55. Bauduy also figures in Nos. 55–56.

87.26 The Davenport brothers, Ira and William, were world-famous American spirit-mediums who flourished between 1855 and 1877. See Slater Brown, *The Heyday of Spiritualism* (New York: Hawthorn, 1970), pp. 184–99.

36. MODJESKA AT THE GRAND.

88.15 Helena Modjeska (1840–1909), a Polish-born actress who fled with her husband to America for political asylum, made her New York debut in *Camille* in 1877. She was outstanding in Shakespearean roles. Otis Skinner (1858–1942), who was often Modjeska's leading man, attained his greatest success as the star of *Kismet* (1911); he was an excellent Shakespearean actor as well.

37. THE THEATERS.

89.8 Fannie Davenport (1850–98) was an American actress known for the variety of her characterizations. Melbourne McDowell was her second husband. The French dramatist Victorien Sardou (1831–1908), best known for *Fédora* (1882), *Tosca* (1887), and *Madame Sans-Gêne* (1893), wrote *Cléopâtre* for Sarah Bernhardt, who first acted in it in Paris in 1890.

89.21 E[dward] S[mith] Willard (1853–1915), English actor known for his romantic leads as well as for his characterization of villains. His greatest success was in J. M. Barrie's *The Professor's Love Story* (1894). See chap. 31 of *ND* for Dreiser's recollection of meeting Willard and his leading lady during this week. *The Middleman* and *Judah* were written for Willard by the English playwright Henry Arthur Jones (1851–1929).

38. JOHN L. OUT FOR A LARK.

90.5 In chap. 26 of *ND*, Dreiser writes that he interviewed Sullivan in St. Louis, but no such interview appeared in the *Globe-Democrat* or the *Republic* while he worked for those newspapers. He may have been remembering this visit to the city by the colorful pugilist.

39. THE BLACK DIVA'S CONCERT.

91.5 Sissieretta Jones (1868–1933), born in Virginia and reared in Providence, Rhode Island, studied at the New England Conservatory in Boston. She sang at the White House for Benjamin Harrison and at the Pittsburgh Exposition of 1892–93; she toured England in 1893 and sang at a New York benefit concert directed by Antonin Dvořák on 23 January 1894. In chap. 31 of *ND*, Dreiser describes how rival newspapers seized upon this review to ridicule *Globe-Democrat* editor J. B. McCullagh for what they saw as his overly sympathetic treatment of a black entertainer. Dreiser's recollection in *ND* of what he wrote is more grandiloquent in tone than the original but is in keeping with its spirit; his epitome of a taunting editorial carried in the *Post-Dispatch* is, however, wholly imaginary, for that paper took no notice of his review. What he must have been remembering was a mocking squib from the Democratic *Chronicle* of 1 April 1893, last edition, p. 4, entitled "A Great Editor and 'Black Patti.'" The *Chronicle* was the only St. Louis newspaper to refer directly to Dreiser's review, but another Democratic paper, the *Republic*, inspired apparently by the *Chronicle* item, published remarks critical of Sissieretta Jones; see "Music and Musicians," 2 April 1893, p. 32.

40. THE THEATERS.

91.27 Archibald Clavering Gunter (1847–1907), English-born civil engineer, chemist, broker, novelist, playwright. His best-known work is the novel *Mr. Barnes of New York* (1887). *My Official Wife*, published in 1891, is by the American novelist Richard Henry Savage (1846–1903).

42. THE THEATERS.

93.3 The libretto of *Ali Baba* was put together by David Henderson, Henry B. Smith, and Lee and John Gilbert. The play had first been performed in Chicago the preceding summer, and Dreiser may have seen it then. Eddie (Edward Fitzgerald) Foy (1857–1928), comic actor and singer, starred in such extravaganzas as *Sinbad*, *Cinderella*, and *Bluebeard*, as well as in *Ali Baba*.

93.21 Jeffreys Lewis, at this point an aging actress, is described by Odell as "the dark-eyed beauty of the '70s" (*Annals*, 15:525). David Belasco (1854–1931) was an American playwright and producer. *La Belle Russe* was first produced in 1882. *Forget-Me-Not* was written in 1879 by the English playwrights Herman Merivale and F. C. Grove.

94.4 Peter Jackson was an Australian black heavyweight prizefighter of the late nineteenth century who fought at the same time as John L. Sullivan, James J. Corbett, and Joe Choynski (see below).

94.18 Joe Choynski was a successful heavyweight Jewish-American prizefighter of the late nineteenth century.

94.22 In America, Ada Gray had for years been virtually identified with *East Lynne*. This famous tear-jerking domestic drama was based on Mrs. Henry Wood's 1861 novel and was first adapted as a play in 1874 by the English dramatist T. A. Palmer.

95.14 See *ND*, chap. 35, for an account of how Dreiser faked several reviews in advance with material culled from press-agent releases because he knew he would not have time to attend the performances. He then learned too late that the Hagan and Pope companies had not reached St. Louis because the railways had been washed out by floods. Realizing that he had once more exposed his chief to ridicule, he left an apologetic letter on McCullagh's desk and never returned to the *Globe-Democrat*. Though he claims that McCullagh later assured him he need not have quit (*ND*, chap. 51), Dreiser probably would have been called on the carpet for his blunder, because two Democratic papers—still smarting from their candidate's defeat in the recent mayoral election—could not pass up the opportunity to twit their prestigious Republican rival (see "An Able Dramatic Critic," *St. Louis Chronicle*, 1 May 1893, p. 4, and "Imaginative Journalism," *St. Louis Post-Dispatch*, 1 May 1893, p. 4). On subsequent days, both newspapers made other barbed references to Dreiser's unlucky blunder (see *St. Louis Chronicle*, 2 May 1893, p. 4, and *St. Louis Post-Dispatch*, 3 May 1893, p. 4). Dreiser's recollection of this episode in *ND* differs in a few details from the actual events: only two, not three, companies were washed out and unable to perform on the evening of 30 April; the Grand was not one of the theaters affected; Sol Smith Russell was not a member of either delayed company and was not scheduled to appear in St. Louis that week; the *Post-Dispatch* did not taunt McCullagh about his interest in spiritualism.

45. HIS OWN STORY.

104.6 **the-entire-seven-in-one** In committing the holdup, Wilson had rather cleverly tricked the trainmen into believing that seven robbers had waylaid them. The truth that he alone had done the job was not discovered until shortly before his arrest.

108.38 A section entitled "From the Robber's Home," two-thirds of a column, is omitted here because, as a "Special to The Republic" from Lebanon, Missouri, it could not have been written by Dreiser.

111.4 **cully** comrade, buddy; **boodle** money; **whack up** divide, share.

46. WHO GETS THE REWARD?

116.11 On 30 June 1893, the St. Louis papers reported that Wilson had been sentenced to fifteen years in the state penitentiary.

47. THE TROUBLE STILL ON.

117.2   Charles Frederick Joy (1849–1921), U.S. representative from Missouri (1893–1903).

48. TEACHERS AT THE FAIR.

121.1   Pizer, Dowell, and Rusch ascribe to Dreiser an article of 16 July 1893 that describes the last-minute preparations for the schoolteachers' excursion to the World's Fair: "To Leave To-Day," No. C93-32. Probably Dreiser did not write this article; its author appears to be familiar with the background of the *Republic* contest dating from before January 1892, well before Dreiser joined the reporting staff. It seems more likely that the article was written by someone who had been on the staff longer than he. Apparently this 16 July item is the last of a series of publicity pieces the paper ran over many months preceding the trip itself.

49. THE REPUBLIC TEACHERS.

125.19   **wiley** Perhaps alluring, enticing, or beguiling; see the first *v.t.* definition of *wile* in *W2*.

51. WILL SEE EVERYTHING.

131.10   **Convent of "La Rabida"** A replica of the convent in which Christopher Columbus was sheltered while seeking Queen Isabella's support.

52. FIFTH DAY AT THE FAIR.

132.18   **Miss White** Sara (Sallie) Osborne White, who eventually became Dreiser's first wife.

54. FEVER'S FRENZY.

146.30   Over the next several days, *Republic* follow-up stories—possibly by Dreiser—report that Willie died, John Finn and the three remaining children survived, and a coroner's jury found the father innocent of his son's death.

55. ALMOST A RIOT.

146.33   Dreiser mentions Jules Wallace in chap. 5 of *Sister Carrie*; see the Pennsylvania Dreiser Edition of the novel, p. 48.

56. THEY MET AND—LUNCHED.

155.24 **moment of closing the forms** The point at which the newspaper was ready to go to press and the forms were closed around the type on the press beds.

158.38 Thomson Jay Hudson (1834–1903), American antispiritualist philosopher. His widely read *The Law of Psychic Phenomena*, first published in 1893, is probably the source of Bauduy's remarks. See *Encyclopedia of Occultism and Parapsychology*.

57. BLINDFOLDED HE DROVE.

159.33 **Alley Sloper** More fully described in chap. 24 of *ND* as "a gruesome-shaped head of *papier-mâché* representing some half-demented creature commonly known in England as Ally Sloper." The name apparently derives from *Ally Sloper's Half Holiday*, a humorous weekly paper published in London, 1884–1916.

160.30 **"Tony Faust's"** A popular 1890s restaurant.

161.22 Tyndall's final sensation in St. Louis is described in "A Perfect Fit" (*St. Louis Republic*, 23 August 1893, p. 6). Clad only in his nightshirt, he went sleepwalking in a downtown district, and when a policeman stopped him, he fell into a cataleptic trance.

59. BANDIT PENNOCK.

170.13 The capture of Pennock's two accomplices, Sam Robinson and Muncie Ray, is detailed in "Caught Another," 8 September 1893, p. 1, and "Ready for the Road," 9 September 1893, p. 5. Dreiser would likely not have had time to cover the events reported in these two stories because he was by then presumably busy collaborating in the writing of a massive exposé, "Jules Wallace, Faker, Fraud, Medium, Healer!", which appeared on 9 September 1893, pp. 1–2. On 24 October, Pennock and Ray were sentenced to fourteen years in the state penitentiary (see "Pathos in This Plea," *St. Louis Republic*, 25 October 1893, p. 11). Robinson's fate is not known, but he probably received a similar sentence, because, like the other two, he signed a full confession.

60. A SPIRITUALIST FRAUD.

170.29 **forked biological specimen** Perhaps an echo of *King Lear*, III.iv.11–14: "unaccommodated man is no more but such a poor, bare, forked animal as thou art."

170.32 **Mrs. Bicknell** In the *Republic*'s recent multipage exposé, "Jules Wallace, Faker, Fraud, Medium, Healer!" (see Appendix, No. 70), on the writing of which Dreiser had probably collaborated, Mrs. Bicknell is identified as one of Wallace's "cappers," a secret accomplice who ferreted out the personal histories of prospective suckers.

172.11 **Dion Boucicault** (1820?–90) Irish-born actor and playwright; a leading figure on the New York stage from 1853 until his death. Wallace fancied himself a thespian as well as a medium and songwriter.

172.21 **alcohol** The *Republic*'s exposé, "Jules Wallace, Faker . . . ," asserted that Wallace's trick of reading a card in a sealed envelope was effected by surreptitiously moistening the envelope with alcohol, thus rendering it temporarily transparent.

172.29 **Schloss** Louis Schloss, or Sloss; exposed in "Jules Wallace, Faker . . ." as another Wallace accomplice; specialized in producing handwritten spirit messages on slate tablets.

174.25 **struck another tartar** Cf. "to catch a Tartar," to attack someone who proves too strong for the assailant.

61. HIS OWN STORY.

176.3 A coroner's jury had ruled earlier that Finn was not responsible for his actions, but a warrant charging him with murder was nevertheless issued. See "Finn Tragedy Complications," *St. Louis Republic*, 7 September 1893, p. 4, and "Sworn Out," 10 September 1893, p. 8.

62. WILL WEAR THE MEDAL.

180.2 The entire notice is set in an ornamental border of conventional design. Beneath the words *Of the Design Shown Below* appear engravings of the front and the back of the medal containing the statements in the remainder of the notice.

63. BRILLIANT BEYOND COMPARE: THE GLITTERING BALLROOM.

184.8 Segments of "Brilliant beyond Compare," the feature coverage in the *Republic* of the sixteenth annual Veiled Prophet's Ball (the most fashionable society costume party of the St. Louis season), which occupied all of pp. 1–3 and col. 4 of p. 6. "The Glittering Ballroom" is preceded by three lead paragraphs and followed by two segments, "The Ball Opens" and "The Grand Entree," after which appears "The Ball at Midnight." The remainder of the space is devoted to long lists of the guests and descriptions of their costumes.

186.16 **"fair, well-spoken dames"** Cf. "fair well-spoken days," *Richard III*, I.i.29.

187.1 **the Veiled Khorassan** Derived from "The Veiled Prophet of Khorassan," the first story in Thomas Moore's *Lalla Rookh* (1817).

187.3 **cheeks of Yezd or Shiraz** Perhaps an echo of "the maids of Yezd and Shiras" from "The Veiled Prophet of Khorassan," pt. 2, l. 230.

187.24   **the roses of Bendemeer stream** From "There's a bower of roses by Bendemeer's stream," in "The Veiled Prophet of Khorassan," pt. 2, l. 247, the opening
line of a lyric that, set to music, became a popular nineteenth-century song.

188.3   **Perian** Apparently an adjective Dreiser derived from *peri*, i.e., a beautiful and
graceful woman.

64. A FAKER'S VICTIM.

188.26   **Rice, Stix & Co.** A St. Louis department store.

192.11   The attribution of this hymn to Mary is questionable. See Antonia Fraser, *Mary,
Queen of Scots* (New York: Delacorte, 1969), p. 534. For the full text see "Scots,
Mary Queen of," in John Julian, *A Dictionary of Hymnology*, rev. ed., 1907 (repr.
New York: Dover, 1957), 2:1589.

192.29   Actually Lincoln liked "Dixie." The incident of his having ordered the playing of
the contraband melody after Robert E. Lee's surrender is well known. See Bruce
Catton, *Never Call Retreat* (New York: Doubleday, 1965), p. 458.

192.37   Following this article are two "specials" to the *Republic:* "Wallace in Denver"
(pp. 1–2) and "Home of the Spooks" (p. 2). They describe some of Wallace's alleged chicanery in Denver and are obviously not Dreiser's work.

65. WARRANTS FOR WALLACE.

193.39   In the 1880s, on a farm near Rockford, Illinois, George Jacob Schweinfurth (1853–
1910) established his "Church Triumphant" on the Christian-socialist principles of
Mrs. C. D. H. F. Beekman. Communal living was practiced after the model of
early Christian congregations. Through the 1890s the members, who referred to
their community as "Heaven," came in for much hostile publicity; they were
charged with licentious practices and with worshiping Schweinfurth as the Mes-
siah. The church disbanded in 1900 after its leader became a Christian Scientist.
(Information supplied by John Molyneaux, Rockford Public Library.)

66. WALLACE'S WORK.

196.25   **"Cleveland Street Gang"** In the fall of 1889, a raid by the London police on a
male brothel in Cleveland Street had exposed scandalous activities of some men of
high social rank, most notably the Duke of Clarence, elder son of the Prince of
Wales. See Piers Compton, *Victorian Vortex* (London: Robert Hale, 1977), p. 183.

196.26   The *Pall Mall Gazette*, under the editorship of William T. Stead, crusaded against
many kinds of sexual vice and crime, particularly child prostitution. See Piers
Compton, *Victorian Vortex* (London: Robert Hale, 1977), pp. 175–76.

200.3   In *ND*, chap. 46, Dreiser says that the landlady, a keyhole peeper, gave him a
rousing description of "Mooney's" activities with the woman in question. A type-

script version of *ND* is more explicit: "She had seen this particular woman, bared to the waist, and even more, on her knees before Mr. Mooney, who was also partially disrobed, and . . . there and then as the law says they were indulging in that relation which she was content to describe as 'unnatural'" (chap. XXXI, p. 8, Box 139, Dreiser Collection).

206.41   With this article, Wandell decided that Dreiser's investigation into Wallace's activities had gone far enough, and "another man—a strange reporter from Salt Lake City and San Francisco" replaced him (MS of *ND*, chap. XXXI, p. 14, Box 139, Dreiser Collection). The fact that the next day's article on Wallace goes into detail about his West Coast and Hawaiian background seems to confirm Dreiser's statement. The remaining articles in the Wallace exposé are "Trail of the Serpent," 31 October 1893, p. 4; "Firm in the Faith," 1 November 1893, p. 7; and "Really Doesn't Know," 2 November 1893, p. 12. The final escapade of Wallace to be reported in the *Republic* during Dreiser's days on its staff was his arrest in Washington, D.C., on a charge of vagrancy, as a result of which he had to give bond as assurance of "future good behavior." See "Jules Wallace Convicted," 13 January 1894, p. 1, and "Wallace the Faker," 17 January 1894, p. 3. By the following November, Wallace was plying his trade in New York, where he was exposed by the *World* shortly before Dreiser began working for that newspaper. See "Nellie Bly and a Spiritualist," 11 November 1894, pp. 25–26, and "Wallace and His Dupes," 12 November 1894, p. 9.

67. MYSTERY OF A MURDER.

221.22   The last report on the McClelland case to appear in the *Republic* while Dreiser was still on the staff was published a few months later: a grand jury had failed to indict McClelland and Martin. See "Not Indicted for McClelland's Murder," *St. Louis Republic*, 27 January 1894, p. 14.

68. ZYTHUM'S EXHILARATION.

222.3   **Lobengula** (ca. 1833–94) His South African kingdom had just been subjugated by the British after the battle of Bulawayo, 23 October 1893.

223.4   **opsympathy** *W2* gives the spelling *opsimathy* for a term so defined.

71. THE HANGING OF WELSOR.

239.7   Dreiser may also have written the brief item "Welsor's Funeral" of Monday, 15 January 1894, p. 8. It reports that on the previous day a crowd of four thousand gathered at Tom Wand's livery stable and undertaking rooms, but that only a few immediate friends were permitted to view the body, which was clad in a black broadcloth suit and laid out in a $150 casket. Twenty-six carriages and twelve buggies followed the hearse to Bellefontaine Cemetery, and on the way back "most of the mourners stopped at the road saloons."

72. THE CHINESE IN ST. LOUIS.

242.11 Wingrave Cook and the source of the quotation from him have not been identified.

243.15 **Bung Loo** A Chinese gambling game, apparently unlike the more familiar Fan Tan in that Bung Loo was sometimes considered illegal. The *Chicago Tribune* printed a story about some Chinese who were arrested for playing it: "Fourteen Players of 'Bung Loo,'" 12 August 1892, p. 3.

246.32 **Six Companies** An organization of merchants in San Francisco's Chinatown that loaned money at interest to Chinese emigrants to the United States and obtained jobs for them. See Herbert Asbury, *The Barbary Coast* (New York: Knopf, 1933), p. 141.

73. THIS CALLS FOR HEMP.

251.20 Dreiser's on-the-scene coverage scooped the other St. Louis newspapers. The *Globe-Democrat*, the rival morning paper, carried nothing about the event on the 17th. The *Post-Dispatch*, appearing that afternoon, gave a fuller account than had the *Republic* but drew heavily on Dreiser's version and even incorporated some of his language.

74. TEN-FOOT DROP.

258.16 The *Republic* printed three more articles on the Buckner lynching, which may have been written by Dreiser: "Mob for Lynching," 19 January 1894, p. 1; "John Buckner's Crimes," 19 January 1894, pp. 1–2; "Lynchers Return Home," 20 January 1894, p. 15. Immediately after No. 74, the *Republic* printed a justification of the lynching that apparently was meant as a statement of the paper's editorial attitude toward such occurrences. The first three paragraphs are reprinted below. They help explain the language and point of view of Dreiser's articles.

SAYS IT WAS NECESSARY.

While there is a general sentiment in St. Louis County condemning mob violence, there is undoubtedly an undercurrent of feeling that John Buckner met with his deserts.

Many say that his death in that ignoble way was necessary to strike terror to the criminal class which infests that part of the county, and makes it the scene of their depredations. There was no color line drawn.

One of Buckner's victims was an aged colored woman and some of those who assisted in his execution belong to his race. The indignant citizens regarded him as a wild beast and destroyed him.

81. NO UNION MEN NEED APPLY TO THE ROBISON COMPANY FOR WORK.

274.9   **Wood County Herald**   Dreiser was considering the purchase of this small Ohio country newspaper. See *ND*, chaps. 62 and 63.

85. M'DOUGALL'S DREAM.

281.11   **whalebacks**   "A form of steam vessel having sides curving in towards the ends, a spoon bow, and very convex upper deck, much used on the Great Lakes, esp. for carrying grain" (*W2*). In *ND*, chap. 66, Dreiser uses the term *turtle-back*, which *W3* cites as a synonym.

86. REED, JUST AS HE STANDS.

285.2   Thomas Brackett Reed (1839–1902), U.S. representative from Maine (1877–99) and Speaker of the House (1889–91 and 1895–99), had come to Pittsburgh to address the Americus Club on its annual celebration of the birthday of General Ulysses S. Grant. Reed was at this time a strong contender for the next Republican presidential nomination. Dreiser later profiled and interviewed him for *Success* 3 (June 1900): 215–16.

285.10   Jacob S. Coxey (1854–1951), a Populist from Massilon, Ohio, had recently led a small "army" of unemployed to Washington, D.C., to present to Congress a petition for work relief.

285.15   Put forward by Democratic congressman William L. Wilson, this bill called for the removal of tariff duties on certain basic commodities and for the imposition of a moderate income tax. The Senate amended the bill drastically, and as the Wilson-Gorman bill it became law in August 1894.

285.35   On 29 March 1894 Grover Cleveland had vetoed a bill prepared by free-silver advocates in Congress that would have permitted coining of the seigniorage, "the silver which remained in the Treasury as gain to the government by the purchase of bullion at a price lower than the value stamped upon the metal when coined, and then put into circulation as money." Ellis Paxson Oberholtzer, *A History of the United States since the Civil War* (New York: Macmillan, 1937), 5:281.

87. HOSPITAL VIOLET DAY.

286.13   Probably a description of "the cool, central, shaded court of the Allegheny General Hospital," where Dreiser, with his friend, the head intern, often "waited for something to turn up" (*ND*, chap. 72).

287.42   **Ayesha Pool**   In H. Rider Haggard's *She* (1887), Ayesha, the white goddess, perpetuates her youth and vigor by bathing in a pool of volcanic fire. A dramatized version of this novel, with which Dreiser might have been familiar, was staged frequently in the early 1890s. In the original text of this article, the phrase "Through the Ayesha Pool" is centered and used as a subheading.

288.17 Dreiser reused material from this article in "Forgotten," *Ev'ry Month* 2(August 1896):16–17.

89. REAPERS IN THE FIELDS.

292.21 **Saturnian** Saturn, or Saturnus, was an ancient Italian king-deity whose reign was thought to have inaugurated a golden age of agricultural fruitfulness.

292.34 A reference to Whittier's poem "Maud Muller" and to the Book of Ruth.

293.11 A reference to the seventh paragraph of "The Legend of Sleepy Hollow": "They are like those little nooks of still water, which border a rapid stream, where we may see the straw and bubble riding quietly at anchor, or slowly revolving in their mimic harbour, undisturbed by the rush of the passing current." See *The Complete Works of Washington Irving* (Boston: Twayne, 1978), 8:274.

90. ODD SCRAPS OF MELODY.

294.17 **French harp** A harmonica.

295.15 Dreiser perhaps heard a concert version of *Cavalleria Rusticana* performed in St. Louis, 24 February 1893, by the Nordica Operatic Concert Company.

295.16 Alfred George Robyn (1860–1935), St. Louis-born musician and composer.

295.30 **"Fatal Wedding"** Attributed by Edward B. Marks to Gussie L. Davis (*They All Sang*, p. 232). Davis's songs were published regularly by Howley, Haviland Company, the firm with which Paul Dresser was associated and which was to become the publisher of *Ev'ry Month*, founded and edited by Dreiser.

296.8 Compare Dreiser's description of steelmaking in *ND*, chap. 74.

91. FENCED OFF THE EARTH.

296.33 This title has overtones of a then-current catch phrase, "Get off the earth!" According to the *St. Louis Globe-Democrat*, the phrase gained currency as the refrain of a Populist rallying song that ridiculed Boston landlords for blacklisting poor tenants. See "Songs of the People," 17 July 1892, p. 29. The expression also occurs in chap. 6 of Stephen Crane's *Maggie* (1893).

299.35 **staving** Big, immense; excessively.

93. SOME DABBLING IN BOOKS.

303.17   Richard Whately (1787–1863), English logician and theologian, author of religious books, and editor of Bacon's *Essays*.

303.32   Perhaps a reference to Elizabeth Simpson Bladen's *Romala: A Tale of Love in a Balloon*, a forty-three-page novel published in Philadelphia, n.d., No. 558 in Lyle H. Wright's *American Fiction, 1876–1900* (San Marino, Calif.: Huntington Library, 1966).

303.34   George Gould (1864–1923), railway financier, son of the financier Jay Gould.

304.7   *Ships That Pass in the Night* was an 1893 novel by the English writer Beatrice Harraden (1864–1935). The title is derived from line 200 of the Theologian's Third Tale in Longfellow's *Tales of a Wayside Inn*. "Do, Do, My Huckleberry, Do" was a popular 1893 song; see Edward B. Marks, *They All Sang*, p. 230.

304.14   Will Carleton (1845–1912), American sentimental poet best known for "Over the Hill to the Poor House." Carl Browne was one of Jacob Coxey's lieutenants; his name figures frequently in the *Dispatch* during the spring and summer of 1894.

304.25   **stogy** Perhaps an allusion to the once-famous "Pittsburgh stogy," a thin, inexpensive cigar then manufactured in Pittsburgh and referred to in several *Dispatch* articles during Dreiser's stay with the paper; or perhaps Dreiser means *stodgy* in the sense of "drab" or "dowdy."

94. SNAP SHOTS AT PLEASURE.

306.36   **"Flobert"** "A breech-loading rifle of small caliber, commonly taking a cartridge with a round ball" (*W2*).

95. NOW THE PILL DOCTRINE!

308.16   **Inferno gate description** See the opening lines of Canto Three of Dante's *Inferno*.

308.17   **the gates ajar** The title of Elizabeth Stuart Phelps Ward's best-selling novel of 1868.

309.3   **From childhood's contentious hour** An echo of the first line of Poe's "Alone": "From childhood's hour I have not been."

309.5   **Buchu** "The aromatic leaves of several South African rutaceous shrubs of the genus *Barosma*, used in medicine as a stimulant, diuretic, and stomachic" (*W2*).

309.37   Edward Payson Roe (1838–88), American author of popular inspirational novels such as *Barriers Burned Away* (1872) and *Opening a Chestnut Burr* (1874). *Dora Thorne* was an 1870s novel by Bertha M. Clay, the pseudonym of the English sentimental author Charlotte Monica (or Marie) Braeme (or Brame) (1836–84). Roe and

Dora Thorne are mentioned together in chap. 35 of the Pennsylvania Edition of *Sister Carrie* (pp. 334–35).

310.2   See the historical note at 304.7.

96. SURVIVAL OF UNFITTEST.

312.12   Floriano Peixoto (1842–95) was president of Brazil (1891–94). His name figured in the news of 1893–94 because he had quelled a naval revolt against his administration.

312.41   David Henderson (b. ca. 1849) was at this time the manager of theaters in Chicago, St. Louis, Pittsburgh, and other cities. See "He Controls the Duquesne," *Pittsburg Dispatch*, 2 September 1894, p. 17. His American Extravaganza Company specialized in Arabian Nights productions. It was of Henderson's *Ali Baba* that Dreiser wrote one of the faked reviews for the *Globe-Democrat* (see No. 42). Henderson's name also appears in the 1900 Doubleday, Page & Co. edition of *Sister Carrie*, p. 270.

97. THE LAST FLY OF FLY TIME.

314.13   **as unto a thousand of bricks** "Vigorously, energetically, thoroughly, very quickly, with a good will" (Partridge, 1984).

99. TALKS AT A BANQUET.

323.19   **Perugini** Pietro Vannucci (Il Perugino) (ca. 1446–1523), painter of the Umbrian school, who in 1499 supervised the decoration of the bankers' guildhall at Perugia into which he placed his own portrait.

103. BETTER TENEMENTS WANTED.

331.25   The Lexow committee at this time was frequently headlined for its sensational exposures of crooked practices by Tammany Hall. Thomas Collier Platt (1833–1910), one-time U.S. representative (1873–77) and senator (1881) from New York, was a powerful boss of the state Republican party.

NOTES ON ATTRIBUTION

Except for some editors and well-known reporters, the writers of 1890s newspaper articles usually were not given bylines. Only two of Dreiser's are identifiable by the presence of his name: No. 7, which is signed "Carl Dreiser," and No. 81, into which he worked "T. H. Dreiser." Other kinds of evidence must be employed to identify the rest.

1. *Articles in Folders 85 and 86 of the Dreiser Collection.* Like most newspaper reporters, Dreiser kept a file of his clippings; today that file is among his papers at the University of Pennsylvania Library. How many clippings this file once held is not ascertainable; over the years its contents have dwindled. At present, of the items reprinted here, it contains Nos. 63, 87, 88, 90, 93, 94, and 98. Robert H. Elias has confirmed that Nos. 55 and 89, now missing from the file, were also among the Dreiser papers when they arrived at the University of Pennsylvania.

2. *Articles identified in another work by Dreiser.* The published version of *Newspaper Days,* supplemented by the original uncut manuscripts, is the primary source for this variety of evidence. (The University of Pennsylvania Dreiser Collection houses the holograph of *Newspaper Days* [Boxes 136 and 137], four typescripts in successively revised states [Boxes 138, 139, 23, and 140], and the galley and page proofs. A final revised typescript [a heavily edited carbon copy of the typescript in Box 140] served as printer's copy; it is in the Department of Special Collections of the Research Library at the University of California, Los Angeles.) On its authority at least 118 articles can be definitely identified as Dreiser's work. General comments in *Newspaper Days* also make it possible to designate other articles as probably by Dreiser: articles that report Third District news for the *Globe-Democrat* and the *Republic;* paragraphs in the *Globe-Democrat*'s "Heard in the Corridors" column; theater reviews appearing in the *Globe-Democrat* when Dreiser was drama critic; Allegheny, Pennsylvania, news stories published in the *Pittsburg Dispatch* during his seven months there; and Nos. 72, 105, and 106.

3. *Two articles attributable to Dreiser on the basis of close analogy to, or reference to, elements in other articles that are unquestionably his.* The two articles in this classification are Nos. 68 and 96.

1. Cleveland and Gray the Ticket: *ND*, chap. 11.
2. Cheyenne, Haunt of Misery and Crime: *ND*, chap. 12.

3. Fate of the Unknown: Probable. This is probably one of the "specials" Dreiser wrote for the Sunday supplement; it is within his range in topic, point of view, and style. See *ND*, chap. 13.
4. Swindlers: *ND*, chap. 14.
5. Fakes: *ND*, chap. 14.
6. Arrested: *ND*, chap. 14.
7. The Return of Genius: *ND*, chap. 13.
8. Greatest in the World: *ND*, chap. 21.
9. Mr. Watterson on Politics: *ND*, chap. 26.
10. Theosophy and Spiritualism: *ND*, chap. 26. The *Globe-Democrat* carried two related stories, "Annie Besant in St. Louis," 19 January 1893, p. 9, and "Lecture on 'Labor Strife,'" p. 12, both of which might also be Dreiser's work. Details in "Theosophy and Spiritualism," however, conform most closely to Dreiser's recollection of this interview in *ND*.
11. Burned to Death: *ND*, chaps. 28–29.
12. Sixteen Dead: *ND*, chap. 29.
13. Guided by Spirits: Remembering the variety of personalities he interviewed for the *Globe-Democrat*, Dreiser writes, "Again, it would be some mountebank or quack of a low order—a spiritualist, let us say, of the Eva Fay stripe, or a mind-reader like Bishop" (Box 140 typescript, p. 204). Elsewhere he recalls that after his big scoop of the Wann disaster, returning to work he found himself "listed for only 'Hotels & Heard in Corridors,' as usual" and was depressed (*ND*, chap. 30). These two statements together warrant this attribution.
14. An Iron Firm Goes Under: In chap. 37 of *ND*, Dreiser recalls interviewing the elderly owner of a large, fifty-year-old southside iron factory that had been forced by hard times to shut down. The remarks attributed to the owner in *ND* are quite different from and far gloomier than those of Arthur Judge, but because No. 14 is the only interview with a bankrupt iron founder to appear in a St. Louis newspaper when Dreiser worked for it, and because Judge's firm was "one of long standing" and was located on the south side, this item can be attributed to Dreiser with reasonable confidence.
15. An Hypnotic Seance: Box 140 typescript, p. 372. Discussing his interest in telepathy as a St. Louis reporter, Dreiser tells of participating with his friends Wood, McCord, and Rodenberger in experiments with "hypnotists, spiritualists and the like. . . . I myself [stood] on the stomach of a thin hypnotized boy of not more than seventeen years of age, while his head was placed on one chair, his feet on another and no brace of any kind being put under his body. Yet his stomach held me up." Of the many articles dealing with hypnosis that appeared in the *Globe-Democrat* and the *Republic* while Dreiser was in St. Louis, No. 15 is the only one to describe the experiment of sitting on the suspended, rigid body of a hypnotized youth. Covering séances like this might have been one of Dreiser's duties as the drama critic for the *Globe-Democrat*.
16. Maj. Bannerman Explains His Defeat—Col. Butler Retires from Politics: Dreiser's recollection of the Bannerman interview in chap. 26 of *ND* differs from the item reprinted here. Dreiser says that the interview occurred *before* the election and that Bannerman severely criticized St. Louisans, particularly "religionists," for their unprogressive outlook, thereby giving such offense to voters that he was "ruined politically." Supposedly, too, the Democratic newspapers angrily denounced the interview as a lie, although McCullagh wrote a tart defense of his reporter's veracity. There is no evi-

dence, however, that rival newspapers took note of Dreiser's postelection interview, although the defeated Bannerman himself did object to it. In a letter to the editor dated 6 April 1893, Bannerman protested: "In politics I have been a life-long Democrat, ever ready to further the interests of my party, but to say that I hate the political opponents of my party is too absurd to give it denial" (*Globe-Democrat*, 7 April 1893, p. 12). On p. 6 of this same issue, the *Globe-Democrat* printed a response insisting that "the publication correctly represented the utterances of Mr. Bannerman in a conversation with a reporter of this paper, which Mr. Bannerman knew was intended for our columns." A preelection interview with Bannerman had appeared in the *St. Louis Chronicle* ("Mayor Himself," 9 March 1893, p. 2). In this interview, Bannerman had sought to dissociate himself from Democratic machine politicians. Throughout the campaign the Republican papers, particularly the *Globe-Democrat*, used these remarks to argue that the entire Democratic ticket should be rejected. Perhaps Dreiser fused the *Chronicle* interview in his memory with the interview he himself had conducted. His recollection of Edward Butler is to be found in *ND*, chap. 19.

17–26. Third District Stories: *ND*, chap. 19.

27. The speaker, Harry Hall, is the Howard Hall of *Dawn* (pp. 391–92), a law student from Michigan who befriended Dreiser at Indiana University.

28. File 86, Dreiser Collection.

29. Paul Dresser was Dreiser's brother.

30. John Maxwell was a copyreader for the *Chicago Globe* who is mentioned frequently in *ND*.

31. The cave adventure Brandon narrates is the one Dreiser describes as having happened to him in *Dawn*, pp. 403–8. He also incorporated this experience into a hotel interview written earlier in 1892 for the *Chicago Globe* (Appendix, No. 16).

32. *Dawn*, pp. 341–46.

33–42. Theatrical Reviews: *ND*, chaps. 30–35.

43. The Boy's Body Found: *ND*, chap. 26. Although Dreiser's recollection in *ND* is of having covered a fire that killed a stable attendant and only seventeen horses, in all other important details his description there corresponds to the circumstances set forth in this story and the related ones carried in the *Republic* that he also probably wrote (see Nos. 34–37 in the Appendix). This stable fire was the only one of magnitude, and the only one to claim a human life, that occurred during Dreiser's stay in St. Louis.

44. "I'm Luckin' fer Mer Wife": In *ND*, chap. 48, Dreiser tells how he outdid Red Galvin, a *Globe-Democrat* rival, by using Negro dialect and waterfront atmosphere to enliven a routine story about a black stevedore who had trailed his wife and her lover from city to city along the river until he finally caught her in St. Louis and nearly killed her with his razor. Galvin, having treated the matter as merely another "low dive cutting affray" worth "only a scant stick," was irritated to have been bettered. He paid Dreiser back later when he scooped him on the story of the capture of train robber Wilson (*ND*, chap. 50). Although No. 44 differs in many details from the romanticized account Dreiser tells us he wrote, no other article printed by the *Republic* while he worked there comes as close to his recollected description.

45. His Own Story: *ND*, chaps. 49 and 50.

46. Who Gets the Reward?: Probable. Dreiser does not mention a jailhouse interview with Wilson in *ND*, but because he wrote the long feature account of the capture, it is probable that he was responsible for this follow-up story. The friendly exchange of greetings

between the prisoner and the reporter suggests that the two were already acquainted and that the reporter was Dreiser.

47. The Trouble Still On: *ND*, chap. 39.

48–53. World's Fair Stories: *ND*, chaps. 40–45.

54. Fever's Frenzy: *ND*, chap. 25. Dreiser, perhaps misremembering, states that he wrote this story while working for the *Globe-Democrat*, and in summarizing it he also seems to have mixed in some details of an earlier, somewhat similar murder; see "A Shocking Tragedy," *St. Louis Republic*, 12 May 1893, p. 2. In chap. 25 he asserts that he wrote "perhaps a column and a half" of this story and submitted his copy to Hartung, the copy editor, and that a reporter named Bellairs supplied "various police theories," but because both men were *Globe-Democrat* employees, the assertion cannot be correct.

55. Almost a Riot: Elias; also *ND*, chap. 46.

56. They Met and—Lunched: Possible. Dreiser almost certainly wrote this follow-up to "Almost a Riot" (No. 55).

57. Blindfolded He Drove: *ND*, chap. 46.

58. He Got a Ride: *ND*, chap. 47. Although Dreiser says that his story about the arrest of an old man and a little girl "never appeared," No. 58 so closely resembles his description in *ND* that his authorship of the item is certain.

59. Bandit Pennock: Probable. "Now again, it was a great train robbery in the centre of the state that took me into the heart of a truly rural region where nothing but farmers and small towns were" (*ND*, chap. 46). Dreiser is referring to his period with the *Republic* following his return from the World's Fair. The circumstances of No. 59 and "On the Scene," the story that preceded it (see Appendix, No. 69), correctly fit his description. The Frisco train robbery was, moreover, the only one that occurred during Dreiser's St. Louis days that was near enough to the city for the newspapers to send reporters out for firsthand coverage. Three sections are omitted from No. 59 because it seems highly unlikely that one reporter would have been able to cover all the ground the story takes in. These sections are "Express Companies Serene," pp. 1–2; "Opening the Strong Box," p. 2; and "No Word from the Doctor," p. 2. Since Dreiser was on the scene shortly after Pennock's capture, it is reasonable to assume that he made personal contact with the prisoner and then wrote the portions of No. 59 that focus on Pennock.

60. A Spiritualist Fraud: *ND*, chap. 46. Although Dreiser calls the fake medium "Mr. Mooney" in *ND*, the story he tells of Mooney follows in all major points the series of articles in the *Republic* exposing Jules Wallace. Two articles precede No. 60: "Jules Wallace, Faker, Fraud, Medium, Healer!" 9 September 1893, pp. 1–2, and "Wallace on Wallace," 10 September 1893, p. 6.

61. His Own Story: In *ND*, chap. 25, Dreiser writes that he tried to interview Finn in his cell shortly after the assault on the children but found him too deranged to make a statement. As No. 54 reveals, however, Finn was confined to a hospital bed at that time. Not until after he had regained his senses was he sent to jail. Dreiser's memory of seeing him in a cell must be of this interview, a month and a half later.

62. Will Wear the Medal: *ND*, chap. 56.

63. Brilliant beyond Compare: The Glittering Ballroom: The two segments are preserved in File 86 of the Dreiser Collection. Perhaps misremembering, Dreiser writes in chap. 25 of *ND* that he wrote this "indiscriminate newspaper tosh" while working for the *Globe-Democrat*.

64–66. Articles on Jules Wallace: *ND*, chap. 46; see attrib. for No. 60.

67. Mystery of a Murder: "Now it was a great murder mystery over in Illinois perhaps that kept me stationed in a small county seat for days" (*ND*, chap. 46). The manuscript version of *ND* specifies that the town was Sandoval and that the murder "came to light twelve years after it had been committed, and that only after an old pond had been drained and the skeleton of a murdered man revealed" (chap. XXI, p. 11, Box 138, Dreiser Collection). Two short articles on this mystery appeared in the *Republic*: "M'Clelland's Skeleton," 11 November 1893, p. 1, and "Murder Will Out," 14 November 1893, p. 1. Both are almost certainly Dreiser's; they present preliminary versions of what is given in detail in No. 67.

68. Zythum's Exhilaration: Judged to be Dreiser's work by virtue of content and style; part of a series of football stories, the other members of which are identified as Dreiser's by Elias (see Appendix, Nos. 90–94).

69. Under the Wheels: In a canceled passage on pp. 192–93 of the UCLA typescript of *ND*, Dreiser recalls writing an account of a streetcar accident in which he "described how the raw country motorman, who had killed a little girl, got off his car and appeared to be dying of cramps, holding his waist, sobbing and groaning." Even though this statement occurs in a passage about his days at the *Globe-Democrat*, No. 69 must be the news story he is remembering because it is the only one to appear during his St. Louis period that describes the death of a girl in a streetcar accident and the grief of the motorman.

70–71. Welsor's Hanging: In *ND*, chap. 54, describing events of some unspecified time during his *Republic* period, Dreiser says, "I remember witnessing a hanging . . . standing beside the murderer when the trap was sprung and seeing him die. . . ." In the next sentence he mentions the lynching of a "negro in an outlying county"—that is, the event he described in Nos. 73 and 74—seeming to imply that this lynching occurred *after* the hanging. His short story "Nigger Jeff," which is based largely on Nos. 73 and 74, lends support to this inference, for there the young reporter who covers the lynching is said to have once before "been compelled to witness a hanging, and that had made him sick—deathly so—even though carried out as a part of the due process of law of his day and place" (*Free and Other Stories*, p. 77). Inasmuch as the execution of Sam Welsor did occur before the lynching of John Buckner and was, in fact, the only one to take place in St. Louis while Dreiser lived there, it must be the one referred to in *ND*. Since Nos. 70 and 71 form a unified narrative sequence culminating in the execution, they can be attributed to Dreiser with confidence. Two short related articles, which he may have written, also appeared: "Scaffold for Welsor," 9 January 1894, p. 10, reporting that the execution was now a virtual certainty, and "Death Watch Begun," 10 January 1894, p. 6, describing the preliminary preparations for it.

72. The Chinese in St. Louis: In *ND*, chap. 32, Dreiser tells of visits he made to the nondescript Chinese restaurants in St. Louis with Dick Wood, the *Globe-Democrat* illustrator. On 2 April 1893 the *Globe-Democrat* printed "A Chinese Dinner," p. 38, which was incorporated almost verbatim into No. 72. The *Globe-Democrat* made no comment on this reuse of its material by the *Republic*. The two newspapers were quick to point out each other's blunders, so one can only assume that no staff member at the *Globe-Democrat* noticed the borrowing. Dreiser apparently felt that since he had written the original story, the text was his to use again.

73–74. Buckner Lynching: *ND*, chap. 54. For a full explanation of the grounds for attribution and a discussion of how Dreiser used Nos. 73–74 as the basis for a short story, see T. D. Nostwich, "The Source of Dreiser's 'Nigger Jeff,'" *Resources for American Literary Study* 8(Fall 1978): 174–87.

75. At the Theatres: If Dreiser himself did not write this item, he surely provided the information on which it is based. Once established at the *Republic*, he helped the drama editor, who would ask him "to see various plays from time to time" (*ND*, chap. 51). See chaps. 58–61 of *ND* for an account of Paul's visit to St. Louis.

76–77. Theater News: *ND*, chap. 51.

78. Plain Murder: *ND*, chap. 37.

79. Whisky Did It: *ND*, chap. 37.

80–84. Strike Reports: *ND*, chap. 65.

85. M'Dougall's Dream: *ND*, chap. 66. Although this article lacks the impressionistic embellishment Dreiser remembers giving to his story about a "bluff old Lake captain" and his "new style grain boat," it is the only article on that subject to appear in the *Leader* during the time he could have been in Cleveland. This version may be a condensation made to satisfy the editor who, according to Dreiser, complained that the original was overly long and loosely written.

86. Reed, Just as He Stands: *ND*, chap. 72.

87. Hospital Violet Day: File 85, Dreiser Collection.

88. After the Rain Storm: File 85, Dreiser Collection.

89. Reapers in the Fields: Elias.

90. Odd Scraps of Melody: File 85, Dreiser Collection.

91. Fenced Off the Earth: *ND*, chap. 87.

92. With the Nameless Dead: See Donald Pizer, "Theodore Dreiser's 'Nigger Jeff'. . . ,'" *American Literature* 41 (November 1969): 331–42.

93. Some Dabbling in Books: File 85, Dreiser Collection.

94. Snap Shots at Pleasure: File 85, Dreiser Collection.

95. Now the Pill Doctrine!: Attributable to Dreiser because he reused this material in "The Gloom Chasers," *Ev'ry Month* 1 (December 1895): 16–17.

96. Survival of Unfittest: Probable. The references to Allegheny and to Darwin, Alfred Russel Wallace, and Thomas Henry Huxley—whose works Dreiser had recently been reading—strongly suggest his authorship. The pessimistic view of evolution seems to coincide with the mood afflicting him at this time. See *ND*, chaps. 6 and 85.

97. The Last Fly of Fly Time: In *ND*, chap. 73, Dreiser recalls incorrectly that a fly story was the *first* feature he wrote for the *Dispatch*. A more detailed description in the manuscript of *ND* leaves no doubt that this is the feature he was remembering. See T. D. Nostwich, "Dreiser's Apocryphal Fly Story," *Dreiser Newsletter* 17(Spring 1986): 1–8.

98. General Booth Says Farewell: File 85, Dreiser Collection. Three related articles, which may be Dreiser's work, also appeared in the *Pittsburg Dispatch:* "A Play in Six Acts," 12 November 1894, p. 2; "To Yield at Once Is Best," 12 November 1894, p. 2; and "Parted in Sorrow," 12 November 1894, p. 2.

99. Talks at a Banquet: "I remember . . . being sent to the Duquesne Club to interview Andrew Carnegie, fresh from his travels abroad . . . , and being received by a secretary . . . who allowed me to stand in the back of a room in which Mr. Carnegie, short, stocky, bandy-legged, a grand air of authority investing him, was addressing . . . the élite of the city on the subject of America and its political needs. No note-taking was permitted, but afterwards I was handed a typewritten address to the people of Pitts-

burgh and told that the *Dispatch* would be allowed to publish that" (*ND*, chap. 73). The address to the Library Board of Trustees was the only one Carnegie gave in Pittsburgh during Dreiser's stay there, so it must be the one he remembered. This article, which is obviously more than a transcript, can therefore be ascribed to him.

100. Educating a Ghost: *ND*, chap. 72.

101. Elopers Captured: *ND*, chap. 72.

102. Used a Horsewhip: *ND*, chap. 72.

103. Better Tenements Wanted: "The city editor . . . told me to attend a meeting of some committee which looked to the better lighting and cleaning of a certain district. . . . I went to the meeting and found that it was of no importance, and made but one inch, as I discovered next morning by a careful examination of the paper" (*ND*, chap. 88). Dreiser is describing his first assignment at the *World*, which he remembers as being carried out sometime during the first weeks of December.

104. Mrs. Moriarity Knocks Out Healy: *ND*, chap. 90. In recalling how he reported on an East Side tenement brawl, Dreiser writes, "Somewhere in the text I used the phrase 'sawing somnolent wood.'" Although No. 104 differs in some details from his recollected version, the "sawed somnolent wood all night long" phrase at 332.14 stamps this item as his.

105. Taken to Potter's Field: Probable. This story and the next one closely fit Dreiser's description of the sort of writing he did for the *World*: "And then after a little while, being assigned to do routine work in connection with the East Twenty-seventh Street police station, Bellevue Hospital, and the New York Charities Department, which included branches that looked after the poor-farm, the morgue, an insane asylum or two, a workhouse and what not else, I was called upon daily to face as disagreeable and depressing a series of scenes as it is possible for a single human being to witness" (*ND*, chap. 92).

106. Did He Blow Out the Gas? See attrib. for No. 105.

TEXTUAL COMMENTARY

In *Newspaper Days* Dreiser indicates that, like most reporters of the 1890s, he wrote his articles in longhand—probably using a pencil—the typewriter not yet being a copy-room fixture.[1] He passed his handwritten draft to a copy editor, at which point his involvement with it usually ceased. The typical procedure from that point on was for the copy editor to correct, prune, embellish, or rearrange the article and also, perhaps, to write the lead paragraph.[2] In addition, the copy editor added the headline and subheads and then sent the article on to the compositor. Occasionally a story might have to be returned to its writer for a major revision, but that did not happen often to a seasoned reporter. Dreiser does not mention its ever happening to him after his early days with the *Chicago Globe*.

The compositor set the text, and a number of proof copies were run off. These were checked for accuracy against the manuscript by staff proofreaders and also were read by the city editor or managing editor for errors in content and for libelous material missed by the copy editor. Practices in proofreading surely varied from paper to paper, but it seems to have been a generally observed rule that reporters did not proofread their own articles. Once the corrected copy was typeset, corrected, and approved, the original manuscript was usually thrown away. No holographs of Dreiser's newspaper articles are known to exist; the only surviving texts are the final printed versions. With the exception of some of the New York *World* stories, these printed versions survive in only one edition of their newspapers. Different daily editions of the 1894 and 1895 New York *World* have been randomly preserved, and in those editions in which duplicate versions of Dreiser's brief articles appear, the versions are identical.

BASIS FOR SELECTION OF THE ARTICLES IN THIS EDITION; SOURCES OF THE TEXTS

Articles have been selected for inclusion here primarily to illustrate the range of work Dreiser undertook and the degree of competence he attained as a reporter. His discussion in *Newspaper Days* of particular articles he wrote has been regarded as a compelling reason for including those articles, although many items not mentioned there are also included in this edition because of their intrinsic merit, or for the additional light they shed on Dreiser's newspaper career.

The arrangement of the material in this edition follows the chronology of Dreiser's jobs. Articles he wrote for each newspaper are categorized by type or "beat" and are chronologically arranged within each category.

Chicago Globe

The *Chicago Globe* articles are reprinted from the unique file owned by the Chicago Public Library.

St. Louis Globe-Democrat

The *St. Louis Globe-Democrat* articles are reprinted from microfilms owned by the Library of Congress.[3]

1. *Third District news stories:* In *Newspaper Days*, Dreiser says that shortly after joining the *Globe-Democrat* he was given the "North Seventh Street" police station as his regular beat. This station had jurisdiction over the section designated as the Third District, which in the 1890s extended from the Mississippi River west to Grand Avenue and was bounded on the south by Washington Avenue and on the north by Cass Avenue.[4] In *Newspaper Days*, Dreiser speaks only of the "North Seventh Street station," but 1890s newspapers in St. Louis always referred to it as the "Third District Station," a term also used in Dreiser's own news stories. According to John L. Given's description of turn-of-the-century journalistic practices, a newly hired reporter on a big-city newspaper was customarily assigned to cover a police precinct station about six months and was responsible for gathering news about accidents, crimes, arrests, fires, and other disturbances in the district.[5] That Dreiser retained the Third District beat throughout his six months at the *Globe-Democrat* is indicated by the *St. Louis Chronicle*'s taunting reference to him in April 1893 as a "police reporter."

Although it is impossible to prove beyond question that Dreiser wrote any particular one of the Third District stories published during his term of employment, it is safe to assume that the majority of them are his. A selection of the more interesting of these articles is included in this edition in order to suggest the kinds of events that regularly occurred in this turbulent slum when Dreiser was covering it.

2. *"Heard in the Corridors"*: During his stint with the *Globe-Democrat*, Dreiser contributed frequently to the daily column "Heard in the Corridors." A typical column consisted of six to twelve paragraphs of remarks supposedly made by people interviewed at the leading hotels. According to Dreiser, as often as not the reporters manufactured fictional characters and comments. Dreiser was certainly not the sole contributor to the column, but immediately after he left the paper on 1 May 1893 the number of paragraphs and the frequency of the column's appearance dwindled rapidly.

From June through November 1893, it did not appear at all. This evidence suggests that Dreiser was the major contributor to the column during his tenure with the *Globe-Democrat*.[6] Reprinted here are six of his representative paragraphs.

3. *Theater reviews:* From the end of January through April 1893, Dreiser was the drama critic for the *Globe-Democrat*. Most of the reviews appearing at this time are little more than notices, almost devoid of critical comment. Occasionally they appear to be canned press-agent releases. Dreiser claims in *Newspaper Days* that he occasionally asked colleagues to review shows for him when McCullagh sent him to cover out-of-town events, but this claim is questionable because no stories like the ones he claims to have written were printed. As the paper's official drama critic, he must have written most of the reviews during this period.[7] Included here are a few items to suggest the quality of the youthful Dreiser's critical perception. They reveal his responses to some of the famous actors and actresses of the day and give something of the flavor of the St. Louis theater in the early 1890s.

St. Louis Republic

The *St. Louis Republic* material is taken from a copy of the Library of Congress microfilm owned by the Center for Research Libraries in Chicago.

Third District news stories: Dreiser began working for the *Republic* no later than mid-May of 1893. In *Newspaper Days* he writes that he was immediately assigned again to cover the Third District police station. It continued to be his regular beat, although Wandell frequently called him away to cover more important happenings. Included here is a small selection of the more interesting items that appeared during his months of employment.

Toledo Blade and Cleveland Leader

The six articles reprinted from the *Toledo Blade* and the *Cleveland Leader* are taken from microfilms owned by the Ohio Historical Society of Columbus, Ohio.

Pittsburg Dispatch

The articles from the *Pittsburg Dispatch* are taken from a microfilm, at the Center for Research Libraries, of files in the Carnegie Library at Braddock, Pennsylvania.[8]

Shortly after joining the *Dispatch*, Dreiser began to contribute to a daily column of commentary on topics of local interest. The published version of *Newspaper Days* implies that he was solely responsible for writing this column, but the manuscript of the book reveals that he was only one of several reporters who provided the material: "For what they craved more than news of a dramatic or disturbing character, was some sort of idle feature stuff they could use in place of news at times and still interest their readers; and this, along with several other reporters who were attempting the same thing at their behest, I was able to supply" (MS of *ND*, chap. LVIII, p. 1, Box 139). These articles, usually printed on page 2 or 3 and illustrated by one to three cartoons, ran nearly every day through most of the summer months of 1894, then appeared much less frequently in September and October and only rarely in November. During Dreiser's time with the *Dispatch*, 187 of them were printed. Of these, twenty-two are either unquestionably or very probably Dreiser's. Eleven of these twenty-two (Nos. 87–97), the best and most interesting, are included in this edition.

Allegheny stories: In *Newspaper Days*, Dreiser states that he was regularly assigned to cover the Allegheny city hall, general hospital, and central police station. This beat seems to have remained his throughout his brief stay on the paper. A small selection of typical Allegheny stories is reprinted to show something of the scene he covered and the sort of writing he did on this assignment.

New York *World*

The New York *World* material is taken from a University of Minnesota Library microfilm of the file in the New York Public Library. Reprinted in this edition are the very few stories definitely attributable to Dreiser on the basis of remarks in the manuscript and printed versions of *Newspaper Days*. Some confusion is caused by Dreiser's mention of an "East Twenty-seventh Street police station" as one of his beats. Volumes of the *World Almanac* for 1894–96 list no station at this address but do list stations at 24 East Twenty-ninth Street and 327 East Twenty-second Street. Perhaps Dreiser meant one of these, but there is no way to choose between them. Consequently, no stories emanating from these two stations are included in this edition.

EDITORIAL PRACTICES

With the exceptions noted below, texts are reproduced exactly as they appear in the newspapers. Only subheadings, lists of names, and resumés of routine business are omitted. Emendations have been made only to eliminate errors in spelling and punctuation and to supply missing letters or words. Such grammatical errors as dangling modifiers and disagreements of subject and predicate have been preserved without comment, as have syntactically awkward sentences. Significant emendations are recorded in the apparatus of this edition. A full record of emendation and correction is available in the Dreiser Collection at the University of Pennsylvania.

Only unquestionable errors in spelling have been corrected. Unusual spellings sanctioned by the *OED* or *Webster's Second* (or *Third*) *International* dictionaries—including those classified as archaic, obsolete, or variant—have been preserved. Turned or broken letters have not been noted.

When the name of a well-known person has a spelling different from the commonly accepted one, the error is corrected. When names of ordinary citizens not known to history have been spelled in different ways from article to article or within the same article, the various spellings have been preserved without comment.[9]

Numerical inconsistencies in amounts, hours, dates, addresses, and ages of people from article to article or within an article are preserved.

Only clear violations of generally accepted English-language punctuation or of a newspaper's customary practice have been emended. Emendations are therefore almost entirely confined to supplying appropriate terminal markings: periods, question marks, quotation marks. Not infrequently the source texts go astray in indicating quotations within quotations. Such confusions are corrected in accordance with the usual practice of the newspaper, invariably today's standard practice as well.

Internal punctuation is another matter. If Dreiser's texts are typical, then the current practice of using commas and semicolons to set off major sentence elements or to prevent misreading was not so strictly followed in newspapers of the 1890s. Occasionally the absence of punctuation may cause a moment's confusion, but as a rule it has not been necessary to impose strict present-day pointing.

The newspapers Dreiser worked for did not always use decimal points in monetary amounts. Occasionally the compositor left an open space. In such instances, the points have been supplied silently in order to spare the reader possible confusion.

When such essential single words as conjunctions and relative pronouns have been omitted, they (or contextually suitable equivalents) have sometimes been supplied for the sake of reading ease.

In the 1890s, standards for word division were different from current practices; in addition, newspapers were often inconsistent in their use of hyphens, even within the same article. This edition reproduces hyphenated words as they occur within lines in the source texts. Of the numerous occurrences in this edition of words divided by a hyphen at the end of a line, all but those listed in the Textual Apparatus are unhyphenated in the source text.

NOTES

1. In response to an interviewer's query, Dreiser once stated that he never used a typewriter "except for correspondence, and not always then." See Diana Rice, "Terrible Typewriter on Parnassus," *New York Times Magazine*, 27 April 1924, pp. 11, 14. The pencil is the writing implement most frequently mentioned in *Newspaper Days*.

2. That Dreiser was used to having copy editors write lead paragraphs for his stories is suggested by his proud observation that, at the *Republic*, Harry Wandell came to call on him to cover "the most difficult stories . . . to which I was always expected to write the lead." Apparently this was a singular distinction in his eyes.

3. Unfortunately the 1892 volume photographed for this microfilm lacks the issue of 31 December. The other libraries listed in Gregory's *American Newspapers 1821–1936* as holders of complete 1892 runs have replaced their bound volumes with the same microfilm. The missing issue apparently no longer exists; whatever Dreiser may have written for it is lost.

4. The exact 1892 boundaries of the Third District were identified by Cathy Reilly, librarian of the St. Louis Metropolitan Police Department.

5. John L. Given, *Making a Newspaper* (New York: Henry Holt, 1907), p. 158.

6. The column was printed only twelve more times in May after appearing on the 2d when it included the last item identifiable as Dreiser's. It then ran nine times the following December and in January 1894 again began to appear regularly six times a week.

7. In *Newspaper Days*, Dreiser implies that his salary was raised to thirty dollars a week when he became drama editor—a five-dollar increase over the twenty-five dollars he had begun to earn as a result of his Wann train disaster scoop.

8. The volume reproduced on this microfilm lacks the issue of 23 July 1894. No. 92, which appeared on that date, has therefore been reprinted from a photocopy made from that issue in the Library of Congress volume.

9. The few exceptions to this rule are in those stories in which a given spelling occurs with enough frequency to establish it conclusively as the correct one. Thus in No. 67, John A. McClelland's middle initial is given once as *F.*, once as *R.*, once as *N.* The initial *A.* is used nineteen times elsewhere in this article.

TEXTUAL APPARATUS

SELECTED EMENDATIONS

This table records significant editorial emendations made in the original newspaper texts in order to produce the texts published in this edition. The page-line reference in each entry is followed by the emended reading—the reading that is printed in this volume. The left-pointing bracket that follows should be read as "emended from." To the right of the bracket is the un-emended reading from the original newspaper text. Below is an example:

90.28   to go on] to on

This entry indicates that at page 90, line 28, of the Pennsylvania text, the word *go* has been added following the word *to*. Explanation of only one emendation (at 259.10) has been necessary; that explanation has been added, within brackets, to the entry in this table.

4.34   heterogenous] homogenous

8.3   unidentified] identified

10.13   places the] places that the

17.14   come] came

40.37   sway] away

73.38   disappeared. A score] disappeared. score

90.28   to go on] to on

99.8   early hour the] early the

136.17   alarm] a am

143.28   linen] lintel

164.18   District, were you not,] District were you not

184.3   boastfulness] bashfulness

201.33   out of their] out their

213.5   John A.] John F.

213.36   John A.] John R.

215.32   John A.] John N.

220.1   Deadmond] Desmond

232.21   man as other] man other

236.34   7:40] 8:40

254.36   Nick] Nic

256.24   11:30 p.m.] 1:30 a.m.

257.27   lanterns] lantern

259.10   reality. To] reality what he writes he has witnessed and felt, ing. To [Two dropped lines apparently caused this garbled text.]

259.14   Meinrad's] Meinard's

293.20   found himself] found him

294.16   together, with which,] together, which,

303.12   Maro] Mars

313.28   do it just] do just

318.41   17:32] 17:3

WORD DIVISION

Words hyphenated at the ends of lines in the copy-texts have been resolved by checking midline renderings of these same words elsewhere in the articles or by ascertaining the customary practice of the newspaper in question. Numerous compound words are hyphenated at the ends of lines in the present volume. When quoting the words in the list below, the critic or scholar should preserve the hyphenation. All other compound words hyphenated at the ends of lines in this edition should be quoted as one word.

9.5	self-evident	116.14	to-day
25.36	one-third	117.10	all-around
27.25	cream-yellow	121.15	light-hearted
28.2	one-third	125.5	water-filled
35.4	free-trade	127.10	never-ending
38.25	twenty-two	130.7	well-heeled
40.23	self-containing	130.34	"nickel-in-the-slot"
40.34	twenty-two	133.2	story-telling
64.2	black-hearted	134.32	To-night
71.31	to-morrow	138.34	sleeping-room
76.36	Twenty-first	149.23	well-inflated
77.11	reddish-brown	153.4	mind-reader
82.32	*Globe-Democrat*	159.17	well-known
94.14	Thespo-pugilistic	165.12	well-shaped
108.15	sickly-looking	170.23	Thirty-fifth

173.18	gray-headed		286.26	long-suffering
181.34	vicious-looking		292.33	time-tried
184.18	milk-hued		301.13	hard-hearted
194.24	"medium-healer"		303.26	laughing-stock
198.38	loud-mouthed		304.22	bridge-tenders
200.14	good-hearted		306.38	blooming-cheeked
200.16	miserable-looking		307.15	rush-snipping
201.33	full-fledged		307.18	over-weighted
203.1	to-morrow		308.8	microbe-killer
215.6	ex-school		308.18	opto-pessimo
219.5	good-hearted		309.3	sugar-coated
253.7	cloud-broken		309.36	good-natured
262.28	ex-Judge			

APPENDIX: STORIES ATTRIBUTABLE TO DREISER THAT HAVE BEEN OMITTED FROM THIS EDITION

(Page and column numbers follow date of publication.)

CHICAGO GLOBE

1.	The Copper Grinned	9/15/92	2.7
2.	At Last	10/7/92	1.8
3.	Robbers	10/8/92	1.1–2
4.	On the Run	10/9/92	2.1
5.	Fakes	10/10/92	1.3
6.	Waiting	10/11/92	2.7
7.	Around the Hotels	10/17/92	2.5
8.	Fakes	10/18/92	1.5–7
9.	Zuckerman	10/20/92	5.3
10.	Reap a Harvest	10/21/92	2.4
11.	Plenty of Suckers	10/22/92	3.3
12.	Still at Work	10/23/92	3.3
13.	Great Profit	10/24/92	1.7
14.	Fakes	10/25/92	1.3
15.	Zuckerman	10/26/92	1.8
16.	About the Hotels	10/29/92	2.4–5

ST. LOUIS GLOBE-DEMOCRAT

17.	Gossip of Chicago's Big Show	10/21/92	6.4–6
18.	Gossip of Chicago's Big Show	10/22/92	4.3–7
19.	Gossip of Chicago's Big Show	10/23/92	23.1–3
20.	Gossip of Chicago's Big Show	10/24/92	4.4–7
21.	Reports and Recommendations	11/17/92	9.2
22.	How a Detective Trapped a Prisoner	11/19/92	8.3
23.	In Wild-Cat Chute	11/20/92	25.1
24.	Seven Runaway Girls	11/23/92	11.4
25.	A Token of Death	11/28/92	9.4

26. Union Depot Construction   12/2/92   12.4
27. Saved in a Burning Hotel   12/18/92   29.6-7
28. Water Works Extension   1/15/93   31.1-7
29. Interviewing a Turk   1/26/93   4.5
30. A Russian Princess Lecturer   2/7/93   9.1
31. A Chinese Dinner   4/2/93   38.1-2
32. 138 "Heard in the Corridors" paragraphs printed from 11/3/92 to 5/2/93
33. 45 columns of theatrical reviews printed from 1/30/93 to 4/30/93

ST. LOUIS REPUBLIC

34. Burned in Bed   5/22/93   1.2-3
35. Curious Controversy   5/24/93   6.5-6
36. The Carcasses Removed   5/25/93   2.4-5
37. The Crum Fire   5/26/93   4.6-7
38. Dey's Mitey Quair Laws   5/26/93   12.2
39. Fast Mail Train   6/19/93   1.1-2
40. The War Fever Spreads   6/21/93   12.4-5
41. With Wrinkled Fronts   6/22/93   12.4-6
42. Jawing and Jabbering   6/23/93   7.1
43. Sphere Twirling Art   6/24/93   8.2
44. Let the Owls Screech   6/25/93   4.1-2
45. Got It in for the Owls   6/28/93   12.2
46. Demands Fair Play   6/29/93   12.4
47. The O. and E. Ball Game   6/30/93   12.4
48. No More Monkeying   7/1/93   11.5
49. Article 4 Hundred 47   7/2/93   2.2-4
50. Pictures from Real Life   7/2/93   23.1-2
51. All Torn Up the Back   7/4/93   12.4
52. White-Winged Peace   7/5/93   5.7
53. Practiced at the Park   7/6/93   7.2
54. The Elks and the Owls   7/7/93   12.5
55. In Grim Dead Earnest   7/8/93   8.2
56. Ready for the Fray   7/9/93   9.4-6
57. Professional Playing   7/11/93   4.7
58. Oraculous Opinion   7/12/93   12.4
59. Here Are the Facts   7/13/93   7.2
60. Portentous Pointers   7/14/93   7.2-3
61. A Presage of Disaster   7/15/93   11.6-7
62. Monday the Day   7/16/93   2.2-5
63. Pictures from Real Life   7/16/93   24.1-2

64.	The Great Game To-Day	7/17/93	2.4–5
65.	Gallagher	8/6/93	9.1–6
66.	Tyndall's Tests	8/9/93	12.5–6
67.	Failed to Connect	8/14/93	2.3
68.	Election of Officers	9/5/93	3.1–7
69.	On the Scene	9/6/93	1.2–3
70.	Jules Wallace, Faker. . . .	9/9/93	1.1–6, 2.2–5
71.	Wallace on Wallace	9/10/93	6.1–3
72.	Going to the Spiritualistic Congress	9/18/93	5.5
73.	Danced for Duncan	9/22/93	9.3
74.	Unprovoked Murder	9/24/93	2.6–7
75.	A Deep Mystery	9/25/93	1.4–6
76.	Awful Wreck!	10/17/93	1.1–6, 2.3–7
77.	A Dear Old Stump	10/22/93	13.2–3
78.	Jules Wallace Denies	10/23/93	2.4
79.	May Have No Visitors	10/26/93	4.6
80.	Wallace Has Skipped	10/29/93	13.2
81.	Chamber of Horrors	11/7/93	6.4
82.	M'Clelland's Skeleton	11/11/93	1.6
83.	Murder Will Out	11/14/93	1.4–5
84.	Poet of Potter's Field	12/3/93	9.1–7
85.	Murdered Fitzwilliam	12/8/93	5.5–6
86.	Murderers Talk	12/9/93	1.3–5, 2.5
87.	Fitzwilliam's Slayers	12/10/93	7.6
88.	Fooled Man and Bird	12/15/93	7.2
89.	A Cosmopolitan Camp	12/17/93	30.1–7, 31.1
90.	Bloodshed May Result	12/30/93	5.2
91.	Miltenberger's Scheme	12/31/93	28.2
92.	That Football Fracas	1/2/94	8.2
93.	Charity Teams Chosen	1/4/94	5.6
94.	Armed for Battle	1/5/94	2.3
95.	The Doomed Man Talks	1/11/94	4.3
96.	Mob for Lynching	1/19/94	1.7
97.	John Buckner's Crime	1/19/94	1.7, 2.3
98.	Lynchers Return Home	1/20/94	15.5
99.	Fighting Now the Fad	1/22/94	3.3–4
100.	The Merry Skaters	1/27/94	1.3–4
101.	Held the Eggs	2/12/94	3.5–6
102.	Graders' Winter Camp	2/18/94	18.4–5
103.	Contentment Afloat	2/25/94	32.3–4
104.	They Both Want Blood	3/2/94	7.2

CLEVELAND LEADER

105. Chicken Thieves   4/29/94   10.3

PITTSBURG DISPATCH

106. And It Was Mighty Blue	5/15/94	2.3
107. Entombed Chinaman Chue	5/15/94	3.3
108. 4 rewritten "Heard in the Corridors" paragraphs	5/18/94	3.2–4
109. Along the River Shore	7/2/94	9.4–5
110. Soldiers of Morganza	7/5/94	3.3
111. In Old Hancock Street	7/18/94	3.3–4
112. Confound the Mosquito!	7/28/94	3.3
113. Sleep During Hot Nights	7/31/94	3.3–4
114. This Settles the Japs	8/1/94	3.3–4
115. Here's to the Sadder Men	8/16/94	3.3–4
116. Where Sympathy Failed	8/25/94	3.3
117. Our Fleeting Shekels	8/26/94	2.4–5
118. Whence Went the Fish?	8/28/94	8.1–2
119. Scenes of the Line	9/12/94	3.1–3
120. In a Rambling Sort o' Way	9/13/94	3.3
121. Are Now Marching Away	9/14/94	2.4–5
122. They're Going, Going, Gone	9/15/94	2.4–5
123. The Theatres	10/16/94	10.3–4
124. A Play in Six Acts	11/12/94	2.2
125. To Yield at Once Is Best	11/12/94	2.2–3
126. Parted in Sorrow	11/12/94	2.3

NEW YORK WORLD

127. Canal Boat's Victim's Body Found	12/30/94	6.2
128. Greatest Evils of the East Side	2/25/95	8.8

INDEX